THE PROGRAMMING PROCESS

An Introduction Using VDM and Pascal

John T. Latham Vicky J. Bush
Ian D. Cottam

Victoria University of Manchester

ADDISON-WESLEY
PUBLISHING
COMPANY

Wokingham, England · Reading, Massachusetts · Menlo Park, California
New York · Don Mills, Ontario · Amsterdam · Bonn
Sydney · Singapore · Tokyo · Madrid · San Juan

Many of the designations used by manufacturers and sellers to distinguish
their products are claimed as trademarks. Addison-Wesley has made every
attempt to supply trademark information about manufacturers and their
products mentioned in this book. A list of the trademark designations and their
owners appears on p. xviii.

Cover design by Crayon Design of Henley-on-Thames
and printed by The Riverside Printing Co. (Reading) Ltd.
Typeset by Times Graphics (Singapore).
Printed and bound in Great Britain by Mackays of Chatham, Kent

First printed 1990.

British Library Cataloguing in Publication Data
Latham, John T. (John Timothy)
The programming process : an introduction using VDM and
Pascal.
1. Computer systems. Programming
I. Title   II. Bush, Vicky J. (Victoria Jane Wright)
III. Cottam, Ian D. (Ian David)
005.1

ISBN 0–201–41661–1

Library of Congress Cataloging-in-Publication Data
Latham, John T. (John Timothy)
    (The programming process : an introduction using VDM and Pascal /
John T. Latham, Vicky J. Bush, Ian D. Cottam.
        p. cm. – (International computer science series)
    Includes bibliographical references.
    ISBN 0–201–41661–1
    1. Pascal (Computer program language)   2. Computer software –
Development. I. Bush, Vicky J. (Vicky Jane).
II. Cottam, Ian D. (Ian David).   III. Title.   IV. Series.
QA76.73.P2L38   1990
005.1–dc20   89–48250
                                                            CIP

THE PROGRAMMING
PROCESS

INTERNATIONAL COMPUTER SCIENCE SERIES

Consulting editors   **A D McGettrick**   University of Strathclyde

J van Leeuwen   University of Utrecht

SELECTED TITLES IN THE SERIES

To: Andrea,
    Elizabeth,
    Scramble,
    and Rummage;

and: Mike,
     Ruth,
     and Saul;

and: Carole
     and Thompson.

Preface

That's right – this is yet another 'introduction to programming' book. But it's different from many of the others – it doesn't claim to teach a *programming language*. Most introductory books are organized around a particular language, making the reader an expert at *reading* programs (in that language), but not really equipped for writing programs, or even knowing what program to write. One wouldn't expect to be a successful writer of French novels by merely studying the French language. Nor would one expect to be a celebrated painter by studying the science of pigments and canvas. Both these respected professions require the study of the *experience* of other respected professionals and the expansion of one's own experience.

The programming process

Programming too is a skill based on experience as well as discipline. Instead of teaching all the places where one may legally write a semicolon in the language XYZ, the aim of this book is to provide the reader with broad practice and experience of the *process* of programming using state-of-the-art techniques. It covers the critical issue of how to know what program to write, as well as how to write it. It takes the (slightly simplistic) view that programming is divided into four distinct stages:

- Requirements analysis – find out what the program must do.
- Formal specification – capture the requirements in unambiguous mathematics.
- Algorithm and data type design – discover how the program will work.
- Implementation – produce the final program and check that it is correct.

Sadly, many books concentrate on the last stage, while some more are also concerned with design. Few introductory texts acknowledge the importance of the first two stages, with the result that many apparently trained programmers also fail to acknowledge that the program produced *must* satisfy the customer's requirements.

Pascal

In conjunction with the programming process, the book also introduces the programming language **Pascal** to a sufficient degree of intimacy for most readers. Knowledge and understanding of that particular language can be increased by complementing this text with any of the many good books describing Pascal. This goes for other languages too – consistent with our view that *programming* is difficult, whilst programming languages are easy.

Formal specification

Similarly, the book exposes the reader to **formal specifications** in the style of the **Vienna Development Method** (VDM), without attempting to cover every detail of that language. Indeed, some VDM concepts which have an almost equivalent Pascal counterpart are not introduced, but rather a generalisation of the Pascal concept is used instead (for example, a generalisation of Pascal records is used instead of VDM composite objects). Moreover, in the early chapters of the book, so that the reader is not bombarded with too much new material and notation at once, some of the VDM constructs are substituted with a more informal, English-language style. Such concepts are then introduced formally in later chapters.

   An area which is not covered in this book is that of formal verification and program proofs. This is not because we don't think this is a worthwhile activity, but simply because it is impossible to do everything at once; we feel that the reader has enough new ideas to assimilate already.

Program design

There are many different program design aids and methods, all seemingly in competition, and all acclaimed as being the best. Rather than teach any one of these, we convey the general principles that lie behind all of them. These are principles such as **top-down, stepwise refinement** and the notion of an **abstract data type.** We believe the best way to learn how to design programs is through the experience of applying these principles and watching other experts apply them – rather like the apprentice and the craftsperson. Thus we teach design by example. However, since we do explicitly present the principles of design, the approach we take does not preclude the use of any particular design aid or method the reader may encounter.

Who can use this book?

We first used this text as the basis of a first-year undergraduate course at the Department of Computer Science of the Victoria University of Manchester, England, in 1986, and it has been running since. In accordance with the normal entrance requirements for this course, we assumed no previous knowledge of computing beyond that of the average, intelligent 18-year-old. In fact, it is still the case that 25% of the students taking the course have no significant computing experience. We have also presented a reduced version as a Post-Experience Vocational Education course to people working in the computing industry without any formal training in programming. In addition to its suitability as a first-year undergraduate text and in industry, we suggest that this book is also appropriate for MSc conversion courses and would be useful as motivation, if not as a course book, in the teaching of formal specification in the second year of an undergraduate course.

The course structure

We do not believe that the best way to learn programming is to be shunted around a *reference* book. This book has been set out to best suit the process of *learning* programming, rather than looking up some detail of a particular programming language. Consequently, the text should be followed through from beginning to end, since later chapters build on the concepts introduced in earlier ones. However, since previously intro-duced ideas and formalisms may be forgotten, all the concepts also appear in an easy-reference form in an appendix.

The book is structured into case studies, each telling a story about the development of a program. For added motivation, these programs come from a variety of backgrounds and are all realistic.

Humour

In addition to the technical details and concepts, the stories in the chapters incorporate scenarios some aspects of which might be described as not wholly unlike humour, although there is no accounting for taste. Whilst it is not intended that the scenarios should be taken seriously, they often do help to get some of the messages across – particularly the importance of requirements analysis and design. Various personalities appear throughout the book (some good and some bad), but Rita Rigorous plays the biggest part in every chapter. She's a sort of heroine, really. Such light seasoning is often very much welcomed by students in material that is usually presented rather dryly.

Notations introduced

We use the specification language VDM (with minor deviations in the interests of clarity) and the programming language BSI/ISO standard Pascal. To keep the amount of notation manageable we use only basic sets, cross-product sets, sequences, records and arrays as abstract models. All the necessary logic and set theory is included. Most of the Pascal language is covered, but again we do not aim to produce 'language lawyers'.

Fundamental technical **concepts** are introduced *exactly* when they are appropriate, if they have not been seen in a previous case study. These descriptions appear like this paragraph, to facilitate the later perusal of the case study without the distraction of the (now understood) concepts.

Summary of chapters, topic coverage and motivation

The Introduction describes the basic philosophy of the book and presents a very simple description of a computer and program compilation. Each of the other chapters in the book is concerned with a particular case study.

Chapter 1 presents the first example, which is to find the average salary of the employees in a certain company. This very small, simple and well understood problem is used to present an overview of the entire programming process and serves as an elementary introduction to programming. At the specification stage, it introduces the concept of a data type with natural numbers and sequences. Operations are also explained. At the implementation stage, all the information needed to write a simple Pascal program is given and the concept of looping is introduced with the while loop.

The introduction in Chapter 1 is reinforced by the case study in Chapter 2 – the example here finds the maximum salary of the employees in the same company. The Boolean data type is introduced, as is the Pascal conditional statement.

Chapter 3 describes the development of a program that plays a variation of the game of Nim. At the specification stage, the example is a vehicle for introducing more details about operations, such as the let expression, and the need in post-conditions to distinguish the values of external variables before and after an operation has been performed. Sequences play an important role in modelling the input to and the output from the game. The design stage shows how operations may be implemented by Pascal procedures. Pascal enumerated types are introduced as being the most appropriate concrete model of one of the types occurring in the specification.

Chapter 4 describes the development of a well known program to analyse telegrams. The initial requirements are full of ambiguities, thus the importance of requirements analysis is motivated. At the specification stage the chapter teaches how to use functions, sets, records and type invariants. Much processing of strings occurs in this case study and the usual Pascal constructs necessary for implementing this are explained. The use of procedures is developed so that they now have local variables.

The case study in Chapter 5 is a program that displays the time and date in a format specified by the user. It further illustrates the use of abstraction in specification, particularly in the representation of data types. Most of the specification is written in a functional style with much reliance on the notion of recursion. Parameters are now introduced for Pascal procedures. Record and set types are used in the implementation.

Chapter 6 develops a program to maintain information about equivalent parts in a warehouse. It concentrates on the importance of program design, in this case to produce an efficient implementation of essentially simple operations. Concepts introduced in the specification include the equivalence relation and quantification. New Pascal constructs are the for loop and the case statement. Reading and writing to non-text files are also demonstrated.

Producing an index of key words in book titles is the subject of Chapters 7 and 8. The abstract data type approach to design and the design method of solving a simpler problem first are exemplified. The implementations of some of the abstract data types are deferred to Chapter 8, and are used as a vehicle for introducing dynamic data structures and linked lists.

Chapter 9 further stresses the abstract data type approach by demonstrating how an abstract data type may be packaged into a reusable component, rather than being specific to the program development in hand. The target here is to write a software tool that will search for the occurrence of a given string in a piece of text. This is implemented using an off-the-shelf unbounded strings package.

Chapter 10 concerns the specification of the unbounded strings abstract data type used in the previous chapter. The Pascal function and procedure headings for the data type operations are written, together with pre- and post-condition specifications. This chapter introduces some more advanced Pascal constructs, such as conformant arrays and the use of procedures and functions as parameters to procedures and functions.

In Chapter 11, the main emphasis is on requirements analysis in the domain of an unfamiliar discipline, namely biology. The task is to produce a program that simulates life in a forest, as experienced by creatures known as birds and bees. The use of two-dimensional arrays is introduced, as are some techniques for improving the efficiency of the program. The topic of error recovery is discussed.

The final chapter describes the realistic implementation of the strings package used earlier, and thus exposes more sophisticated dynamic data structures, though still based on linked lists. This chapter may be ignored at a first reading since the data structure chosen is very complex for a beginner.

Appendix A collects together all the concepts introduced throughout the book, which are here ordered so that related concepts appear together. Entries in the main index refer to the place in the text where a concept is defined and also to its appearance in this appendix.

A list of Pascal reserved words and the syntax of the language are given in Appendix B. The final appendix, C, presents the full implementation of the strings package described in Chapter 12.

Exercises

As has already been mentioned, this book should be read from beginning to end. There are numerous small exercises interspersed with the case studies, and tutorial and longer laboratory exercises at the end of some chapters. The answers to *all* the small exercises are included in the book. The tutorial exercises are designed to work best as a discussion between a group of students and a teacher. They have all been tried and tested in this mode. The laboratory exercises each involve the implementation of part of, or some variation of, a case study from the book. They are designed to occupy a *good* student for about 30 hours of laboratory time, over the period of the course. The software needed to run the laboratory exercises on UNIX Pascal systems, their solutions, tutorial guides and transparency masters are all available to bona fide educational establishments, at a cost to cover expenses only. Those interested should write to the authors at the following address:

Dr John T. Latham
TPP Teachers' Guide
Department of Computer Science
The Victoria University of Manchester
Oxford Road
Manchester
M13 9PL
UK

Or send electronic mail to:

Internet: jtl%cs.man.ac.uk@nss.cs.ucl.ac.uk
JANET: jtl@uk.ac.man.cs   UUCP: ..!mcvax!ukc!man.cs!jtl

Acknowledgements

We would like to thank firstly our respective families, to whom this book is dedicated, and whose continued support, understanding and silent suffering was instrumental in completion of the text: a million thanks.

Then there are the hundreds of guinea-pigs who had the dubious fortune of surviving the first year as students of the Manchester course; their feedback was invaluable and without them this book would never have happened: one thank each.

Thanks also to Graham Gough, who is currently teaching part of the course, for his comments on some of the chapters and for contributing some of the exercises; and to Cliff Jones for his support and advice on VDM matters; and to the rest of our colleagues in the University, and, indeed, to the dear old Victoria University of Manchester itself.

To the staff of Addison-Wesley, especially Simon Plumtree, Lynne Balfe and the team, we extend our profound thanks for their professionalism and unswerving patience: thanks (profoundly). Sorry we were late – we overslept.

Thanks are due to Douglas Adams who through his *Hitch Hiker's Guide to the Galaxy* quite unwittingly inspired the manner of reporting, if not the facts of *some* of the wilder aspects of some of the adventures of our heroine, Rita: even poor imitation is sincere flattery.

Finally, dues must be paid (perhaps these will be exacted!) to the IPSE 2.5 and Flagship research groups: so long and thanks for all the laser toner.

John T. Latham
Vicky J. Bush
Ian D. Cottam

Victoria University of Manchester
April 1990

Contents

Introduction

Imagine two people and a book. One person is called 'Ian Mark' and the other is called 'Irene Mary'. Their surnames are 'Lost' and 'Found'. The book is this one. 'I.M. Lost' has already done some programming, in BASIC, and Pascal, and COBOL, and FORTRAN, and . . . . 'I'm pretty much an expert – this book will teach me nothing' he or she thinks. 'I.M. Found', on the other hand, has done absolutely no programming at all, not a jot.

I.M. LOST: Right. Programming is all about making a computer do something. All you have to do is give it instructions written in a programming language, and it simply obeys those instructions.

I.M. FOUND: You make it sound easy. . .

LOST: Oh, it is easy. Now, there's lots of different programming languages, and it's important to know as many as you can.

FOUND: Oh dear – I don't know any yet.

THE BOOK: Ummm – perhaps you should not listen too much to 'I.M. Lost'. Programming is *hard* but programming *languages* are easy. In this book, you'll learn how to program and, at the same time, you'll learn just *one* programming language.

LOST: That's all very well for you to say – I already know how to program, and I find it easy. I want to learn more languages.

FOUND: I wish I knew how to program – how many languages do you already know?

BOOK: Wait, wait. Can either of you speak French?

LOST: Yes, well I'm not bad.

FOUND: Me too.

BOOK: Okay, can you write a French novel?

LOST: Err . . .

FOUND: I doubt it.

BOOK: Exactly! Writing novels is hard, whilst learning French is easier. A programming language is just the way we express our programs. Creating the programs is hard.

LOST: But I don't find it hard.

BOOK: So, what is the most important aspect of a program?

LOST: It must be fast, and use as little space as possible.

FOUND: I'm lost.

BOOK: No, you're found. What about whether or not the program does the right thing?

LOST: Well, obviously.

FOUND: What do you mean by 'the right thing'?

BOOK: Exactly – half of this book is just about knowing what 'the right thing' is.

LOST: But that's not programming!

FOUND: I don't know – if programming is about making the computer do something that needs to be done, then it must be very important to make sure it does just that.

LOST: Well of course! That's called debugging. That's when you've written the program and it doesn't seem to do what's needed. You try lots of different things – changing bits of it and so on – until it starts to work properly.

FOUND: That sounds a bit messy. And in any case, how do you *know* it doesn't work, if you don't know what it is supposed to do?

LOST: Well, that depends. Usually, it doesn't matter too much what the program really does, as long as it does certain things. In any case, you don't really decide exactly what it is supposed to do until after it's written. I've written lots of adventure games, and they're all different from how I originally thought they would be.

BOOK: But, in the *real* world, there are *real* customers, who have *real* problems that must *really* be solved. It's no good starting to write the program until you know *exactly* what it has to do.

LOST: I don't believe that – I've been programming for years, and I've never known what I was doing.

BOOK: Alright, what about the time taken to produce the program?

LOST: Pah! I don't mind that. I often spend hours and hours making my programs fast and small.

BOOK: But what does it cost to make your programs fast and small?

LOST: Cost? Nothing! Well, I suppose you could work out the electricity!

FOUND: Do you mean, you actually enjoy working for hours and hours with a computer?

LOST: Of course! It's great fun – isn't that why you want to learn to program too?

FOUND: I'm not really sure.

BOOK: Well, there's nothing wrong with programming being good fun. But what if someone was paying you to program? What then?

LOST: I'd be very lucky, wouldn't I!

BOOK: Yes, but you couldn't spend hours and hours and hours on every program then, or else you'd be sacked!

LOST: What do you mean? If I could make the program more efficient, my boss would be pleased.

BOOK: Only if it was worth the *cost* of your time.

LOST: True, I suppose.

BOOK: And, also true is that if you only find out *after* writing the program what it is *really* supposed to do, then it takes longer overall than if you find out properly before you start.

FOUND: So what is this book going to teach then?

BOOK: Listen to this story:

There was a caveman who had a great idea. He realized one day that rather than look for caves and make do with whatever he could find, he would make a cave. This he did, and he was very pleased. It took him ages because he kept having better ideas and making silly mistakes. In the end it had windows, and doors, and separate rooms. He put a chimney in after a few weeks, so that the smoke from his fire could escape. All his friends were very impressed. They asked him if he would make them some caves too, and, in return, they promised to pay him lots of antelope steak. The first house he built was finished in two days! The new owner was very pleased, and handed over a huge pile of nicely grilled steaks. Alas, when he tried to open the door, it fell off. 'Never mind', he said, 'it's still better than a real cave'. A few days later, he discovered a room in the house that he could get into, but he couldn't get out! He yelled, and yelled. The man who made the house came running, and set him free. 'I'm sorry', he said, 'I didn't realize that you would want to close this door while you were inside the room.' He put a handle on the inside of the room, so that the mistake wouldn't happen again. 'I'll fix your front door while I'm here too', he added. This went on for several years – every now and then the owner would find a fault or something that didn't suit him, and it would be fixed immediately, or a little later, depending upon how serious it was. The owner didn't mind, because it was still better than living in a cave.

LOST: Is this about programming or ancient history?

BOOK: Well, you'll see.

Several million years later, a descendant of the owner of the new house bought a dwelling from a descendant of the caveman builder. Another amazing coincidence was that the rest of the story was also the same – it took just two days to build, the front door fell off, there was a room that locked you in and all the other faults and unsuitable aspects were there too; and it took several years to get sorted out. The only difference was that the modern owner was furious and called the builder a 'cowboy', among other less polite titles. To make things worse, a different builder was building a house next to his. This one took several weeks to build, but when it was finished there was nothing wrong with it. So really, it took less time to build than the one that was first finished in two days, but was not right until several years later.

FOUND: I think I can see what you're getting at.

LOST: I don't, and I'm bored. Can we learn some programming languages now?

BOOK: The craft of programming is just like house building – there are customers and they have needs. The difference is that programming is a relatively new craft, but that doesn't excuse programmers from being professional. In fact, the modern customer is beginning to get rather sick of paying cowboys for programs that have lots of faults and don't do what they *really want.*

What *is* this book about?

This book is not obsessed with teaching you all the details of any programming language. We want to teach you the *process* of programming. That includes how to know which program to write, as well as how to write it so that it does the correct job as soon as it is finished. If all we did was teach you the details of a particular programming language, then you'd only know how to *read* programs, and only in that language.

The programming process

A computer is a moronic machine that is capable of pedantically obeying some pedantic instructions. The nature of those instructions depends on the nature of the computer – they might involve complex numerical calculations, for say predicting weather patterns, or perhaps involve movement of robot arms in a car factory. Programming is all about producing the instructions, called the **program** for the computer to obey. Obviously, those instructions must make the computer do what is desired of it – and this means satisfying a **customer's** requirements.

The skill of programming is based on experience. The aim of this book is to provide you with a broad practice and experience of programming using state-of-the-art techniques. The **process** of programming is divided into four distinct stages:

- **Requirements analysis**   This is where the programmer talks to the customer to ascertain what is needed. This is not as easy as it sounds, since the customer may have absolutely no appreciation of computers, but is often a skilled practitioner in some domain that the programmer knows very little about. So it is easy for the two to misunderstand each other, and for the customer to omit many of the details that the programmer will need to know.

- **Formal specification**   This involves describing the intended behaviour of the program using unambiguous mathematics and logic. The production of the specification confirms that the programmer understands the customer's needs. It can be used as the basis of the *programmer* describing their understanding of the requirements to the *customer*. Many ambiguities and misunderstandings can be exposed by this process. The finished specification can then be used as a definitive reference for the later stages of development.

- **Program design**   This is where the programmer considers *how* the program will work, and involves the creation of an **algorithm** or method of solution. This is usually the hardest stage of the process, since it is based largely on pure creativity.

- **Program implementation**   This final stage is when the design is turned into a finished program, presented to the computer and **tested.**

Naturally, the rest of the book is going to elaborate on this description of the process.

Formal specifications – VDM

The book exposes you to **formal specifications** in the style of the **Vienna Development Method** (VDM) without attempting to cover every detail of that language. This notation was originally developed at IBM's research laboratories in Vienna. Since then there have been many alterations to it and, at the time of writing this book, work is ongoing to produce a BSI/ISO VDM standard (British Standards Institution, 1988). A good reference to VDM is Jones (1990), although it is not an introductory programming book. We have found it useful to deviate from the notation he uses in minor ways, in the interests of clarity. However, to all intents and purposes, all the formal specifications appearing in this book are written in VDM.

Program design

There are many different design aids and methods, all of which are claimed to be the best. Rather than teach any one of these, we expose the underlying principles of design common to all of them. We feel that the best way to learn how to design programs is through the experience of applying these principles and watching other experts apply them.

Pascal

To study and construct specific programs, the book introduces the programming language **Pascal.** Why Pascal? It is not the theoretically ideal language for learning to program, but it is a good compromise between that and what is widely available. Apart from where explicitly stated, we use only BSI/ISO standard Pascal (British Standards Institution, 1982), but we don't attempt to train you as Pascal 'language lawyers'. You may of course increase your knowledge of the language by complementing this text with any of the many good books describing it in more detail, but remember the distinction between knowing a programming language and knowing how to program.

Structure of the book

The book is structured into case studies, each telling a story about the development of a program. Technical concepts are introduced precisely when they are needed by the case studies, so the form of the book is suited to *learning* programming, rather than acting as a reference source. The consequence of this is that the text should be followed through from beginning to end. However, there is an appendix containing all the technical concepts in an easy reference form, to facilitate quick revision of definitions and principles that have been previously introduced, but which you have temporarily forgotten.

When technical concepts are introduced in the text, the descriptions appear like this paragraph so that you can later re-read the case studies without their distraction.

IF you have programmed before THEN

Although you are a reader who already has some previous programming experience, you will nevertheless benefit from being exposed to the wider aspects of programming. Our message to you is: there is more to a program than it doing *something* quickly. There is no point in concentrating on developing a super-efficient program if it performs the wrong operations. The emphasis in this book is on getting things right first – efficiency is definitely a lesser consideration. Beware, also, of skipping concepts that you think you already know. At least make sure your understanding agrees with our view.

ELSE {or OTHERWISE}

Although you are a reader with absolutely no previous programming experience, you can relax. You should not be at a disadvantage, since all the concepts are presented assuming only a reasonable familiarity with basic mathematics (such as simple algebra). Indeed, there is an argument that suggests you have an advantage over the others, at least initially. This is because the best way to first learn programming is to learn the best way first!

Some fundamentals of computers

Before launching into the programming process, it is worth looking more closely at some of the fundamental aspects of computers and their programs. As has already been stated, a computer is a machine that is capable of obeying certain instructions. Computers are *not* intelligent; in fact, they are more moronic than any person you are ever likely to meet. For most applications it is precisely because they are ideal morons that they are useful. For example, they can continue churning out telephone bills a long time after any intelligent beast would have died of boredom. They are very pedantic in that they do *exactly* what their instructions tell them to, regardless of whether that was what the programmer *intended*.

Outline structure of a computer

A simple computer may be regarded as consisting of a **central processor**, **memory**, and **input** and **output** devices. As shown by Figure 1, the central

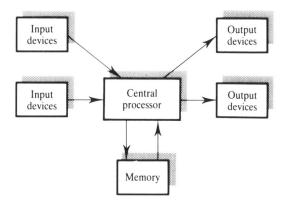

processor is the heart of the machine. This can understand and obey a limited range of very simple instructions called **machine codes**. The program the computer obeys or **executes** is written in these machine codes. The memory is used to store information. Part of that information is the machine code program that the computer is executing, and the rest of the information is **data** for the program. An example of data is the names and addresses of the clients who will receive telephone bills. This would be part of the data for a program that produces those bills.

There are various forms of input device, but the most obvious is a **keyboard**, which allows a user to type **text** directly into a computer. The most obvious output devices are **visual displays**, which show text on television screens, and **printers**, which can write text on pieces of paper.

Machine code instructions

The instructions that the central processor can understand are very simple indeed. For example, it knows how to take a number from a location of its memory and add it to a number stored in a different location, placing the result in a third piece of the memory. However, many computers don't know how to multiply! Such advanced operations have to be programmed using repeated addition. No typical computer can directly understand expressions like

$$10 + 23 - 17$$

That result would have to be evaluated in stages by a number of separate instructions of the program. Some of the instructions are concerned with input and output, but these too are very simple. For example, there is typically an instruction to display a single character on a visual display, but not one that will display a whole string of characters.

Computer memory

The memory of a computer has a certain size, corresponding to the amount of information that can be kept in it. Memory **internal** to the computer is built from electronic devices, called **random access memories**. These are designed to be very fast, meaning that the information can be **stored** and **recalled** very quickly. However, such memory is relatively expensive and bulky, so most computers also have **backing** memory. This is usually based on some magnetic media, such as **tapes** or **disks**. It is much slower than random access memory, but it is also much cheaper. Most general-purpose computers have about 100 times more backing memory capacity than internal memory capacity. For example, a typical personal computer might be able to hold a quarter of a million **bytes** of information internally, and 20 million bytes on a magnetic disk. A byte is equivalent in size to one **character** of text. (There are over 20 thousand characters of text in this chapter.) Backing storage also has the advantage that the information stored is not lost when the computer is switched off, in much the same way as the music recorded on your cassette tapes does not disappear when you remove them from your cassette player. On the other hand, the information stored in random access memories vanishes when the electric power is removed.

High-level languages

Machine code instructions consist only of numbers. These are stored in the computer using the **binary** system of 0s and 1s. The early programmers had to write programs in machine code, and enter them through toggle switches on the front of the computer! You are lucky, in that better ways of programming computers have been invented which make the whole task more reliable and efficient. A **high-level language** is a language of instructions, in the same sense as machine code, but such that each instruction is quite powerful and is expressed in a form which is convenient to the human programmer, rather than to the computer. In a typical high-level language, a programmer *can* write such expressions as

    10 + 23 - 17

A **compiler** is a special program, usually supplied by the manufacturer of a computer, which can translate another program, written in a high-level language, to an equivalent one written in machine code. This is necessary because the computer cannot directly understand the instructions of the high-level language. Thus the input data to the compiler is the programmer's high-level program, and the output data from the compiler is in machine code and is called the **object program** corresponding to the given high-level program.

Program errors

'To err is human, but to really mess things up takes a computer.'

Programmers do make mistakes in their programs. **Compile-time** errors are those detected and reported by the compiler, whereas **run-time** errors are those detected while the object program is being executed. When a compiler detects errors in the high-level program, it usually does not produce an object program. Such errors may be **syntax** or **semantic** errors. A syntax error occurs when the programmer has written something grammatically incorrect, according to the rules of **syntax** of the high-level language. An example of a grammatically incorrect sentence in English is the sign (seen strapped to the back of a poodle) 'My other an alsatian dog is'. Semantic errors occur when the programmer has written syntactically correct statements that have no meaning. An example in English is another sign 'My other dog is a Porsche'. That is meaningless because a Porsche is a kind of car, not a kind of dog. On the other hand, the sentence is grammatically correct.

Run-time errors occur when the program attempts to perform some impossible task. An obvious one is when the evaluation of an expression involves dividing some number by zero. When a run-time error occurs, the execution of the program stops, and it is said to have **crashed.**

That's enough fundamentals to get you going. Many readers will no doubt develop an interest in finding out more about how computers work, but such knowledge is not essential in order to be a successful programmer.

How you should use this book

As already stated, the text should be followed through from beginning to end. You will find exercises inserted in several places in each chapter. For the best effect you should attempt these as you reach them. All the answers are located at the back of the book. At the end of each chapter you will find a summary table of the notation it introduces. If you don't feel familiar with all the concepts listed, you should re-read the chapter before moving on to the next one. At the end of some chapters you will find tutorial and laboratory exercises. The tutorials are best attempted individually and then discussed in small groups. The laboratory exercises should be undertaken individually for maximum understanding.

Our heroine – Rita

This is where you meet her. Her name is Rita Ursula Rigorous (R.U. Rigorous). She is not likely to be anyone you've heard of – she's just a computer programmer. However, she *is* good at her job. The case studies in this book are part of her adventures. As authors we merely present to you an account of how and why Rita works as she does. As a reader you are invited to share her experience and follow her example.

Once you have digested the book, you should be a long way along the even longer road towards being an excellent and cost-effective programmer.

Meanwhile, we hope you enjoy the scenery.

Find the average of some numbers

1

MOTIVATION
This first short case study provides an introductory overview of the entire programming process, covering the stages of requirements analysis, specification, design and implementation. To achieve this aim, some fundamental concepts are defined, including: **data types**, **sequences**, **operations**, and **assignment**, **write** and **loop statements**.

The programming process is concerned with producing a program to solve a problem. It may be divided into four stages of development:

Requirements The requirements of the user are expressed informally, ambiguously and often incompletely in English. Requirements analysis is intended to give the programmer a full understanding of the problem.

Specification With the insight and understanding gained from the requirements analysis, the specification part of the process produces a precise and complete statement of the program behaviour, as the basis of a contract between the customer and the programmer. Unambiguous, formal mathematical concepts are used to define the **effect**, but *not* the **method** of the program.

Design This informal process produces an algorithm for solving the problem described in the specification.

Implementation This stage is the (relatively straightforward) task of converting the design into a program written in some formal computer programming language, and testing it on a computer.

1.1   Requirements

Rita Rigorous is a computer programmer, working for May Kit engineering construction company. Rita's boss, Beatrice Business, has been attending a management course all week. Rita arrives at the office one morning to find Beatrice has left a memo on her desk. It says:

> Write me a program to find the average of some numbers. I'll pop in to use it during coffee break this morning.

Exercise 1.1   If you are familiar with a high-level language, why don't you try to write this program *before* you read on?

The requirements are initially put forward by the customer. They are written (or spoken!) informally in English and are not always complete. This can be because the customer has not considered the problem deeply enough, or, more usually, simply does not have a sufficient appreciation of computer programming to be aware of the absolute exactness needed. It is the task of what is normally called the **systems analyst** to discuss the requirements with the originator of the problem and make them more precise. This is often difficult because not only may the user not know about programming, but also the systems analyst may not know about the user's application area.

Another source of defects is that natural language is not formal, and therefore is not always precise. Consequently, anything written in natural language can be interpreted in different ways by different people, or by the same person at different times. A change of wording can sometimes improve the precision of the requirements statement, but in many cases it is not possible to write the requirements precisely until the formal specification stage.

Rita reads the memo:

RITA: Just look what I have to put up with! I wish my boss had gone on a programming course, rather than another management course! I'd better go and catch her before her lecture starts and get some more information.

Rita just catches her in time, and a couple of minutes' conversation is all that is needed to elicit the required information. Rita now proceeds to write down a more comprehensive description of the program requirements.

It is required to find the mean average annual salary of all the
programmers in our department, to an accuracy of at least one
pound. Head office needs this information every month to assess
the overall trends in salary scales.

This description, though not much longer than the one in the memo,
clears up the vagueness of the initial requirements. Firstly, Rita knows
whether the average that is required is the mean, mode or median.
Secondly, she now knows what sort of numbers are being averaged.
Thirdly, she knows that the program must find the average of a variable,
rather than a fixed amount of data, as the number of programmers in the
department varies from time to time. Fourthly, since all the details of the
department's employees are stored on computer **file,** she knows from
where to access the data.

A computer **file** is a unit of information in a computer system. A file has a beginning and
an end, and may be written and read like a book (or even a ring-file). A file may contain
data (for example the information concerning all employees of a certain business) or a
program.

Finally, she can deduce where the program must put the answer. Since it
is going to be sent to head office as part of the monthly report, which is
a handwritten form, her boss would simply like the result to appear on
the screen.
    Having obtained what Rita believes to be an adequate understand-
ing of the requirements, she next attempts to formalize them.

1.2   Specification

A **specification** is a formal description of the required program using notation based on
logic and mathematics. This describes the data and program operations in an abstract
manner, without any stipulations about how these should be implemented. The
specification should be complete and unambiguous. It may form the basis of a contract
between the customer and the programmer. It should be possible later to verify whether
the program (which is also formal) does in fact implement the specification, and thus
whether the contract has been satisfied.

1.2.1   Specification of the data types used by the program

A **data type** in specifications is a collection (set) of values. For example, the set of all natural numbers (that is, whole numbers greater than or equal to 0).

The only input data that the average salary program is interested in is the salary of employees. Hence, Rita decides that it is most appropriate in the specification to regard an employee as a single number, that number being the salary. All other employee details can be ignored. Salaries are always a whole number of pounds (in May Kit), and nobody has a negative salary! Thus they can be represented by **natural numbers**.

We assume the existence of some elementary types when writing specifications. Among these is

$\mathbb{N}$

which contains all the natural numbers: 0,1,2... .

Sometimes it is helpful to give an alternative name to a type which is already defined. This can greatly aid the clarity of the specification. We write:

A = B

to indicate that the type A is the same as B. For example:

Employee = $\mathbb{N}$

Employee = $\mathbb{N}$ {that is, just their salary}

The employee details supplied as input to the program are simply a **sequence** of employees.

A **sequence** is a list of elements, possibly with duplicates, where the order in which they occur is important. When we write:

Y-seq = Seq of Y

we are defining a type called Y-seq. This contains all possible sequences such that each ∃∀ element of those sequences is one of the values of type Y.

A sequence may be **empty**, that is contain no elements. Whatever the type of sequence, the empty sequence is denoted in specifications as:

[ ]

Non-empty sequence values may be written by listing the elements, separated by commas and inside square brackets.

Example elements of the type

Seq of N

are the sequences

[ ]
[153]
[5 , 1 , 8 , 1]

Note that 1 occurs twice in the last example.

Employees = Seq of Employee

The mean average salary will be a **real number** of pounds.

Another assumed type in specifications is

R

This contains all the **real** numbers between negative and positive infinity. For example: 3.141 592 6.

Exercise 1.2   Assuming a data type Nat-seq is defined as

Nat-seq = Seq of N

say whether the following are elements of this type:

(a)   [1, 3, 3, 7, 11]
(b)   the sequence 2, 4, 6, . . . ad infinitum
(c)   [1.8, 1.9, 2.0, 2.1]

(d)   [0]

(e)   the data type $\mathbb{N}$

1.2.2   Specification of the program

Having identified the basic data types of the problem, Rita is ready to define the effect of the program. She decides to specify the program as an **operation** that reads the employee details and produces a real number.

An **operation** is some action which is part of a user's requirements. An operation has a name and generally has a **state** consisting of external entities (variables) that it may access and/or update. It also may have a **pre-condition** and a **post-condition**. A specification of an operation typically looks like the following:

```
NAME
ext .... *** external variables ***
pre ... *** pre-condition ***
post ... *** post-condition ***
```

The **external** variables in the state of an operation are listed at the beginning of the operation specification, each with its type. These types denote the set of values that the variables may possess. The variables have different access modes depending on whether they are **read only** (rd), indicating that the operation may not change the value, or **read and write** (wr), indicating that it *may* both access the value and change it.

The name of Rita's operation is AVERAGE-SALARY. It has two external variables – the employee-details, which is read only; and the output, which may be written to.

```
AVERAGE-SALARY

ext rd  employee-details : Employees
    wr output : ℝ
```

Next, Rita has to write an **expression**, called the **pre-condition**, that characterizes everything her operation can assume.

An **expression** is a structured sequence of symbols, consisting of **operators** (such as + and –), **variables**, function names and curly brackets. An expression has a value which depends upon the value of any variables occurring in it.

An operation may have a **pre-condition**. This is an expression, either true or false, which characterises all the assumptions the operation may make concerning the values of its state (and so on) before the operation executes.

The AVERAGE-SALARY operation may assume that the list of employees is **not equal to** the **empty sequence** (that is, there is at least one employee in the department).

All types in specifications have an **equality operator**, denoted:

$$=$$

This takes two values from the same type and gives true if they are the same value, and false otherwise. It is an **infix** operator (that is, the operator symbol is written between the two arguments). Thus in an expression we write:

$x = y$

to mean true if and only if x and y have the same value.

The opposite of equality, not-equality, is denoted:

$$\neq$$

and is used in the same way.

Hence the **pre-condition**, written formally, is

pre employee-details $\neq$ [ ]

To define that the program calculates the mean average salary, Rita must write a **post-condition**.

∃∀

An operation **post-condition** characterizes all the things that must be accomplished by the operation by the time it has finished executing; provided that the pre-condition is satisfied before its execution.

> The post-condition must say something like: take the sequence employee-details and add up each item in it. Divide the total by the number of items (that is, its length) and that is the final value of output.

There exists a function in specifications called **len** which can be applied to all sequence values and which gives the length of the sequence, that is, the number of elements in it. Thus, for example, if S is a sequence from the type:

Seq of $\mathbb{R}$

then the meaning of:

len(S)

is the number of real numbers in the sequence S. If S is the sequence

[1.3 , 2.4 , 8.1 , 0.2]

then

len(S) = 4

Note that a sequence length is always a natural number, and that

len([ ])

is zero.

There exists a function which may be applied to any sequence, S and a natural number, i, which returns the ith element in S, counting from 1 upwards. The value of i must be in the range 1 to the length of S. The function is applied by following the sequence with square brackets enclosing the value of i. For example, for a sequence X of type

Seq of $\mathbb{N}$

containing the natural numbers

[1 , 7 , 9 , 3 , 8]

the value of

X[4]

is the fourth element in the sequence X, that is, the natural number 3.

She states the required property formally, as

post

$$output = \frac{\sum_{i=1}^{len(employee\text{-}details)} employee\text{-}details[i]}{len(employee\text{-}details)}$$

Thus her complete specification is:

Employee = $\mathbb{N}$ {that is, just their salary}

Employees = Seq of Employee

AVERAGE-SALARY
ext rd employee-details : Employees
    wr output : $\mathbb{R}$
pre employee-details ≠ [ ]
post

$$output = \frac{\sum_{i=1}^{len(employee\text{-}details)} employee\text{-}details[i]}{len(employee\text{-}details)}$$

(Note that the entire operation has been specified without giving a method or recipe for *how to perform* the operation.)

An operation may be defined solely by its pre- and post-conditions. This is called an **implicit** (or **input–output**) **specification** of an operation (or, less formally, an **implicit operation**), since, in general, absolutely no indication is given as to how it might be implemented.

An operation specification gives no hint as to what the operation will do if the pre-condition is not satisfied before the operation executes. This is because an implementor is *free* to assume that the condition is satisfied. For example, one implementation might never stop, another might stop with a run-time error, a third might give the wrong answer, and so on.

Rita attempts to satisfy herself that this specification does indeed capture the intentions of her boss. Having done so she is ready to proceed with the program design.

Exercise 1.3   Study the following implicit operation specification:

```
DOUBLE
ext wr in  : N
     wr out : N
pre in > 0
post 2 * in = out
```

One suggested implementation of this operation is to set in to have the value 1, and out to have the value 2. Is this valid? Assuming that the intention was for out to be given double the value that in has to begin with, and no other effect, what change must be made to the specification to make it correct with respect to that intention?

Exercise 1.4   What would it mean if a pre-condition was specified as follows?

```
pre true
```

What about if it was specified as false?

Exercise 1.5   What is the meaning of

```
X [ - 42]
```

where X is any sequence?

 # 1.3 Design

Program **design** is the activity of transforming a formal specification, which defines the **effect** of a program, into some other notation (similar to a formal programming language) which defines **how** this effect is going to be achieved.

Data structures implementing the data types, and algorithms that produce the effect of the operations defined in the specification, must be designed.

Program designs are expressed in an informal notation, usually quite closely resembling the implementation programming language, but with the finer details omitted. This allows the programmer to concentrate on the often difficult process of algorithm construction.

The purpose of the design process is to produce an algorithm that correctly implements the specification. The clearer the algorithm, the more likely it is to be understood. Thus a simple algorithm which is thought to be correct is more likely to be correct than a complex one. Related to this is the fact that very often a program is altered after it is completed because of changes in the requirements of the customer. Modifying a program is likely to introduce errors, unless the program is very clear to understand. (A program is most often modified by a programmer who did not write it originally.)

On the other hand, efficiency of space and time can be important, as the program must produce results within an acceptable period, and must be able to run on the resources available. There is no point, however, in having a fast solution that produces the wrong answer. There is usually a trade-off between the clarity and simplicity of the method used, and its efficiency. When considering how efficient an algorithm needs to be, the programmer must bear in mind the cost of the design and implementation process, and that of future modifications. It may be that a very efficient algorithm is possible, but would take a long time to develop, and hence cost more. This may be justified if, say, the application is time critical. But a program that runs occasionally, and which can be left running overnight, does not need to be very fast.

Sometimes, a good way to approach a problem is to ask yourself how you would do it if you, not the computer, had to do it. This can cause you to think of a good and simple solution – since humans seem to have an instinct for avoiding doing more than is required!

The first question Rita asks herself is this: 'How would I do it?' If someone was standing near her, shouting out a number every time she nodded her head, she would not need to remember all the numbers (on the other hand, she might need ear plugs!). Instead, she would only need to remember how many numbers she had had so far, and the sum of all those numbers. Then, at the end, she would simply divide the total by the number of numbers she had so far, and give the answer. Ah! How would she know she was at the end? Well, there would have to be some signal to indicate that all the numbers had been given.

Rita is now in a position to write down the program design.

Designing a program is no different from any other difficult task – generally, it cannot be done in one go. The designer of a motor car does not start by drawing the front bumper, then working through in every detail until the back bumper is drawn. There is too much complexity to be contained in the mind all at once, so the job is split into meaningful parts – first the overall shape, with labels for the various sub-parts, such as 'engine'. Then

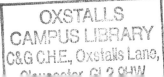

each sub-part can be designed in the same manner – engine split into combustion part, cooling part, transmission part, and so on.

Similarly, in program design, one can **control the complexity** by **abstracting** away from the unnecessary detail early on. This is called **top-down stepwise refinement** (TDSR) because the process starts at the top level of the problem and works downwards, refining each step.

It is just another form of the age-old axiom 'divide and conquer'.

The program needs at least two **variables**, one for the number of employees processed so far, and the other for the total of their salaries.

A program **variable** is a named object which contains a value from a specified type (for example a real number) during execution of the program. (It may be thought rather concretely as being similar to a labelled pigeonhole, in which only a specified type of pigeon may be placed.) A variable represents a unique entity of the problem being solved by the program, and this should be reflected in its name. For example, in a program that controls a model train on a track, one may expect a variable called train-position which might contain the number of a sensor which the train has just passed. A program may explicitly examine and change the value of its variables during execution. A good design rule is that the value of a variable should *always* reflect the meaning of the entity it represents. For example, every time the train passes a sensor, the program should change the value of train-position accordingly.

Rita's first draft of the design (we shall express designs informally in a notation resembling Pascal) is:

```
program average-salary
var
  count-of-employees-so-far,
  sum-of-salaries-so-far : ℕ
  . . . . .
```

The names Rita has chosen for the variables indicate that they do not necessarily hold values corresponding to all employees, but only those that have been processed so far. Inappropriate names for variables is one of the biggest sources of confusion in program development.

Rita decides also to use a variable to hold the final average, so she adds this in too:

```
final-mean-salary : ℝ
```

By giving the variable this name, she is unlikely to make the mistake of computing the average too soon, that is, before all numbers have been processed. (If for some reason she wished to compute it as the numbers were being processed, a good name would be mean-salary-so-far.)

Her first view of the actual algorithm is that it has four steps:

```
begin
    initialize count-of-employees-so-far and
        sum-of-salaries-so-far
    read in all the salaries, counting them and summing them
    compute final-mean-salary
    output final-mean-salary
end
```

The first three of these four stages require some design refinement. The fourth may be coded into Pascal very easily.

As a general guide in TDSR designs, when faced with the choice of which step to refine next, it is usually a good idea to pick the one that looks most complex. This is because there may be some influence between the steps which becomes apparent only when you examine them in more detail. These dependencies could affect the appropriateness of the choice of steps you have made, thus it is preferable that they show up early. They are more likely to show up in complex steps.

Starting with the refinement of the second stage, this being the most complex, Rita sees that a **loop** is needed.

A **loop** is a programming concept involving the repeated execution of some actions. This iteration is usually controlled by some true or false condition involving the values of program variables. The loop stops when the condition becomes true or false, depending on the kind of loop.

One particular form of loop is called the **while loop**. This has a **continuation condition** and a body of actions. The condition is evaluated (tested) *before* the loop body is executed. If the value of the condition is **true**, the actions in the body of the loop are executed and then the condition is tried again, and so on. When the condition is evaluated and is **false**, the loop execution stops. For example, the following loop reads and processes all the remaining elements of a sequence:

```
    while the sequence is not empty
       remove the next element from the front of the sequence
       process the removed element
    end-of-while
```

Note that, if the condition is false to begin with, the body of the loop will not be executed at all.

She writes:

```
        while not all of the employees have been read
           add one to count-of-employees-so-far
           read an employee salary and add it to sum-of-salaries-so-far
```

Even this requires some design refinement – in the second sub-part within the loop. Consideration of this causes her to introduce another variable to store the current salary, just read from the file. She adds this to the list of variables:

```
        current-salary : ℕ
```

Then she rewrites the loop:

```
        while not all of the employees have been read
           add one to count-of-employees-so-far
           read current-salary from employee-details file
           add current-salary to sum-of-salaries-so-far
```

Next she goes back to the main top level of the program and refines the design of the first and third stage. Her eventual design is:

```
        program average-salary
        var
           count-of-employees-so-far,
           sum-of-salaries-so-far : ℕ
           final-mean-salary      : ℝ
           current-salary         : ℕ
        begin
           set count-of-employees-so-far to zero
           set sum-of-salaries-so-far to zero
           while not all of the employees have been read
              add one to count-of-employees-so-far
              read current-salary from employee-details file
              add current-salary to sum-of-salaries-so-far
           set final-mean-salary to sum-of-salaries-so-far divided by
              count-of-employees-so-far
           output final-mean-salary
        end
```

Before embarking on the implementation, Rita also needs to consider how to make the actual file of employee details look like a simple list of salaries. This is not difficult for her, but has been omitted to avoid this introductory case study being over-complicated.

Now that the design is supposedly complete, it is important that Rita convinces herself that it is correct. She does this by studying the specification and the design, and reasoning about their consistency. She checks that the algorithm reads all of the salaries by inspecting the condition of the while loop. She checks that every salary is added to the total exactly once. She ensures that it counts the employees correctly, by observing that the count is initially set to zero, and exactly one is added for every salary read.

So, having dealt with all aspects of the design, Rita is ready to take the relatively simple step of implementing the program.

1.4 Implementation

Once the design of the program has been formulated, the implementation stage is the relatively straightforward phase of translating the design into the syntax of the programming language being used (in our case, Pascal). The programmer must then ensure that the resulting program actually implements the specification. This is done by both comparing the program with the specification and also by running the program and testing all the different logical paths. (The relationship can be proved **formally**, but that is beyond the scope of this book.)

A **program** is a formal and executable description of a method to undertake some task, written as a set of instructions. During **execution** of the program, the computer pedantically obeys these instructions regardless of whether this results in the behaviour expected or desired by the programmer. In Pascal, a program consists of a **heading**, various **declarations** and a **statement body**. The heading introduces the name of the program and specifies the domain of its interaction with the outside world. The declarations define the names and characteristics of various objects in the program. The statement body contains instructions for execution of the program.

A **program comment** is a piece of text which is part of a program, but which is ignored by the computer during execution. Its purpose is to help document the program, so that humans (programmers) looking at the text may have a better understanding of what it does and how it does it. Every program should have a comment near the front that states what it does, and in various places throughout, explaining interesting parts. In Pascal, comments occur between left and right curly brackets: { }. They may extend over many lines, and may be placed anywhere in a program. The computer treats each comment as a space. For example:

> { *This is a*
> *comment in*
> *Pascal* }

Rita first writes the **program heading** and a **comment** briefly describing the action of the program:

> **Program** *AverageSalary(EmployeeDetails,output)*;
> { *Program to compute the mean average of a number of salaries.*
> *These are obtained from the departmental employees file. The average*
> *is displayed as a real number of pounds.* }

An **identifier** is a word used to name an object (such as a program). In Pascal, identifiers start with a letter and contain only letters and digits. Upper and lower case letters are interchangeable throughout Pascal. For example:

> *EmployeeDetails1988*

The identifiers enclosed within brackets after the program name specify the limit of the program's interaction with the outside world. The occurrence of the identifier *input* states that the program may accept data from the standard input list (usually the keyboard). The occurrence of the identifier *output* states that the program may send data to the standard output (usually the display). The occurrence of other names indicates that the program can access and/or update items (usually files) of those names. In order for it to be known what kind of objects these are, they must be declared as variables later in the program. This is not required for *input* and *output*. For example, the program

> **Program** *double(input,output)*

may accept data from the standard input and write data to the standard output.

Next she writes the list of **variables**, each of which has a **type**.

A **program type**, like the types used in specifications, is a set of values. However, program types also have an associated collection of functions defined on them. In Pascal, types are named by identifiers. There are a few built-in types including one, containing all the whole numbers (between two implementation dependent limits) above and below zero, and zero itself. This is identified as *Integer*. The real type (subject to implementation dependent precision and bounds) is also built-in and identified as *Real*. The operators on integers and reals include addition (+), subtraction (–), multiplication (*), division (/) giving a real number result, and the usual comparisons, and so on.

Her program must use the Pascal type *Integer* as an implementation of the type ℕ used in the specification and the design. This does not cause a problem, since although *Integer* contains negative whole numbers, Rita may assume that all the salaries are non-negative by the fact that the specification declares them to be of the type ℕ.

(It is not quite true that *Integer* can be used as a complete implementation of ℕ, because there is a limit on the size of integers in Pascal, whereas natural numbers in specifications are unbounded. None of Rita's colleagues are paid so much that their total salaries are greater than this restriction, so let's ignore it.)

A **variable declaration** in Pascal defines a new variable, by giving its name and type. The name of a variable is an identifier. For example, the declarations

```
Var sum   : Integer;
    mean : Real;
```

define two variables – *sum* of type *Integer* and *mean* of type *Real*.

```
Var
    CountOfEmployeesSoFar,        {how many salaries so far processed}
    SumOfSalariesSoFar : Integer; {sum of salaries so far processed}
    FinalMeanSalary     : Real;   {mean salary, once all been summed}
    CurrentSalary       : Integer; {salary last read from file}
```

As required by Pascal, Rita declares the *EmployeeDetails* file. The details of the file, and reading data from it, have been omitted to avoid excessive complication in this first chapter.

```
    EmployeeDetails    : {detailed bit omitted from here};
```

Then she implements the algorithm.

A **statement sequence** is a list of program statements, which are executed by the computer in the order in which they textually appear. In Pascal the statements in the list are separated by semicolons (;).

A **reserved word** is a word, consisting only of letters, which is used as part of the Pascal language (for example **Program**) and may not be used as an identifier. The complete list of Pascal reserved words appears in Appendix B.

The algorithm of a Pascal program is contained in the **program body**. This is a statement sequence occurring between the reserved words **Begin** and **End**, and followed by a full stop (.).

Begin
  {detailed bit omitted which opens the input file}

Rita needs to use an **assignment** statement to initialize the count and sum of salaries.

An **assignment** statement contains a variable and an expression. When executed, the expression is evaluated, and its value is placed in the named variable. (Hence the types of the named variable and that of the expression must be compatible.) In Pascal, the variable name and the expression are separated by the := symbol. For example

  sum := sum + next

In this example, *sum* has the value of *next* added to it.

CountOfEmployeesSoFar := 0;
SumOfSalariesSoFar := 0;

Next she writes the Pascal for the while loop in her design. She must identify the Pascal **condition** for continuation of the iteration.

A **condition** is a program expression having either a true or false value when evaluated.

Like all program expressions, these conditions may contain variables, constant values and 🖭
operations. The values of such variables are used when the expression is evaluated, thus
it is possible (in fact, likely!) that sometimes the condition is true, and sometimes false.

The loop must continue reading salaries while it has **not** arrived at the
end of the employee details **file**.

There is a pre-declared function in Pascal which takes a file and returns as its result *true*
or *false* depending on whether the file is at its end point, that is whether there is no more
data to be read from the file. It is written:

   eof(f)

where *f* is the file.

There is a built-in operator in Pascal which takes a true or false value and negates it. That
is, if it is given *true*, it returns *false*, and vice-versa. It is called **Not**. Thus, for example,

   Not *eof(f)*

is true when the file *f* has *not* had all of its data read.

Thus, the condition of the loop is

   Not *eof (EmployeeDetails)*

The Pascal **while loop** she needs to construct has this condition, and also
a body corresponding to the body of the loop in the design.

A **compound** statement is a sequence of statements which is treated as a single statement.
This can sometimes help the clarity of the program, but is mostly used for writing a
statement sequence in places where only a single statement is syntactically legal. In Pascal
a compound statement is constructed by surrounding the sequence with the reserved
words **Begin** and **End**.

In Pascal, one form of loop construct is the **While** statement, which tests a condition
before executing the iterative part. It involves the keywords **While** and **Do**. The syntax

rules of Pascal insist that the loop body is a single statement. Thus, in cases where a sequence of statements is required for the body, a compound statement is used. For example

While *next* > 0 **Do**
Begin
    sum := *sum* + *next*;
    next := *next* – 1
End

Rita writes the loop:

While Not *eof*(*EmployeeDetails*) **Do**
Begin
    CountOfEmployeesSoFar := *CountOfEmployeesSoFar* + 1;
    {*detailed bit omitted which reads CurrentSalary from EmployeeDetails*}
    SumOfSalariesSoFar := *SumOfSalariesSoFar* + *CurrentSalary*;
End;

After the loop, the design places the required result in *FinalMeanSalary*. Hence, Rita writes

FinalMeanSalary := *SumOfSalariesSoFar* / *CountOfEmployeesSoFar*;

The last part of the design outputs the result. To do this in Pascal, she needs to use a **write** statement.

A **write** statement is a program statement which causes data to be written out from the program, to the standard 'output' (or elsewhere – see later). One way to achieve this in Pascal is via *writeln*, which also produces a new line after the data is written. (*writeln* is in fact a procedure, not a statement – see later.) For example

writeln(*sum*)

This example causes the value of the variable *sum* to be written to the standard output.

She writes this, followed by the final **End** of the program and the required full stop.

writeln(*FinalMeanSalary*);
End.

Pascal has a statement that has no spelling, and no effect. It is called the **empty** statement. For example, if one places a semicolon immediately before an **End**, there is said to be an empty statement between them. This is because semicolon is used as the statement separator.

The complete program (apart from the omitted bits) is:

```
Program AverageSalary(EmployeeDetails,output);
{ Program to compute the mean average of a number of salaries.
  These are obtained from the departmental employees file. The average
  is displayed as a real number of pounds. }

Var
  CountOfEmployeesSoFar,     {how many salaries so far processed}
  SumOfSalariesSoFar : Integer; {sum of salaries so far processed}
  FinalMeanSalary     : Real;   {mean salary, once all been summed}
  CurrentSalary       : Integer; {salary last read from file}
  EmployeeDetails     :         {detailed bit omitted from here};

Begin
  {detailed bit omitted which opens the input file}
  CountOfEmployeesSoFar := 0;
  SumOfSalariesSoFar := 0;
  While Not eof(EmployeeDetails) Do
  Begin
    CountOfEmployeesSoFar := CountOfEmployeesSoFar + 1;
    {detailed bit omitted which reads CurrentSalary from
    EmployeeDetails}
    SumOfSalariesSoFar := SumOfSalariesSoFar + CurrentSalary;
  End;
  FinalMeanSalary := SumOfSalariesSoFar / CountOfEmployeesSoFar;
  writeln(FinalMeanSalary);
End.
```

Rita finishes testing the program as Beatrice arrives to produce the required statistics.

RITA: Is it all okay?

BEATRICE: Oh, the program is fine. But ... comparing your salary with the average, you seem to be overpaid!

Exercise 1.6   How many times would the number 42 be printed by the following loop?

```
While false Do
  writeln(42);
```

What about this one?

```
While true Do
    writeln(42);
```

Exercise 1.7 Find the maximum length of a Pascal identifier by looking at the syntax diagrams in Appendix B.

Exercise 1.8 What is the difference between the following?

$$x = x + 1$$

and

$$x := x + 1$$

Exercise 1.9 What is the effect of the following program?

```
Program trivial(output);
Var sum, next : Integer;
Begin
    sum := 0;
    next := 10;
    While Not next > 0 Do
    Begin
        sum := sum + next;
        next := next - 1;
    End;
    writeln(sum)
End.
```

SUMMARY

This chapter has introduced the four stages of the process of programming, together with some fundamental specification and programming concepts. The next chapter reinforces this introduction with a different, but similar case study.

The following notations were introduced in this chapter.

Specification notation

Data types	$\mathbb{N}$, $\mathbb{R}$
Type naming	A = B
Sequence type	Employees = Seq of Employee
Sequence values	[ ] , [3, 8, 7, 4]
Operation	
External variables	ext rd employee-details : Employees
Equality operator	=, $\neq$
Pre-condition	pre employee-details $\neq$ [ ]
Post-condition	post output = ...

| Sequence length | len(employee-details) |
| Sequence index | employee-details[i] |

Pascal notation

Program heading	**Program** *average(EmployeeDetails,output)*
Program comment	*{ this program ... }*
Identifier	*average, EmployeeDetails, output, CountOfEmployeesSoFar ...*
Program parameter	*EmployeeDetails, output*
Program types	*Integer, Real, + , − , * , /*
Variable declaration	*var SumOfSalariesSoFar : Integer*
Statement sequence	*..... ; ..... ; .....*
Reserved word	**Program, Begin, End, While, Do,** ....
Program body	**Begin** ..... **End**
End of file	*eof (EmployeeDetails)*
Not operator	**Not**
Condition	**Not**(*eof (EmployeeDetails)*)
Writeln statement	*writeln(FinalMeanSalary)*
Assignment statement	*SumOfSalariesSoFar := 0*
Compound statement	**Begin** ..... ; .... ; ..... **End**
While statement	**While** ..... **Do** .....

TUTORIAL EXERCISE

This tutorial asks some general questions about the programming process and then some more specific ones using the Average case study as an example.

1 – General

(a)   Why is it important to separate out the four phases/activities of software development?

(b)   In which of the four phases must you be completely formal, and in which do you have some freedom in the level of formality?

2 – Specification

(a)   Explain what a pre-condition is. What are the implementor's obligations with respect to a pre-condition?

(b)   What happens in the case of the Average program if you run it with an empty input file? Do you consider this behaviour reprehensible in any way, and, if so, why?

(c)   Explain what a post-condition is. What are the implementor's obligations with respect to a post-condition?

(d)   What is the value of the Average post-condition if the pre-condition is false?

3 – Design

Briefly, what is meant by the design rule (heuristic) 'Top-down stepwise refinement'?

4 – Implementation

(a)   What is the difference between an expression and a statement?

(b)   What is the difference between equality (=) and assignment (:=)?

(c)   How many times is the while loop, in the Average program, executed? Why doesn't it continue looping forever?

What is the
maximum salary?

MOTIVATION
This second short case study is intended to reinforce the overview of the entire programming process introduced in Chapter 1. Only two new concepts are introduced: the **Boolean** data type, and **conditional** statements.

2.1 Requirements

Rita is not at all happy with Beatrice's insinuation.

> RITA: I might be paid more than the average, but I'm sure I don't have the highest salary. I'll prove it.

Rita storms off, intent on finding out what the maximum salary is. There are two approaches she can use: ask everyone, or write a program to examine the same data as before. She decides on the latter course of action.

2.2 Specification

The 'maximum' problem involves the same data types as the 'average' program, that is:

Employee = $\mathbb{N}$ {that is, just their salary}

Employees = Seq of Employee

Rita jots down a specification of the program. Rather than formally introduce all the concepts required at this early stage, we'll show you only an informal version of her operation. (We will do this from time to time in order to show you worthwhile examples without having to expose you to all the formalisms at once.)

```
MAXIMUM-SALARY
ext rd  employee-details : Employees
    wr output           : Employee {that is, a natural number}

pre employee-details ≠ [ ]

post output is a member of the elements of employee-details
     and
     for every element, E, of employee-details, it is true that E ≤ output
```

The post-condition states that the result, output, is one of the salaries from the input and that *all* of the salaries in the input are less than or equal to the result. Thus output must contain the maximum salary from the input salaries.

Exercise 2.1 Before you read on, which of the following statements are true?

(a) $2 + 7 * 4 = 91$

(b) $2 * 3 + 4 = 14$
(c) $13 - 2 / 3 = -3.666$
(d) $14 - 4 * 2 + 8 = 28 / 2$
(e)   Professor Bodmas invented operator precedence.

Even though it has the same meaning as the informal English word of the same spelling, **and** is a formal **operator** in specifications (and also programs).

An **operator** is something that combines expressions to form larger expressions. Examples are addition of natural or real numbers $(+)$, subtraction $(-)$, multiplication $(*)$ and so on. Operators have a **precedence**, indicating how powerful they are at competing with other operators for their arguments. For example, without precedence it would not be possible to say whether the expression

$$34 + 16 + 56$$

meant

$$(34 + 16) + 56$$

or

$$34 + (16 + 56)$$

Luckily, the value of both expressions is 106, and so the parentheses are immaterial. However, this is not true for expressions like

$$34 + 16 * 56$$

which has the value 2800 or 930 depending on which operator is applied first. In specifications and in programs, multiplication has higher precedence than addition. Division has the same precedence as multiplication and, likewise, subtraction has the same precedence as addition.

There is a type which we assume to exist in specifications known as **Boolean** and written $\mathbb{B}$. This has only two values, **true** and **false**. Actually, pre- and post-conditions are expressions of this type. Such expressions are also known as **truth-valued expressions** or **predicates**.

∃∀

There are various Boolean operators which can be used to combine Boolean expressions. One of these is **conjunction** otherwise known as **and**. This takes two Boolean expressions, called **conjuncts**, and returns one Boolean result.

It can be described by way of a table called a **truth table**:

and:

P	Q	P and Q
T	T	T
F	T	F
T	F	F
F	F	F

Another Boolean operator which takes two values is **disjunction** otherwise called **or**. This takes two **disjuncts** and is defined as:

or:

P	Q	P or Q
T	T	T
F	T	T
T	F	T
F	F	F

A third operator of the Boolean type is **negation** otherwise called **not**. This takes one Boolean value and gives a Boolean result:

not:

P	not(P)
T	F
F	T

not has a higher precedence than **and**, which has a higher precedence than **or**.

Exercise 2.2 Verify that

    not p and q

is the same (has the same truth table) as

    not (p or not q)

Exercise 2.3 Imagine you have a car. You go to a garage to fill up with petrol. Unbeknown to you, the petrol pump puts water instead of petrol in your tank. What will happen to your car? Does this mean that assuming that petrol pumps deliver petrol is not a reasonable pre-condition of driving a car?

2.3 Design

Rita considers how the program will work. Clearly, all of the salaries need to be looked at in order to find the highest. As before, she considers how she would do it if somebody was calling out the numbers. She would only need to remember the highest one she had heard so far, rather than all of them. As she hears each number, she needs to compare it with the highest so far, and remember the higher of the two. What should the highest one be to start with? Well, at the start no numbers have been called, and hence there is no highest one. However, since all of the numbers are salaries, and are not less than zero, the method will work if the highest so far is set to zero to begin with. On the other hand, since in this case there is definitely at least one number, the highest so far can be set to the *first* number initially and then she could use the method for the remaining numbers, if any. Of the two alternatives, Rita prefers the second because it is less contrived and slightly more efficient.

Exercise 2.4 Why is it more efficient?

Her first draft of the design is:

```
program maximum-salary
var
   highest-salary-so-far : ℕ
begin ... end
```

Her first view of the actual algorithm is as follows:

```
begin
   read highest-salary-so-far from employee-details file
      { that is, first number is the highest to begin with }
   read in all the remaining salaries, keeping track of the
      largest
   writeln highest-salary-so-far
end
```

The second of these stages requires some design refinement. As before, a variable is to be used to store each salary as it is read. Rita adds this to the design:

current-salary : $\mathbb{N}$

Then she refines the second stage into a while loop:

```
while not eof(employee-details)
    read current-salary from employee-details file
    compare current-salary with highest-salary-so-far
        and set latter accordingly
```

In order to refine the comparison of salaries in the loop body above, Rita needs to use a **conditional statement**.

A **conditional statement** is a programming concept that involves some action or sequence of actions which must be executed if and only if a certain condition is satisfied (true) just beforehand. In designs we tend to write, for example:

```
if a = b
    c := d
    e := f
```

This means that the two assignment statements will be executed if and only if a = b when execution reaches the conditional statement. Note that Pascal insists on the use of the word **Then** in **If** statements.

Our heroine refines the comparison design into

```
if current-salary > highest-salary-so-far
    highest-salary-so-far := current-salary
```

Thus, her eventual design is:

```
program maximum-salary
var
    highest-salary-so-far,
    current-salary : ℕ

begin
    read highest-salary-so-far from employee-details file
    while not eof(employee-details)
        read current-salary from employee-details file
        if current-salary > highest-salary-so-far
            highest-salary-so-far := current-salary
    writeln highest-salary-so-far
end
```

Again we shall hide the details of how Rita makes the real employee details file look like a simple list of salaries.

At this point, Rita convinces herself that the design she has just produced is correct with respect to the specification. Every salary is examined, and by the end the variable highest-salary-so-far will contain the maximum salary in the input.

Rita is now ready to implement the program.

2.4   Implementation

The final program is not much different from the design. Again she uses the type *Integer* as an implementation of ℕ:

> **Program** *MaximumSalary(EmployeeDetails,Output)*;
> { *Program to compute the highest of a number of salaries.*
>   *These are obtained from the departmental employees file. The result is*
>   *displayed as a natural number of pounds.* }
> **Var**
>   *HighestSalarySoFar,*   {*current maximum*}
>   *CurrentSalary*   : *Integer*; {*salary last read from file*}
>
>   *EmployeeDetails*   :   {*detailed bit omitted from here*};

In Pascal, the standard **conditional** statement is the **If** construct. The syntax rules of the language insist that the conditional part is a single statement. In cases where more than one statement is to be conditionally executed, those statements are formed into a compound statement with **Begin** and **End** round them. The **If** construct involves the reserved words **If** and **Then**.

For example:

> **If** *x* > *y* **Then**
> **Begin**
>   *swap* := *x*;
>   *x* := *y*;
>   *y* := *swap*
> **End**

> **Begin**
>   {*detailed bit omitted to open the input file*}
>
>   {*detailed bit omitted to read HighestSalarySoFar from*
>   *EmployeeDetails*}

```
While Not eof(EmployeeDetails) Do
Begin
    {detailed bit omitted to read CurrentSalary from
        EmployeeDetails}
    If CurrentSalary > HighestSalarySoFar Then
        HighestSalarySoFar := CurrentSalary;
End;
writeln(HighestSalarySoFar);
End.
```

As she types the program, Rita is careful to make sure it is all correctly **indented** and well laid out, as she has learned from experience that attention to this sort of detail pays off when it comes to avoiding or tracking down any errors in her programs.

A program can be very large indeed, and thus quite difficult for humans to read. One excellent way of improving the clarity of the program is to use **indentation** to make the structure more obvious. This involves laying out the program text very carefully, so that, for example, **Begin**s and **End**s line up vertically. There are many different styles in common use, but in this book all Pascal programs (and designs) are indented in one style. However, all successful styles are based on the principle that the more the structure of the program is nested, the more the lines are indented. Thus here, for example, we indent inwards after a **Begin** and outwards before an **End**. We also indent within a **While** loop and **If** statement (and so on) even if the body is not compound. There are other places where we use indentation to add to the clarity, as you will see. At least two spaces should be used, although more than four cause the lines to become too short if they are still to fit on a reasonably sized page. It is well worth indenting programs as they are implemented, rather than as a final step, as the clarity added will help greatly with the implementation process itself (in particular, with finding typing mistakes).

Rita runs the program to discover that the highest salary seems to be *exactly* the same as her own!

RITA: Oooops! Sorry. I was wrong. Don't worry, I've been wrong once before.

BEATRICE: I told you.

RITA: Hmmm . . . if I'm the highest paid programmer here, maybe I should leave . . .

BEATRICE: Errr . . . would you like a rise?

SUMMARY

This chapter has served to reinforce the overview of the four stages of programming, and has also introduced the **Boolean** data type and the **conditional (If–Then)** statement. The next chapter presents the first sizeable case study – a game-playing program. This is used as a vehicle for introducing many more specification and programming concepts.

The following notations were introduced in this chapter:

Specification notation

Boolean type   {true, false}
And, or, not   (. . . and . . .) or not . . .

Pascal notation

If statement   **If** . . . **Then** . . .

Match–Snatch – a variation on Nim

3

MOTIVATION

This third case study is longer and more involved than the two previous chapters, and consists of Rita writing a game-playing program. It acts as a vehicle for introducing more basic concepts of formal specification and programming, whilst sticking with **sequences** as the main data type. Of particular interest is the analysis that Rita performs in order to understand the game, and the use of a sequence to model the input to the program from the user.

3.1   Requirements

Rita is given the pay rise Beatrice suggested, and she decides to celebrate by calling an old college friend to arrange a date. She rings Urmston Upwardly-Mobile.

> *Ring, ring . . .*

> VOICE OF URMSTON: Hello, this is Minitropolis 342335. I'm sorry but Urmston is unable to take your call personally. If you'd like to leave your name and number I'll, I mean, he'll contact you as soon as possible. Oh, you can also leave a message, it says here. Speak when you hear the tone, err please.

> *Bleep. . .*

> RITA: Hello Urmston, this is Rita . . .

> *. . . bleep, bleep, bleeeeep.*

> RITA: Err, hello Urmston, it's Rita here. I'm celebrating my new pay rise. Do you fancy a drink? I'll be in the Spread Sandwich on the corner of Tap-juice Close and Milky Way. Byee.
> VOICE OF URMSTON: Byee – I'll tell him.

The Spread Sandwich is almost unique in the centre of Minitropolis. Most of Rita's acquaintances have never heard of it. It lacks the flashing lights and sound systems audibly disguised as top-loading washing machines. It lacks the perpetual foliage that never grows in the other bars of Minitropolis. It lacks carpets. It lacks records on its juke box that are younger than 13 years – the same length of time that its walls have lacked new imagination. Above all, it lacks pretence. Most of Rita's acquaintances believe a picture paints a thousand words. When they celebrate the start of the weekend they appear as pictures, but with little else to say. Luckily their silence is smothered by the washing machines so lacking in the Spread Sandwich. The Spread Sandwich lacks most of Rita's acquaintances, which is only partly why it is her favourite bar.

Seeing Rita enter causes Urmston to jump, not completely unlike a condemned man hearing of his reprieve.

> URMSTON: Where are we going now?
> RITA: There's a nice table just over here. . .
> URMSTON: Hmmm. I've, er, never been in here before.

RITA: I'll forgive you in time.
URMSTON: It's different, I'll say that.

Urmston begins to get more relaxed after a few full strength beers. He tells Rita about his own little celebration.

> URMSTON: Yes, it's not every day one gets voted *regional chairperson* of SOFAPONG.
> RITA: SOFAPONG? What on earth (dare I ask?) is that?
> URMSTON: Society of Friends And Players Of Nimmy Games!
> RITA: Nimmy games? You are joking?
> URMSTON: Certainly not! Nimmy games are perfectly respectable. They make Go and Othello seem complicated.
> RITA: But they are complicated.
> URMSTON: Exactly. Nimmy games are much more fun, okay? Yah!
> RITA: Hmmmm. So what's a Nimmy game then?
> URMSTON: You have heard of Nim, haven't you? The ancient Chinese used to play it with marbles, or something. Nowadays, matchsticks are all the rage.
> RITA: Obviously.
> URMSTON: My favourite Nimmy game is called Match–Snatch – good name, eh?
> RITA: It might be.
> URMSTON: Let me explain . . .

Said to be of ancient Chinese origin, the game of Nim is played with three piles of matches, and two players. The players take turns to remove matches until all matches have been removed. A turn consists of choosing one of the three piles, and removing from it at least one match, but not more than some agreed maximum. By prior agreement, removing the last match results in either winning or losing the game.

There is a wide variety of games similar to Nim, one of which is called Match–Snatch (previously used as an example by Conway *et al.* (1976)). The informal rules are as follows:

(1) There are two opposing players.
(2) A known (but not fixed) number of matchsticks are placed in one pile.
(3) The players take turns removing a number of matches from the pile – at least one match but not more than a move-limit agreed before the game starts.
(4) The player who removes the *last* match *loses* the game.

The move-limit ensures that the game is not trivial – without it, the first player would always win by taking every match except one (unless they were stupid).

Typically, a game might start with 20 matches in the pile, and an agreed move-limit of 5.

RITA: Let me clarify: do you mean this?

Rita describes a more formal view of the game to Urmston:

(1)   There are two players, player 1 and player 2.

(2)   Before the game begins, the number of matches in the pile > 0.

(3)   Player 1 starts and each player takes it in turns to make their move.

(4)   This produces a sequence of moves, S (each move being a number of matches removed), such that after the game has finished:

- each element in $S > 0$ and $\leqslant$ the move-limit

  and

- the sum of all the elements in S = the number of matches in the pile

  and

- (the length of S is odd and the winner = player 2

  or

- the length of S is even and the winner = player 1)

URMSTON: Wow – that's it exactly! Where did you learn to talk like that? Never mind, do you want a game?

Several exciting games later, Rita is wondering why Urmston keeps winning – except for once, when he appeared to be completely frustrated by Rita's moves. They're each taking it in turns to start the game, and the number of matchsticks in the pile to begin with and the move-limit are being varied. There must be a trick, she muses. When she next goes to the bar, Urmston fails to notice her scribbling on the inside of a beer mat. He does not fail to notice that from then on she wins as often as he does.

URMSTON: Okay – you've played this before haven't you. It's a good trick.

RITA: No, I just thought about it.

URMSTON: Gosh! I've known the trick for ages, but I don't know why it works. One starts with the number of matches in the pile, takes away one, then divides that by one more than the move-limit. That leaves a remainder which is the best move to make. The problem is that sometimes the remainder is zero, but one has to take at least one match.

RITA: What a confusing way of saying it!

Rita shows Urmston her beer mat. Below several lines of scribble is clearly written the formula:

(pile – 1) mod (move-limit + 1)

URMSTON: What's mod? And how did you work it out?

RITA: I'll explain it all, if you like . . . .

3.1.1   The winning strategy

There is an algorithm for playing the game which allows the player who makes the first move to win in most random cases, as long as the algorithm is followed unfailingly. If the first player errs on even one move, this same algorithm can be successfully employed by their opponent. Rita explains the sneaky algorithm as follows.

Suppose the move-limit is move-limit matches. If you can take enough matches to leave just one in the pile, your opponent will lose on their next move. So if the pile presented to you on some move contains pile number of matches, where:

2 ≤ pile ≤ move-limit + 1

you will simply take

pile – 1

matches and leave your opponent with one. For example, if the move limit was five, and the pile contained six matches, then you would take five of them.

But if

pile > move-limit + 1

it is not that simple since you cannot take enough matches to leave only one. However, if you manage to leave

move-limit + 2

matches in the pile after your move, your opponent is not allowed to take more than move-limit matches and so cannot leave you with one.

However, they must take at least one match which means that there will be at most

move-limit + 1

matches left, and thus you will be able to leave them with one on your next move. For example, if the move-limit was still five, but the pile contained nine matches, you would take two of them, leaving seven. Suppose your opponent then took one match. That would leave you with six, and you could win by taking five of them as before. Suppose, instead, your opponent took two matches. That would leave five and you could win by taking four of them. Similarly, you could win if your opponent took three, four or five matches. You would respond by taking three, two or one of them respectively, leaving only one match in each case. Your opponent would not be able to leave you with only one match, since the move-limit is five.

By similar reasoning, if you leave

2 * move-limit + 3

matches after some move you will surely be able to leave

move-limit + 2

after the next move and hence leave only one on the move after that.

In general, if you can arrange to leave

m * (move-limit + 1) + 1

matches in the pile after your move, for m = 0,1,2,3, . . . , you will be able to win the game (in m more moves). But if you ever fail to leave

m * (move-limit + 1) + 1

matches after your move then your opponent can move to leave you that many and thus take control.

The person who makes the first move is able in most cases to win by following the above algorithm. However, when the number of matches in the initial pile is equal to

m * (move-limit + 1) + 1

for some m, the person who makes the first move is not in control. In these cases, the second player can always win the game by following the same algorithm. For example, sticking with a move-limit of five, your opponent can win if it is your move and the number of matches in the pile is seven, or thirteen, or nineteen, and so on.

The following analysis and result requires use of the **mod** operator.

Another operation over ℕ is the infix **mod**. This takes two arguments, divides the first by the second, and returns the remainder. **div** is the operator that returns the result of the division, hence the following is always true for every n, m : ℕ:

    (n div m) * m + (n mod m) = n

For example,

    17 mod 4 = 1
    17 div 4 = 4

The calculation of what constitutes a move to retain control of the game (if you already have it) may be arrived at by the following reasoning. Suppose there are pile number of matches before the move, such that

    pile ≠ m * (move-limit + 1) + 1

for any m (that is, you are in control). You must leave

    m * (move-limit + 1) + 1

matches for *any* m. Thus the number you must remove, good-move (⇔ means 'is equivalent to'), is:

    good-move   = pile − (m * (move-limit + 1) + 1)
  ⇔ good-move + m * (move-limit + 1) = pile − 1
                                         [by adding m * (move-limit + 1) to both
                                         sides]
  ⇔ (good-move + m * (move-limit + 1))
    mod (move-limit + 1)   = (pile − 1) mod (move-limit + 1)
                                         [by mod (move-limit + 1) to both sides]
  ⇔ good-move mod (move-limit + 1)   = (pile − 1) mod (move-limit + 1)
                                         [by (x + y * z) mod z = x mod z]

Since also good-move ⩽ move-limit (by the rules of the game):

    good-move = (pile − 1) mod (move-limit + 1)   [by x mod z = x if x < z]

Thus, in general, the number of matches to remove is:

(pile – 1) mod (move-limit + 1)

unless this value is zero (indicating that you are not in control).

> URMSTON: This is exciting! Wait until I tell the society.
> RITA: Why don't you let me write a computer program to play the game?
> URMSTON: Oh would you? You're such a darling.
> RITA: No problem. Will Pascal on a PC be okay?

Exercise 3.1   What is the best number of matches to remove from

(a)   a pile of 21 matches with a move-limit of 6?

(b)   a pile of 31 matches with a move-limit of 9?

3.1.2   The computer program

Rita is going to write a program that plays Match–Snatch following the sneaky algorithm. The program user will act as the other player, and will choose the initial pile size and move-limit. The only question is what the computer should do if the best move is zero? Urmston suggests that in such cases it should try to prolong the game by taking only one match. That means there are more chances for the opponent to make a mistake.

The program is to play such that the user will always lose whenever the computer finds itself in control of the game. Of course, since the user chooses the game's parameters, they should always be able to win if they know the method and as long as they don't make a mistake!

In addition to acting as one player, the program will operate the game. It will accept the initial conditions from the user, ask the user to make their moves, keep track of the number of matches and announce the outcome. The computer will use the winning strategy above when choosing its own moves and will read its opponent's moves from the keyboard.

3.2   Specification

Later that evening, Rita constructs a specification of the program while sitting in bed, sipping her usual nightcap.

3.2.1   Data types

Rita starts by identifying a data type for the two players of the game.

In specifications, a new type may be constructed by simply listing the values as a set, written between curly brackets and separated by commas. The values may be part of another type defined elsewhere, or may be completely new values. For example:

Player = {human, computer}

Player = {human, computer}

One of the interesting aspects of formalizing the behaviour of this program is the program user, upon whom the behaviour depends. Rita muses that the user is (probably) a human, and humans are very complex indeed! However, for the purpose of specifying the program, she may regard the user as nothing more than a sequence of numbers. These are the initial pile size, then the move-limit, then an indication of who goes first, followed by all the moves made by the user throughout the execution of the *whole* program. In other words, Rita specifies the behaviour of the program in terms of the entire list of input typed by the user throughout the game. This Rita shall simply call input, as it is the input to the program.

3.2.2   Operations

Initializing the parameters of the game

Rita specifies an operation to initialize each of the parameters of the game. These are: the number of matches that is in the pile to begin with; the maximum number of matches that is allowed to be taken away in one move; and the choice of which player starts the game. The parameters are entered by the user each time the game is played.

   An operation is needed that allows the user to set the initial size of the pile. This has two external variables: the pile of matches, and the list of input values.

SET-INITIAL-PILE-SIZE

ext wr pile   : $\mathbb{N}$
     wr input : Seq of $\mathbb{N}$

The operation must remove a number from the input sequence, and put the value in the variable pile. The number must be greater than zero, although it might be preceded by some invalid values. Rita adds the pre-condition:

pre for some index, n, it is true that input[n] > 0

Any numbers that might occur before the first acceptable one, are erroneous and should be rejected by the operation (with an error message to the user and a prompt for another number). It is reasonable to assume that eventually the user will learn how to play the game, or cease mistyping, and enter a number greater than zero (or abort the game, in which case the result is irrelevant anyway).

Turning to the post-condition, Rita gives a name to the position in the input sequence at which the first acceptable number is found, by means of a **let expression**.

As a convenience and/or to aid clarity, when we write expressions in a specification, we can give a simple name to some sub-expression, and then use that name rather than the sub-expression. This might avoid repetition of a lengthy term, or simply give some intuitive name to a part of an expression.

The format is:

let X : X-type   be   Sub-expression   in   expression

For example:

let quotient : $\mathbb{R}$ be total / count
in quotient * quotient – total

This is equivalent to

(total / count) * (total / count) – total

During the execution of SET-INITIAL-PILE-SIZE, the input is altered, as numbers are read from it, until the first acceptable one is found. That number and all those preceding it must be removed from the input, so that the next operation which takes values from the input does not use the same number. To specify this, Rita needs to refer to the value of input before SET-INITIAL-PILE-SIZE executes.

In the post-condition of an operation we often wish to refer to the external state occurring before the operation was executed. To differentiate between the state before and after execution of the operation, the value of any variable before execution is referred to by the variable name **hooked** with a back-pointing arrow drawn above it. For example, the value of the variable

input

before execution of an operation is written

$\overleftarrow{\text{input}}$

Note that it is never necessary to hook a variable which has read only access mode, because the final value and the initial value must be the same.

She also needs to denote a **sub-sequence** of the input.

All sequence types have a function to extract a (proper) **sub-sequence** of a sequence. The function takes a sequence and two indices, and returns the sub-sequence occurring between the two indices inclusive. The function is denoted as:

s [i1 , . . . , i2]

where s is a sequence, and i1 and i2 are the two indices.
Thus, for example, if s was the sequence

[A, B, C, D, E, F, G]

then s[3 , . . . , 6] would be the sequence

[C, D, E, F]

She writes the post-condition of SET-INITIAL-PILE-SIZE:

post let n : $\mathbb{N}$ be the smallest number such that $\overleftarrow{\text{input}}$[n] > 0
    in
    (pile = $\overleftarrow{\text{input}}$[n]
    and
    input = $\overleftarrow{\text{input}}$[n + 1 , . . . , len($\overleftarrow{\text{input}}$)])

Exercise 3.2 Remove all the let expressions from the following, to result in equivalent but perhaps more long-winded expressions:

(a)   let discriminant : $\mathbb{R}$ be $(b^2 - 4ac)^{1/2}$
       in $(-b + discriminant)/2a$

(b)   let diff : $\mathbb{R}$ be x $-$ y in diff/(1 $+$ diff $*$ diff)

(c)   let s : $\mathbb{R}$ be $(a + b + c)/2$ in $(s * (s - a) * (s - b) * (s - c))^{1/2}$

Rita specifies a similar operation for setting the move-limit. This number cannot be zero or else it would not be possible to have a legal move! Rita thinks it is also a good idea to ensure that the number is not greater than the number of matches in the pile.

SET-MOVE-LIMIT

ext rd pile   : $\mathbb{N}$
     wr move-limit : $\mathbb{N}$
     wr input   : Seq of $\mathbb{N}$

pre for some index, n, it is true that 1 $\leqslant$ input[n] $\leqslant$ pile

post let n : $\mathbb{N}$ be the smallest number such that 1 $\leqslant$ $\overleftarrow{input}$[n] $\leqslant$ pile
     in
     (move-limit $=$ $\overleftarrow{input}$[n]
     and
     input $=$ $\overleftarrow{input}$[n $+$ 1 , . . . , len($\overleftarrow{input}$)])

Rita's third operation sets the first player of the game, depending on the input of a 0 for human, or a 1 for computer. This is not a good interface, but at least it keeps the specification from being conceptually too complicated at this stage.

SET-WHO-GOES-FIRST

ext wr current-player : Player
     wr input   : Seq of $\mathbb{N}$

pre for some index, n, it is true that 0 $\leqslant$ input[n] $\leqslant$ 1

post let n : $\mathbb{N}$ be the smallest number such that 0 $\leqslant$ $\overleftarrow{input}$[n] $\leqslant$ 1
     in
     (((current-player $=$ computer
          and $\overleftarrow{input}$[n] $=$ 1)
       or
       (current-player $=$ human
          and $\overleftarrow{input}$[n] $=$ 0)
)
     and
     (input $=$ $\overleftarrow{input}$[n $+$ 1 , . . . , len($\overleftarrow{input}$)])
)

Exercise 3.3   What would be the values of current-player and input after the SET-WHO-GOES-FIRST operation has been performed with the following input:

input = [3,2,1,6]

Rita decides to group together the operations she has written so far into another operation, INITIALIZE-GAME, which simply executes each of them in turn. She notices that it is important that SET-INITIAL-PILE-SIZE be executed before SET-MOVE-LIMIT but it is immaterial when SET-WHO-GOES-FIRST is executed. She specifies INITIALIZE-GAME **explicitly**.

An operation may be specified by giving an algorithm for it, similar to a program, but not as pedantic on syntax, and so on. The algorithm may call other operations as commands. Such a definition is called an **explicit** specification of an operation (or less formally, an **explicit operation**). A typical skeleton explicit operation is

```
NAME
ext . . .
pre . . .
begin
   . . .
end
```

```
INITIALIZE-GAME

ext wr pile          : ℕ
    wr move-limit    : ℕ
    wr current-player : Player
    wr input         : Seq of ℕ

begin
  SET-INITIAL-PILE-SIZE
  SET-MOVE-LIMIT
  SET-WHO-GOES-FIRST
end
```

A single turn in the game

When taking a turn in the game the program must ascertain how many matches are to be removed from the pile. If it is the user's turn this involves asking them how many matches they will remove. Otherwise the computer must calculate the number of matches it will remove. Rita constructs an operation called HUMAN-MOVE, which reads the user's move, and another operation called COMPUTER-MOVE, which calculates the computer's move. Both operations leave the number of matches to be removed in the external variable move-sticks.

HUMAN-MOVE

ext   rd pile   : ℕ
      rd move-limit   : ℕ
      wr move-sticks : ℕ
      wr input   : Seq of ℕ

pre   for some index, n, it is true that
          0 < input[n] ⩽ move-limit
          and input[n] ⩽ pile

post let n : ℕ be the smallest number such that
          0 < input[n]↼ ⩽ move-limit
          and input[n]↼ ⩽ pile
      in
      (move-stick = input[n]↼
      and
      input = input[n + 1 , . . . , len(input)]↼)

Exercise 3.4   Why is it necessary to include the condition

    input[n] ⩽ pile

in the pre-condition of HUMAN-MOVE, when it was originally ensured in
SET-MOVE-LIMIT that the move-limit is not bigger than the pile?

Next Rita specifies the strategy used by the computer as follows:

COMPUTER-MOVE

ext   rd pile   : ℕ
      rd move-limit   : ℕ
      wr move-sticks : ℕ

pre   pile > 0

post let good-move : ℕ be (pile − 1) mod (move-limit + 1)
      in
      ((good-move > 0 and move-sticks = good-move)
       or
       (good-move = 0 and move-sticks = 1)
)

Exercise 3.5   In cases when

    good-move = 0

move-sticks has the value 1 after COMPUTER-MOVE has been performed.

(a)   Explain why this is a special case.
(b)   Could this special case have been specified so that move-sticks has
       a different value? Explain.

HUMAN-MOVE and COMPUTER-MOVE obtain the number of matches to be removed from the pile and store that value in move-sticks. Rita also needs to specify an operation which will actually remove the matchsticks from the pile:

```
MAKE-MOVE

ext  wr pile        : ℕ
     rd move-sticks : ℕ

pre  (pile > 0)
     and
     (move-sticks ≤ pile)

post pile = ⎺pile⎺ – move-sticks
```

Playing the whole game

To play the game, the program must repeatedly make moves and swap the current player until the pile is empty. The winner is then the current player, that is, the player whose turn it would have been next if the pile had not just become empty. Rita specifies all this by a single explicit operation, PLAY-GAME:

```
PLAY-GAME

ext rd move-limit     : ℕ
    wr move-sticks    : ℕ
    wr pile           : ℕ
    wr current-player : Player
    wr winner         : Player
    wr input          : Seq of ℕ

begin
  while pile ≠ 0
    if current-player = human
       HUMAN-MOVE
    else
       COMPUTER-MOVE
    MAKE-MOVE
    if current-player = human
       current-player : = computer
    else
       current-player : = human
  end-of-while
  winner : = current-player
end
```

Finally, Rita specifies the whole game. This involves initialization, playing the game and reporting the result.

```
MATCH-SNATCH

ext wr pile            : ℕ
    wr move-limit      : ℕ
    wr current-player  : Player
    wr move-sticks     : ℕ
    wr winner          : Player
    wr output          : Player
    wr input           : Seq of ℕ

begin
  INITIALIZE-GAME
  PLAY-GAME
  output := winner
end
```

The specification abstractly regards the output as being of type Player, identifying the winner of the game. It makes no mention of the interface in terms of prompts for user input, and so on, and messages to tell the user how many matches are left in the pile. (A more advanced specification would at least formally include the reporting by the computer of the number of matches it has taken in each turn. This is clearly needed for the human player to know what the computer is doing!) It can be regarded that such messages are not part of the abstraction which treats the output as merely the winner of the game. Thus Rita is free to decide on a suitable interface during the design of the program. Although a version which gave no intermediate messages could still be *technically* a valid solution of the specification, the messages the user sees are clearly an important part of the general acceptability. Rita notes that a well engineered implementation will involve helpful messages to:

- Prompt for the game's parameters.
- Ask what move the user will make.
- Report the move made by the computer.
- Say how many matches are left on the pile.

And then she goes to sleep.

Exercise 3.6 Consider the following specification:

```
WHAT-DOES-IT-ALL-MEAN
ext wr x : ℕ
    wr y : ℕ
pre true
post y = 10
```

What will be the value of x when an implementation of the
operation completes?

3.3   Program design

The next day is Saturday and, quite unusually, Rita does not have to go
to work. Instead, she proceeds to design the Match–Snatch program over
a bowl of Scrummy Poppers breakfast cereal. She decides to exploit the
structure of the specification, and produce a program design with much
the same structure. This is made even easier by the fact that she has
specified some of the higher level operations explicitly – already consti-
tuting part of the program design. Nevertheless, she still applies the
process of design in a number of stages, working from the specification in
a top-down manner.

     When Rita wrote the specification of the program she found it
convenient to split it into various sub-tasks called operations. The same
is true of program designs and implementations, and in this case Rita will
split the program into the same parts as the specification. (This is what
was meant by saying that, in this case, the specification and the program
have the same structure.) Programs are split up via **procedures**.

A **procedure** is a programming concept. It is a sub-part of a program, designed to achieve
some part of the overall task performed by the program. Procedures have a name and a
body consisting of statements to be executed. They are referenced by a **procedure call**
statement. When such a call is executed, the computer executes the body of the
procedure, and then continues execution from the point after the call. (Thus it behaves
as though the body of the procedure was written in place of the procedure call.) Large
programs should *always* be split into procedures, as this is the only way to make their
design and implementation a manageable task. This fits in extremely well with the
TDSR method of program design, as the various design steps can be refined as separate
procedures. An added benefit, but which is only a *secondary* motive, is that procedures
can be called from different places in a program, thus removing the need for great textual
repetition of code. In designs we normally indicate where a procedure is to be called by
simply inserting its name as a statement.

     For the Match–Snatch program, Rita will eventually write proce-
dures in Pascal, which have the same names as the corresponding operations of the specification (except written slightly differently, as Pascal

does not allow the use of hyphens in identifiers). Hence, the statement to initialize the game will be simply:

InitializeGame

and to play the game, until someone wins:

PlayGame

Rita's first draft of the *design* of the program corresponds closely to the operation MATCH–SNATCH:

```
match-snatch (input,output)

Player  =  {human, computer}

var pile            : ℕ
    move-limit      : ℕ
    current-player  : Player
    move-sticks     : ℕ

begin
  initialize-game
  play-game
  {write who won to output}
end
```

According to the specification, the program is expected to report who won the game after it ends (abstractly represented by an assignment to the variable output). To do this the program needs to produce a message on the output, using a write statement. The messages required can be produced by two write statements, such as:

write 'I won, bad luck!'

and

write 'You won, well done!'

However, only one of these statements is to be executed, depending on who won. Hence Rita requires a **conditional statement**.

An extension of the concept of a **conditional statement** involves *two* alternative actions or sequences of actions. The first must be executed if a certain condition is true just beforehand, otherwise the second must be executed. For example:

```
if x > y
   write x
else
   write y
```

This would cause the largest value of x and y to be output.

Her *design* to produce the final message is:

```
if winner = computer
   write 'I won, bad luck!'
else
   write 'You won, well done!'
```

So far, her program looks like:

```
match-snatch (input, output)

Player = {human, computer}

var pile           : ℕ
    move-limit     : ℕ
    current-player : Player
    move-sticks    : ℕ
    winner         : Player

begin
   initialize-game
   play-game
   if winner = computer
     write 'I won, bad luck!'
   else
     write 'You won, well done!'
end
```

Subsequent stages of the design are concerned with the various procedures required.

First Rita concerns herself with the most complicated – the
play-game procedure. Her explicit specification of this has again
incorporated the basic design:

```
play-game
begin
   while pile > 0
   begin
```

```
        if current-player  =  human
          human-move
        else
          computer-move
        make-move
        if current-player  =  computer
          current-player : =  human
        else
          current-player : =  computer
      end
    winner : =  current-player
  end
```

So next she turns her attention to the procedure **computer-move**.

RITA: Ughh!

Rita removes a small plastic soldier from her mouth. Unfortunately, it was kitted out in desert camouflage uniform – the same colour as Scrummy Poppers.

RITA: Why do they have to make these so realistic?

The computer has to work out how many matches to take based on the specification given earlier. The procedure can assume that the pile is greater than 0 when it starts. Rita notes from the post-condition that the result is either the expression represented by **good-move** or 1 if **good-move** is 0. One standard way of achieving something like this is to assume that the result is **good-move**, then after assigning it to **move-sticks**, compare it with 0 and change it to 1 if necessary. Rita writes:

```
computer-move
begin
  move-sticks : =  (pile  –  1) mod (move-limit  +  1)
  if move-sticks  =  0
    move-sticks : =  1
  if move-sticks  =  1
    write 'I take 1 match'
  else
    write 'I take' move-sticks 'matches'
end
```

It is obviously useful for the computer to tell the other player how many matches it is taking. Rita uses a conditional statement for this to enable the message to be grammatically correct.

The procedure **human-move** is required to read the first number in the move-limit range less than or equal to the number in the pile. Thus Rita needs to design a loop to read and reject all other numbers occurring before the valid one. When the loop finishes, the value of move-sticks must be within the correct range, that is:

(move-sticks ≥ 1) and (move-sticks ≤ pile) and
   (move-sticks ≤ move-limit)

Hence the condition of the loop to *reject* values entered by the user is exactly the opposite (not) of this, that is:

(move-sticks < 1) or (move-sticks > pile) or
   (move-sticks > move-limit)

Exercise 3.7 Convince yourself that the above reasoning is indeed correct, and then complete the following truth table:

P	Q	NOT(P AND Q)	(NOT P) OR (NOT Q)
T	T		
F	T		
T	F		
F	F		

So, Rita's complete design of the procedure is:

```
human-move
begin
  write prompt
  read move-sticks from input
  while (move-sticks < 1) or (move-sticks > pile) or
    (move-sticks > move-limit)
    if move-sticks < 1
      write 'You must take at least one'
    else
    if move-sticks > move-limit
      write 'That is more than we agreed'
    else
    {if move-sticks > pile}
      write 'There are not that many'
    write re-enter prompt
    read move-sticks from input
  end-of-while
end
```

Note her use of different write statements for the different rejection conditions. This improves the interface with the user.

The next procedure she designs is **make-move**. Looking back at its specification, she sees that all it has to do is remove **move-sticks** from pile. It does not need to check whether that amount is too much, because of the pre-condition. However, it is nice to make it report to the user how many matches are left (as, in a real game, they would be able to see the pile). Thus for **make-move** Rita constructs:

```
make-move
begin
  pile := pile  –  move-sticks
  if pile = 1
    write 'there is 1 left'
  else
    write 'there are' pile 'left'
end
```

Like **play-game**, the design of the procedure **initialize-game** is also similar to its explicit specification:

```
initialize-game
begin
  write 'Welcome to the game of Match-Snatch'
  set-initial-pile-size
  set-move-limit
  set-who-goes-first
end
```

Next Rita constructs the three procedures associated with initialization, namely **set-initial-pile-size**, **set-move-limit** and **set-who-goes-first**. Starting with **set-initial-pile-size**, she observes that its specification requires it to remove the first number greater than zero from the input and place it in the variable pile. The first item of data typed by the user may be less than one, thus it is again necessary to use a loop to reject numbers, until an acceptable number has been entered. After the loop is finished, the value entered must be greater than zero, and must be stored in pile. Consequently she makes

```
pile < 1
```

the condition of the rejection loop. She also places sensible write statements to produce messages to the user, so they know what is required of them and what is happening when they enter the wrong data.

```
set-initial-pile-size
begin
  write a prompt
  read pile from input
```

```
      while pile < 1
        write 'There must be at least one match'
        write a re-enter prompt
        read pile from input
      end-of-while
    end
```

Rita's design of set-move-limit is very similar:

```
    set-move-limit
    begin
      write a prompt
      read move-limit from input
      while (move-limit < 1) or (move-limit > pile)
        if move-limit < 1
          write 'There must be at least 1'
        else
        {if move-limit > pile}
          write 'There are not that many matches'
        write a re-enter prompt
        read move-limit from input
      end-of-while
    end
```

The third initialization procedure, set-who-goes-first has a specification requiring it to read a number which is either 0 or 1, and reject any before that. Rita can achieve this by a loop which continues while the number read is not 1 *and* not 0. There is a minor complication with this procedure: it has to read a number from the user and, depending on this, set a value in the variable current-player. It needs a place to store the number read so that it can be compared with 0 and 1. Rita uses an extra variable, first-player-no of type ℕ for this purpose, and adds it to her list of variables:

```
      . . .

      first-player-no : ℕ
```

Then she designs the procedure as:

```
    set-who-goes-first
    begin
      write a prompt (including 'you – 0 , computer – 1')
      read first-player-no from input
      while (first-player-no ≠ 1) and (first-player-no ≠ 0)
        write a re-enter prompt
        read first-player-no from input
      end-of-while
```

```
        if first-player-no = 1
          current-player := computer
        else
          current-player := human
      end
```

As always, Rita studies the piece of design she has just written to check that it is correct. She smiles as she remembers how, when she was first learning to program, she would have written

while first-player-no ≠ 1 or 0

as the condition of the while loop, as that is how one might say it in human language. Her tutor would have pointed out that

1 or 0

is a meaningless sub-expression, and Rita, accepting this, would have altered her design to

while (first-player-no ≠ 1) or (first-player-no ≠ 0)

This would have been worse, because it is not meaningless, but it is the wrong condition (in fact, it is always true)! She has come a long way since then!

So, now, Rita has designed the entire program. As a final check, she compares each procedure with its corresponding specification to convince herself that the designs do not contain any (different) mistakes. Then she finishes breakfast, which has gone very soggy indeed.

 ## 3.4   Implementation

After dressing, Rita struggles with an old wooden deckchair that used to belong to her grandfather. It is a gloriously sunny day, and she is intent on making the most of it. When she finally does beat the chair into a form of submission, she is able to sit down with her portable PC and implement the program.

Converting the completed design to a final program involves Rita arranging the various procedures in an appropriate order, filling in the missing syntax and comments, and so on, and choosing appropriate prompt messages. She starts with the program heading.

Program *MatchSnatch* (*input, output*);

{ *to play the game of match-snatch between the computer and a human, with the human choosing the variations of the game.* }

The best Pascal implementation of the Player data type is a **type declaration** of an **enumerated type**.

In Pascal, an **enumerated type** is a new type defined by a programmer, for which all the values are explicitly listed as identifiers. These values are written between round brackets ( ) and are separated by commas. There are few operations associated with enumerated types. For example:

> (*monday, tuesday, wednesday, thursday, friday*)

This defines a type with five values, as listed.

A **type declaration** in Pascal associates a name with a type definition. The name is an identifier. The form is:

> **Type** *Weekday* = (*monday, tuesday, wednesday, thursday, friday*)

This defines a type with five values as listed, and calls the type *Weekday*.

Type *Player* = (*human, computer*);

Var	*pile*	: *Integer*; {*No. of matches in the pile*}
	MoveLimit	: *Integer*; {*Maximum no. of matches allowed to be removed in a go*}
	MoveSticks	: *Integer*; {*No. of matchsticks removed from pile in current go*}
	CurrentPlayer	: *Player*; {*Whoever's turn it is – swaps between human, computer*}
	winner	: *Player*; {*The winner at the end of the game*}
	FirstPlayerNo	: *Integer*;

Each procedure of the design needs implementing as a **procedure declaration**.

A **procedure declaration** defines a procedure used elsewhere in the program via procedure calls. It starts with a **procedure heading** which names the procedure with an identifier (and defines any parameters – see later). The procedure heading is followed by the procedure's statement body. Every procedure should contain a comment after the heading, explaining what it does. Like all declarations, a procedure must be declared textually before it is used. For example:

Procedure *XthPowerOfY*;
{ *pre x >= 0* }
{ *power := y to the power x; x := 0* }
Begin
  power := 1;
  While *x > 0* **Do**
  Begin
    power := power * y;
    x := x – 1
  End
End;

The first procedure declaration in Rita's implementation is *MakeMove*. The body of this requires a Pascal **If–Else** statement.

An extension of the Pascal **If** statement is the **If–Else** statement. This involves *two* alternative conditional statements and the reserved words **If Then** and **Else**. The first statement is executed if the condition is true just beforehand, otherwise the second is executed. For example:

If *x > y* **Then**
  max := x
Else
  max := y

The same procedure also requires a **writeln** statement to produce the required messages to the user.

The procedure **writeln** can be used to write out a constant message enclosed in single quotes. For example:

writeln('There is 1 left')

Note that, this is not how one would quote in English (using an open and a close quote); instead, the same quote character is used for both starting and ending the message in Pascal.

writeln is a procedure which is pre-declared in Pascal. It takes an arbitrary number of parameters, separated by commas. If the first parameter is a text file variable, the output

is written to that file. Otherwise it is written to the file *output*. The other parameters are
expressions which are evaluated and then output in the order they appear in the
statement. The expressions may be of mixed types; in particular they may be string
constants or integer values. A new line is produced on the output file after the data is
written. For example:

> *writeln(output, 'The date today is', date, 'of', month)*

```
Procedure MakeMove;
{ remove 'MoveSticks' matches from the pile }
Begin
    pile := pile - MoveSticks;
    If pile = 1 Then
        writeln(output, 'There is 1 left')
    Else
        writeln(output, 'There are', pile, 'left')
End; {MakeMove}
```

The next procedure declaration is *SetInitialPileSize*. The body of this
needs to use **less than** on integers, the **write** procedure and the **readln**
procedure.

Most Pascal data types allow an equality comparison operator, denoted as =. For these
types, there is also the converse not-equality comparison, denoted <>. The result of such
comparisons is of type *Boolean*.

In addition to equality and not-equality, Pascal allows the normal four comparison
operators for the *Integer* (and *Real*) data type. These are written as the normal symbols
for **less than** and **greater than** (< and >) and as an approximation to the normal symbols
for **less than or equal** and **greater than or equal** (<= and >=).

Pascal has a pre-declared procedure called **write** which is used to write items to files.
When used with text files, such as *output*, it is exactly like *writeln*, except that a new line
is not written after the data.

There is a pre-declared procedure in Pascal, called **readln**. This is used to read items of
data from a text file, such as input, placing the values in named variables. After this any
data following on the same line is ignored, and the read position is arranged to be the start
of the next line (if there is one). For example:

:=   *readln(input, pile)*

would read the next item of data from the input file and place the value in the variable
pile. Spaces preceding the data are ignored. Any text after the data up to the end of the
line is also ignored. An error occurs if the data is not compatible with the type of the
variable.

Procedure *SetInitialPileSize*;
{ *determines the number of matchsticks in the initial pile* }
Begin
    write(output, 'How many matches in pile to start?');
    readln(input, pile);
    While *pile* < 1 **Do**
    Begin
        writeln(output, 'There must be at least one match');
        write(output, 'Re-enter: how many matches in pile to start?');
        readln(input,pile);
    End
End; {*SetInitialPileSize*}

Exercise 3.8   Write a program to read in two integers from the standard
input and report the greater of the two on the standard output. Produce
prompts for the input and accompany the output with an explanatory
message.

The *SetMoveLimit* procedure needs to use the **Or** operator on *Boolean*
values.

As seen in specifications, the Boolean data type, $\mathbb{B}$, has two values for true and false
respectively and there are various associated functions. In Pascal, this type is called
Boolean, and is pre-declared in the same way as *Integer*. All conditions of **While** loops
and **If** statements are in fact expressions of type *Boolean*. The two values are the
pre-declared identifiers *true* and *false*. The result of comparisons, such as < on integers,
is of the *Boolean* type. For example, the value of

    (*sum* > 0)

is either *true* or *false*.

There is a built-in operator on the Pascal *Boolean* data type called **And**. This takes two
arguments and returns *true* if both are true, and *false* otherwise. Another is **Or**. This takes

two Boolean arguments and returns *true* if at least one of the arguments is true, and *false* 🔲
if both of them are false.

And and **Or** are reserved words (as is **Not**). For example,

   $(sum < 0)$ **And** $(sum > 0)$

always has the value *false*.

```
Procedure SetMoveLimit;
{ determines the maximum number of matches allowed to be removed in
  a go }
Begin
    write(output, 'How many maximum in any move?');
    readln(input,MoveLimit);
    While (MoveLimit < 1) Or (MoveLimit > pile) Do
    Begin
      If MoveLimit < 1 Then
         writeln(output, 'There must be at least 1 match')
      Else
         writeln(output, 'There are not that many matches');
         write(output, 'Re-enter – how many maximum in one move?');
         readln(input,MoveLimit);
    End
End; { SetMoveLimit }

Procedure SetWhoGoesFirst;
{ determines which player has the first go }
Begin
    write(output, 'Who moves first – you (type in 0) ',
                  'or the computer (type in 1)?');
    readln(input,FirstPlayerNo);
    While (FirstPlayerNo <> 1) {computer} And
          (FirstPlayerNo <> 0) {you} Do
    Begin
       write(output, 'Which – you (type in 0) ',
                     'or the computer (type in 1)?');
       readln(input,FirstPlayerNo);
    End;
    If FirstPlayerNo = 1 {computer} Then
       CurrentPlayer := computer
    Else
       CurrentPlayer := human
End; {SetWhoGoesFirst}
```

The *ComputerMove* procedure needs to use the **Mod** operator.

The operator **Mod** in Pascal takes two integer arguments and returns an integer. The second argument *must* be greater than zero. If the first argument is non-negative, the result is the remainder when the first argument is divided by the second (exactly as our notion of mod in specifications). (A more general interpretation applies if the first argument is negative.) The following is *always* true of the result:

$$0 \leq i \textbf{ Mod } j < j$$

Procedure *ComputerMove*;
{ *calculates how many matches the computer is to remove from the pile. The number to be removed is stored in 'MoveSticks'.*}
Begin
  MoveSticks := (*pile* – 1) **Mod** (*MoveLimit* + 1);
  If *MoveSticks* = 0 **Then**
    MoveSticks := 1;
  If *MoveSticks* = 1 **Then**
    writeln(*output*, *'I take* 1 *match'*)
  Else
    writeln(*output*, *'I take* ', *MoveSticks*, *'matches'*)
End; {*ComputerMove*}

Procedure *HumanMove*;
{ *reads how many matchsticks the user will remove from the pile. The number to be removed is stored in 'MoveSticks'.*}
Begin
  write(*output*, *'How many matches do you take?'*);
  readln(*input*, *MoveSticks*);
  While (*MoveSticks* < 1) **Or**
    (*MoveSticks* > *pile*) **Or** (*MoveSticks* > *MoveLimit*) **Do**
  Begin
    If *MoveSticks* < 1 **Then**
      writeln(*output*, *'You must take at least one'*)
    Else
    If *MoveSticks* > *MoveLimit* **Then**
      writeln(*output*, *'That is more than we agreed'*)
    Else
    If *MoveSticks* > *pile* **Then**
      writeln(*output*, *'There are not that many'*);
    write(*output*, *'Re-enter: how many do you take?'*);
    readln(*input*, *MoveSticks*);
  End
End; { *HumanMove* }

Exercise 3.9   Is the following condition equivalent to the condition of the **While** loop in the procedure *HumanMove* above?

Not ((*MoveSticks* >= 1) **And** (*MoveSticks* <= *pile*)
                      And (*MoveSticks* <= *MoveLimit*))

The *PlayGame* procedure involves a **procedure call.**

In Pascal, a (parameterless) procedure is **called** by a statement consisting simply of the name of the procedure. For example the statement

  HumanMove;

executes the body of the procedure *HumanMove.*

```
Procedure PlayGame;
{ assumes pile > 0, plays moves until empty. Assigns winner }
Begin
  While pile > 0 Do
  Begin
    If CurrentPlayer = human Then
      HumanMove
    Else
      ComputerMove;
    MakeMove;
    If CurrentPlayer = computer Then
      CurrentPlayer := human
     Else
      CurrentPlayer := computer
  End; {of move loop}
  winner := CurrentPlayer
End; {of PlayGame}

Procedure InitializeGame;
{ initializes the parameters of the game}
Begin
  writeln(output, 'Welcome to the game of Match-Snatch');
  writeln(output);
  SetInitialPileSize;
  SetMoveLimit;
  SetWhoGoesFirst
End; { initialize game}

Begin {main program – Match-Snatch}
  InitializeGame;
  PlayGame;
  If winner = computer Then
    writeln(output, 'I won, bad luck!')
  Else
    writeln(output, 'You won, well done!')
End. {Match-Snatch}
```

Having completed the program, Rita tests it. She creates cases for which the computer can and cannot win, and makes sure that it behaves appropriately.

The following day, Rita calls Urmston who then drops by to pick up the completed program. He also brings Rita a thank-you present – life membership of SOFAPONG. Rita accepts the honour.

URMSTON: Great, that makes seven members now!

3.5   Comment

Some of Rita's design decisions (both in the specification and in the program) are a matter of taste. For example, the decision in the specification to have an extra level of operation to initialize a game, which merely calls the three subsidiary operations, could have been replaced by a decision just to use the operations directly in PLAY-GAME, rather than indirectly via INITIALIZE-GAME. However, introducing an extra level does emphasize that the group of operations have a related purpose, namely, they all initialize parts of the game.

SUMMARY

This chapter has presented a more complicated case study than the two preceding chapters. This has served to give more experience of specification and programming, and to introduce more concepts. The main specification concepts introduced were **explicit operations**, **let expressions** and **sub-sequences**. The main programming concepts were the *Boolean* type, **procedures**, **type declarations** and **enumerated types**. The following notations were introduced in this chapter.

Specification notation

Mod and div	19 mod 3 = 1, 19 div 3 = 6
Type as enumerated set	{human, computer}
Variable initial value	$\overline{\text{input}}$
Let expression	let good-move: $\mathbb{N}$ be (pile – 1) mod (move-limit + 1) in . . .
Sub-sequence	input[n + 1, . . . , len(input)]

Pascal notation

Enumerated type	*(human, computer)*
Type declaration	**Type** *Player* = *(human, computer)*
Procedure declaration	**Procedure***MakeMove*; **Begin** . . . . **End**
If–Else statement	**If** . . . . **Then** . . . . **Else** . . . .
Writing string constants	*writeln('Hello!')*
File name in writeln	*writeln(output, 'there are', pile, 'left')*
Write	*write(output,'How many matches to start?')*
Readln	*readln(input,pile)*

Boolean type	*true, false*
And, or, not	(.... **And** ....) **Or Not** ....
Equality operator	= , <>
Comparisons	<> <= >=
Integer mod	(*pile* – 1) **Mod** (*MoveLimit* + 1)
Procedure call	*UsersMove*

TUTORIAL EXERCISE

This tutorial reinforces simple specification using pre- and post-conditions.

1

What do you think *should be* the values, if any, of the following expressions?
Assume that s is some sequence.

(a)   [ ][5]

(b)   [2,3,4] [2 , . . . , 7]

(c)   [5,0,8] [2 , . . . , 1]

(d)   s[1 , . . . , len(s)]

2

The following is a *proposed* formal specification of one of the operations from
the Match–Snatch program:

SET-MOVE-LIMIT

ext   wr pile   : N
        wr move-limit : N
        wr input   : Seq of N

pre   true

post let n : N be the smallest number such that $1 \leqslant \overline{input}[n] \leqslant \overline{pile}$
        in
        (move-limit = $\overline{input}[n]$
        and
        input = $\overline{input}[n + 1 , . . . , len(\overline{input})]$)

(a)   What does it mean for a pre-condition to be specified as 'true'?

(b)   Apart from any consideration of the actual Match–Snatch program, what
         is wrong with the pre-condition being simply 'true' in this operation? (Hint:
         does the post-condition make sense?) What should the pre-condition be?

(c)   Assuming that the pre-condition is replaced by the one in your answer to
         (b), the specification of SET-MOVE-LIMIT is actually too loose, in that it
         allows the implementor more freedom than is intended for the context of
         the Match–Snatch program. What is wrong with it, and why is this
         wrong?

(d)   Propose *two* ways of fixing the fault you have identified in (c). Which do you think is the best way?

LABORATORY EXERCISE – To implement part of a variation on Match–Snatch

Purpose

Implementation in Pascal of a specification, with emphasis on using logical relations. You should invest plenty of time in understanding the specification, before proceeding with the design.

Problem

The rules of Match-Snatch2, a simple variation of Match-Snatch are as follows:

(1)   There are two players.

(2)   Two equal piles of matchsticks of a given size are placed between the two players.

(3)   A 'move' is for a player to remove some number of mtches from those remaining. To be a valid move, he or she must take at least one match, and not more than some number agreed upon as a move-limit before the game begins. The matches may be removed from either or both piles. The players alternate moves and the object of the game is to avoid being the player who has to take the last match.

For this exercise, it is sufficient to study only the parts of the specification given below. Assume that the full specification has been partially implemented in Pascal and you are required to complete the program by designing and writing the code for the following two procedures:

(i)   HUMAN-MOVE – This reads from the terminal how many matches the human player wishes to remove from each pile, checking for any values which are not allowed;

and

(ii)   COMPUTER-MOVE – This calculates and reports the value of the move to be made by the computer.

You must study the specifications below to find the precise definition of these procedures. Failure to study the specification will almost certainly result in you producing the wrong implementation! Even if *you* consider your implementation to be *better* than is required by the specification, a solution which does not satisfy the specification is, in general, worthless.

Specification

There are six external variables used in the specification of HUMAN-MOVE
and COMPUTER-MOVE. There are two piles of matches – called pile1 and
pile2. The number of matches to be removed from each pile are stored in the
external variables move-sticks1 and move-sticks2 respectively. The variables
move-limit and input are as in MATCH-SNATCH.

   HUMAN-MOVE reads values from input and places them in
move-sticks1 and move-sticks2. COMPUTER-MOVE calculates values for those
variables from the values of pile1, pile2 and move-limit. Note also that the
HUMAN-MOVE specification dictates a particular rejection strategy for invalid
input.

HUMAN-MOVE

ext rd pile1,pile2   : $\mathbb{N}$
    rd move-limit   : $\mathbb{N}$
    wr move-sticks1,move-sticks2 : $\mathbb{N}$
    wr input   : Seq of $\mathbb{N}$

pre
    for some natural number, n, it is true that
    input[2 * n + 1] $\leqslant$ pile1 and
    input[2 * n + 2] $\leqslant$ pile2 and
    0 < input[2 * n + 1] + input[2 * n + 2] $\leqslant$ move-limit

post
    let n: $\mathbb{N}$ be the smallest number such that
            input [2 * n + 1] $\leqslant$ pile1
        and input [2 * n + 2] $\leqslant$ pile2
        and 0 < input [2 * n + 1] + input [2 * n + 2] $\leqslant$ move-limit

    in

    move-sticks1 = input [2 * n + 1]
    and
    move-sticks2 = input [2 * n + 2]
    and
    input = input [2 * n + 3 , ... , len input]

COMPUTER-MOVE

ext rd pile1,pile2   : $\mathbb{N}$
    rd move-limit   : $\mathbb{N}$
    wr move-sticks1,move-sticks2 : $\mathbb{N}$

pre (pile1 > 0) or (pile2 > 0)

post
    let good-move : $\mathbb{N}$ be (pile1 + pile2 - 1) mod (move-limit + 1)
    in

    (move-sticks1 $\leqslant$ pile1) and (move-sticks2 $\leqslant$ pile2)
    and
    (((good-move > 0) and (move-sticks1 + move-sticks2 = good-move))
        or ((good-move = 0) and (move-sticks1 + move-sticks2 = 1)))

Implementation

Design and implement the operations in the form of two procedures which must have the headings:

Procedure *HumanMove*;
Procedure *ComputerMove*;

Assume the following global declarations, and no others:

Var *pile1, pile2,*
    MoveLimit,
    MoveSticks1, MoveSticks2 : Integer;

Telegram analysis

MOTIVATION

The Telegram Analysis problem is concerned with processing a number of telegrams to discover various attributes of each telegram (such as how many words it contains) and outputting them in a neat listing. The user's requirements are written informally in English and have a number of defects. The purpose of this chapter is to identify these defects, obtain (from the customer) appropriate resolutions of them, develop a formal specification, and then design and implement the program. The specification involves **functions**, **sets** and **records**. The implementation involves strings of characters, and thus the chapter introduces the Pascal type **Packed Array Of** *Char*. In addition, the Pascal **sequential file** is looked at in more detail, including **text** and non-text files.

4.1   Requirements

> BEATRICE: Now that you're paid so much, you're ideal for this latest
> assignment.
> RITA: Oh, what's that then?
> BEATRICE: Our branch in Polygonia have won a contract to supply
> telegraphic equipment to the Polygonian National Tele-
> graph. They're short of programmers, and I'm lending you
> to them.
> RITA: Oh! Well, what do I have to do?
> BEATRICE: Here's your plane tickets – you fly out tomorrow at 6
> a.m. I dare say they'll tell you what you do when you get
> there.

Rita certainly has the impression that Beatrice expects a lot from her, a
thought she has more than enough time to contemplate on the bumpy 18
hour flight to Polygonia. It's a small country surrounded almost entirely
by oblivion. Well, at least, according to the only guide book she could
find, that is the preferred belief of the local inhabitants. Rita's luggage,
which mainly consists of three bikinis, 12 bottles of sun lotion, malaria
cream and a portable PC with 20 Mbyte hard disk, ideally reflects the
spicy mixture of simplicity and hi-tech sophistication that Polygonia has
become. May Kit built a small factory there two years ago, to service the
growing markets of the whole of the Geometrica continent. Uncannily,
it's exactly 6 a.m. the same day local time when she arrives – not ready
for a full day's work. The heat slaps her lungs into overtime as she
descends the steps to the swimming tarmac. It's hot. So are the hotel, her
bed and her dreams.

The next day she drives to the factory and meets her new boss –
Mr P. Portly. Rita never did find out what his first name is. The air
conditioning is broken and her T-shirt is ashamed of her.

> MR P. PORTLY: Hello Miss, err, Rigorous – welcome to May Kit
> Polygonia. I trust you had a nice flight, and your hotel is
> comfortable?
> RITA: I . . .
> MR P. PORTLY: Good. Well, I'm a great believer in time. Time waits
> for no man, so they say. I suppose Mr Business told you
> what we want you to work on?
> RITA: Ms Business – no *she* did not.
> MR. P. PORTLY: Oh! Well, err, you'll be working with, well, under
> Mr Solitude – let's take you to him, hmmm?

Mr Portly leads Rita down a glass-topped corridor. He rivets her to a stop
outside a door marked 'Mr S. Solitude', whilst he rumbles through it.

Apparently unaware of the propensity for sound to travel in all directions at once, Mr Portly explains directly to the occupant of the room that Rita will be working for him, and that 'she's a woman'.

> MR S. SOLITUDE: Hello – I'm Simon. Don't worry about old Piggy Portly – you won't have to work with him.

Simon explains the work to Rita over a cup of locally grown coffee. The factory has a contract to supply a new telegraph system for the country. Simon normally designs the hardware and software for systems like this, but because of the very tight schedule he wants Rita to write the computer program to control one part of it. He gives her a written description of what's needed:

> A program is required to process a stream of telegrams. This stream is available as a sequence of letters, digits and blanks on some device and can be transferred in sections of predetermined size into a buffer area where it is to be processed. The words in the telegrams are separated by sequences of blanks and each telegram is delimited by the word ZZZZ. The stream is terminated by the occurrence of the empty telegram, that is a telegram with no words. Each telegram is to be processed to determine the number of chargeable words and to check for occurrences of overlength words. The words ZZZZ and STOP are not chargeable and words of more than 12 letters are considered overlength. The result of the processing is to be a neat listing of the telegrams, each accompanied by the word count and a message indicating the occurrence of an overlength word.

> SIMON: As you can see, I've written it out very precisely.
> RITA: Do you have a formal specification?
> SIMON: Errr, no. I've got the original requirements from the government. Err, I've heard of formal specifications, but we don't need them here. I do everything.

It's quite clear to Rita that Simon has never worked in a team before.

> RITA: Okay. Suppose I study this and come back to you?

4.1.1 Case study history – an aside

This requirement statement was originally given by Peter Henderson (a computer scientist) and his experience is described by Henderson and

Snowdon (1972). It is also discussed (with an abstract specification) by Jones (1990). The purpose of the exercise was to demonstrate the method of top-down, structured programming to his students. The method he used and the resulting program were subsequently analysed. Of particular interest was the discovery of a **bug** and the analysis of how this occurred.

A **bug** is a term for an error in a program.

Henderson and Snowdon attributed it to the introduction of unnecessary detail too early in the design of the solution. If the programmer had been more formal about the assignment of meanings to the concepts he introduced, they reasoned, it could be expected that the inconsistency between these formal meanings would become obvious then, rather than showing up as a bug later. The conclusion that they drew from the exercise was that Henderson should have described the problem more formally. Thus, the problem description was written by a programmer with the intention of being precise and yet it still contained several ambiguities.

4.1.2 Inadequacies of the requirements

Rita takes the document to her new office. It's hot. So she takes it, some paper, a pen and a bikini to the nearby beach instead. Having found a quiet secluded spot, she slips in and out of the cool sea and then settles under a palm tree to study the requirements. There are a great number of ambiguities and omissions. She divides her questions into two basic categories.

Questions about the net effect (meaning) of the program

These include:

(1)   Are overlength words charged as normal words?

(2)   Are overlength words modified (truncated, for example) for output?

(3)   The definition of 'overlength' states that only letters should be considered. Is this really the intention, or should digits be included too?

(4)   Should the number of overlength words be counted, or just the fact that some exist?

(5)   What is the meaning of 'word count' in the results? Does it really mean all words, or just chargeable words?

(6)   Is the delimiting word ZZZZ to be transferred to the output?

(7)   Should there be a report for the empty telegram?

(8)   What error detection and recovery is to be provided? (That is, can the input be assumed to be reliable?)

Questions about how the information is to be presented

These include:

(9)   What is the meaning of 'delimit'? For example, does the delimiter occur before and after the telegrams, or afterwards only, or only between telegrams?

(10)   What is the exact meaning of 'sequence' in the requirements? For example, does this allow empty occurrences?

(11)   What is, or, at least, what determines the buffer size?

(12)   Can words span blocks?

(13)   What is an 'empty telegram'?

(14)   Are leading spaces allowed before words and at the beginning of a buffer?

(15)   And, quite importantly, what is a 'neat listing'? For example, one word per line, or right justified to some fixed width, and so on? Can words span lines?

Rita clearly has to ask her 'customer', Simon, for clarification of these issues. So she returns to the factory, but not before another quick dip.

When faced with such a set of questions, the analyst (who is often the programmer also) would need to ask the customer for more information, or clarification. In general, some of the questions may only come to light after the specification is started. Even in these cases, the specifier (who is often the analyst, and hence often the programmer) must obtain resolutions from the customer. In some simple cases, it might be convenient to make temporary educated guesses, in order to enable more of the specification to be attempted, and thus pester the customer less often. Of course, these guesses must still be checked with the customer, before the specification is considered complete; and if they are wrong – then the specification must be corrected.

Exercise 4.1 The following is a customer's requirement statement for a taxi fleet control program. Identify as many inadequacies as you can find and suggest sensible resolutions where appropriate.

> A program is required to control a taxi fleet. It must work out the best car to answer some call and keep track of the whereabouts of a car. It must be able to work out the best route between two points, or the cost.

4.2 Specification

Once Rita has obtained the answers she needs, she starts to construct a formal specification. Work out what Simon said yourself from the specification that Rita writes.

To simplify the specification, Rita decides to write it in two parts. The first assumes a rather abstract view of the input and output, omitting complications like buffer blocks and telegram delimiting words. The second part is more concerned with the relationship between the abstract specification and the required form of the input and output. Thus, the first stage is primarily concerned with the processing done, and the second with the representation of the data.

4.2.1 Abstract specification

In the abstract specification, Rita views the input as a sequence of telegrams. The empty telegram, which is used as a delimiter in the actual representation, is not needed in this abstraction.

    Telegrams = Seq of Telegram

Similarly, telegrams are viewed as sequences of words, and the delimiting word ZZZZ is not needed in this abstraction. However, none of the telegrams are empty (as the empty telegram marks the end of the list in the actual representation). Rita uses a **data type invariant** to specify this.

Sometimes when defining a type we know more about it than can be deduced from standard constructions, such as Seq of . . . . These additional characteristics are called **invariants**, as they are extra things which are always true about the type. Invariants can be written explicitly after a type definition.

```
Telegram = Seq of Word
              excluding [ ]
```

She defines a word as being a non-empty sequence of alphanumeric **characters**, but excluding the word ZZZZ (because that would end the telegram in the actual representation).

Another data type which is usually assumed to exist in specifications is **Char**. This is the set of characters, such as 'A', 'b', '2' and '?' The exact content of the set is context dependent. In this book it is considered as being the same as the corresponding type in Pascal.

```
Word = Seq of Alpha-num
            excluding [ ] and ['Z','Z','Z','Z']
```

She specifies alphanumerics as being a **set** of characters. She does this by denoting the sets of digits and letters, and then defining alphanumerics as being the **union** of these.

As said before, a data type is a set of values. A **set** is an unordered collection of distinct objects – there is no order of the elements in a set. What is more, a value cannot be an element of some set more than once – either it is in the set or it is not. For example, the set containing only 4, 6, 2, 4 and 2 is the same as the set containing only 4, 2 and 6.

In specifications, a set may be denoted by simply listing all of its elements separated by commas within curly brackets. For example,

{6,2,90,12}

This of course is the same as

{12,2,90,6}

and

{12,2,12,90,2,6}

and so on.

$$\text{Digit} = \{\text{'0', '1', '2', '3', '4', '5', '6', '7', '8', '9'}\}$$
$$\text{Letter} = \{\text{'A', 'B', 'C', 'D', 'E', 'F', 'G', 'H', 'I', 'J', 'K', 'L', 'M',}$$
$$\text{'N', 'O', 'P', 'Q', 'R', 'S', 'T', 'U', 'V', 'W', 'X', 'Y', 'Z'}\}$$

A function on sets (and thus on specification types) is **set union**. This takes two sets and produces the set containing all values that were in either of the two given. In specifications we use the infix $\cup$ operator for union. For example:

$$\{4,3,10,1\} \cup \{25,10,2,1,15\} = \{4,10,25,3,15,1,2\}$$

$$\text{Alpha-num} = \text{Letter} \cup \text{Digit}$$

Each element of Alpha-num is either an element of Digit or of Letter. Thus, for any sequence from the set Word, each element of that sequence is either a Digit or a Letter.

Exercise 4.2   What is the value of each of the following sets?

(a) $\{A,B,C\} \cup \{A,B,C\}$

(b) $\{[\,]\} \cup \{\{\,\}\} \cup \{\{\{\,\}\}\}$

(c) $\{X,Y,Z\} \cup \{x,y,z\}$

Thinking next about the result of the progam, Rita views the output as a sequence of reports, one for each telegram in the input.

$$\text{Reports} = \text{Seq of Report}$$

Each report consists of a number of related pieces of information about a telegram, namely: the message itself, the charge count and whether there are any overlength words. She groups these items together using a **record** type.

A **record** is a value consisting of several separate items collected together. The items are called **fields** of the record. A **record type** is a data type (that is, a set), containing all the record values of a particular form. The types of the fields might not be the same as each other, but they are fixed for a given record type.

The fields of a record type each have a name. Record types are defined in our specifications by listing these names, and with each, the type of the values which may occupy the field. For example,

```
Personal-details = Record
                    first-name : Seq of Letter
                    surname : Seq of Letter
                    age : ℕ
                    sex : {female , male}
                  end
```

This defines the type Personal-details as the set of all possible records with those fields described.

```
Report = Record
            message       : Telegram
            charge-count : ℕ
            overlength    : 𝔹
         end
```

Exercise 4.3 Define a record type that describes different wines. It should include characteristics such as name, age, colour, price per bottle, country of origin, taste and whether there is some currently in stock.

The word STOP is significant in the abstract specification, and Rita finds it convenient to define it as a **constant**.

It is possible to give a meaningful name to a constant value. Such a name can then be used instead of the constant value, thus aiding the clarity of the specification. Such associations also make a specification easier to change, should that be necessary. For example:

```
basic-tax-rate = 25.0
```

```
stop-word = ['S','T','O','P']
```

She decides to define the behaviour of the program, at this abstract level, as a **function** rather than an operation.

A **function** is a mapping or correspondence between sets of values. A function is **applied** to values, called the **arguments** of the function, and yields a value called the **result** of the function. The type of the arguments is called the **arity** (sometimes called the domain – but see later) and the type of the result is called the **value sort** (sometimes called the range

∃∀ – see later). When a function is applied to different arguments it may yield the same result but it is not possible to yield different results for different applications of the function to the same arguments. For example:

```
multiply (4,2)   = 8
multiply (8,1)   = 8
multiply (7,3)   = 21
multiply (8,1)   = 8   (still!)
```

From the point of view of specification, it is extremely useful to state the arity and value sort of a function. This information, together with the function name, is presented in the function **signature**. For example, len is a function that takes a sequence and returns a natural:

$$\text{len} : (s : \text{Seq of } X) \rightarrow (l : \mathbb{N})$$

s is being used here as a name for the argument, within the function, and l as a name for the result.

The arity of a function of more than one argument is given as a list of all the argument sets separated by commas. For example:

$$\text{multiply} : (x : \mathbb{N}, y : \mathbb{N}) \rightarrow (m : \mathbb{N})$$

A function can only be applied to the set of values specified in its arity and will always yield a result in the value sort. Note that a function does not have external variables (state).

Sometimes it is convenient to specify a program, or part of a program as a **function** rather than a more general operation. This is merely a specification technique, and should not affect the approach taken to the implementation.

She writes the signature of the function:

$$\text{analyse} : (\text{tels} : \text{Telegrams}) \rightarrow (\text{reps} : \text{Reports})$$

A function specification may include a **pre-condition**. This true or false expression characterizes all things that an implementation of the function may assume about its arguments (that is, its input).

The program assumes nothing about its input.   ∃∀

The **pre-condition** of an operation or function may be written as, simply,

> true

A pre-condition characterizes all that may be assumed to be true before the operation executes, or the function is applied. Thus, if a pre-condition is merely true, this means that *nothing* may be assumed.

> pre true

Rita defines the result of the function via a **post-condition**.

A function may be specified via a **post-condition**. This characterizes all required things about the relationship between the function arguments and the function result.

The length of the result and the input sequences are the same, and for each telegram in the input sequence, the corresponding item in the result sequence is a report relating to it. To refer to the indices of the two sequences, Rita uses the **inds** function.

Two more functions on sequence data types are **inds** and **elems**. They are both functions from a sequence to a set. inds yields the set of indices of the elements in a given sequence and elems yields the set of elements in a sequence:

> inds : (s : Seq of X) → (i : Set of $\mathbb{N}$)
> inds (s) is the set of all naturals from 1 to len(s)
>
> elems : (s : Seq of X) → (e : Set of X)
> elems (s) is the set of all elements of s

For example, if s = [a,b,b,c], inds(s) = {1,2,3,4} and elems(s) = {a,b,c}.

Assuming another function, analyse-telegram, for specifying the report corresponding to a single telegram, Rita writes the post-condition of analyse:

post len(reps) = len(tels) and
    for every member, i, in inds(tels), it is true that
        reps[i] = analyse-telegram(tels[i])

Exercise 4.4   What does the following function specify?

$F : (n : \mathbb{N}) \rightarrow (r : \mathbb{R})$
pre true
post $r \geqslant 0$ and $r * r = n$

Thus, her whole specification so far is

Telegrams = Seq of Telegram

Telegram = Seq of Word
               excluding [ ]

Digit = {'0', '1', '2', '3', '4', '5', '6', '7', '8', '9'}

Letter = {'A', 'B', 'C', 'D', 'E', 'F', 'G', 'H', 'I', 'J', 'K', 'L', 'M',
            'N', 'O', 'P', 'Q', 'R', 'S', 'T', 'U', 'V', 'W', 'X', 'Y', 'Z'}

Alpha-num = Letter $\cup$ Digit

Word = Seq of Alpha-num
          excluding [ ] and ['Z','Z','Z','Z']

stop-word = ['S','T','O','P']

Reports = Seq of Report

Report = Record
        message   : Telegram
        charge-count : $\mathbb{N}$
        overlength : $\mathbb{B}$
     end

analyse : (tels : Telegrams) $\rightarrow$ (reps : Reports)

pre true

post len(reps) = len(tels) and
    for every member, i, in inds(tels), it is true that
        reps[i] = analyse-telegram(tels[i])

If a function is defined for *all* the values in its arity, it is said to be a **total function**. If it is defined for only some of the values, it is a **partial function**. For example, the function div over two natural numbers is a partial function, because it is not (usually) defined for dividing by zero. A function that has a pre-condition of true is a total function, because it assumes nothing about the values of its arguments, and hence must be defined for all values in its arity. The **domain** of a function is the sub-set of its arity, for which it is [∃∀]ᴾ defined. Thus, the domain of a total function is exactly its arity. (Sometimes the arity is called the domain, even for partial functions.)

Similarly, the **range** of a function is the sub-set of its value sort, containing the elements yielded by the function for at least one argument in its domain. (Sometimes the value sort is called the range.)

Rita has not given an indication of how the program can be implemented, she has merely defined the output in relation to the input. That is, she has defined it **implicitly**.

Like operations, functions may be completely specified using pre- and post-conditions. Such a definition is called an **implicit specification** of a function (or, less formally, an **implicit function**), because it (generally) gives no hint as to how the function might be implemented. If no pre-condition is given for an **implicit** function specification, the pre-condition true is assumed.

Exercise 4.5 If the post-condition of the analyse function did not include the condition that len(reps) = len(tels), what would a valid implementation be allowed to do?

Next she considers the analyse-telegram function. This function produces a report for a telegram, **constructing** the **record value** from its constituent parts.

In specifications we **construct** a **record value** by making use of an automatically defined function based on the name of the record type. Every record type, for example,

```
Rtype = Record
           field1 : Type1
           field2 : Type2
           . . .
        end
```

has an associated function, for example, mk-Rtype with a signature of

```
mk-Rtype : (field1 : Type1 , field2 : Type2 , . . .)  ⊳ Rtype
```

This takes an argument from each of the appropriate types and produces the corresponding record value. For example, with the record type

```
Pencil-sharpener = Record
                   diameter    : ℕ
                   blade-angle : ℕ
                   material    : {plastic, steel}
                   colour      : {silver, red, blue, yellow, green}
                 end
```

the value of

```
mk-Pencil-sharpener (10, 20, plastic, blue)
```

is a record of type Pencil-sharpener with diameter of 10, blade-angle of 20, material of plastic and colour of blue.

Rita decides to define analyse-telegram **explicitly** in terms of two other functions, charge-word-count and any-overlength.

Functions may be defined explicitly by presenting an expression in terms of the arguments, as the function result. This is *instead* of a post-condition. Such a definition is called an **explicit specification** of a function (or, less formally, an **explicit function**). The result expression is written after the symbol

$$\triangle$$

which may read as 'is defined to be'. For example,

```
increment : (i : ℕ) → ℕ
increment (i) △ i + 1
```

Note that the name of, and the parentheses round, the result in the signature *may* be omitted.

An explicit function may also be given a pre-condition. However, if a pre-condition is omitted, then rather than assuming simply true, the actual pre-condition is deduced from the result expression, and is exactly the weakest pre-condition (that is, the one that assumes the least) required for the result expression to be defined. The weakest possible pre-condition is true.

```
analyse-telegram : (tel : Telegram) →• (r : Report)
analyse-telegram(tel) △
    mk-Report(tel, charge-word-count(tel), any-overlength(tel))
```

This states that the report for a telegram consists of the telegram itself, the number of chargeable words, and whether or not there are any overlength words.

Next, Rita considers the charge-word-count function. This must take a telegram and count the number of occurrences of words that are not STOP. One way to specify this is to construct the set of indices into the telegram such that the word at that index is not STOP. The desired result is the size, or **cardinality**, of that set.

---

card is a function that says how many elements there are in a (finite) set, that is it yields the **cardinality** of a given set. For example,

```
card ({a,d,c,a,e,e}) = 4
```

To specify the set of required indices, Rita uses **set comprehension** and **membership**.

Another function on sets is a test for **membership** of a set, written as

```
∈
```

This returns true if a given value is an element of a given set. For example,

```
c ∈ {a,b,c}
```

is true, but not

```
d ∈ {a,b,c}
```

A general way of specifying the elements in a set is by what is called **set comprehension**. This defines a set which contains all elements from another set, that satisfy some property. One form involves a logical variable from a given type, which is a typical member of the set being constructed. For example,

∃∀ $\{i \in \mathbb{N} \mid 1 \leqslant i \leqslant 3\}$

This means the set ({}) of *all* elements, i, from the set $\mathbb{N}$, such that (|) $1 \leqslant i \leqslant 3$. It is the same as the set $\{1,2,3\}$. One could imagine constructing the set by taking all the natural numbers and removing those for which the property is *not* true. Another example is:

$\{s \in$ Seq of $\{1,2,3\} \mid$ len(s) $= 2$ and s[1] $<$ s[2]$\}$

This is the same as:

$\{ [1,2] , [2,3] , [1,3] \}$

Set-comprehension is, of course, most useful for denoting very large (or even infinite) sets, or sets dependent on an unknown, such as a function argument or operation external variable.

The function is defined as

charge-word-count : (tel : Telegram) $\rightarrow$ (r : $\mathbb{N}$)
charge-word-count (tel) $\triangle$
    card ($\{ j \in$ inds (tel) $\mid$ tel[j] $\neq$ stop-word$\}$)

Informally, this says: construct the set of all indices of words in the telegram for which the word at that point is not the stop word. The number of chargeable words is the size of that set. To convince herself, Rita considers an example:

charge-word-count([['H','E','L','L','O'], ['A','U','N','T'], ['N','E','L','L'],
                    ['S','T','O','P'], ['H','A','P','P','Y'],
                    ['B','I','R','T','H','D','A','Y'], ['S','T','O','P']])

By the definition of the function, this is

card ($\{$j $\in \{1,2,3,4,5,6,7\}$
        |
        [['H','E','L','L','O'], ['A','U','N','T'], ['N','E','L','L'],
          ['S','T','O','P'], ['H','A','P','P','Y'],
          ['B','I','R','T','H','D','A','Y'], ['S','T','O','P']]
        [j] $\neq$ stop-word $\}$)

which is

card ($\{1,2,3,5,6\}$)

which equals

5

Finally, Rita specifies any-overlength as:

```
any-overlength : (tel : Telegram) → B
any-overlength(tel) △
    for some member, w, ∈ elems(tel), it is true that
        len (w) > 12
```

This states that the answer is true if and only if there can be found some word in the telegram for which the length is greater than 12.

Exercise 4.6   Given any sets, a and b, and any sequence, s, which of the following expressions are always true?

(a)   a ∪ { } = a

(b)   card(a) + card(b) = card(a ∪ b)

(c)   card(inds(s)) = len(s)

(d)   card(elems(s)) = len(s)

Exercise 4.7   List the elements of the following set defined by set comprehension:

```
{s ∈ Seq of {a,b,c} | (lens s < 3) and (card elems s = card inds s)}
```

Exercise 4.8   The abstract specification contains the answers Rita received from Simon to some of the questions about the net effect of the program. Only the first five questions are relevant to the abstract specification; the others are covered by the specification of the representation details. Find the answers to those five questions.

4.2.2   Representation details

Having formed an abstract specification, Rita's next task is to relate it to the required representations. She specifies the concrete input as a sequence of blocks, where each block is a fixed length sequence of alphanumeric characters and spaces:

```
Blocks = Seq of Block

Block  = Seq of Symbol
            of length block-size

block-size = 150

Symbol = Alpha-num ∪ {' '}
```

Similarly, the concrete form of the output she specifies as

Lines = Seq of Line

Line   = Seq of Symbol
            of maximum length max-line-length

max-line-length = 80

Now she has two major tasks left: one to define a function to turn the
Blocks into Telegrams, and another to turn Reports into Lines. She defines
these informally. The first function takes a value of Blocks and *abstracts*
it into the corresponding value of Telegrams. As a kind of convention, she
uses the function name abs-Blocks, to indicate that the function abstracts
from the type Blocks.

abs-Blocks : (bs : Blocks) → (tels : Telegrams)

Informal definition   This takes a sequence of blocks of symbols (letters,
digits and spaces). The block structure is removed by concatenating all
the blocks together to produce a simple sequence of symbols. Non-space
symbols are then grouped into words, without changing the order of the
symbols, to form a sequence of words; by treating a non-empty sequence
of spaces as a word separator. The spaces are discarded. Finally, these
words are grouped into sequences of words, again without changing the
order of the words; by regarding the word ['Z','Z','Z','Z'] as a sequence
terminator. All the ['Z','Z','Z','Z'] words are discarded. An empty sequence
of words marks the end of the input, the word sequences before that form
the resulting sequence of telegrams.

Her second function relates Reports to their representation as Lines.
Thus the function *represents* a given Reports value, and she calls it
rep-Reports.

rep-Reports : (reps : Reports) → (ls : Lines)

Informal definition   This takes a sequence of reports. The result is a
sequence of lines, formed by concatenating smaller sequences of lines.
These smaller sequences each correspond to a report in the input, and are
concatenated in the same order as the order of the corresponding reports.
The sequence of lines corresponding to a single report consists of an
(even) smaller sequence of lines corresponding to the message of the
Report, concatenated with a line containing a decimal representation of
the charge-count of the report, concatenated with another line containing
a textual representation of the overlength field of the report.

The sequence of lines corresponding to a message is formed as
follows. Words from the message are grouped together into smaller
sequences of words without changing their order. Each group, apart from
the last one, has as many words as possible such that the summed lengths
of the words in each group plus the number of words in the group minus

one (for space separators) is less than or equal to 80. Words that are longer than 80 characters are truncated to 80. Each group is turned into a line by concatenating the words, with one space between them, thus forming a sequence of lines overall. Then all lines of the message, apart from the last, are right-justified according to the function right-justify:

right-justify : (this-line : Line) → (result : Line)

pre there does not exist a number, i, such that
     this-line[i] = ' ' and this-line[i + 1] = ' '
   and len(this-line) ≤ max-line-length

Informal definition If there is only one word in this-line, the result is this-line. Otherwise the length of the result is max-line-length. The words in the resulting line are the same and in the same order as in the argument. The number of spaces between adjacent words in the result is N, or N + 1, for some N.

4.2.3 Complete specification

Rita finally writes an operation specification that precisely states how the three parts of the specification fit together:

TELEGRAM-ANALYSIS

ext rd tel : Blocks
     wr rep : Lines

pre abs-Blocks(tel) is defined

post rep-Reports(analyse(abs-Blocks(tel))) = rep

The pre-condition above signifies that Rita is assuming that the input to the program is in the correct format; that is, that it really does represent an abstract sequence of telegrams. This is perfectly reasonable as the input is generated by another reliable device controlled by a program.

    Now she has completed the specification, she takes Simon for a beer while she describes it to him. He is not convinced that she hasn't just wasted her time, but at least confirms that she seems to have understood him properly.

4.3 Design

Rita next considers how the problem is going to be solved. Essentially, her solution will consist of a loop that reads and processes telegrams until an empty telegram is input. This loop will presumably be preceded by some initialization, the details of which will become clear as the design proceeds.

She now needs to know the exact details concerning the format of the input and output. She asks Simon.

The input comes in blocks of 150 characters, from a special device connected to the PC on which the program will run. However, as far as the program is concerned, this will appear as a normal file, called *telegrams*, consisting of these blocks. The last block is filled at the end with spaces, if necessary, to make it a total of 150 characters. The output is to be written to a text file, called *reports*.

Rita makes a first approximation of the design, starting with the **program heading**. This contains the names of the input and the output file accessed by the program.

program telegram(telegrams, reports)

She defines a **program constant** for the block size.

As in specifications, the ability to declare entities which have a constant value in a program greatly increases its readability. This may be done in Pascal via a **constant declaration**. The name given to the constant value is written in place of the constant wherever it is needed in the program. It also means that, if the value of the constant is ever changed, a simple change to the constant declaration is all that is needed, rather than looking through the program to change each occurrence of that particular value. For example,

Const *BasicTaxRate* = 25.00;

---

const block-size = 150

The input blocks consist of **characters**.

There is another built-in data type in Pascal, called **Char**, which contains characters. The character sets may vary from one computer to another but they include the upper-case and lower-case alphabets, 'A'...'Z' and 'a'...'z', the decimal digits '0'...'9' and the space character, ' '.

A character constant is represented by writing it enclosed in single (close) quotes. For example,

'a', 'B', '*', '8'

The input blocks are actually Pascal **array** values.

An **array** type is a **structured** Pascal data type. Each array value comprises a fixed number of separate components, or **elements**. These elements are values from another Pascal data type. Each element of an array has an **index**, distinct from the indices of the other elements. The indices are chosen from another Pascal data type, and are often integers.

An array is typically declared as follows:

> **Type** *column* = **Array** [1 .. 10] **Of** *Integer*;

In this example, each value of the type *column* is an array consisting of ten separate integers. These ten elements are indexed from 1 to 10.

Arrays indexed from 1 upwards are very similar to sequences in our specifications, but it is important not to confuse the two concepts.

Unlike in a file, elements of an array may be accessed randomly. In Pascal, it is possible to alter particular components of an array without having to update all the elements in the array.

```
type block = array [1 .. block-size] of char
```

The telegrams are input as a **file** of such blocks.

The **sequential file** is the basis of all input and output in Pascal. A sequential file may be created by adding new elements, one at a time, to the end of an originally empty file. An already existing sequential file may be read, an element at a time, starting at its beginning. A file type is denoted:

> **File Of** *X*

where *X* is the type of the items in the file.

(Note that there is no Pascal operator to test for equality between two files.)

```
var telegrams : file of block
```

The report file is a Pascal **text** file.

Pascal **text files** are sequential files whose elements are of type *Char*. They are a pre-declared type called **Text**. For example,

   Var *x* : *Text*;

They are not quite the same as **File Of** *Char*, because they are structured into lines.

Actually, the files *input* (usually keyboard) and *output* (usually display) are pre-declared variables of type *Text*.

```
          reports : text
    ⋮
    begin
      initialize {procedure call}
      analyse   {procedure call}
    end
```

Rita's next level of refinement is the design of the procedure **analyse**. This contains the loop to process telegrams. It requires a variable to hold the number of words in the most recent telegram processed, so that the final empty one can be detected. She adds this variable to the design of the program:

   word-count : ℕ

Then she writes the design of **analyse**:

```
    analyse
    begin
      analyse-telegram
      while word-count ≠ 0
        analyse-telegram
    end
```

The procedure **analyse-telegram** is her next piece of refinement. This must copy words, one by one, from the input to the output, until it finds the ending word, **ZZZZ**. Then it will write out the analysis of the telegram, unless the telegram was the empty one (in which case, no words would have been copied). While it copies the words, it must count them (excluding the ending word), count the chargeable words, and see if any words are too long. Accordingly, Rita adds new variables to the top-level design:

```
    charge-count    : ℕ
    any-overlength : 𝔹
```

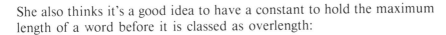

She also thinks it's a good idea to have a constant to hold the maximum length of a word before it is classed as overlength:

    const max-non-overlength = 12

She also needs a variable to store each word while it is being copied. This of course will eventually require her to choose an appropriate Pascal type to represent a sequence of alphanumeric characters. Although this is not difficult to implement, she finds it is convenient to regard the variable more abstractly during the design. This also applies to the representation of the ending word and the stop word:

    current-word : Seq of Alpha-num
    end-word   = ['Z','Z','Z','Z']
    stop-word = ['S','T','O','P']

Analysing a telegram involves reading words from the input until the end-word is encountered. These words must be output in lines, right-justified to 80 characters. Rita postulates that this can be achieved by adding words to a line, and only right-justifying and writing the line when a word will not fit on it. Using this approach, she needs a variable to store the line before writing it. As with words, she considers this variable abstractly in the design.

    current-line : Seq of Char

In the actual design of **analyse-telegram**, she assumes a number of other procedures as follows:

- Get-word will read a word from the input.
- Add-word-to-line will add a word stored in current-word to the current-line, right-justifying and writing the line first if it does not fit.
- Write-line will write current-line to the report file (without right-justifying).
- Write-analysis will write the analysis of the telegram to the report file.

```
analyse-telegram
begin
  charge-count := 0
  word-count := 0
  any-overlength := false
  get-word
  while current-word ≠ end-word
    word-count := word-count + 1
    if (current-word ≠ stop-word)
      charge-count := charge-count + 1
```

```
                    if len(current-word) > max-non-overlength
                       any-overlength := true
                    add-word-to-line
                    get-word
                 end-of-while
                 write-line
                 if word-count ≠ 0
                    write-analysis
              end
```

Rita regards get-word as a likely next candidate for refinement. This must build up the current word from the input buffer, refilling the buffer if necessary. The procedure must skip any leading spaces, and then loop through building the word until it finds another space. She assumes another procedure, get-char, to obtain the next character from the input into the variable input-char. An important aspect of the design of get-word is that it may be assumed that there exists at least one more word in the input. This can be shown from the overall program assumption that the input is in the correct form, and from the manner in which the procedure is called. Also, since she knows that the last block of input is space-filled, the get-word design can also assume that there is at least one space *following* the word it is about to extract. This would be untrue only if the last word of the input happened to end at the last position of the last block of input. However, that can be dealt with by pretending there is an extra space in the input, if it is required to read another block when all of them have been read. Observations such as these can make an implementation easier, but they should also be documented in the program.

```
         input-char : Char

         get-word
         { Note: assumes that there is at least one more word to get,
                 followed by at least one space (see get-char) }
         begin
            while input-char = ' '
               get-char

            current-word := [ ] {Note: this is abstract, and not Pascal!}

            {read current-word from buffer}
            while input-char ≠ ' ' {Note: can assume a space eventually}
               append input-char on end of current-word
               get-char
            end-of-while
         end
```

Get-char must take the next character to be processed from the input and place it in the variable input-char. Because the input comes in blocks of 150 characters, it is necessary to have a variable, which Rita calls input-buffer, to hold one whole block (array of *Char*). The procedure will read the next block of data from the file into the buffer, if it is needed. Then it will copy one of the characters from the buffer into the variable input-char.

To select an element of an **array,** the array is subscripted by an **index** in a similar way to the selection of an element from a sequence in our specifications. For example,

     InputBuffer[5]

denotes the element indexed by the value 5 in the array *InputBuffer*.

       To take the characters out of the buffer, Rita sees that there will need to be an index, referencing either the next to be removed or the previous one that was removed. She decides on the latter. This means it is time to refill the buffer when this index is equal to the buffer size.

```
input-buffer        : block
previous-buffer-pos : ℕ {position of last character that was
                          'removed'}
get-char
{ get next character from input, or space after end }
begin
  if previous-buffer-pos < block-size
    previous-buffer-pos := previous-buffer-pos + 1
    input-char := input-buffer[previous-buffer-pos]
  else
  if not eof(telegrams)
    read input-buffer from telegrams
    input-char := input-buffer[1]
    previous-buffer-pos := 1
  else
    input-char := ' '
end
```

The next stage of design is concerned with the procedures add-word-to-line and write-line. add-word-to-line takes the value of current-word and adds it on the end of current-line, including also a space before it, unless it is the first word on the line. If the word won't fit, current-line is first right-justified, written to the reports file and set to empty. write-line writes the current-line to the reports file (without right-justifying) and sets it back to empty.

       At this point, Rita sees Simon walking across the beach towards her.

SIMON: I've some bad news for you – old Piggy has assigned yet another body to the project. He'll work for you.

RITA: That's not bad news, is it?

SIMON: You haven't met him – whenever he does anything for me, he gets it wrong.

RITA: Why?

SIMON: I don't know. He never seems to understand what I want. That's why I prefer to work on my own.

RITA: Does anybody else ever work for you?

SIMON: No, you're the only person apart from him.

RITA: Ahhh. Well, never mind – I'm sure we'll muddle through.

Rita meets her new colleague – Hugh Reader.

RITA: I'm pleased to meet you, Hugh.

Hugh is a junior programmer, but at least has seen some formal specifications before.

RITA: Good – I'll be giving you the specifications of some pieces of the telegram analysis program.

Rita has just decided to ask Hugh to do the add-word-to-line and the write-line procedures. She knows it is wise to provide specifications, so that the correct implementations may be produced. Hugh won't be starting until the next day, so that gives Rita time to prepare. She decides to write the specifications after it is clear how current-word and current-line are to be represented.

Despite the fact Hugh is going to design and implement the add-word-to-line procedure, it is clear that the operation requires an algorithm to write a right-justified line to the report file. To make it a little easier for Hugh, Rita decides to design that part herself. (This, of course, is not strictly top-down. However, it does mean that the design and implementation of add-word-to-line and write-line are reasonable exercises for Hugh, the Reader.)

Rita thinks about the right-justifying routine. It could start by counting the number of separators (spaces) already on the line. Then it could go through the line writing out the non-space characters, or a number of spaces instead of each space. The number of spaces would be based on how many spaces need to be written in total, divided by the number of separators left. This algorithm requires some variables, such as the number of separators, which are used only by the procedure, and not by any other part of the program. Rita will design these as **local variables.**

A **local variable** in a procedure is one which is defined and used only within that procedure. It has no meaning outside the procedure. Local variables are good for reducing the complexity of a program, since entities that are related to only one procedure can be hidden from the rest of the program, thus overall reducing the number of entities at the top level of the program.

```
write-line-right-justified
var no-of-separators, line-position,
     no-of-spaces-needed, no-of-spaces-here : N
begin
   { first count the separators }
   no-of-separators : = 0
   line-position : = 1
   while line-position ≤ len (current-line)
     if current-line[line-position] = ' '
        no-of-separators : = no-of-separators + 1
     line-position : = line-position + 1
   end-of-while

   { work out how many spaces needed in total }
   no-of-spaces-needed : = max-line-length –
                          len (current-line-len)
                          + no-of-separators

   {write the line}
   line-position : = 1
   while line-position ≤ len (current-line)
     if current-line[line-position] ≠ ' '
        write(reports, current-line[line-position])
     else
        no-of-spaces-here : = no-of-spaces-needed div
                             no-of-separators
        write no-of-spaces-here spaces
        no-of-separators : = no-of-separators – 1
        no-of-spaces-needed : = no-of-spaces-needed –
                               no-of-spaces-here
     end-of-if
     line-position : = line-position + 1
   end-of-while
   writeln (reports)
end
```

Apart from initialize, there is just one simple procedure left for Rita to design: write-analysis. This reports the number of chargeable words and whether there were any overlength words. A suitable design, which ignores the question of what messages might accompany the output, is

```
        write-analysis
        begin
           write charge-count and overlength to reports
        end
```

Now all that remains is for Rita to consider what initialization is needed. The files need opening, the first character of the input needs to be obtained, and the output line needs setting to the empty sequence.

```
        initialize
        begin
           open telegrams for input
           open reports for output
           current-line := [ ]
           previous-buffer-pos := block-size
           get-char
        end
```

There is likely to be some more initialization than this in the actual program, associated with the way that words and the output line are represented. That will become clear during the implementation.

:= 4.4 Implementation

Much of the implementation is straightforward given the design. The major work involves the representation of words and the output line. Rita decides to use a **packed array of characters** for the representation of words.

There is a standard way of manipulating *fixed* length strings of characters in Pascal. This is through an **Array Of** *Char* indexed from 1 to some number greater than 1, which is also **packed**. These packed arrays (may) occupy less space than unpacked ones, but, more importantly, Pascal offers more facilities, such as comparison, simply because they are packed.

An array is a fixed length sequence, but Rita's design assumes the more general non-empty sequence of characters. To implement sequences of varying lengths, Rita will associate an integer typed variable with each array. The second variable will hold the length of the sequence stored in the array. So a sequence of, say, five characters will be implemented by having those characters stored in the first five positions in the array, and a value of five in the associated length variable. This gives flexibility, but it is still not as general as the design, because the *maximum* length of a word is fixed by the size of the array. However, words are truncated to 80 characters on output anyway (see rep-Reports). Rita convinces herself that if words longer than 80 characters are truncated and the excess discarded when they are *input*, this will have the same effect.

She needs the array to be packed so that words can be compared with STOP and ZZZZ. In order for such comparisons to be well defined, she will ensure that words shorter than 80 characters are space-filled to the end of the array. This will avoid comparing undefined array elements, and/or pieces of a word that were the previous value of a variable, being longer than the current value.

Rita decides to store the output line similarly in an array, with an associated length variable. However, the array does not need to be packed because lines are not compared. Using an array for the line does not impose a restriction, as report lines are required to be of a fixed maximum size.

Having made these representation decisions, Rita may now provide Hugh with the specifications of write-line and add-word-to-line. She hands him the paper, and watches his reaction.

HUGH: Oh, VDM – we did that at college.

The specifications are as follows:

Line   = Seq of Char
Word = Seq of Char

max-line-length = 80

The specification of write-line requires the sequence **concatenation** operator, to state that the current output line is added on the end of the reports file.

A function on sequences, **concatenation**, written

⌢

takes two sequences and joins them together in order. It is an associative infix operator, that is:

$(s1 \frown s2) \frown s3 = s1 \frown (s2 \frown s3)$

for all sequences s1, s2 and s3. For example:

$[4,1,3] \frown [5,3] \frown [2] = [4,1,3,5,3,2]$

:=

WRITE-LINE

ext   wr reports   : Seq of Line
        wr current-line : Line

post reports = $\overline{\text{reports}}$ $^\frown$ [current-line]
        and current-line = [ ]

Exercise 4.9   Which of the following statements are true for all sequences s1, s2?

(a)   len s1 $^\frown$ s2 = len s1 + len s2

(b)   elems s1 $^\frown$ s2 = elems s1 $\cup$ elems s2

(c)   inds s1 $^\frown$ s2 = inds s1 $\cup$ inds s2

Exercise 4.10   The following is not true for s1, s2 : Seq of $\mathbb{N}$ in general:

        s1 $^\frown$ s2 = s2 $^\frown$ s1

Is it true for any particular values of s1 and s2? What is the most general single condition characterizing all pairs of sequences for which it holds?

By the fact that words are to be truncated on input to a maximum length no bigger than the maximum line length, the add-word-to-line procedure is entitled to assume that the word in current-word is not bigger than the maximum line length. Rita has stated this in the pre-condition:

ADD-WORD-TO-LINE

ext rd current-word : Word
        wr reports   : Seq of Line
        wr current-line   : Line

pre len current-word $\leqslant$ max-line-length

The post-condition essentially describes two cases: when the word will fit on the current line, and when it will not. Rita finds it convenient to write this using an **if–then–else expression**.

In specifications, we can write an **if–then–else** (or **conditional**) expression to denote two alternative expressions depending on a condition. The general form is

        if b then e1 else e2

where b is any **predicate** (condition) and e1 and e2 are expressions of the same type. The type of the if–then–else is the same as the type of e1 and e2. The meaning of the

expression is e1 if b is true, or e2 otherwise. This is similar to the Pascal if–then–else :=
statement, but should not be confused with it.

```
post
    let delimiter : Seq of Symbol be
        if current-line = [ ] then [ ] else [' ']
    in
        if (len (current-line ⌢ delimiter ⌢ current-word)
            ⩽max-line-length) then
        (current-line = current-line ⌢ delimiter ⌢ current-word)
        and (reports = reports)
    else
        (current-line = current-word)
        and (reports = reports ⌢ [right-justify (current-line)])
```

Rita explains the rather complicated post-condition to Hugh. The first
part is giving an intuitive name (delimiter) to a sub-expression which is
either the empty sequence or a sequence containing exactly one space.
This value is used in the specification to signify the gap between words,
inserted before the current word being added to the line. Naturally, if the
line is empty beforehand, there should be no gap (hence the empty
sequence). Then there are two possible (and mutually exclusive) cases:
either the word will fit on the line or it won't. The first case is signified
by the condition that the combined lengths of the line, the delimiter and
the word are not bigger than the maximum line length. In this case, the
final value of the line is the initial value with the delimiter and the word
added on the end. For the other case, the final value of reports is the
initial value with the right-justified initial line added on the end; and the
final value of the line is the same as that of the given word.

In addition to the specification, Hugh needs the details of how the
lines and words are represented, the variable names, the exact interface
to the procedures, and about the write-line-right-justified procedure.
Rita tells him all this, and he goes away to get started.

Rita then implements the rest of the program:

Program *telegram* (*telegrams, reports*);
{ *program to process a stream of telegrams and output a neat listing of*
   the telegrams, each accompanied by the word count and a message
   indicating the occurrence of an over-length word.

}

```
Const BlockSize          = 150;
      MaxLineLength      = 80;
      MaxWordLength    = MaxLineLength;
                              { words longer than this are truncated }
      MaxNonOverlength = 12; { words longer than this are
                                 overlength }

Type  Block =            Array [1 . . BlockSize]        Of Char;
      Line =             Array [1 . . MaxLineLength] Of Char;
```

Any Pascal structured type (record, array, set, file) may be declared as **Packed** by simply adding that word in front of the type construction. This may cause values of the type to occupy less space, at the cost of execution taking a little longer. However, the behaviour of the type is not affected *except* for arrays of *Char* indexed from 1 upwards. These have more operations available than their unpacked counterparts, in that they may be compared.

```
Word = Packed Array [1 . . MaxWordLength] Of Char;

Var telegrams : File Of Block; { input stream of telegrams }
    reports     : Text; { output file containing neat listing of telegrams,
                          chargeable word count and indication of
                          overlength words }
    InputBuffer       : Block;   { buffer area where stream is to be
                                   input }
    PreviousBufferPos : Integer; { position in InputBuffer of previous
                                   character removed }
    InputChar : Char;
```

As well as an array variable to store the text of the current output line, Rita uses another variable to hold the length of the line actually stored in the array.

```
CurrentLine       : Line;   { holds one line of the output report }
CurrentLineLength : Integer; { length of line stored in CurrentLine }
```

Similarly, *CurrentWordLength* holds the length of the actual word stored in *CurrentWord*.

```
CurrentWord       : Word;   { current word being processed }
CurrentWordLength : Integer; { length of current word }

ChargeCount : Integer; { number of chargeable words in telegram }
WordCount   : Integer; { total number of words in a telegram }

AnyOverlength : Boolean; { indicates occurrences of overlength words}
```

To aid with the space filling of words, Rita uses a word containing just spaces. She also has two variables to store the spellings of the stop-word and end-word. (She could have used constants for these, but that would require typing a large fixed-size string of 80 characters for each of them. As well as being a little ugly, the maintainability of the program would be adversely affected, because changing the maximum size of words would necessitate editing the constants.)

```
EmptyWord,      { word containing all blanks }
StopWord,       { 'STOP' - non-chargeable word }
EndWord : Word; { 'ZZZZ' - telegram delimiter, non-chargeable }
```

The implementation of **get-char** needs to **read** blocks from the telegrams file.

A **read** statement is a program statement that causes data to be taken from a file and copied into program variables. In Pascal, one of the ways of accomplishing this is via the pre-declared procedure **_read_**. This reads data from a file variable and places the value read in another variable. The format is:

```
read( file-variable, result-variable)
```

```
Procedure GetChar;
{ get next character from input buffer, refilling it if necessary, or space
  after end}
Begin
  If PreviousBufferPos < BlockSize Then
  Begin
    PreviousBufferPos := PreviousBufferPos + 1;
    InputChar := InputBuffer[PreviousBufferPos]
  End
  Else
  If Not eof(telegrams) Then
  Begin
    read(telegrams, InputBuffer);
    InputChar := InputBuffer[1];
    PreviousBufferPos := 1
  End
  Else
    InputChar := ' '
End;
```

The _initialize_ procedure must also set the values of the variables _EmptyWord_, _EndWord_ and _StopWord_, in addition to the operations identified in the design, such as opening the files.

There are two pre-declared procedures, **reset** and **rewrite**, which initialize files so that they are in the correct state for reading from or writing to respectively. *Reset(f)* causes the next read statement to file *f* to read the first element in that file. *Rewrite(f)* sets *f* to be the empty file so that any previous contents of the file are discarded.

```
Procedure initialize;
{ initializes input files and program variables }
Var WordIndex : integer;

Begin
  { initialize files: }
  reset(telegrams); { telegrams is to be read from }
  rewrite(reports); { reports is to be written to }

  WordIndex := 1;
  While WordIndex <= MaxWordLength Do
  Begin
    EmptyWord[WordIndex] := ' ';
    WordIndex := WordIndex + 1;
  End;

  EndWord := EmptyWord;
  WordIndex := 1;
  While WordIndex <= 4 Do
  Begin
    EndWord[WordIndex] := 'Z';
    WordIndex := WordIndex + 1;
  End;

  StopWord := EmptyWord;
  StopWord[1] := 'S';
  StopWord[2] := 'T';
  StopWord[3] := 'O';
  StopWord[4] := 'P';

  { initialize CurrentLine: }
  CurrentLineLength := 0;

  PreviousBufferPos := BlockSize;
  GetChar;
End; { end initialize }
```

Rita needs to give the *GetWord* procedure required some extra thought, because of the implementation of words. Most notably, the length of the word must be explicitly counted, and truncated if longer than the maximum allowed. This truncation is easily implemented within the loop to build up the word, by only storing the input character in the word if the word length is not already at the maximum:

Procedure *GetWord*;
{ *get next word from the InputBuffer. Note that words may pass over*
block boundaries }
{ *Note: assumes that there is at least one more word to get, followed by*
at least one space }
Begin { *GetWord* }
  { *remove any leading spaces* }
  While *InputChar* = ' ' **Do**
    GetChar;

  { *initialize word to empty:* }
  CurrentWord := *EmptyWord*;
  CurrentWordLength := 0;

  { *read CurrentWord from buffer* }
  While (*InputChar* <> ' ') **Do** { *Note: can assume a space eventually* }
  Begin
    If *CurrentWordLength* < *MaxWordLength* **Then**
    Begin
      CurrentWordLength := *CurrentWordLength* + 1;
      CurrentWord[*CurrentWordLength*] := *InputChar*;
    End;
    GetChar;
  End;
End; { *GetWord* }

The implementation of write-line-right-justified has some **local variables**.

Local variables can be defined within procedures just as in the main program. They exist only when the procedure is being executed and cannot be referenced by the main program. They do *not* retain their value between calls of the procedure defining them.

Her procedure uses a **field specifier** on a *writeln* statement, to obtain the appropriate spacing between the words.

Items to be written by the *writeln* statement (and write on text files) can be suffixed by an integer **field specifier** indicating how many characters the representation of that value should occupy. Field specifiers must always be greater than zero. They are written in the program after a colon (:) following the item to which they refer.

In the *write* and *writeln* statements, the **field specifier** of an item which is a character, or a string of characters (**Packed Array Of** *Char*), defines the exact number of characters that will be written for that item. If the field specifier is less than the length of the string, the string is truncated on the right. (That is, if the field specifier is *N*, only the first *N* characters are written.) If the field specifier is greater than or equal to the length of the string, a number of spaces are written before the string. For example,

> *write*('*A*': 7)

writes six spaces and then the letter A; and

> *writeln*(*CurrentWord*:10)

writes the first ten characters of *CurrentWord*, followed by a new line, if *CurrentWord* is a **Packed Array Of** *Char*, indexed from 1 to some value greater than or equal to 10.

The procedure also uses the Pascal **Div** operator.

The operator **Div** in Pascal takes two integer arguments and returns an integer. The second argument *must not* be zero. The result is the value of the first argument divided by the second, truncated towards zero to the nearest integer. Thus, where *abs* means absolute value (in other words ignore the sign):

> $abs(i) - abs(j) < abs((i \text{ \textbf{Div} } j)* j) <= abs(i)$

The sign of the result will be positive if the signs of the arguments are the same, otherwise negative.

```
Procedure WriteLineRightJustified;
Var NoOfSeparators, LinePosition,
      NoOfSpacesNeeded, NoOfSpacesHere : Integer;
Begin
  { first count the separators }
  NoOfSeparators := 0;
  LinePosition := 1;
  While LinePosition <= CurrentLineLength Do
  Begin
    If CurrentLine[LinePosition] = ' ' Then
      NoOfSeparators := NoOfSeparators + 1;
    LinePosition := LinePosition + 1
  End;
```

```
{ work out how many spaces needed in total }
NoOfSpacesNeeded := MaxLineLength - CurrentLineLength
                          + NoOfSeparators;

{ write the line }
LinePosition := 1;
While LinePosition <= CurrentLineLength Do
Begin
  If CurrentLine[LinePosition] <> ' ' Then
    write(reports,CurrentLine[LinePosition])
  Else
  Begin
    NoOfSpacesHere := NoOfSpacesNeeded Div NoOfSeparators;
    write(reports,' ':NoOfSpacesHere);
    NoOfSeparators := NoOfSeparators - 1;
    NoOfSpacesNeeded := NoOfSpacesNeeded - NoOfSpacesHere
  End;
  LinePosition := LinePosition + 1
End;
writeln(reports);
End;
```

Exercise 4.11   Given

Word : **Packed Array** [1. .6] **Of** *Char*

where *Word* contains the characters *'monkey'*, what will the following statements output?

(a)   *write(Word:8)*

(b)   *write(Word:4)*

(c)   *writeln('The animal is a',Word:7)*

(d)   *writeln(' ':11)*

```
Procedure WriteLine;
{ waiting for Hugh }
⋮
End;

Procedure AddWordToLine;
{ waiting for Hugh }
⋮
End;
```

:=

Character string constants can be written in Pascal as a sequence of characters surrounded by single quotes ('). The type of such a string with N characters in it is:

Packed Array $[1 .. N]$ **Of** *Char*

(Consequently, string constants may be assigned into string arrays of the same size.)

```
Procedure WriteAnalysis;
{ Write the analysis of the telegram out to the file 'reports' }
Begin
    writeln(reports,'The number of chargeable words is  ', ChargeCount);
    If AnyOverlength Then
        writeln(reports,'Overlength words present')
    Else
        writeln(reports,'No overlength words');
    writeln(reports)
End; { WriteAnalysis }

Procedure AnalyseTelegram;
{ process telegram word by word until reach telegram terminator,
  EndWord}

Begin { AnalyseTelegram }
    ChargeCount := 0;
    WordCount := 0;
    AnyOverlength := false;

    GetWord;
    While CurrentWord <> EndWord Do
    Begin
        WordCount := WordCount + 1;

        { charge words: }
        If (CurrentWord <> StopWord) Then
            ChargeCount := ChargeCount + 1;

        { check words }
        If CurrentWordLength > MaxNonOverlength Then
            AnyOverlength := true;

        { write CurrentWord to report: }
        AddWordToLine;
        GetWord;
    End; { of loop to process words }
    WriteLine;

    { write out analysis of telegram to the report: }
    If WordCount <> 0 Then
        WriteAnalysis;
End; { AnalyseTelegram }
```

Procedure *analyse*;
{ *process telegrams one by one and output analysis to a report* }

Begin { *analyse* }
  { *retrieve and analyse telegrams:* }
  AnalyseTelegram;
  While *WordCount* <> 0 { *empty telegram* } **Do**
    AnalyseTelegram
End; { *analyse* }

Begin { *main program* }
  initialize;
  analyse
End. { *telegram* }

By the time Rita has finished typing the program, Hugh has completed the two parts he was asked to implement. Rita glances at his file – the procedures seem to be alright. Hugh assures her that they conform to the specification she gave him. She incorporates his file into hers, and tries the program on some test data. It works, of course! Rita knows it is important to test it using enough data to span several input blocks. She temporarily decreases the block size to help with this. She has already written a simple program to produce data in the correct format for the telegram analysis program, from text typed at the keyboard.

    She tells Simon that the job is complete, and that Hugh produced good work. He is surprised, but refuses to believe that the specification helped him. Simon does not expect that her program will work with the rest of the system that he has been producing, and wants her to stay for the full testing. Rita knows it will work, because she is sure that she properly understood his requirements, and has correctly satisfied them. But she does not mind waiting another day – with nothing to do but sunbathe.

SUMMARY

A main emphasis in this chapter was that of requirements analysis, and the importance of knowing what is required of a program before work is started on its eventual implementation. Specification concepts introduced included **functions**, **sets** and **records**. The main programming concepts were **packed array of char** and **sequential files**, including **text** and non-text files.

    The following notations were introduced in this chapter.

Specification notation

Type invariant	Telegram = Seq of Word excluding [ ]
Set type	
Set enumeration	{6,2,90,12}
Set union	Alpha-num = Letter ∪ Digit
Record type	Report = Record . . . end
Named constant	stop-word = ['S', 'T', 'O','P']
Function, application, arguments, domain, range, signature	len : (s: Seq of X) → (l: ℕ)
Index and element set	inds(tels) , elems(tel)
Record construction	mk-Report(tel, charge-word-count(tel), any-overlength(tel))
Membership of a set	j ∈ inds(tel)
Set comprehension	{ j ∈ inds(tel)	tel[j] ≠ stop-word}
Cardinality of a set	card ({ j ∈ inds(tel)	tel[j] ≠ stop-word})
Sequence concatenate	reports ⌢ [CurrentLine]
If-then-else expressions	if . . . then . . . else . . .

Pascal notation

Named constants	**Const** *BlockSize* = 150
Type *Char*	*Char, 'a', '*'* . . .
Array type	**Type** *block* = **Array** [1..*BlockSize*] **Of** *Char*
File type	**Var** *telegrams* : **File Of** *Block*
Text file type	*reports* : *Text*
Array element	*InputBuffer*[*PreviousBufferPos*]
Packed types	**Packed**
Character string	**Packed Array** [1 . . *MaxLineSize*] **Of** *Char*
Local variable declaration	**Var** *NoOfSpacesHere* : *Integer*
Read statement	*read*(*telegrams, InputBuffer*)
File opening	*reset, rewrite*
Writeln character field specifier	*write*(' ':*NoOfSpacesHere*)
Div operator	*NoOfSpacesNeeded* **Div** *NoOfSeparators*
String constant	*'Overlength words present'*

TUTORIAL EXERCISE

This exercise is designed to reinforce your knowledge of the details of the Pascal programming language. We also introduce the notion of **ordering** of characters in Pascal.

The values of the Pascal type *Char* are ordered. Each character has an **ordinal number**, sometimes called a **character code**, which starts from 0 and goes up to the cardinality of the character set, minus one. Each distinct character has a distinct ordinal number. The actual value associated with each character is implementation dependent, as is the actual set of characters supported. However, in a standard implementation, the codes for the digits, '0' to '9', are guaranteed to be ascending and consecutive. The codes for each of the two alphabets, 'A' to 'Z' and 'a' to 'z', are guaranteed to be ascending, but not necessarily consecutive (for example, the code for 'B' is greater than the code for 'A', but not necessarily just one more). Most, but not all, computers nowadays use the **ASCII** character set and codes, in which the digits, and also each of the alphabets, are consecutive.

The relational operators $<, >, \leqslant, \geqslant$ on characters are supported in Pascal, and are defined as the corresponding relation on integers acting on the ordinal numbers of the characters.

The following is a specification for a piece of code to read a word from the input. A word is defined, in this context, to be a sequence of one or more letters with a maximum permitted length of 30.

```
Short-string = Seq of Char
               where the length = 30

READ-WORD
ext  wr input : Seq of Char
     wr word : Short-string
pre  len(input) > 1 and
     is-letter(input[1]) and
     not is-letter(input[len(input)])

post let n : ℕ be the first number such that
        (not is-letter (input[n + 1]))
     in
        ((n < 30 and input[1 , . . . , n] ⌢ spaces(30 – n) = word)
         or
        (n ≥ 30 and input[1 , . . . , 30] = word)
        )
        and
        (input [n + 2 , . . . , len(input)] = input)

is-letter : (c : Char) → 𝔹
is-letter(c) △ 'a' ≤ c ≤ 'z' or 'A' ≤ c ≤ 'Z'
   Assuming letters are consecutive

spaces : (n : ℕ) → (r : Seq of Char)
pre  true
post len(r) = n and
     for all indices i in r, it is true that
        ' ' = r[i]
```

Here is our hopelessly inadequate attempt at implementing READ-WORD.

```
Procedure ReadWord;
{ – See spec. for pre/post conditions }
Const ShortStringLength = 30; { Max length of word }
Type ShortString = Packed Array [ 1..ShortStringLength ] Of Char;
Var word : ShortString;
        i : Real;    { Index into word }
       ch : Integer; { Temp. for Input[i] }
Begin
   read(Input, word [0]);
   i := 2;
   read(Input, ch);
```

```
                While (('a' <= ch) Or (ch <= 'z'))
                    And (('A' <= ch) Or (ch <= 'Z')) Do;
                Begin
                    word[i] := ch;
                    i := i + 1;
                    read(Input, ch)
                End
            End { of ReadWord };
```

1

List all the errors in the procedure that are violations of the Pascal programming language.

2

List all the errors that are correct Pascal, but are certainly blunders!

3

Modify the procedure so that it satisfies the given specification.

LABORATORY EXERCISE – to implement WRITE-LINE and ADD-WORD-TO-LINE

Problem

Hello Hugh. Your job is to design and implement the write-line and add-word-to-line components of the program that analyses telegrams.

Special note: To make it easier to *assess* whether you have correctly implemented the exercise, why not use a '_' character to separate words in the output, rather than a space as in the case study. (This means that any separators incorrectly written after the end of the line will be clearly visible.)

Specification

The formal specification of the procedures are duplicated below for convenience:

```
Line  = Seq of Char
Word  = Seq of Char

max-line-length = *** some natural of no concern to this exercise, > 0 ***

right-justify : (this-line : Line) → (result : Line)

pre there does not exist a number, i, such that
        this-line[i] = '_' and this-line[i + 1] = '_'
    and len(this-line) ≤ max-line-length
```

Informal definition   If there is only one word in this-line, the result is this-line. Otherwise the length of the result is max-line-length. The words in the resulting line are the same and in the same order as in the argument. The number of spaces between adjacent words in the result is N, or N + 1, for some N.

WRITE-LINE

ext   wr reports   : Seq of Line
        wr current-line   : Line
post reports = reports ⌒ [current-line]
        and current-line = [ ]

ADD-WORD-TO-LINE

ext   rd current-word : Word
        wr reports   : Seq of Line
        wr current-line   : Line

pre   len current-word ≤ max-line-length

post let delimiter : Seq of Symbol be
            if current-line = [ ] then [ ] else ['_']
      in
          if (len (current-line ⌒ delimiter ⌒ current-word)
                   ≤ max-line-length) then
              (current-line = current-line ⌒ delimiter ⌒ current-word)
              and (reports = reports)
          else
              (current-line = current-word)
              and (reports = reports ⌒ [right-justify(current-line)])

Implementation

Your procedures must have the following headings:

   Procedure *WriteLine*;

   Procedure *AddWordToLine*;

The procedures can assume (only) the following global declarations:

   Const *MaxLineLength*   = { *a positive integer of no concern* };
          MaxWordLength = *MaxLineLength*;

   Type   *Line* =   **Array** [1 . . *MaxLineLength*] **Of** *Char*;
          Word = **Packed Array** [1 . . *MaxWordLength*] **Of** *Char*;

   Var   *reports* : *Text*;

          CurrentLine   : *Line*;   { *holds one line of the output*
                                                      report }
          CurrentLineLength : *Integer*; { *length of line stored in*
                                                      CurrentLine }

          CurrentWord   : *Word*;   { *current word being processed* }
          CurrentWordLength : *Integer*; { *length of current word* }

Procedure *WriteLineRightJustified;*

{ Right justifies CurrentLine according to the specification of the right-justify function, and writes the result to Reports. }

Note that the types *Word* and *Line* are here bounded approximations of the corresponding unbounded sequences in the specification. You may assume that this is an acceptable restriction. You may also assume that *CurrentLineLength* holds the actual length of the line stored in *CurrentLine* before your procedures are called. Your procedures must maintain this relationship explicitly. Similarly *CurrentWordLength* always holds the actual length of the word stored in *CurrentWord*.

Time–date display program

MOTIVATION

This case study is intended to illustrate further the use of abstraction in specification, particularly in the modelling of the data types. It also serves as a vehicle for learning more specification techniques, and more Pascal. Most of the specification is done in a functional style (writing functions rather than operations), with much use of the notion of **recursion**. The chapter also introduces **procedure parameters,** and the use of **sets** and **records** in Pascal.

5.1   Requirements analysis

A little while after Rita's jaunt to Polygonia, she got so fed up with May-Kit that she left them to realize her true ambition. She is now the proud owner of her own software house – Slow-Haste Software Services. It's small but it keeps her busy. She undertakes contract programmer work, and also produces one-off application software – in fact, she'll consider doing *almost* anything!

One day she gains a customer, a Mr Naive. Actually, most days she gains at least one customer, but for reasons not yet apparent we shall concern ourselves only with this one particular character.

5.1.1   The customer's initial requirements

CUSTOMER: Hello. Naive's my name. But you can call me Norman.

RITA: Good morning Norman. Nice weather for the time of year, don't you think?

NORMAN: Yes, it's not raining anywhere near as much as normal. Do you take United Speed credit cards?

RITA: That will do nicely, sir! Well, what can I do for you?

NORMAN: Ah yes. I'd like you to write me a program that displays the time in any format required – when can I collect it?

RITA: Hmm. Can you be more specific?

NORMAN: What I mean is, when will it be ready – will it be too big for me to carry?

RITA: You had better sit down sir.

After a tortuous hour Rita has managed to write a more complete specification of the requirements. She reads it to her client:

A program is required that continually displays the current time, updating the display as often as possible, but no more often than every second. The time is displayed in a format decided by the user. This format may contain items of time (for example, year, second) mixed with fixed strings of characters (for example, o'clock). The format is defined by the user using some suitable means, when the program starts. The format always consists of one line of textual output. The format is read from the standard input, and the time display is written on the standard output as a sequence of lines.

NORMAN: Seems okay – when will it be ready?

RITA: I'd like to study this, design a user interface and construct a more formal specification for your approval. This will confirm that we are talking about the same thing.

NORMAN: Is this necessary?

RITA: Certainly – there may still be questions I need to ask you. By the way – what machine will it need to run on?

NORMAN: My latest acquisition – I'm very proud of it. It's a Cruncher 3 Mega-Boulder. I got it from an advert in *Swap and Barter* Magazine; it's only got 50 000 hours on the clock.

RITA: Hmm, does it support Pascal?

NORMAN: Who? I'm not sure – it's got space invaders.

Rita makes an appointment to visit the machine to survey the documentation, and then disposes of her visitor. Studying the improved requirements Rita makes two lists:

(1)   To find out

- What language is supported on the machine?
- How is the system time accessed, and in what form?
- What are the rules concerning time? For example, days in a month, and leap years.

(2)   To design

- Means for user definition of time format.
- Suggested set of time items available.

5.1.2   The monster

When Rita does visit the Cruncher and consults the documentation, she is relieved to find that it supports Pascal and, what is more, provides a routine called *wallclock* to access the current time as the number of seconds since the beginning of 1 January 1970. She presents Norman with an informal description of how a user of the program will specify the format:

> The format is submitted as a single line of text. Dollar signs ($) are treated specially in that a sub-string between an oddly occurring and an evenly occurring dollar is a mnemonic for a time item. The output format is a copy of the input format, except with the time mnemonics and dollar signs replaced with the corresponding time item.

NORMAN: What?

Rita provides an example:

date = da/mo/ye time = ho:mi:se

produces a display like

date = 5/11/87 time = 11:30:00
date = 5/11/87 time = 11:30:01
date = 5/11/87 time = 11:30:02
⋮

Rita also gives Norman a list of the time items to be supported, together
with their corresponding mnemonics:

ho – *hour*
mi – *minute*
se – *second*
da – *day number in month*
mo – *month number*
ye – *year number in century*

NORMAN: What about century and month name?
RITA: I'll add those two if you wish:

ce – *century*
MO – *month name*

NORMAN: Fine. When will it be ready?
RITA: Next I'd like to construct the formal specification to make
      sure we've covered everything. I'll hopefully have it ready in
      a day or so.

5.1.3   Research

After this Rita obtains a definition of the size of the various months, and
the rules for leap years. These include:

	Jan	Feb	Mar	Apr	May	Jun	Jul	Aug	Sep	Oct	Nov	Dec
Days	31	28–9	31	30	31	30	31	31	30	31	30	31

Leap years: Every fourth year is a leap year, including 1900.

(Actually the real rule for leap years has been slightly simplified for this
case study, without affecting the validity of the example.)
     Having identified all the requirements and the necessary informa-
tion, she proceeds with a construction of the formal specification.

5.2   Specification

5.2.1   Abstractions

To make the specification easier to construct, and clearer to read, Rita decides to use various levels of abstraction in it. Each level defines some of the properties of the program, but modelled in terms of different abstract views of the data types. The most abstract view defines the program as working with very abstract data types, and the other parts of the specification characterize the relationship between the abstract models of data and their real structure in the final program.

Rita splits the specification into six parts.

Part 1

The most abstract view of the program behaviour regards the user's definition of the format as a sequence of strings of characters, rather than as a single string of characters. These sub-strings are separated by dollar signs.

In specifications, we often write a sequence of characters as a string inside quotes ("). This is an abbreviation for the full format written with individual characters. For example,

    "fred"

is an abbreviation for

    ['f','r','e','d']

Thus:

    "mo/da/ye"

an abbreviation for:

    ['$','m','o','$','/','$','d','a','$','/','$','y','e','$']

is regarded in the most abstract specification as:

    ["mo" ,"/" ,"da" ,"/" ,"ye"]

In the final program, the output is an infinite sequence of lines, where each line is a string of characters. In the most abstract specification, the output is viewed as an infinite sequence of displays, where each display is a sequence of display items. For example, the concrete output

```
[ "The time now is 20:35:15" ,
  "The time now is 20:35:16" ,
  "The time now is 20:35:17" ,
   ... ]
```

would be regarded abstractly as

```
[ ["The time now is " , 20 , ":" , 35 , ":" , 15 ] ,
  ["The time now is " , 20 , ":" , 35 , ":" , 16 ] ,
  ["The time now is " , 20 , ":" , 35 , ":" , 17 ] ,
   ... ]
```

Lastly, the time, which is actually presented to the program via a routine that it calls, is viewed as an infinite sequence of records, where each record represents time as a number of fields for century, year, and so on.

Part 2

The second part of the specification defines the relationship between time viewed as a sequence of records as above, and time viewed as an infinite, sorted sequence of natural numbers without duplicates. Each item in this sequence is the number of elapsed seconds since the start of 1970.

Part 3

The third part defines the relationship between time viewed as a sequence of natural numbers as above, and how it really is presented to the final program via the *wallclock* routine.

Part 4

Part four of the specification defines the relationship between the input format as typed by the user and the abstract view of it assumed in part 1.

Part 5

The fifth part similarly specifies the relationship between the real

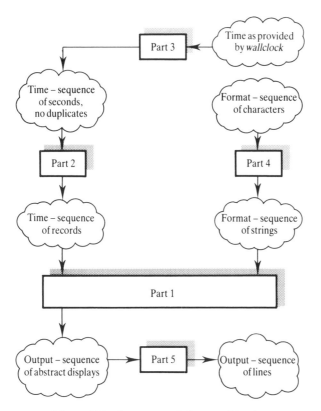

Figure 5.1   Structure of the specification.

structure of the output from the program and how it is viewed abstractly in part 1.

Part 6

Finally, part six specifies the relationship between all the other parts of the specification, thus overall forming a complete description of the program. This relationship is illustrated in Figure 5.1.

5.2.2   The specification

Part 1 – Most abstract specification

Having identified these abstractions, Rita proceeds to specify the program as a function producing an infinite abstract sequence of displays, taking an abstract format and an abstract sequence of time records. First she defines the types used in the specification, starting with the output values:

String = Seq of char

Rita defines hours and minutes, and so on, as **sub-ranges** of **integers**.

Another elementary data type used in specifications is

$$\mathbb{Z}$$

which contains all the whole numbers, including negative ones:

..., -2, -1, 0, 1, 2, ...

The set of natural numbers, $\mathbb{N}$, is a sub-set of $\mathbb{Z}$.

In specifications, a set may be defined as a **sub-range** or **interval** of the set of integers, $\mathbb{Z}$. The sub-range is the set of integers between two given values, inclusive. These limits are written as two expressions separated by dots. For example,

{5 , . . . , 12}

is the same as:

{5,6,7,8,9,10,11,12}

The formal specification of the notation is given below. In such descriptions of **infix** (two arguments with the operator between) or, as in this case, **mixfix** or **distfix** (a mixture of arguments and operator symbols) operators, underscores are used to mark the argument places in the signature.

{ _ , . . . , _ } : (i : $\mathbb{Z}$, j : $\mathbb{Z}$) → (rs : Set of $\mathbb{Z}$)

{i , . . . , j} $\triangleq$ {k ∈ $\mathbb{Z}$ | i ≤ k ≤ j}

This means that the set is empty if i is greater than j.

Hour	=	{0 , . . . , 23}
Minute	=	{0 , . . . , 59}
Second	=	{0 , . . . , 59}
Day	=	{1 , . . . , 31}
Month-no	=	{1 , . . . , 12}

Exercise 5.1 What is the value (if any) of each of the following expressions?

(a)   card { 27 , ... , 37 }

(b)   { − 1 , ... , − 7 }

Rita defines the set of values for month names and centuries:

Month-name = {"jan","feb","mar","apr","may","jun","jul","aug", "sep", "oct",
              "nov", "dec"}
Year   = {0 , ... , 99}
Century   = $\mathbb{N}$

The output is a sequence of displays, where each display is a sequence of items. Each item is either a string or one of the components of time. Thus, the set of possible display items is the **union** of strings and the various time components.

Display-item = String ∪ Hour ∪ Minute ∪ Second ∪ Day ∪
               Month-no ∪ Month-name ∪ Year ∪ Century

Display = Seq of Display-item

Display-seq = Seq of Display (infinite)

Next she defines the data type of time values:

Time = Record
          time-second : Second
          time-minute : Minute
          time-hour   : Hour
          time-day   : Day
          time-month : Month-no
          time-year   : Year
          time-century : Century
       end

Time-seq = Seq of Time (infinite)
                 ordered in ascending Time with no duplicates

Finally, she defines the type of the abstract format:

Display-format = Seq of String

She next defines the program as a **recursive function** over the two inputs, namely, the format and the time sequence.

A **(self) recursive function** is one that is defined in terms of itself. For example, the well known factorial function:

```
fact : (n : N) → N
fact (n) △
    if n = 0 then 1
    else n * fact (n – 1)
```

For a finite recursive function to be well defined, there must be a **base case** involving no recursion, and each recursive application must be applied to an argument value that 'gets nearer' the base case value (in some sense). The base case for the above factorial example is the value zero, and the function can be shown to be well defined because given a number greater than zero, the argument for the recursive application is nearer to zero.

It is possible to have infinite recursive functions, which do not need a base case. The most typical examples act over an infinite sequence, yielding a corresponding infinite sequence. For example:

```
increment : (s : Seq of N) → Seq of N
increment (s) △ [hd s + 1] ⌢ increment(tl s)
```

Rita's recursive function takes a sequence of time records, displays the **head** of that sequence, and recursively displays the **tail** of the sequence.

Two simple functions on sequences are:

```
hd : (s : Seq of X) → (h : X)
tl  : (s : Seq of X) → (t : Seq of X)
```

hd returns the first item in the given sequence; **tl** returns all but the first item. For example,

```
hd ([3,1,2]) = 3
tl ([3,2,1])  = [2,1]
```

She calls the function display-times. It assumes another function called format-display.

display-times : (t : Time-seq, f : Display-format) → Display-seq
display-times(t, f) △
   [format-display(hd(t), f)] ⌢ display-times(tl(t),f)

Rita notes that display-times does not need a base case as it is an infinite function, taking and producing an infinite sequence.

Exercise 5.2 What is wrong with the following definition of factorial?

   fact (n) △ n * fact(n − 1)

Exercise 5.3

(a) What is the value of the following expression?

   tl tl tl [1,2,3]

(b) What is the value of the following expression?

   hd tl [1,2,3]

(c) Give a value for the sequence s so that the following expression is defined:

   hd hd s

Exercise 5.4 Write a recursive function, reverse, that will reverse the order of the elements of a sequence. (Hint: reverse the tail, and add on the head.)

The function format-display takes a time record and a format and produces a display, using another function that produces an individual display-item from a format and a time. Rita also defines this function recursively. It does have a base case, because it takes a finite sequence of format strings and produces a finite sequence of display items.

   format-display : (t : Time, f : Display-format) → Display
   format-display(t,f) △
     if f = [ ] then [ ]
     else [format-display-item(t,hd(f)] ⌢ format-display(t,tl(f))

Format-display-item takes a time record and a string, and produces the corresponding display item. For given strings which are mnemonics, the result is obtained by **referencing** the appropriate **field** from the time record.

Fields of a record are selected in our specifications by means of a **field access** function. There is one of these functions for each field in a record. The name of the function is a

∃∀ dot (.) followed by the field name. The result type of the function is the type of the field. For example, if we have the type and variable:

```
Car = Record
         make : Seq of Char
         wheels : N
         colour : { red, blue, yellow, pink }
         sun-roof : B
      end

SOME-OP
ext rd my-car : Car
. . .
```

then, assuming that the variable my-car contains the details of my car, its colour, its number of wheels and whether it has a sun-roof are respectively:

```
my-car.colour
my-car.wheels
my-car.sun-roof
```

The definition of format-display-item causes Rita to think about strings from the format that are surrounded by dollar signs but which are not mnemonics:

```
format-display-item : (t : Time , f : String) → Display-item
format-display-item(t,f) △
        if f = "$ho$" then t.time-hour
    else if f = "$mi$" then t.time-minute
    . . .
    else if f = "$MO$" then name-of-month(t.time-month)
    . . .
    else if f = "$ce$" then t.time-century
    else if hd(f) = '$' then [ ]
    else f
```

Finally, the above function uses name-of-month to convert a month number to its corresponding name:

```
name-of-month : (m : Month-no) → Month-name
name-of-month(m) △
    ["jan","feb","mar","apr","may","jun","jul","aug","sep","oct","nov","dec"][m]
```

Note that in this function the month number must be in the range 1 to 12 (see definition of month-no).

Having completed this most abstract specification, Rita discusses the implications of it with Norman, who agrees that it abstractly describes the program required.

Part 2 – Time seconds as time records

Rita's next task is to relate the various abstractions involved in the previous specification to the concrete domain in which the program is to be implemented. A possible starting point is to relate the abstraction of time, as a sequence of time records, to the abstraction of time as a sequence of natural numbers. One way to do this is to write a function that converts a sequence in the latter abstraction to one in the former, using definitions from the previous specification as much as possible. Rita writes:

```
Time-second      = ℕ
Time-second-seq  = Seq of Time-second (infinite)
                        ascending order without duplicates

abstract-time-seq : (t : Time-second-seq) → Time-seq
abstract-time-seq(t) △ [ abstract-time(hd(t)) ] ⁀ abstract-time-seq(tl(t))
```

The function abstract-time is used to specify the relationship between a time expressed in seconds and a time as a record. To construct an explicit function which converts from a Time-second to the corresponding Time record is not entirely straightforward. However, there is a one-to-one correspondence between the two views of time, thus there must be an **inverse** function which converts in the other direction. As it happens, this latter function is easier to specify than the one we actually want! Given that the emphasis in specification is stating what must be done, rather than how it must be done, Rita considers it appropriate to define the inverse function retrieve-time-second explicitly, and define abstract-time implicitly in terms of its inverse. Thus, first assuming the inverse function, she writes:

```
abstract-time : (ts : Time-second) → (t : Time)
pre   true
post retrieve-time-second(t) = ts
```

Then she defines this inverse function, assuming several other functions, as:

```
retrieve-time-second : (t : Time) → Time-second
retrieve-time-second(t) △
      century-seconds(t.time-century)
```

```
    +  year-seconds(t.time-year)
    +  month-seconds(t.time-month,t.year)
    +  day-seconds(t.time-day)
    +  hour-seconds(t.time-hour)
    +  minute-seconds(t.time-minute)
    +  t.time-seconds

    -  century-seconds(19)
    -  year-seconds(70)
    -  month-seconds(1,70)
    -  day-seconds(1)
    -  hour-seconds(0)
    -  minute-seconds(0)
    -  0
```

Here, century-seconds is to be a function returning the number of seconds occurring since the epoch (that is, in theory, midnight on New Year's Eve at the end of the year 1 BC) up to the start of a given century. The other functions will have similar interpretations, but returning the number of seconds since the start of the next largest time field.

Exercise 5.5 Can you think of any widely used simple mathematical functions that are more easily defined implicitly in terms of their explicitly defined inverse, than defined explicitly themselves?

In the 20th century, century number 19, there have been 19 centuries previously, so generally:

```
century-seconds : (c : Century) → Time-second
century-seconds (c) △ four-year-size * c * 25

four-year-size  = day-size * (3 * 365 + 366)

day-size     = 24 * hour-size

hour-size    = 60 * minute-size

minute-size = 60
```

The number of seconds occurring between the start of a century and the start of a given year depends on the occurrence of leap years. The function year-seconds returns the total number of seconds within a century, up to the start of a given year:

```
year-seconds : (y : Year) → Time-second
year-seconds(y) △
    if y = 0 then 0
    else
```

```
        day-size * ( if (y  -  1) mod 4  =  0 then 366
                    else 365)
        + year-seconds(y  -  1)
```

Similarly, the number of seconds up to the start of a given month depends on the month and the year. The function month-seconds returns the total number of seconds in each month of a given year, up to but excluding a given month:

```
month-seconds : (m : Month-no , y : Year)  →  Time-seconds
month-seconds(m,y) △
if m  =  1 then 0
else
   (day-size * ( if (m  -  1) ∈ {1,3,5,7,8,10,12} then 31
                 else
                 if (m  -  1) ∈ {4,6,9,11} then 30
                 else
                 if y mod 4  =  0 then 29
                 else 28
                 )
    + month-seconds(m  -  1 , y)
   )
```

(Here, the value of 12 is included only for completeness.)

The number of seconds in a day, an hour and a minute are constant:

```
day-seconds : (d : Day)  →  Time-second
day-seconds(d) △ (d  -  1) * day-size

hour-seconds : (h : Hour)  →  Time-second
hour-seconds(h) △ h * hour-size

minute-seconds : (m : Minute)  →  Time-second
minute-seconds(m) △ m * minute-size
```

Exercise 5.6 Suppose a year is divided into four quarters:

```
first quarter    : January – March
second quarter : April – June
third quarter    : July – September
fourth quarter  : October – December
```

(a)   What is the following function, q-s, calculating?

```
Quarter-no = {1 , . . . , 4}

q-s : (q : Quarter-no , y : Year)  →  Time-seconds
q-s(q,y) △ month-seconds ((q  -  1) * 3 + 1, y)
```

(b)   Write a function, quarter-year-size, to find out how many seconds there are in a given quarter of a given year. You may use any of the functions already defined above.

Part 3 – System time as time sequence

As the next stage of specification Rita defines the relationship between the system time and the abstraction as an ascending sequence of naturals without duplicates. This is difficult to specify formally. Rita imagines an external variable, called wallclock (the same name as the built-in function on the final machine), with a natural number value which periodically increases. She defines the abstraction as an object with function-like syntax, but which is actually non-deterministic (in the sense that it produces different results depending on the unpredictable behaviour of wallclock).

```
abstract-time-second-seq : → Time-second-seq
abstract-time-second-seq △ remove-adjacent-duplicates (wall-clock-ticks)

wall-clock-ticks : → Seq of Time-second
ext ?? wallclock : ℕ { special time updating value }
wall-clock-ticks △ [wallclock] ⌢ wall-clock-ticks
```

Next she writes the function that removes duplicates. She only needs to specify this for infinite sequences, as that is all she is concerned with.

```
remove-adjacent-duplicates :
   (dupseq : Seq of Time-second) → (ts : Time-second-seq)
remove-adjacent-duplicates (dupseq) △
   (if dupseq[1] = dupseq[2] then
      [ ]
   else
      [dupseq[1]]
   ) ⌢ remove-adjacent-duplicates(tl(dupseq))
```

(Note here the slightly non-obvious use of the brackets around the if expression. Also note that, although no pre-condition is written, the implicit pre-condition is not true. In this case the pre-condition is that the input sequence dupseq is infinitely long, as that is what is required for the function to be defined.)

Part 4 – Input format as abstract format

This part of the specification relates the concrete input from the user to the abstract format by taking a sequence of characters and returning a sequence of strings. Here Rita (reasonably) regards the input from the user as being a finite sequence of characters. In the implementation, the actual format will be a single line of text.

Conc-display-format = Seq of Char

abs-display-format : (s : Conc-display-format) → Display-format
pre even-dollars(s)
abs-display-format(s) △
  if s = [ ] then [ ]
  else [first-item(s)] ⌒ abs-display-format(tail-items(s))

first-item : (s : Conc-display-format) → String
pre even-dollars(s) and s ≠ [ ]
first-item(s) △
  if hd(s) = '$' then
    let end-dollar : N be smallest natural > 1 such that
      s[end-dollar] = '$'
    in s[1 , . . . , end-dollar]
  else
    let start-dollar : N be smallest natural such that
      (s ⌒ ['$'])[start-dollar] = '$'
    in s[1 , . . . , start-dollar − 1]

tail-items : (s : Conc-display-format) → (r : Conc-display-format)
pre even-dollars(s) and s ≠ [ ]
post first-item(s) ⌒ r = s

even-dollars : (f : Conc-display-format) → B
even-dollars(f) △
  let dollar-count : N be
    card { i ∈ inds(f) | f[i] = '$' }
  in
    (dollar-count mod 2) = 0

It is not reasonable to expect that the user will *always* type an even number of dollars in the input, but the specification above does assume this. Accordingly, Rita writes:

make-even-dollar-conc-display-format : (format : Conc-display-format) →
                                   (even-format : Conc-display-format)
post even-dollars(even-format) and
    ((even-format = format) or (even-format = format ⌒ ['$']))

This function is to be used in addition to abs-display-format to characterize the full relationship between the concrete and abstract format.

Exercise 5.7 Explain the function first-item. Why is there a need for a conditional expression in its definition? What sort of strings will be in its result?

Part 5 – Output format as abstract display

The relationship between the abstract display sequence and the real output format is similarly identified, by writing a function from the abstract to the concrete. For this the concrete output is regarded as a sequence of lines where each line is a sequence of characters:

Concrete-output = Seq of Conc-display (infinite)

Conc-display = Seq of Char

rep-concrete-output : (ds : Display-seq) → Concrete-output
rep-concrete-output(ds) △
  [rep-display(hd(ds))] ⌢ rep-concrete-output(tl(ds))

rep-display : (d : Display) → Conc-display
rep-display(d) △
  if d = [ ] then [ ]
  else rep-display-item(hd(d)) ⌢ rep-display(tl(d))

rep-display-item : (di : Display-item) → Conc-display
red-display-item(di) △
  { as expected, numbers converted to Seq of char, and so on }

Part 6 – Complete specification

The various levels of the specification are fitted together by an operation definition for the whole program:

CLOCK-PROGRAM

ext wr input-file   : Conc-display-format
    wr output-file : Concrete-output
    ?? wallclock   : ℕ { special time updating }

pre true

post input-file = [ ]
     and
     output-file =
       rep-concrete-output(
         display-times(
           abstract-time-seq(abstract-time-second-seq)

           ,
           abs-display-format(
             make-even-dollar-conc-display-format (input-file)
)
)
)

Rita notes that the input file and the output file are still specified as abstractions, but that the difference between these abstractions and the concrete Pascal text files is trivial.

She discusses the implications of the completed specification with Norman, who gladly gives her the go ahead for the implementation.

NORMAN: When can I try it?

5.3   Implementation?

Being a little pressed for time, and having arrived at a rigorous specification of the program, Rita decides to leave the implementation to a contract programmer, allowing herself time to run her business and attract more customers. She telephones The OK-Corral Software Bureau:

RITA: Hello. Slow-Haste Computer Services here. I'd like a temporary for a short while to implement a program. I've already got the specification.

BUREAU: The what? Oh. Err, I think I, err, might have just the man; when does he need to start?

RITA: This afternoon?

BUREAU: No problem. The rate is ten pounds per hour. I'll send him round; his name is a Mr Hackit.

RITA: That's fine.

Later on in the afternoon Rita discovers an odd-looking form as it filters into her office. Not the sort of form that she is so begrudgingly competent at satisfying in triplicate. No, the sort of form one does not expect to observe shuffling across the floor of a modern software office. The strange shape stoops under the weight of a vast library of computer manuals nestling deep inside the duffel bag so carelessly misarranged on its shoulder. Almost slithering from a left-hand coat pocket is a crumpled and grubby copy of *Fiddle-Bits* magazine. In case his bearing (and indeed what he is carrying) does not speak for itself, Rita recognizes him as the new employee from the red pools with dark surrounds, below which great bags hang poised over, and as if about to avalanche down, his cheeks. Clearly Mr Hackit is not the sort of person to waste time sleeping. The red eyes scan the room, and then settle distantly on Rita.

MR HACKIT (*politely*): Good afternoon. Hackit, Harry.

RITA: What? Oh – your name. Hello. I've been expecting you.

HARRY: Yes. Where is the machine?

Rita leads Harry to a terminal, hands him the customer requirements and the program specification, then leaves him to work – having been assured that he knows what he is doing. Thirty seconds later she hears her new employee tapping the keyboard with the furiousness of a demented woodpecker.

By the end of the afternoon our heroine has completed several VAT (sales tax) forms (in triplicate), entered tenders for various mind-degrading jobs and entertained one or two possible clients.

Approaching Hackit she finds him engrossed in a fervent battle of wits with her unlucky Pascal compiler. Unlucky, because it is so robust against attack that it is still suffering.

RITA: How are you getting on?
HARRY: Ah. I'll finish it tonight. About 11 o'clock, I think.
RITA: Oh. I was just about to go home now.
HARRY: Really? I do my best work after dark.
RITA: May I see?

There is a blur of fingers and key-clicks while Harry commands a printer listing of his creation, before he briefly beams at Rita. That very same lull in his attention towards the compiler enables it to slip out another dozen unnoticed error messages. The printer bursts into life and relentlessly gnaws at a previously virginal ribbon of paper until the entire afternoon's work lies limply on the stacker. This takes just a few seconds. Rita's worst fears materialize into concrete panic as she sifts through the mis-construction:

```
program hh1(input,output);
type tim:record h,m,s,d,mo,y,c:integer; end;
var t,ot:tim; f:array[1. .1000]of char; i,j,k:integer;
procedure get2;
begin { later } end;
begin
i := 0; get2;
while not eoln do begin i := i + 1; read (f[i]); end;
while true do begin j:= 1;while j<i do begin
if f[j] = '$' then if f[j + 1] = 'c' then if f[j + 2] = 'e' then write(t.c)else
else if . . .
⋮
end.
```

HARRY: Just got a few errors, and then the procedure. I do like to
        have a procedure, even though it's a bit slower. I read that
        somewhere.
RITA: You haven't indented it very well.

HARRY: Takes more room. I can do that later, if you think it's
    important.
RITA: And the variable names aren't very good.
HARRY: I like short ones – it's quicker. I read that somewhere too.
RITA: Procedure 'Get2'?
HARRY: I wanted to call it 'get', but that's already used in Pascal.

The screen is overflowing with a seemingly endless list of compilation errors, and Rita begins to realize the folly of her ways. Even if this program nearly works by midnight, which would be a miracle, it will be impossible to maintain or modify. And that will be *Rita's* responsibility.

RITA: I don't like it at all. You're fired.
HARRY: What?
RITA: Where's your design?
HARRY: I can write one later if you want.
RITA: Forget it. Just take your fee and go.

Poor old Hackit leaves, puzzled and disheartened. This, he thinks, is not how it happens in the movies. Rita shudders at the thought of the afternoon's experience. She consoles herself: she is a little poorer, but a lot wiser.

Exercise 5.8   Why don't you format Harry Hackit's program so that it is correctly indented to reflect its structure?

5.4   Design!

Wearing her absolutely rosiest spectacles the next day, Rita starts to design the program herself. The program basically involves reading the format from the user, and then, in an infinite loop, displaying the time in that format.

    The display format needs to be stored. She could use some mechanism that allows the format to be of an unlimited length, but she considers an array variable to be suitable, even though it imposes a maximum length.

Often a specification may be regarded as an **idealization** of the actual requirements, such that an **approximate implementation** is sufficient. For example, in specifications we regard integer (or natural) numbers as being the full infinite set, but it is usually sufficient (and hence appropriate) to implement them using the Pascal type *Integer*, which is bounded.

It is quite common, for another example, to specify some structured data using unbounded sequences, when in fact a bounded array implementation is acceptable.

A second variable is used to hold the length of the format:

const   max-format-length = 100

type display-format   = array[1. .max-format-length] of
                                 Char
       display-format-length = 0 . . max-format-length

var user-format   : Display-format
     user-format-length : Display-format-length

The major problem with the upper limit on the format length is the specification of make-even-dollars-conc-display-format. This requires that an extra dollar is added to the format if there is an odd number of dollars in it. If the format typed by the user is truncated to the maximum length and it does contain an odd number of dollars, it is not possible to add an extra one because there is no room! Consequently, Rita loosens the specification to accommodate this:

make-even-dollar-conc-display-format : (format : Conc-display-format) →
                                        (even-format : Conc-display-format)

post even-dollars(even-format)
    and
      ((even-format = format)
      or (even-format = format ⌢ ['$'])
      or (even-format = format [1 , . . . , len(format) – 1] ⌢ ['$'])
      or (even-format = format [1 , . . . , len(format) – 1])
)

Exercise 5.9   Why might the result of the above function be the given format up to, but excluding, the last character?

Looking at the top level of the specification, Rita sees that the program is to display the time only as it changes, thus two variables are needed, to hold the current time and the previous displayed time so that they can be compared. The type of these variables is the same as that she defined in the specification:

current-time,previous-time : Time

In the design of the top-level algorithm, Rita assumes the existence of procedures to read the format, get the current time and display a given time in the required format. These will have **parameters**.

Although well named and sized procedures contribute greatly to the clarity of a program, it is not always immediately clear what interaction an individual procedure has with the rest of the program. For example, a procedure might be given some value which is stored in a variable in the main program, or might return some value in some variable, or both. A comment in the procedure which describes the interface can help, but many languages provide a formal mechanism for stating (at least part of) it. A **parameter** is such a mechanism and is rather like a function argument. The two kinds of parameters which are most frequently used in Pascal are **value** and **variable** parameters. The first is a value passed to the procedure by the piece of program that calls it. The second is a variable which is similarly passed.

A procedure **value parameter** is a value which is explicitly presented to a procedure when it is called. The principle is the same as function arguments in our specifications, where a function is applied to a value. For consistency with Pascal, parameters in our designs are defined within brackets in the procedure heading and the values actually applied to the procedure are written in brackets after the procedure name in the procedure call. For example, the procedure

```
write-money-with-leading-asterisks(number : Real; field-width : Integer)
begin
    . . .
    { loop to write the lead chars }
    . . .
        write(output, '*')
    . . .
    { write the number with two decimal places }
    write(output,number:1:2)
    . . .
end
```

is designed to take two value parameters (in the following order): a *Real* number, which will be displayed with two decimal places, and an *Integer* field which will be filled up with leading asterisks. We can write the statement

```
write-money-with-leading-asterisks(tax-rate * taxable-pay, 10)
```

assuming that **tax-rate** and **taxable-pay** are *Real* variables. This statement will execute the body of the procedure **write-money-with-leading-asterisks**, which will act on the values supplied.

Suppose that later, during the design, it became clear that sometimes asterisks, sometimes spaces and sometimes zeros were needed as the leading character. The above procedure could be altered to

```
write-money-with-leading-char(number : Real;
                             field-width : Integer; lead-char : Char)
begin
  . . .
  { loop to write the lead chars }
  . . .
    write(output,lead-char)
  . . .
  { write the number with two decimal places }
  write(output,number:1:2)
  . . .
end
```

Then the same effect as before would be achieved by

```
write-money-with-leading-char(tax-rate * taxable-pay, 10, '*')
```

(As another example, the Pascal predeclared procedure *writeln* takes value parameters which are displayed on the output file.)

In contrast to procedure value parameters, through a **variable parameter**, a procedure may be given a variable from which it can read a value, and to which it can write a value. A variable parameter is similar to an external variable with read/write access in our specifications, except that the actual variable referenced may be different, depending on the call of the procedure. For consistency with Pascal, variable parameters are defined within brackets after the word var in the procedure heading in our designs. Similarly, the variables to which the procedure is actually applied are written in brackets after the procedure name in the procedure call. For example, suppose we wished the **write-money-with-leading-char** procedure to write the result to a different file in different parts of the program. The file to be used could be passed to the procedure as a variable parameter. Thus, the heading could be

```
write-money-with-leading-char(var result-file : Text;
                             number : Real; field-width : Integer;
                             lead-char : Char)
begin
  . . .
  { loop to write the lead chars }
  . . .
    write(result-file,lead-char)
  . . .
  { write the number with two decimal places }
  write(result-file,number:1:2)
  . . .
end
```

Then a call to the procedure might be

write-money-with-leading-char(audit-file, tax-rate, 5, '0')

(As another example, the Pascal predeclared procedure *readln* takes variables as parameters and places values in them from the input file.)

The procedures to read the format and access the current time are to use variable parameters to return their results. The procedure to read the format will also make sure there are an even number of dollars, by adding one on the end if necessary, as hinted at in the specification. The procedure to display the time in the required format is to be given the time and the format as value parameters. This procedure can assume there are an even number of dollars. After reading the format, the program should access the current time, and then in an infinite loop, display that time and wait until the time changes. Thus Rita's design is:

```
clock(input,output)

begin
  read-format(user-format,user-format-length)
    { Note: must make sure even dollars }
  get-time(current-time)
  while true { that is, do forever }
    display-time(user-format,user-format-length,current-time)
    previous-time := current-time
    while current-time = previous-time
      get-time(current-time)
  end-of-while
end
```

Next Rita turns her attention to the get-time procedure, this being the most complicated of those left to be refined.

Exercise 5.10 Can you think of any other programs like clock which are designed to run forever (well, until stopped by external interrupt from the user)?

5.4.1 Design of get-time

The get-time procedure must access the system time as a number of seconds, and convert it into the corresponding record format. This record format can be obtained by starting with the time expressed as seconds, repeatedly comparing that value with the number of seconds in the largest time component, removing that many seconds and counting components until the residual number of seconds is too small. The residue can then be compared with the size of the next largest time component, and so on until all components larger than a second have been considered.

This alone would not take account of the time before 1970, because the number of each component counted in the time would start at zero. A simple way to add on this unconsidered time is to start counting centuries from 19, years from 70, months from 1, days from 1 and the rest from 0.

A consequence of this, however, is that when counting the number of a certain component it is possible to accumulate more than the allowed number of that component in a date (for example, more than 30 years since 1970). In such cases, when the overflow condition occurs, the number of components must be set to zero and the number of outer ones incremented. This overflow can occur for any component (except the largest) that does not start counting at its smallest possible value.

Rita draws up a table of the various components and their relevant attributes:

Component	Start count	Overflow?	Fixed size?
Century	19	no	yes
Year	70	yes	no
Month	1	no	no
Day	1	no	yes
Hour	0	no	yes
Minute	0	no	yes
Second	0	no	yes

Looking at her table Rita notices that year and month are not fixed in size, but depend on the current year, and upon the current month with current year respectively. In the worst case, it is possible for there to be 99 years, and this would involve 99 tests for leap years. Consequently she decides to introduce another component, a four-year, which has a fixed size. However, when these are counted, the algorithm must add four to the number of years, still checking for overflow.

As an optimization on the general method, she observes that the components that have a fixed size can be processed using division and remainder, because, for example, the number of centuries in a number of seconds is that number of seconds divided by the number of seconds in a century.

Our heroine is now in a position to design the algorithm for the conversion procedure:

```
get-time(var current : Time)

var residual-time : ℕ
    four-year-count : ℕ
    begin

      get system time into variable residual-time

      { now calculate the century, and new residual time within century }
      current.time-century := 19 + residual-time div century-size
      residual-time := residual-time mod century-size

      { now the year: first deal with the initial value }
      current.time-year := 70

      { now deal with four year chunks: }
      four-year-count := residual-time div four-year-size
      residual-time := residual-time mod four-year-size

      { overflow adjustment: }
      current.time-century := current.time-century +
                              (current.time-year + 4 * four-year-count) div 100
      current.time-year := (current.time-year + 4 * four-year-count) mod 100

      { now the remaining years: }
      while residual-time ⩾ year-size(current.time-year)
        residual-time := residual-time – year-size(current.time-year)
        if current.time-year = 99
          current.time-year := 0
          increment current.time-century
        else
          increment current.time-year
      end-of-while

      { now the months: }
      current.time-month := 1
      while residual-time ⩾ month-size(current.time-year,current.time-month)
        residual-time := residual-time –
                         month-size(current.time-year,current.time-month)
        increment current.time-month
      end-of-while

      { now the days: }
      current.time-day := 1 + residual-time div daysize
      residual-time := residual-time mod daysize

      { now the hours: }
      current.time-hour := residual-time div hour-size
      residual-time := residual-time mod hour-size

      { now the minutes: }
      current.time-minute := residual-time div minute-size
      residual-time := residual-time mod minute-size
```

```
        { and finally, the seconds: }
        current.time-second := residual-time
    end
```

All that remains in the refinement of this procedure is the consideration of the various time component sizes. Most of these are constant, except year-size and month-size. These latter two are best designed as **program functions.**

```
        minute-size = 60

        hour-size = 60 * minute-size

        day-size = 24 * hour-size
```

In many languages, a programmer may define **functions** algorithmically. These are used to split a program into parts in a similar way to procedures. However, rather than being sub-routines executed as one statement, they are used in program expressions as functions taking a number of arguments and returning a value result. A program function has a body of statements which is executed during the evaluation of each program expression containing an application of the function.

For consistency with Pascal, in our designs the result of the function is returned by assigning the desired value to the name of the function.

For example, the design of a function that returns the largest of two given *Integers* is

```
largest-number(n1,n2 : Integer) : Integer
begin
  if n1 > n2
    largest-number := n1
  else
    largest-number := n2
end
```

With this design, a statement to write the largest of three given *Integer* exam marks, might be

```
write(output,largest-number(CS110-exam-mark,
                   largest-number(CS120-exam-mark,
                           CS130-exam-mark)))
```

assuming that CS110-exam-mark, CS120-exam-mark and CS130-exam-mark are declared as Integer variables.

```
month-size(this-year : Year; this-month : Month-no) : ℕ
var days : day
begin
  if this-month ∈ { 1,3,5,7,8,10,12 }
     days := 31
  else
  if this-month ∈ { 4,6,9,11 }
     days := 30
  else
     if this-year mod 4 = 0
        days := 29
     else
        days := 28
  month-size := days * day-size
end

year-size(y : year) : ℕ
begin
  if y mod 4 = 0
     year-size := day-size * 366
  else
     year-size := day-size * 365
end

four-year-size = (3 * 365 + 366) * day-size

century-size = 25 * four-year-size
```

5.4.2   Design of display-time

The next candidate for design is the procedure to display the time in the required format. This essentially involves looping through the format array and looking for dollar signs.

Many algorithms are primarily concerned with processing some form of structured data. In such cases, the most natural solution is often one that has the same structure as the data. So, if the data involves the repetition of some form (for example, a sequence), the algorithm will have a loop to process that repetition. If the items of data involve alternative forms, the algorithm will have alternative parts to process each of the forms. Thus, identifying the structure of the data that an algorithm must process can often lead to the most appropriate structure for the algorithm itself.

The abstract specification that treats the format as a sequence of strings provides Rita with a good clue as to the best way to design the procedure. The format array can be regarded as a sequence of sub-strings, each either to be copied to the output or interpreted as a mnemonic corresponding to a time item. This suggests the use of an outer loop, inside which one of these sub-strings is processed. Another loop is required to process a sub-string, so the body of the outer loop will consist of two alternative inner loops. She makes a start:

```
display-time( format:Display-format;
              format-length:Display-format-length;
              this-time:Time)
begin
  format-point := 1
  while not reached end of format
    if at a mnemonic
      while not at the end of the mnemonic
        extract character at format-point and add to mnemonic
        format-point := format-point + 1
      end-of-while
      compare the mnemonic with those allowed and display
        appropriate time item
    else
      while not at the end of the literal string
        extract character at format-point
        write character at format-point
        format-point := format-point + 1
      end-of-while
    end-of-if
  end-of-while
end
```

She then goes on to add more detail, such as inventing a variable for storing the mnemonic and initializing it to empty just before the inner loop, and so on. She does complete the design, but, she prefers not to talk about it. So, regrettably, we have no choice but to leave it as a laboratory exercise (see later). Sorry.

One thing that she will mention, though, is that when she designs the procedure she decides it is convenient to have the names of the months stored in an array indexed by month number. Although these are really constant throughout the execution of the program, it is necessary to store them in a variable in Pascal, because constants may only be numbers or simple packed arrays of characters, and not arrays of packed arrays of *Char*. Having completed the design of display-time Rita adds the following variable to the design:

month-names : array[1..12] of packed array[1..3] of Char

These values need initializing, so she adds an appropriate procedure call at the start of the top level of the program design:

init-month-names

The design of this latter procedure is trivial. It has 12 assignment statements and nothing else in its body. So trivial, in fact, that Rita designs it next!

> RITA: Well, it only takes one minute, and it might take two minutes
> if I do it later.

```
init-month-names
begin
  month-names[1] := 'jan'
  ⋮
  month-names[12] := 'dec'
end
```

5.4.3 Design of read-format

The procedure to read the format must read the first line of text from the input file and place it in the format array, ignoring any characters that will not fit. It must also make sure there are an even number of dollars, by adding one on the end if required. The simplest way to achieve all this is to have a loop that reads a character from the input until all the characters on the first line have been read. While this is being done, the characters are being counted to determine where to put them in the array, if there is room. To keep track of whether there are an even number of dollars, Rita uses a Boolean variable. This is initially set to true, and then negated each time a dollar is read. Then, having read the format, an extra dollar can be added if necessary to make the number of dollars even. Unfortunately, there is a subtle complication, regarding the possibility of having read a format of maximum length (or maybe a truncated one) which is found to have an odd number of dollars. It is not possible to add an extra dollar in this case, as there is no room for it. Instead, the last character is changed to become a dollar *unless* it already is a dollar! In this latter case, Rita decides simply to remove the last character. A lesser heroine than Rita may well have overlooked the possibility that the last character of a format of maximum length with an odd number of dollars could itself be a dollar. Such a case is unlikely to occur by accident during testing. That is the nature of bugs that sneak up from behind when least expected, years after a program has happily matured!
    To get back to the point, Rita's design is:

```
            read-format(var format:Display-format;
                          var format-length:Display-format-length)
            var ch:char
                dollar-even:Boolean
            begin
              dollar-even := true
              format-length := 0
              while more data on input line
                read(input,ch)
                if format-length < max-format-length
                  format-length := format-length + 1
                  format[format-length] := ch
                  if ch = '$'
                    dollar-even := not dollar-even
                  end-of-if
                end-of-if
              end-of-while
              if not dollar-even { then must add a dollar }
                if format-length < max-format-length
                  format-length := format-length + 1
                  format[format-length] := '$'
                else
                  if format[format-length] = '$' then
                    format-length := format-length - 1
                  else
                    format[format-length] := '$'
                  end-of-if
                end-of-if
              end-of-if
            end
```

⬛ 5.5 Implementation

As with previous chapters, much of the implementation is straightforward from the design. The complete program follows, with explanation
as necessary:

Program *clock(input,output)*;

Const *MaxFormatLength* = 100;

Pascal allows the definition of **sub-range** types, denoted similarly to sub-ranges of sets in
our specifications. Any of the Pascal types with the notion of successor may be
sub-ranged. These include: *Integer, Char, Boolean,* (*false* is less than *true*), but not *Real.*

(*Real* numbers do not have a unique successor.)

Array index descriptions in the form v1..v2 are actually sub-range types.

```
Type Hour = 0..23;
     Minute = 0..59;
     Second = 0..59;
     Day = 1..31;
     MonthNo = 1..12;
     Year = 0..99;
```

Just as in specifications, we may assign an alternative name to an existing type in Pascal. For example,

```
Type Century = Integer;
```

```
Century = Integer;
```

Just as in specifications, we may define **record** types in Pascal. The fields are listed by name and type, and the field access operations may be used in a similar way to those seen in specifications.

However, Pascal offers no operation to construct record values from the collection of values for the fields (that is, the mk-Blah-blah functions in our specifications). Hence it is not possible to have a constant record value written in a program, and all record values have to be stored in variables, constructed by assignment to the individual fields.

Records may be copied completely in one assignment statement, but in standard Pascal two record variables may not be compared for equality.

```
Time = Record
         TimeHour    : Hour;
         TimeMinute  : Minute;
         TimeSecond  : Second;
         TimeDay     : Day;
         TimeMonth   : MonthNo;
         TimeYear    : Year;
         TimeCentury : Century;
       End;

DisplayFormat = Array[1..MaxFormatLength] Of Char;
DisplayFormatLength = 0..MaxFormatLength;
```

Var *UserFormat*   : *DisplayFormat*;
    UserFormatLength : *DisplayFormatLength*;

CurrentTime,PreviousTime : *Time*;

MonthNames : **Array**[1. .12] **Of Packed Array**[1. .3] **Of** *Char*;

Pascal procedure or function variable parameters are declared in the procedure or function heading after the procedure name, and between brackets. For each parameter, a name is given, followed by the type of the variable expected for that parameter. To distinguish a variable parameter from a value parameter, the word **Var** is written before it. The names given in the heading are called **formal variable parameters,** and are used to reference the variable throughout the body of the procedure or function.

For example, the following procedure has one formal variable parameter, called *current*:

Procedure *GetTime*(**Var** *current* : *Time*);
Begin
    . . .
    current := . . .
    . . .
End;

As well as declaring local variables, a procedure or function may **locally declare** constants, types, procedures and functions. The declared items may be used only within the declaring procedure.

Constant declarations in Pascal may not employ an expression to produce the value. This is an unfortunate deficiency in the current version of standard Pascal, which is remedied in the proposed new standard for 'Extended Pascal'.

Procedure *GetTime*(var *current*:*Time*);
{ *get current time as time record* }

Const *MinuteSize*   = 60;
     HourSize   = 3600;   { 60 * *MinuteSize* }
     DaySize   = 86400;   { 24 * *HourSize* }
     FourYearSize = 126230400;   { (3 * 365 + 366) * *DaySize* }
     CenturySize = 3155760000; { 25 * *FourYearSize* }

Var *ResidualTime* : *Integer*;
    FourYearCount : *Integer*;

The function *MonthSize* is declared within the procedure *GetTime*, and has value parameters.

Pascal procedure or function value parameters are declared in the procedure or function heading after the procedure name, and between brackets. For each parameter, a name is given, followed by the type of the value expected for that parameter. The names given here are called **formal value parameters**, and are used to reference the value throughout the body of the procedure or function.

For example, the following function has two formal value parameters called *This Year* and *ThisMonth*.

```
Function MonthSize(ThisYear : Year; ThisMonth : MonthNo) : Integer;
Begin
   . . .
   . . . ThisMonth . . .
   . . . ThisYear . . .
   . . .
End;
```

A procedure or function may have a mixture of both value and variable parameters. For example, the following procedure heading defines three variable parameters, *a*, *b* and *e*; and three value parameters, *c*, *d* and *f*:

```
Procedure MixtureOfValueAndVariable ( Var a,b : Integer; c,d : Boolean;
                         Var e : Real; f : Char);
```

A **function declaration** defines a program function consisting of a heading, local declarations and a body. The heading defines the name of the function, the formal value (or variable) parameters and the result type. Within the body of the function, the name is treated as a **write-only** variable, in order to assign the function result. For example:

```
Function factorial (n : Integer) : Integer;
{ Assumes n >= 0 }
Var result : Integer;
Begin
   result := 1;
   While n > 0 Do
   Begin
      result := result * n;
      n := n - 1;
   End;
   factorial := result
End;
```

Note that it is necessary to have a local variable in the above example. This is because the name of the function is treated as a write-only variable for assigning the result. It is

:= not allowed to replace the variable *result* with the function name *factorial*, that is, to have the statement:

> *factorial* : = *factorial* * *n*;

because that would be reading the value associated with *factorial*. (The reason for this is clear when one considers that Pascal allows functions that have no parameters, and also allows functions to be recursive.)

A final note about variable parameters of functions. Pascal allows this, but there are few cases where their use is justified. The main reason for this is that functions should have all their input through their parameters (arguments) and all their output through their result. Variable parameters, on the other hand, are an explicit means for allowing a procedure or function to change the value of a variable. As hinted, though, there are cases for exception to this general principle, but they are rather subtle for introduction at this point.

The body of the *MonthSize* function involves the use of Pascal **sets**.

Set types may be used in Pascal, although the type of elements and the size of sets is restricted. Membership test is implemented as an infix operation, called **In**. Set constants are written in a notation slightly divergent from traditional mathematics, using square rather than curly brackets. (Unfortunately, these look rather like the sequences we write in specifications – do not confuse them!) For example,

> [1,3,5,7,8,10,12]

denotes a value of type **Set Of** *Integer*, containing only the elements listed.

```
Function MonthSize(ThisYear : Year; ThisMonth : MonthNo) : Integer;
Var days : Day;
Begin
  If ThisMonth In [1,3,5,7,8,10,12] Then
    days := 31
  Else
  If ThisMonth In [4,6,9,11] Then
    days := 30
  Else
    If ThisYear Mod 4 = 0 Then
      days := 29
    Else
      days := 28;
```

MonthSize := *days* * *DaySize*;
End;

Function *YearSize*(*y* : *Year*) : *Integer*;
Begin
  If *y* **Mod** 4 = 0 **Then**
    YearSize := *DaySize* * 366
  Else
    YearSize := *DaySize* * 365;
End;

The (non-standard) function used by the program to access the system time on the Cruncher 3 Mega-Boulder is pre-declared as:

Function *wallclock* : *Integer*;
Begin
  wallclock := *number of seconds since beginning of* 1970
End;

Humming quietly to herself, Rita writes the body of the procedure *GetTime*. In this she uses the Pascal mechanism for **referencing** individual **fields** of a record.

As in our specifications, **fields** of a record are **referenced** in Pascal by suffixing the record variable with a dot followed by the field name.

The statements of *GetTime* call the various time component size functions, supplying **actual value parameters** to those functions.

Procedure or function value parameters actually passed to a procedure are written as expressions within parentheses after the name of the procedure in the procedure call. These values are called **actual value parameters,** and are associated with the procedure's formal parameters by the order in which they are written. The type of an actual parameter must be compatible with the type of the corresponding formal parameter. There is no relationship between the name of a formal parameter and any variable or constant involved in the associated actual parameter.

For example, assuming the function *MonthSize*, which takes two value parameters, one might construct the expression:

10 * *MonthSize*(89,7)

:=

```
Begin { of GetTime }
  { first get the time from the system }
  ResidualTime := wallclock;

  { now calculate the century, and new residual time within century }
  current.TimeCentury := 19 + ResidualTime Div CenturySize;
  ResidualTime := ResidualTime Mod CenturySize;

  { now the year: first deal with the initial value }
  current.TimeYear := 70;

  { now deal with four year chunks: }
  FourYearCount := ResidualTime Div FourYearSize;
  ResidualTime := ResidualTime Mod FourYearSize;
  current.TimeCentury := current.TimeCentury +
                          (current.TimeYear + 4 * FourYearCount) Div 100;
  { now the remaining years: }
  current.TimeYear := (current.TimeYear + 4 * FourYearCount) Mod 100;
  While ResidualTime >= YearSize(current.TimeYear) Do
  Begin
    ResidualTime := ResidualTime - YearSize(current.TimeYear);
    If current.TimeYear = 99 Then
    Begin
      current.TimeYear := 0;
      current.TimeCentury := current.TimeCentury + 1
    End
    Else
      current.TimeYear := current.TimeYear + 1;
  End;

  { now the months: }
  current.TimeMonth := 1;
  While ResidualTime >= MonthSize(current.TimeYear,current.TimeMonth) Do
  Begin
    ResidualTime := ResidualTime -
                    MonthSize(current.TimeYear,current.TimeMonth);
    current.TimeMonth := current.TimeMonth + 1;
  End;

  { now the days: }
  current.TimeDay := 1 + ResidualTime Div DaySize;
  ResidualTime := ResidualTime Mod DaySize;

  { now the hours: }
  current.TimeHour := ResidualTime Div HourSize;
  ResidualTime := ResidualTime Mod HourSize;

  { now the minutes: }
  current.TimeMinute := ResidualTime Div MinuteSize;
  ResidualTime := ResidualTime Mod MinuteSize;

  { and finally the seconds: }
  current.TimeSecond := ResidualTime;
End;
```

```
Procedure InitMonthNames;
Begin
   MonthNames[1] := 'jan';  MonthNames[2] := 'feb';
   MonthNames[3] := 'mar'; MonthNames[4] := 'apr';
   MonthNames[5] := 'may'; MonthNames[6] := 'jun';
   MonthNames[7] := 'jul';  MonthNames[8] := 'aug';
   MonthNames[9] := 'sep';  MonthNames[10]:= 'oct';
   MonthNames[11]:= 'nov';  MonthNames[12]:= 'dec';
End;
```

Reading the format involves reading characters until the **end of line** has
been reached.

There is a pre-declared Pascal function called ***eoln***. This takes a file of type *Text* which
has been opened for reading, and returns a *Boolean* result. The result is true when the
current reading position in the file is at the end of a line, and is false otherwise.

```
Procedure ReadFormat(Var format:DisplayFormat;
                     Var FormatLength:DisplayFormatLength);
                     Var ch:Char; DollarEven:Boolean;
Begin
   DollarEven := true;
   FormatLength := 0;
   While Not eoln(input) Do
   Begin
      read(input,ch);
      If FormatLength < MaxFormatLength Then
      Begin
         FormatLength := FormatLength + 1;
         format[FormatLength] := ch;
         If ch = '$' Then DollarEven := Not DollarEven;
      End
   End;
   If Not DollarEven Then
   Begin
      If FormatLength < MaxFormatLength Then
      Begin
         FormatLength := FormatLength + 1;
         format[FormatLength] := '$';
      End
      Else
         If format[FormatLength] = '$' Then
            FormatLength := FormatLength - 1
         Else
            format[FormatLength] := '$';
   End;
End;
```

> **Procedure** *DisplayTime(format:DisplayFormat;*
> *FormatLength:DisplayFormatLength;*
> *ThisTime:Time);*
>
> *{ Note: Assumes an even number of dollars in format }*
>
>   *{ an exercise }*
> **End**;

The design of the main program compares the *current-time* and *previous-time* variables to wait until they are different.

Unfortunately in standard Pascal it is not permitted to compare two record values to see whether they are the same. Instead, one must explicitly compare all or a sufficient sub-set of the fields of the records.

Rita realizes that it is sufficient to compare only the *TimeSecond* fields, as it is extremely unlikely that exactly a whole minute will have elapsed between starting and completing the display of a time!

Procedure variable parameters actually passed to a procedure are variables written within parentheses after the name of the procedure in the procedure call. These are called **actual variable parameters,** and are associated with the procedure's formal parameters by the order in which they are written. The type of the actual parameters must be compatible with the type of the formal parameters. Note that actual variable parameters are not expressions – they are variables. There is no relationship between the names of the formal parameters and the names of the corresponding actual parameters.

For example, the procedure with the heading:

> **Procedure** *GetTime* (**Var** *current* : *Time);*

might be called as:

> *GetTime(TimeNow)*

Rita finally implements the main body of the program:

```
Begin
  InitMonthNames;
  ReadFormat(UserFormat,UserFormatLength);
  GetTime(CurrentTime);
  While true Do
  Begin
    DisplayTime(UserFormat,UserFormatLength,CurrentTime);
    PreviousTime := CurrentTime;

    { can't compare records }
    While CurrentTime.TimeSecond = PreviousTime.TimeSecond Do
      GetTime(CurrentTime);
  End
End.
```

Exercise 5.11   Design a Pascal implementation of the following specification:

```
elapsed-time : (time1 : Time , time2 : Time) → Time
elapsed-time(time1, time2) △
    abstract-time( retrieve-time-second(time1)
                 – retrieve-time-second(time2)
                 )
```

abstract-time and retrieve-time-second are defined earlier in this chapter. Naturally, you may consult the design of get-time also given earlier, if you think it will help!

Exercise 5.12

(a)   Give an informal but clear and precise explanation of the following formal specification. Avoid simply translating the symbols into English.

```
Perfect-list : (N : ℕ) → (s : Seq of ℕ)
pre N > 1
post let perfect-set be {x : ℕ | x > 1 and x ≤ N and perfect (x)}
        in
            elems s = perfect-set
            and
            len s = card perfect-set

perfect : (N : ℕ) → 𝔹
perfect(N) △ N = sum-of-factors(N – 1, N)

sum-of-factors : (N : ℕ , M : ℕ) → ℕ
sum-of-factors(N,M) △
    if N = 1 then
       1
    else
```

```
                       if M mod N = 0 then
                          N + sum-of-factors(N - 1, M)
                       else
                          sum-of-factors(N - 1, M)
```

(b)   Write a procedure that implements the specification below. You may assume that the Pascal type *Text* is an adequate representation of Seq of ℕ.

```
WRITE-PERFECT-LIST (N : ℕ)
ext wr output : Seq of ℕ
pre N > 1
post output ⌢ Perfect-list(N) = output
```

Exercise 5.13

(a)   Pascal allows program functions to call themselves, in much the same way as functions in our specifications can be recursive. Argue that the following Pascal function terminates:

Function *multiply* (*x,y* : *Integer*) : *Integer*;
Begin
   If *x* < 0 **Then**
     multiply := − *multiply*(− *x, y*)
   Else
   If *x* = 0 **Then**
     multiply := 0
   Else
     multiply := y + *multiply*(*x* − 1,*y*)
End;

(b)   Write an iterative version of the above function, without using the Pascal multiplication operator, but instead based on the principle of repeated addition.

SUMMARY

This case study emphasized the use of abstraction in specification, particularly in the modelling of the data types. The main concepts introduced were **recursion, procedure parameters,** and the use of **sets** and **records** in Pascal.

   The following notations were introduced in this chapter.

Specification notation

Character sequence constant	"This is a sequence of 36 characters."
Set sub-range	{0 , . . . , 59}
Recursive function	display-times(t,f) △ . . . display-times(. . . , . . .)
Head and tail of sequences	hd(t), tl(t)
Record field access	t.time-hour

Pascal notation

Sub-range type	**Type** *hour* = 0..23
Alternative type names	*Century* = *Integer*
Record type	*time* = **Record** ... ;...;...;... **End**
Function declaration	**Function** *MonthSize*(.. .....):*Integer*; ... **Begin** ... **End**
Formal value parameter	**Function** *MonthSize*(*y:Year*; *m:MonthNo*):*Integer*
Formal variable parameter	**Procedure** *GetTime*(**Var** *current:Time*)
Set type	[1,3,5,7,8,10,12]
Record field access	*current.TimeMonth*
Text end of line	**While Not** *eoln*(*input*) **Do** ....
Actual value parameter	*DisplayTime*(*UserFormat*, *UserFormatLength*, *CurrentTime*)
Actual variable parameter	*ReadFormat*(*UserFormat*, *UserFormatLength*)

There is a potential in the laboratory exercise at the end of this chapter for the reader to fall into a **Wally trap.** Avoiding the exercise does not make such traps go away, so we introduce the concept here.

A **Wally trap** happens when the programmer has written a condition which is apparently sensible, but which may cause a run-time error because some part of it has an undefined value. There are two usual forms, based respectively on the **And** operator and the **Or** operator.

In an **And-based Wally trap,** one part of the **And** (conjunct) may be undefined when the other part is false. For example, assuming the variables

x : **Array** [1 .. 10] **Of** *Integer*
i : *Integer*

the following condition is an **And**-based Wally trap:

(i **In** [1 .. 10]) **And** ($x[i]$ = 100)

When the first conjunct is true, the expression is evaluated to true or false depending on the value of $x[i]$. The problem is that if the first conjunct is false, the second one is undefined. This happens, for example, when the value of i is 11. The mistake occurs when the programmer expects the **And** operator to be generous and return a false result when one of its conjuncts is false, regardless of whether the other is undefined. However, in Pascal (and similar languages) such undefined expressions cause a run-time error when they are detected. So, at best, the computer will evaluate both conjuncts of the expression (even though this is not optimally efficient) and always give a run-time error. At worst, the computer that the program is tested on might evaluate the first conjunct, find that it is false and not look at the second one, but return false as the result. This is disastrous because sooner or, worse still, later the program will be run on a computer that always computes both conjuncts or computes the second one first! So the program you tested and found to be working does not run on the customer's machine! Don't you feel a Wally?

An example of an **Or-based Wally trap,** based on the same variables as above, is

$(i > 10)$ **Or** $(x[i] = 20)$

This problem does not occur in specifications, because there the operators are defined more generously to return a result whenever possible. That is, **And** returns false when either of its conjuncts is false (even if the other would be undefined) and **Or** returns true if either of its disjuncts is true. Jones (1990) gives a more detailed discussion of this for the interested reader.

TUTORIAL EXERCISE

This exercise is designed to reinforce the process of design from a specification to a Pascal implementation. In keeping with the time–date case study, part of the specification is a recursive function.

One of the assumptions about computer character sets that Pascal makes is that the decimal digits '0' ... '9' are included, in that order and directly following one another. Each character has a position number in the computer character set called the **ordinal** number. The ordinal numbers always range from zero to one less than the number of elements in the computer's character set. The position of a particular character may vary from computer to computer, but the ordinal number for '0' is always one less than the ordinal number for '1', and so on. It is possible to access the ordinal number for a particular character value, c, using a standard Pascal function $ord(c)$, which yields the ordinal number of c. There is also the standard function, $chr(i)$ which yields the character whose ordinal number is the value, i, where i is an integer expression.

1

What is the effect of each of the following Pascal statements?

  Var i : *Integer*; ch : *Char*; b : *Boolean*;

(a) $ch := chr(ord(ch))$;
(b) $ch := chr(ord('0'))$;
(c) $i := 8$; $ch := chr(ord('0') + i)$;
(d) $b := (ord(ch) < ord('Z'))$ **And Not**$(ch < 'Z')$;

2

The following is a specification for a piece of code which converts numbers to a required output format:

short-string-length = 10

Short-string = Seq of Char
                         of length short-string-length

The conversion is specified as an operation taking a number, n, as a parameter, and writing the representation in the external variable, rep-of-n.

NUM-TO-STRING (n : $\mathbb{Z}$)
ext wr rep-of-n : Short-string
pre true
post
    let num-string : Seq of Char be
        if n < 0 then ['–'] $\frown$ posnum-to-string(– n)
        else   posnum-to-string(n)
    in
        rep-of-n = (if len(num-string) > short-string-length then ''*OVERFLOW*''
                          else
                          spaces(short-string-length – len(num-string)) $\frown$ num-string)

The function posnum-to-string is recursively defined as:

posnum-to-string: (i : $\mathbb{N}$) $\rightarrow$ Seq of Char
posnum-to-string(i) $\triangle$
    if i < 10 then [digit-rep(i)]
    else posnum-to-string(i div 10)
        $\frown$ [digit-rep(i mod 10)]

digit-rep: (n : $\mathbb{N}$) $\rightarrow$ (ch : Char)
pre 0 $\leqslant$ n $\leqslant$ 9
post chr(ord('0') + n) = ch

The function spaces is defined as in the last tutorial:

spaces : (n : $\mathbb{N}$) $\rightarrow$ (r : Seq of Char)
pre   true
post len(r) = n and
        for all i $\in$ inds(r), it is true that
        ' ' = r[i]

The (Pascal pre-declared) functions *chr* and *ord* are implementations of the following:

chr : (n : $\mathbb{N}$) $\rightarrow$ (ch : Char)
pre   n $\leqslant$ (card(Char) – 1)
post ord(ch) = n

```
ord : (ch : Char) → (n : ℕ)
pre   true
post chr(n) = ch
        and  ord('0') = ord('1') – 1
        and  ord('1') = ord('2') – 1
        and  ...
        and  ord('8') = ord('9') – 1
```

Design and implement a piece of Pascal code that will satisfy the above specification, justifying your choice of data structures, procedures, functions, local variables, control constructs, and so on.

LABORATORY EXERCISE – to implement the display procedure

Purpose

To implement a component of a program, given the formal specification. The design stage is of particular concern in this exercise, as the specification does not provide much clue to a reasonable solution.

Problem

Write a procedure that displays a given time in a given format. The definition of the output format is given to the procedure as a one line string of text (stored in an array). This string appears literally in the output, except for any portion between an oddly and evenly occurring dollar sign ($). A sub-string between such dollars is to be interpreted as follows:

ho	hours
mi	minutes
se	seconds
da	day number
mo	month number
MO	month name (or abbreviation)
ye	year without century
ce	century (for example, 19)

All other string values between oddly and evenly occurring dollars are to be ignored.

For example, the format

ho:mi:se mo/da/ye

may produce time like:

15:21:32 3/24/87

(American format date)

Similarly,

> mi minutes and se seconds past ho o'clock

may produce:

> 21 minutes and 32 seconds past 15 o'clock

For a precise explanation, you *must* study the following specification of the procedure.

Specification

As in the case study, the specification here has been divided into levels of abstraction to assist with the clarity.

Most abstract specification

The abstract input format given to the procedure may be regarded as a sequence of strings (separated by $s). Based on this, the abstract output from the procedure is specified as a sequence of Display-seq, as follows:

```
String      = Seq of char
Hour        = { 0 , . . . , 23 }
Minute      = { 0 , . . . , 59 }
Second      = { 0 , . . . , 59 }
Day         = { 1 , . . . , 31 }
Month-no    = { 1 , . . . , 12 }
Month-name  = { "jan","feb","mar","apr","may","jun","jul","aug",
                "sep","oct","nov","dec" }
Year        = { 0 , . . . , 99 }
Century     = ℕ

Display-item  =  String ∪ Hour ∪ Minute ∪ Second ∪ Day ∪
                 Month-no ∪ Month-name ∪ Year ∪ Century

Display  =  Seq of Display-item

Display-seq  =  Seq of Display (infinite)

Time  =  Record
              time-hour    : Hour
              time-minute  : Minute
              time-second  : Second
              time-day     : Day
              time-month   : Month-no
              time-year    : Year
              time-century : Century
         end
```

Display-format = Seq of String

format-display : (t : Time , f : Display-format) → Display
format-display(t,f) △
   if f = [ ] then [ ]
   else [format-display-item(t,hd(f))] ⌢ format-display(t,tl(f))

format-display-item : (t : Time , f : String) → Display-item
format-display-item(t,f) △
    if f = "ho" then t.time-hour
   else if f = "mi" then t.time-minute
   . . .
   else if f = "MO" then name-of-month(t. time-month)
   . . .
   else if f = "ce" then t.time-century
   else if hd(f) = '$' then [ ]
   else f

name-of-month : (m : Month-no) → Month-name
name-of-month(m) △
   ["jan","feb","mar","apr","may","jun","jul","aug","sep","oct","nov","dec"][m]

Input format as abstract format

This part relates the concrete input from the user to the abstract format, by
taking a sequence of characters and returning a sequence of strings. Here we
(reasonably) regard the input from the user as being a finite sequence of
characters. In the implementation, the actual format will be a single line of
text.

Conc-display-format = Seq of Char

abs-display-format : (s : Conc-display-format) → Display-format
pre even-dollars(s)
abs-display-format(s) △
  if s = [ ] then [ ]
  else [first-item(s)] ⌢ abs-display-format(tail-item(s))

first-item : (s : Conc-display-format) → String
pre even-dollars(s) and s ≠ [ ]
first-item(s) △
  if hd(s) = '$' then
    let end-dollar : $\mathbb{N}$ be smallest natural > 1 such that
      s[end-dollar] = '$'
    in s[1 , . . . , end-dollar]
  else
    let start-dollar : $\mathbb{N}$ be smallest natural such that
      (s ⌢ ['$'])[start-dollar] = '$'
    in s[1 , . . . , start-dollar − 1]

tail-items : (s : Conc-display-format) → (r : Conc-display-format)
pre even-dollars(s) and s ≠ [ ]
post first-item(s) ⌢ r = s

even-dollars : (f : Conc-display-format) → 𝔹
even-dollars(f) △
  let dollar-count : ℕ be
    card { i ∈ inds(f) | f[i] = '$' }
  in
    (dollar-count mod 2) = 0

Output format as abstract display

The relationship between the abstract display sequence and the real output
format is similarly identified, by writing a function from the abstract to the
concrete. For this the concrete output is regarded as a sequence of lines where
each line is a sequence of characters:

Concrete-output = Seq of Conc-display (infinite)

Conc-display = Seq of Char

rep-concrete-output : (ds : Display-seq) → Concrete-output
rep-concrete-output(ds) △
  [rep-display(hd(ds))] ⌢ rep-concrete-output(tl(ds))

rep-display : (d : Display) → Conc-display
rep-display(d) △
  if d = [ ] then [ ]
  else rep-display-item(hd(d)) ⌢ rep-display(tl(d))

rep-display-item : (di : Display-item) → Conc-display
rep-display-item(di) △
  { as expected, numbers converted to Seq of char and so on }

Complete specification of procedure

The various levels of the specification are fitted together by an operation
definition for the whole procedure:

Conc-display-seq = Seq of Conc-display { that is, text file }

DISPLAY-TIME (format : Conc-display-format; this-time : Time)

ext   wr output : Conc-display-seq

pre   even-dollars(format)

post output = $\overline{\text{output}}$ ⌢
    [rep-display(format-display(this-time, abs-display-format(format)))]

Implementation

Your implementation may assume the following global declarations, and no others:

Const
        MaxFormatLength = 100;

Type
        Hour   = 0..23;
        Minute   = 0..59;
        Second   = 0..59;
        Day   = 1..31;
        MonthNo = 1..12;
        Year   = 0..99;

        Century = *Integer*;

        Time = **Record**
                        TimeHour   : *Hour*;
                        TimeMinute : *Minute*;
                        TimeSecond : *Second*;
                        TimeDay   : *Day*;
                        TimeMonth   : *MonthNo*;
                        TimeYear   : *Year*;
                        TimeCentury : *Century*;
                End;

        DisplayFormat   = **Array**[1..*MaxFormatLength*] **Of** *Char*;
        DisplayFormatLength = 0..*MaxFormatLength*;

Var *MonthNames* : **Array**[1..12] **Of Packed Array**[1..3] **Of** *Char*;

{ *The file output is declared in the program heading.* }

The type *DisplayFormat* is used as a restricted but acceptable approximate implementation of the data type *Conc-display-format* in the specification.

        The variable *MonthNames* has been initialized to contain the required three-character string spellings of the respective month names.

        The file *output* is to be used for the results. Thus you may assume that the Pascal type *Text* is an appropriate representation of *Conc-display-seq* (where each text line represents one *Conc-display*). You should write your solution as a procedure with the heading:

        Procedure *DisplayTime*(*format:DisplayFormat*;
                        FormatLength:DisplayFormatLength;
                        ThisTime:Time);

The parameter *FormatLength* always contains the length of the actual format stored in the parameter *format* (hence *FormatLength* ≤ *MaxFormatLength*). Note that it is not necessary to store a display before its output.

        Finally, don't be a Wally – avoid a condition like this:

> **While** (*FormatPoint* <= *FormatLength*) **And**
>   (*format*[*FormatPoint*] <> '$') **Do**

or, just the same really:

> **Until** (*FormatPoint* > *FormatLength*) **Or** (*format*[*FormatPoint*] = '$')

Interchangeable parts system

MOTIVATION

The primary emphasis in this case study is the importance of program design, which here corresponds to an efficient, but non-obvious, implementation of some essentially simple operations. The resulting program looks very little like the original specification, which is short and abstract. So the example also illustrates the potential conciseness of specifications.

The example is based on the concept of an **equivalence relation**. The main specification concepts introduced include a formalization of **data type invariants**, **implication** and **universal** and **existential quantifiers**. The Pascal concepts introduced include the **file read buffer** and the **For** and **Case statements**.

6.1   Scenario

Rita's business has now become established. She has several current contracts and a few regular clients. One *quiet* afternoon, while almost effectively attempting to complete the documentation for a hair dresser's accounting package, juggling with a faulty printer data cable in her left hand, and fending off a truly awkward customer in her right hand (and being comfortable in the knowledge of the distance between the two telephones being employed in this latter effort), she is completely oblivious to her impending fate of being swiftly removed from *this* normality into that of providing the Fordge Motor Company, Galactica, with a much needed **on-line equivalent parts management system**. Of course, this lack of insight should not surprise her: she has never had much time for the fortune telling business, in the past.

Anyway, meet Henry.

 # 6.2   Requirements

Later that same day, our heroine receives another phone call. Within two days she is hurtling towards the headquarters of the Fordge Motor Company, Corporative Foundation Galactica, aided only by a comfortable seat attached to a wide-bodied flying restaurant, and a rather liberated air-line host. On arrival she is escorted directly to the president himself.

> HENRY: Hi! You must be the non-sexist-term person come over to give us a mega on-line interactive equivalent parts management system! Hey!
>
> RITA: Err, I think so. You couldn't write it down could you?

After much discussion, the problem turns out to be fairly simple in essence. The company uses about one million different components in their manufacture of cars. Well, it seems that many of these parts are equivalent, in the sense of being interchangeable. Now, Joe has just retired; he was the parts store boss, and he knew which parts were interchangeable with each other. The point is, now that he's not around they want a computer to remember the equivalences. Joe had a great memory – the engineers would tell him which parts were the same, and he never forgot.

Rita spends a couple of hours talking to people on the shop floor – most of them think Joe was a great asset. Her summary of the requirements is as follows:

There are one million consecutive part numbers. Some of these identify interchangeable parts. A test engineer can state that two parts are equivalent. A test engineer can ask whether two parts are equivalent. If, say, Tom states that part 23 and part 87 are the same, Dick states that part 87 and 13 are interchangeable, then when Harry asks if 23 and 13 are the same, the computer must reply 'yes'.

HENRY: That's just really amazing! – did Tom, Dick and Harry tell you that?

Rita recognizes that the problem is actually an instance of an **equivalence relation**.

A **relation** is something that relates two objects (arguments). If R is a relation then

R(X,Y)

is either true or false. For example, 'less than' (<) on integers is a relation: for any two integers, X, Y, the expression

X < Y

is either true or false.

An **equivalence relation** is a relation which also has the three following properties. Firstly, an equivalence relation is **reflexive**, that is all objects are related to themselves:

R(X,X) = true

regardless of X. An equivalence relation is also **symmetric**, that is:

R(X,Y) = R(Y,X)

regardless of X and Y. Finally, an equivalence relation is **transitive**. This means:

if R(X,Y) and R(Y,Z) then R(X,Z)

'Less than' on integers is not an equivalence relation, whereas equality is. A more illustrative example comes from hypothetically ideal beasts called white mice, and the relation 'is nice to'. This relation is an equivalence relation on pairs of idealized white mice, resulting from the following invariant principles of their conduct: all mice are nice to themselves (reflexive); all mice are nice to every mouse that is nice to them (symmetric); and all mice are nice to every mouse that is nice to some mouse they are also nice to (transitive). This does not stop mice being horrible. In some colonies, mice are only nice to themselves, but the relation is still an equivalence relation. In most colonies, there are gangs of mice such that the members of each gang are really nice to each other, but each gang is pretty nasty to each other gang. 'Is nice to' is still an equivalence relation in these places.

Exercise 6.1 Is it possible for an idealized white mouse to be a member of two gangs, each containing other mice which are not members of the other gang?

The main problem as Rita sees it is devising an appropriate data structure that can record all the equivalences, and efficiently support the operations:

- initialize-parts – make all parts different.
- equate-parts – make two parts equal (transitively).
- test-parts – see if two parts are equal.

Of course, the initialize operation will be performed rarely, perhaps only once.

Exercise 6.2 The following is a customer's requirement statement for a payroll program. Identify as many inadequacies as you can find and suggest sensible resolutions where appropriate.

A program is required to update a sequential file of employee payroll records. Each employee record contains a number, which uniquely identifies that employee, and details of the employee's salary. Some employees are paid monthly and others weekly. Errors must be handled appropriately. You may assume that each salary is a whole number of pounds.

 ## 6.3 Specification

The information concerning the equivalences is to be stored in a simple parts database. Rita postulates that a good abstract model of the database is a set of sets of part numbers, such that two parts are interchangeable if and only if they are in the same set. The initialize operation is to be specified as producing the parts database with each element being a singleton set. Equating two parts removes at most two sets from the database, and inserts their union. The test operation merely involves seeing if the two parts are in the same set.

Rita commences writing the specification:

Part-number = {1 , . . . , 1000000}

When we write:

Y-set = Set of Y

we are defining a type called Y-set. This contains all possible (finite) sets such that each element of those sets is one of the values of type Y.

A set may be empty, that is contain no elements. Whatever the type of set, the empty set is denoted in specifications as { }.

As an example, the type

Set of $\mathbb{B}$

is the set

{ { } , {true} , {false} , {true,false} }

Parts-database = Set of (Set of Part-number)

She realizes that a parts database is not as general as just a set of sets, but that there are more specific properties which can be expressed by a **data type invariant**.

In specifications a **data type invariant** may be written formally by defining a predicate function associated with the type. The name of the function is inv- followed by the name of the type. The function always takes a value of the type as one parameter, and yields true or false as the result. For example, for a type called S, the associated invariant predicate could be:

inv-S : (s : S) → (p : $\mathbb{B}$)
pre . . .
post . . .

Or the function could be defined explicitly:

inv-S : (s : S) → (p : $\mathbb{B}$)
inv-S(s) $\triangle$ ...

The names of the parameter and the result (s and p in the above example) are not fixed by any convention, whereas the name of the function (inv-S) is. The function expresses formally the extra properties that are true for all members of the type.

Datatype invariants are actually a convenient form of set comprehension, as illustrated by the following example:

S = Seq of ℕ
inv-S(s) △ (len s = 10)

is equivalent to:

S = { s ∈ Seq of ℕ | len s = 10 }

So what properties of the parts database, in addition to those of a set of sets, should be invariant over all the operations? Firstly, none of the sets of part numbers can be **empty** – that would make no sense. Secondly, all of the part numbers must be somewhere in the database – including ones that are not interchangeable with any other. This is equivalent to saying that the **distributed union** of all of the sets in the database must be equal to the set of all part numbers.

The **distributed union** of a set of sets is the union of all the element sets. For example,

∪ ({ {3,5,10} , {4,10} , {9,3,2} })
 = {3,5,10} ∪ {4,10} ∪ {9,3,2}
 = {2,3,4,5,9,10}

Finally, none of the sets may overlap since no part number may be in more than one set. That is, for all pairs of sets in the parts database, their **intersection** must be empty.

A function on sets which is similar to union is **intersection**. This takes two sets and returns the set of elements which are in *both* sets. For example:

{2,7,8,2,5} ∩ {4,2,9,8,3} = {2,8}

and

{ [2,4], [ ], [5] } ∩ { [4,2], [0,5] } = { }

She writes:

Parts-database = Set of (Set of Part-number)
inv-Parts-database(pdb) △
    ...
and
    ...
and
    ...

The invariant has three conjuncts, corresponding to the three properties she has identified informally. To express these formally, Rita needs to use a **quantifier**.

In our specifications we often wish to express the truth of some proposition (Boolean expression) applied to some or all values of a certain set (type). The general form of such expressions is:

Q i ∈ S • P(i)

where Q is a **quantifier**, i is a **logical variable**, S is a set and P(i) is a proposition involving i. Such expressions are themselves propositions, either true or false. There may be more than one logical variable, from more than one set. The two most common quantifiers are the **universal quantifier** ('for all') written

∀

and the **existential quantifier** ('exists'), written

∃

The quantifiers have a lower precedence than the logical operators, and, or and not.

She needs to use the **universal quantifier** in this invariant.

The **universal quantifier**, written as

∀

and pronounced **for all**, expresses the truth of some proposition for every member of a set. For example,

∀ i ∈ ℕ • i ≥ 0

is true. (Every natural number is greater than or equal to zero.) On the other hand,

∀ i,j ∈ ℕ, s ∈ Seq of ℕ • s[i] = s[j]

is false. (It is not true that for every pair, i and j, of natural numbers and sequence, s, of natural numbers; the ith and jth elements of s are the same.) Note the small extension allowing more than one logical variable (i,j) to be quantified in the same expression.

If the set of values for the logical variable (or one of the logical variables) is empty, the expression is defined to be true. For example:

    let s : Seq of $\mathbb{N}$ be [ ] in
        $\forall\ i \in$ inds(s) • s[i] = 10

is true. (All the elements of the empty sequence are 10!)

She also needs to express a logical dependency, for which she will use the **implication** operator.

Another function on Booleans is **implication**, written

    $\Rightarrow$

This takes two Boolean arguments and returns a Boolean result:

    $\_\Rightarrow\_ : (p : \mathbb{B}, q : \mathbb{B}) \rightarrow \mathbb{B}$

The result of $p \Rightarrow q$ is always true, unless q is false and p is true.

$\Rightarrow$:

p	q	$p \Rightarrow q$
T	T	T
F	T	T
T	F	F
F	F	T

For example,

    $(3 < 5) \Rightarrow ($len$([1,0]) = 2)$

is true

It is often used with variables (such as quantified or function arguments) to express a dependency of some value on another. For example,

    $\forall\ x \in \mathbb{N} • x < 10 \Rightarrow x + 1 < 11$

She completes the specification of the type Parts-database:

Parts-database = Set of (Set of Part-number)
inv-Parts-database(pdb) △
  (∀ ps ∈ pdb • ps ≠ { })
and
  (∪(pdb) = Part-number)
and
  (∀ ps1,ps2 ∈ pdb • (ps1 ≠ ps2) ⇒ (ps1 ∩ ps2 = { }))

Exercise 6.3   What are the values of the following expressions?

(a)   ∀ x ∈ ℕ • x ⩾ 0

(b)   ∀ x ∈ ℕ • ∀ y ∈ ℕ • (x * y ∈ ℕ)

(c)   ∀ x ∈ {a,b,c} • x ∈ {a,d,e,f} ∪ {b,d,f,g}

Exercise 6.4   What does the third conjunct of the invariant for Parts-database say about a pair of element sets of pdb which are the same?

Exercise 6.5   Can you think of a value for the type T, for which the following is true:

     ∀ s ∈ Seq of T • ∀ i,j ∈ inds s • s[i] = s[j]

Next Rita specifies the input to the program as a sequence of commands. Abstractly, these can be described as:

Command = {init} ∪ Arg-command
Arg-command = Record
               name:{test,equate}
               part1,part2:Part-number
       end

Commands = Seq of Command

The data type Command includes the value init and all pairs of part number with the value test as an Arg-command record, and similarly for the value equate.

Exercise 6.6   What is the cardinality of the set (type) Command?

To specify the behaviour of the program, Rita decides to write an explicit operation, which calls the three operations of main interest already identified but not yet formally specified. These operations will have **parameters** for the part numbers, and so on, and access the database as an external variable.

Operation specifications may be given (value) **parameters** in a similar way to function arguments. Operations cannot change the values of these parameters.

In explicit operations, when the algorithm calls another operation that requires value parameters, the actual values passed are written in brackets after the called operation name.

The program has three external variables: the database, the input commands and the output test results.

```
IPS

ext wr pdb : Parts-database
    wr input : Commands
    wr output : Seq of {yes,no}

begin
    while input ≠ [ ]
    begin
        if hd(input) = init
            initialize-parts
        else
        if hd(input).name = test
            test-parts(hd(input).part1,hd(input).part2)
        else
            equate-parts(hd(input).part1,hd(input).part2)
        input := tl(input)
    end
end
```

All that remains is to specify the three main database operations. Initialize produces the parts database where each set contains just one part number (and each part number is contained in just one set). She uses a generalization of **set comprehension** introduced earlier to achieve this.

There is an alternative form for writing **set comprehensions**. Rather than say the members of the set are the values of some logical variable satisfying a given property, it is often more convenient to state that the members of the set are the values yielded after applying some function to all the values of one or more logical variables having certain properties.

For example, the set of factorials of all prime numbers can be specified, assuming ⊒∀⌐
definitions of fact and is-prime as:

    { fact(i) | i ∈ ℕ and is-prime(i) }

More generally, the elements of the set being defined are all the possible values of some
expression, written before the |, involving some functions and/or operators applied to
each other and to some logical variables. The types of these logical variables are given on
the right-hand side of the |, together with their other properties.

For example, the set of squares of all distances from the origin in integer coordinate
geometry is:

    { x * x + y * y | x ∈ ℤ and y ∈ ℤ }

---

    initialize-parts
    ext wr pdb : Parts-database
    post pdb = { { e } | e ∈ Part-number}

The equate operation must alter the database by replacing the sets
containing the two parts by their union:

    equate-parts(p1,p2 : Part-number)

    ext wr pdb : Parts-database

    post pdb = { s ∈ $\overleftarrow{pdb}$ | not (p1 ∈ s) and not (p2 ∈ s) }
          ∪
          { s1 ∪ s2 | s1 ∈ $\overleftarrow{pdb}$ and s2 ∈ $\overleftarrow{pdb}$
                 and p1 ∈ s1
                 and p2 ∈ s2 }

Exercise 6.7   Convince yourself that the above specification of equate-parts is
correct, even if the two parts were already equated in the parts database
before the operation.

    Finally, the test operation must append a yes or a no to the output,
depending on whether the two parts are in the same set. Above all, it
must not alter the parts database, so Rita gives only read access to it for
this operation. She needs to use an **existential quantifier** to specify the
post-condition.

The **existential quantifier**, called **exists**, expresses the truth of a proposition for at least one member of a set. For example,

∃ s ∈ Seq of ℕ • s[3] = s[4]

is true. (There does exist at least one sequence of natural numbers having the third and fourth elements the same.) On the other hand,

∃ i,j ∈ ℕ, s ∈ Seq of {1,3,5} • s[i] = j * 2

is false. (There do not exist two natural numbers and a sequence of {1,3,5} such that the ith element is 2 times j.)

If the set of values for the logical variable (or one of the logical variables) is empty, the expression is defined to be false. For example:

let s : Seq of ℕ be [ ] in
  ∃ i ∈ inds(s) • s[i] = 10

is false. (There does not exist an element of the empty sequence such that its value is 10!)

test-parts(p1,p2 : Part-number)

ext   rd pdb : Parts-database
     wr output : Seq of {yes, no}

post output = $\overline{\text{output}}$ ⌃ (if (∃ s ∈ pdb • p1 ∈ s and p2 ∈ s)
                    then [yes]
                    else [no])

Rita discusses the implications of the specification with Henry. He seems rather pleased.

HENRY: That's just really amazing! I mean, well, you know – this is gonna put Fordge back on the map!

RITA: Err, yes. I suppose so.

Exercise 6.8 What are the values of the following expressions?

(a)   ∃ x ∈ ℕ • x ⩾ 0

(b)   not ∃ x,y ∈ ℕ • not (x * y ∈ ℕ)

(c)   ∃ x ∈ {a,b,c} • x ∈ {a,d,e} ∩ {b,c,f }

(d)   ∃ s ∈ Seq of ℕ • ∀ i ∈ inds s • s[i] = i

(e)   ∀ s ∈ Seq of ℕ • ∃ i ∈ inds s • s[i] = i

There are a few concrete considerations missing from the specification presented so far. In particular, the specification regards the input from the user as being an abstract sequence of commands. In reality, the input is text typed by the user. Apart from the structural difference, the concrete input may be erroneous, that is, the user may type things that make no sense when viewed abstractly. If the exact form of the input were considered important by the customer, the relationship between the concrete text typed by the user and the abstract view in the specification would have to be formalized. However, in this case it is sufficient for Rita to choose any concrete form which can represent the abstract commands already agreed.

It is necessary to have some way for the user to indicate the end of the command sequence. Perhaps the nicest way to achieve this is to introduce an extra command for quitting. In addition, Rita feels it is a good idea to have a simple on-line help message, invoked by a help command. She defines the concrete command syntax (using a derivative of the BNF system of syntax definition (Naur, 1963)):

commands = {command} 'q' eoln.

command = 't' eoln part eoln part eoln

    |

    'e' eoln part eoln part eoln

    |

    'i' eoln ('y' | 'Y' | 'n' | 'N') eoln

    |

    'h' eoln.

part = integer.

eoln = *** end of input line ***.

In the above description, items in quotes (') denote literal characters, that is, characters that actually appear in the input. Unquoted names refer to other syntax definitions (such as command). Curly brackets denote repetition zero or more times, and a vertical line (|) denotes alternatives.

The first character of each command corresponds to the operation being invoked: 't' for test, 'e' for equate, 'i' for initialize and 'h' for help. The 'q' following the list of commands corresponds to a quit operation. The initialize command requires a confirmation or rejection, after a simple prompt.

Rita has to decide what to do with input that doesn't take the above form. Any text appearing after a command but before an end of line is to be completely ignored. Also, if a character not in the set {'t','e','i','h','q'} is typed when one of those is expected, it is to be treated as being the same as 'h'. Any part number entered which is outside the allowed range should be rejected, and immediately re-input until an acceptable one is entered.

The test operation should have a clear message indicating whether the result is 'yes' or 'no'.

Exercise 6.9   According to the above BNF syntax, which of the following are legal input to the program, that is, which are strings of the form 'commands'?

(a)   'q' eoln

(b)   'h' eoln

(c)   'i' eoln '3' eoln 'q' eoln

(d)   't' eoln '3' eoln '4' eoln 'i' eoln 'N' eoln 'q' eoln

Exercise 6.10   What is the purpose of the characters 'y', 'Y', 'n' and 'N' after the 'i' command? What do you think should be done if a character which is not one of these is typed instead?

6.4   Design

Next Rita concerns herself with the program design. The obvious point she notes is that Pascal (or, for that matter, most similar languages) does not directly support sets of sets of numbers. She must think of a data structure that will efficiently support the test and equate operations, and for which the storage requirements are not excessive.

Exercise 6.11   Before reading on, try to think of a Pascal data structure that could be used to implement the type Parts-database.

6.4.1   How about an obvious solution?

Perhaps the most obvious way of recording the equivalences between parts is to have a static matrix (that is, a two-dimensional table) of Boolean values. The matrix is indexed (labelled) on both sides by part numbers. To see if two parts are equivalent, one merely needs to look at the matrix cell indexed by the two parts. The test operation would be fast with this structure; however, the equate operation would be very slow, as it would have to compute the transitively equivalent parts explicitly. (This is called the **transitive closure**.) As if this were not enough, the matrix itself would be huge! One million million cells, even if each cell is a single binary digit (representing true or false) is big by any current standard. Needless to say, Rita rejects this idea quite early.

6.4.2 How about another obvious solution?

What if we store only the explicitly equated parts in a single list (such as an array of pairs, or a file of pairs)? This certainly gets round the storage problem of the previous proposal, since only the equated pairs need be stored. Even the worst case of all parts being equivalent can be represented by only 999 999 pairs. The equate operation, if it did not check whether the two parts are already equated, would be extremely fast: all it would have to do is add on another pair. Unfortunately, the test operation would be remarkably slow – it would have to try all pairs over and over to find a transitive equality.

6.4.3 How about a nice cup of tea?

That's a good idea! So, over a cup of tea Rita thinks about the required operations of the data type. What is needed, it seems, is some single entity for each part number which is the same for all interchangeable parts, but different for non-interchangeable parts. How silly, she thinks – the answer was there all the time. In the specification that entity is the set (or perhaps some identification of the set, such as its 'name') in which the part resides. Two parts are interchangeable if and only if they are in the same set. All we need to do is to efficiently implement these sets, together with the various operations.

So, what is a good way to implement these sets? Well, an important thing to consider is that all parts must be in exactly one set at any time. This suggests that an implementation of general sets, allowing some parts to be not present, and others to be in several sets, is likely to be over-complicated for this system.

By studying the specification of test-parts Rita sees that, if the implementation could tell which set a given part number was in, it would be easy for it to satisfy the existential quantifier in test-parts. To check her reasoning here, she finds it helpful to rewrite that specification, assuming such a function:

```
test-parts(p1,p2 : Part-number)

ext  rd pdb : Parts-database
     wr output : Seq of {yes,no}

post output = output ⁀ (if (set-containing(p1,pdb) = set-containing(p2,pdb))
                        then [yes]
                        else [no])
```

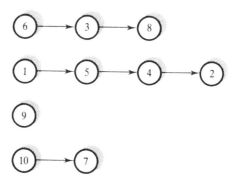

Figure 6.1 A linked list model of the set of sets {{3,6,8}, {1,2,4,5}, {9}, {10,7}}.

Suppose the sets were modelled as lists. In these lists, each part is linked either to another part in the set, or to nothing. An example, using only ten part numbers, is shown in Figure 6.1.

These lists would be easy to implement in Pascal. Each part number appears in exactly one list, and hence has exactly one follower, unless it is at the end of a list. The structure needs only to store the follower of each part number. This can be held in a single array indexed by part numbers. Each cell would contain the part number of the next part in the same list, or itself if it were the last in the list. The example of Figure 6.1 would be represented by the array shown in Figure 6.2. In this, 5 is the follower of 1, 2 is the follower of itself (since it is at the end of a list), 8 is the follower of 3, and so on.

The 'name' of each set could be the part number at the end of the list. In this case, it would be easy to find the name of the set that any part number resides in, by simply following the chain. Thus the test operation would be easy to implement: follow the chain for both given parts, and then see if the two ends are the same.

If the sets were modelled this way, the equate operation would somehow have to join together the two lists containing the given parts. This would have the desired effect of both removing the old two sets and adding the new set. (Of course, if the two parts were already equated, the lists would already be joined so there would be no net effect.) The problem is: how can we join two lists like this? Obviously, we need to have one 'front end' and one 'back end' which we join together, but so far we have only got a mechanism for finding one kind of end. For

Index	1	2	3	4	5	6	7	8	9	10
Value	5	2	8	2	4	3	7	8	9	7

Figure 6.2 Array implementation of the lists in Figure 6.1.

example, suppose it was required to equate parts 3 and 5 in the above example. To join the two lists, we have to make 6 the follower of 2, or make 1 the follower of 8. We have no problem finding parts 8 and 2 by following the chains from parts 3 and 5. However, we so far have no way of finding the other ends, namely parts 6 and 1.

If Rita were rash, she might have thought that the solution was to have both forward and backward links in the chains, so that it was easy to find the two different ends needed to join the chains together. It's a good job she is not rash, because such a solution would be unnecessarily complicated.

6.4.4   How about a nice cup of really hot tea?

Over the next cup of tea Rita asks herself: 'Do they have to be lists?' At this, the room turns embarrassingly quiet. 'No!', she shouts even louder. Everyone assumes she is hallucinating, perhaps suffering from 'nozzle insulate' – a curious, unfortunate, but temporary consequence of an undoubtedly round earth. Everyone, that is, except a nearby ancient mathematician, who, while momentarily distracted from his pie, looks up and nods his head in understanding.

The problem of joining chained lists is that they have two kinds of end and it must be possible for both of these to be found. However, the *crucial* property required of the lists is that they have *one* unique end of some kind which can be used for identifying the sets they represent, and this end can be found for any part number. Lists are just one specific case of a more general structure that has this property: trees. Trees have one end of one kind (called the **root**) and many ends of another kind (called **leaves**). An example, again using ten part numbers, of a general tree representation is shown in Figure 6.3. It could be implemented by the Pascal array shown in Figure 6.4.

To join two trees together, given any two part numbers belonging to them, the equate operation merely has to find the root of one tree and graft it on to the other tree at any point by changing the chain at that

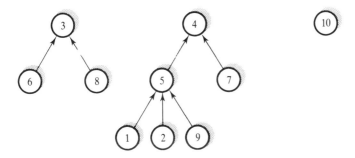

Figure 6.3   A tree model of the set of sets {{3,6,8}, {1,2,4,5,7,9}, {10}}.

Index	1	2	3	4	5	6	7	8	9	10
Value	5	5	3	4	4	3	4	3	5	10

Figure 6.4   Array implementation of the trees in Figure 6.3.

root. One obvious place to graft it on the other tree is at the given part number. However, if the two parts are already in the same tree, the operation must make sure that it does not connect the root of that tree to one of its own lower nodes – that would produce a cyclic graph structure. The only place in this model where cyclicity is allowed to occur is at the actual root of the tree, as root part numbers are chained to themselves. Thus the trees should be joined at both the roots.

Also, by grafting trees together at the roots, there will be a tendency towards shallower (bushy) trees. Bushy trees means that there are fewer steps required to find the root of any part number. (If test time became critical, one could implement a version of equate that *always* made the trees completely bushy, with one node in each tree being the root, and all other nodes being leaves. However, this would require chain links in both directions, or a scan through the entire parts database.)

Bearing this in mind, Rita decides that the trees will be grafted at the roots. If they are the same tree after all, the operation has no effect.

To convince herself, Rita considers the simple example shown in Figure 6.3. Suppose part 8 and part 9 are to be equated. The operation would find the roots of the the two trees, that is parts 3 and 4, and graft them together. The new tree structure would be as shown in Figure 6.5, or Figure 6.6, depending on which way the trees were grafted.

What about the initialize operation? All this has to do is set up the array so that each element chains to itself. This represents one million single node trees, corresponding to the desired abstract structure of a singleton set for each part number, containing that number.

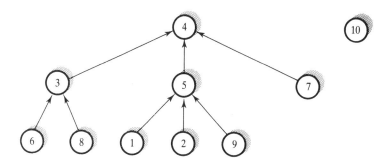

Figure 6.5   Equating parts 8 and 9 of the trees in Figure 6.3, grafting the tree of part 8 on to that of part 9.

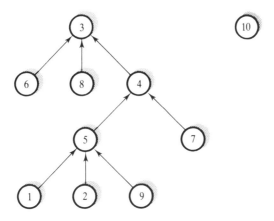

Figure 6.6   Equating parts 8 and 9 of the trees in Figure 6.3,
grafting the tree of part 9 on to that of part 8.

6.4.5   The program

Having chosen the data structure, Rita is now in a position to sketch out
the program design:

program IPS(input,output)

const max-part-number = 1000000

type Part-number = 1 .. max-part-number

The parts database is stored in an array indexed by **Part-number**, where
each cell contains a **Part-number**. She deliberates as to what the
variable should be called. Abstractly, it represents the parts database, and
so database is a good name. On the other hand, it concretely represents
a 'follower' function, giving for each part number, the part number that
follows it in a list. Thus follower is also a good name. In the end, she
decides to call it by *both* names! She achieves this by having a record with
only one field:

type Parts-database = record
                    follower: array[Part-number] of
                                        Part-number
           end

var database : Parts-database

When she wants to think of it as abstract, she will call it database. When
she needs to think of it as concrete, that is, when she needs to use the
follower function, she will call it database.follower. The two variables
are different. However, she knows that any compiler worth its price will

treat them as the same, because the record has only one field. So she is confident that using this record structure will not make the program less efficient.

The main program body is concerned with accepting user commands and executing the appropriate operations. The specification itself, which was explicit at this level, can be here regarded as a skeleton design. What is missing is the processing of the concrete input and the fact that the database will need to be stored somewhere between executions of the program. Rita sketches a more complete design:

```
var command-char : Char

begin { main program }
  read the database from permanent file
  writeln(output, '(Type h if you need help)')
  write(output,'Command: ')
  readln(input, command-char)
  while not (command-char ∈ {'q','Q'})
    if command-char ∈
      {'t','T'} : read-part-numbers(part1, part2)
                  test-parts(part1, part2)

      {'e','E'} : read-part-numbers(part1, part2)
                  equate-parts(part1, part2)

      {'i','I'} : ask if sure (y or n)
                  readln(input, command-char)
                  if command-char ∈ {'y', 'Y'}
                    initialize-parts
                    write confirmation of initialization
                  else
                    write not-initialized message
        otherwise : write the help message
    end-of-if
    write(output,'Command: ')
    readln(input, command-char)
  end-of-while
  write database to file
end { main program }
```

Rita next designs the procedure to read the part numbers for the equate and test commands.

```
read-part-numbers(var part1, part2: Integer)

begin
  read-part-number(part1,'First   ')
  read-part-number(part2,'Second')
end
```

The First or Second prompt can be implemented as a Pascal packed array.

```
type Short-word = packed array[1..6] of Char

read-part-number(var part : Integer; prompt : Short-word)
begin
  write(output,prompt,' part number: ')
  read-number(part)
  while (part < 1) or (part > max-part-number)
    writeln(output,'Part numbers must be in the range 1 to ',
                                          max-part-number)
    write(output, '(try again) ',prompt,' part number: ')
    read-number(part)
  end-of-while
end
```

When reading the actual numbers, it is important that the program does not crash if the user types some other form of input.

```
read-number(var part : Integer)
begin
  if current head of input is a digit ('0' .. '9')
    readln(input, part)
  else
    part := 0 { assume zero value, so causes error message }
    readln(input) { ignore whatever is there }
  end-of-if
end
```

Then she moves on to the more interesting parts of the program. She designs the initialize operation using a **for loop**.

The **for loop** executes a controlling statement ('the body') a number of times with the aid of a **control variable** and a range of values. Each time the body of the loop is executed, the control variable assumes one value from the range, in ascending order, until each value has been thus used. If the range is empty (that is, the start value is greater than the end value) the loop body is not executed at all. For loops should (only) be used where the required number of iterations can be computed *before* the loop starts. The body should *not* explicitly change the value of the control variable. The use of for loops is often *suggested* by the occurrence of a universal quantifier in a specification.

```
initialize-parts
{ initialize the database }
var i : Part-number
begin
  for i := 1 to max-part-number
    database.follower[i] := i
end
```

The equate operation is even shorter – all it has to do is find the two roots and chain one to the other. Rita decides to have a 'root' function to find the root part number of a given part number. This function will be given the part number as a parameter, but will access the database directly as a global variable. This means that the function is not strictly a function in the mathematical sense, since some of its input is hidden, rather than all being supplied as arguments. However, Rita considers this as an exception to her usual rule, because the database is *the* fundamental data structure for the whole program and, as such, it is appropriate for every part of the program to refer to it directly.

```
equate-parts(p1,p2:Part-number)
{ equate parts p1 and p2 }
begin
    database.follower[root(p1)] := root(p2)
end
```

Testing two parts boils down to merely comparing the two roots:

```
test-parts(p1,p2:Part-number) {test if parts p1 and p2 are equal}
begin
    writeln(root(p1) = root(p2))
    { Note: we actually want 'yes' or 'no', not 'true' or 'false' }
end
```

Finally, the root of the tree containing a given part number is found by repeatedly following the chain until no further progress is made. Rita's algorithm for this changes the value of the given parameter to its own follower, until doing so would make no difference to it.

Value parameters in Pascal behave like pre-initialized variables, in the sense that they are given a value by the statement that calls the procedure; but that procedure may change the value during its execution. However, such a change does not affect anything outside the procedure.

```
function root(p:Part-number):Part-number
{ find the root of p }
begin
    while database.follower[p] ≠ p
        p := database.follower[p]
    root := p
end
```

Having completed the design, and convinced herself that it does in fact satisfy the specification, Rita begins the implementation.

Exercise 6.12   Normally speaking, it is regarded as very bad practice for a program function to have any side-effects on the variables of the program. All the output from the function should be through the function result. However, some variables can be viewed at different levels of abstraction. For example, the database in this case study can be viewed abstractly as a set of sets or concretely as a collection of trees represented by a follower array. It might be appropriate for a function to have a side-effect at the concrete level on some variable, as long as it does not alter the abstract value of that variable. For example, the root function, which finds the root of a part-number in the database, must not alter the abstract value of the database, but it would be alright for it to change the concrete value to another that represents the same abstract value.

Propose a simple improvement to the design of the function root so that it has a side-effect on the concrete but not the abstract value of database, which causes a tendency for the trees to become bushy (and hence efficient) at hardly any expense.

6.5   Implementation

Rita must now decide how the database is to be stored between executions of the program. The simplest way to achieve this in Pascal is to use a file which can contain items of the type Parts-database. However, the file is used to hold just one element – the value of the database variable. This way, the entire parts database can be input in one read and output in one write!

Rita starts to construct the program:

```
Program EquivalentParts(input, output, DatabaseFile);

Const MaxPartNumber = 1000000;
Type  PartNumber     = 1 .. MaxPartNumber;
      PartsDatabase  = Record
                          follower : Array [ PartNumber ] Of
                                        PartNumber;
                       End;
Var   database       : PartsDatabase;
      DatabaseFile   : File Of PartsDatabase; { for saving database }

      part1, part2   : Integer; { used in user dialogue }
      CommandChar : Char;   { used in user dialogue }
```

```
Function Root(p : PartNumber) : PartNumber;
{
  – Find the root of the tree containing p
}
Begin
  While database.follower[p] <> p Do
    p := database.follower[p];
  Root := p
End{ Root };
```

The *InitializeParts* procedure uses a Pascal **For** loop.

The for loop concept is used in Pascal by the **For** statement. This involves the reserved words **For**, **To** and **Do**. The rules of the language insist that the loop body is a single statement, so in practice it is often a compound statement, with a **Begin** and **End**. The control variable must be declared within the same program block (for example, procedure) as the one in which the statement occurs. The value of the control variable cannot be altered by assignment inside the loop body (which would be bad practice anyway). Also, the value of the control variable is **undefined** after the loop execution terminates.

```
Procedure InitializeParts;
{
  – Make finest partition on database
}
Var i : PartNumber;
Begin
  For i := 1 To MaxPartNumber Do
    database.follower[i] := i
End{ InitializeParts };
```

Exercise 6.13   What is the value of each of *start* and *i* at the end of the following program fragment?

```
start := 0;
For i := 1 To 4 Do
Begin
  start := start + i;
  start := start * i
End
```

Procedure *EquateParts(part*1*, part*2 *: PartNumber)*;
{
– *Make part numbers part*1 *and part*2 *equivalent.*
– *Graft the root of part*1 *onto the root of part*2.
}
Begin
   database.follower[*Root(part*1)] := *Root(part*2)
End{ *EquateParts* };

The *TestParts* procedure is required to state whether the two given parts are interchangeable or not. Rita decides that it would be nice to include the part numbers in the message. An example message she has in mind is:

Yes, part number 10 is interchangeable with part number 25

She implements this so that there is no unnecessary space around the part numbers by using **field specifiers**.

For integer items in the *writeln* (or *write* on text files) statement, the **field specifier** is interpreted as follows. If the decimal representation of the integer being written requires fewer characters than the width specifies, the representation is space filled on the left to make it up to the width. Otherwise, the representation is written using as many characters as are required for the value without any space filling. For example:

   *writeln(count:*7)

If, say, *count* has the value 57, then the output for the above statement would be five spaces followed by the string '57'.

   *writeln(MaxPartNumber:*1)

The value 1 as a field specifier causes the number to be written using exactly as many characters as required by its decimal representation, without any spaces.

   writeln(salary:MaxWidth + 2)

The above example illustrates that the field specifiers may be expressions involving program variables.

Procedure *TestParts(part*1*, part*2 *: PartNumber)*;
{
– *Inform the operator whether part*1 *is an*
– *equivalent part to part*2.
}

```
Begin
  If Root(part1) = Root(part2) Then
    writeln(output,
            'Yes, part number ', part1:1,
            ' is interchangeable with part number ', part2:1)
  Else
    writeln(output,
            'No, part number ', part1:1,
            ' is not interchangeable with part number ', part2:1)
End{ TestParts };
```

Exercise 6.14 What will be output by the following statement, when *part1* has the value 3 and *part2* has the value 361?

writeln(output,'Part number ', part1:1,'is equivalent to ', part2:1)

Rita implements *ReadPartNumbers* next. This consists of three procedures, as designed, but one is defined in another, which in turn is defined inside the third. The innermost one *ReadNumber* defines a set of characters as a **range** of values to determine whether the input character is a digit or not.

The values of the Pascal type ***Char*** are ordered. Each character has an **ordinal number**, sometimes called a **character code**, which starts from 0 and goes up to the cardinality of the character set, minus one. Each distinct character has a distinct ordinal number. The actual value associated with each character is implementation dependent, as is the actual set of characters supported. However, in a standard implementation, the codes for the digits, '0' to '9', are guaranteed to be ascending and consecutive. The codes for each of the two alphabets, 'A' to 'Z' and 'a' to 'z', are guaranteed to be ascending, but not necessarily consecutive (for example, the code for 'B' is greater than the code for 'A', but not necessarily just one more). Most, but not all, computers nowadays use the **ASCII** character set and codes, in which the digits, and also each of the alphabets, are consecutive.

The relational operators <, >, ≤, ≥ on characters are supported in Pascal, and are defined as the corresponding relation on integers acting on the ordinal numbers of the characters.

When denoting a **set** value in Pascal, as well as enumerating the elements, one may specify **ranges** of elements which are members of the set. For example:

[3 .. 21 , 50, N + 1, 105]

['A' .. 'Z' , 'a' .. 'z', '0' .. '9' , ' ']

The same procedure also uses the input **buffer variable** to look at the next character on the input without actually removing it.

When reading a file in Pascal, one may examine the element at the current reading position without moving on to the next element. This is because Pascal associates with each file a **buffer variable**. For a file, F, the buffer variable is called

$F\hat{\ }$

and it contains the element at the current position. This is most useful if one wishes to read the file conditionally, when the condition is based on the value that would be read. When the file is opened for reading (reset), the buffer variable contains the first element, if there is one.

The buffer variable associated with the standard input file,

input^

is initially set to the first character of the input, if there is one. However, to allow for sensible use of interaction, the language implementation usually delays the association of keyboard characters until the value is needed in the program.

```
Procedure ReadPartNumbers(Var part1, part2: Integer);
{
  - Read in part1 and part2 checking within range
}
Type ShortWord = Packed Array[1..6] Of Char;
  Procedure ReadPartNumber(Var part: Integer; prompt:ShortWord);
  {
    - read one part number, and check within range
  }
    Procedure ReadNumber(Var part: Integer);
    {
      - to avoid program crashing if no integer on input file
    }
    Begin
      If input^ In ['0' .. '9'] Then { is a number }
        readln(input, part)
      Else
      Begin
        part := 0; { assume zero value, so causes error message }
        readln(input); { ignore whatever is there }
      End
    End;
```

```
Begin { of ReadPartNumber }
  write(output,prompt,' part number: ');
  ReadNumber(part);
  While (part < 1) Or (part > MaxPartNumber) Do
  Begin
    writeln(output,'Part numbers must be in the range 1 to ',
            MaxPartNumber:1);
    write(output, '(try again) ',prompt,' part number: ');
    ReadNumber(part);
  End;
End;

Begin { of ReadPartNumbers }
  ReadPartNumber(part1,'First   ');
  ReadPartNumber(part2,'Second ');
End { ReadPartNumbers };
```

Rita implements the body of the program:

```
Begin { main program }
  writeln(output, 'Interchangeable Parts recording system');
  writeln(output);
  writeln(output, 'initializing system. . .');
  reset(DatabaseFile);
  If Not eof(DatabaseFile) Then
    read(DatabaseFile, database)
  Else
    InitializeParts;

  writeln(output, '(Type h if you need help)');
  write(output,'Command: ');
  readln(input, CommandChar);
  . . .
```

Rita implements the alternative executions for the different commands as a **Case** statement.

The Pascal **Case** statement is a specialized form of alternatives command (like if–then–else), based on the value of a single expression. It comprises an expression (called the **case-index**) of some ordinal type (for example, *Integer, Char, Boolean*; but not *Real*) and a collection of non-overlapping lists of distinct values from the same type, each list associated with an action (statement). The general form is:

```
Case e Of
  c1,c2,c3 : st1;
  c4 : st2;
  . . .
End
```

where e is an expression, $c1$, $c2$, and so on, are constants of the same type, and $s1$, $s2$, and so on are single statements (perhaps compound, with **Begin** and **End**). On execution of a **Case** statement, the given expression is evaluated and the value compared with the lists of constants. If the value of the expression occurs in one of the lists, the action associated with it is performed. If the value of the expression does not appear in one of the lists, a run-time error occurs. It is for this reason that a **Case** statement is often written inside an **If** statement, the latter checking that the value of the expression is one of those covered by the former. (Some non-standard implementations of Pascal allow a very convenient addition to the **Case** statement which enables the programmer to state what should be done if the value of the expression does not occur in any of the lists. This usually involves the keyword **Otherwise**. Of course, the disadvantage of using non-standard features is that the program can only be run on that, or similarly non-standard, implementations.)

```
. . .
While Not (CommandChar In ['q','Q']) Do
Begin
  If Not (CommandChar In ['i', 'I', 't', 'T', 'e', 'E']) Then
    writeln(output,'Type t for a test, e to equate two parts,',
                   ' i to re-initialize system, q to quit')
  Else
    Case CommandChar Of
      't','T': Begin { Testing parts }
                 ReadPartNumbers(part1, part2);
                 TestParts(part1, part2)
               End;
      'e','E': Begin { Equating parts }
                 ReadPartNumbers(part1, part2);
                 EquateParts(part1, part2)
               End;
      'i','I': Begin { Re-initializing system }
                 write(output, 'Are you sure you want to re-initialize',
                               ' the entire system? (y or n)');
                 readln(input, CommandChar);
                 If CommandChar In ['y', 'Y'] Then
                 Begin
                   InitializeParts;
                   writeln(output, 'system re-initialized')
                 End
                 Else
                   writeln(output, 'system re-initialization aborted')
               End
    End { of case };
    write(output,'Command: ');
    readln(input, CommandChar);
End;
. . .
```

To save the database, the implementation uses a **write** statement (so far used only with *Text* files).

There is a pre-declared procedure in Pascal, called **write**. When used with non-text files, it takes a file variable and an expression, evaluates the expression and writes the value on to the end of the file. The expression must be of the correct type for the file, and the file must be open for writing (that is, a rewrite must have been performed on it).

. . .

rewrite(DatabaseFile);
write(DatabaseFile, database)
End { *main program* }.

When she has finished testing the program, Rita shows it working to Henry. He seems to be impressed that it didn't take very long.

Credit

The algorithm described in this case study was originally invented by Fischer and Galler (1964).

Exercise 6.15

(a)   Give an informal but clear and precise explanation of the following formal specification. Avoid simply translating the symbols into English.

X
ext wr s : Seq of $\mathbb{N}$
pre s $\neq$ [ ]
post $\exists$ n $\in$ elems $(\overleftarrow{s})$ •
      (not ($\exists$ m $\in$ elems $(\overleftarrow{s})$ • m < n)
      and
      ($\forall$ k $\in$ (elems $(\overleftarrow{s})$ $\cup$ elems (s)) – { n } •
        multiplicity($\overleftarrow{s}$, k) = multiplicity(s , k))
)
      and
      multiplicity $(\overleftarrow{s}, n)$ – 1 = multiplicity(s , n)

multiplicity : (s : Seq of $\mathbb{N}$, n : $\mathbb{N}$) $\rightarrow$ (r : $\mathbb{N}$)
post r = card { i $\in$ inds(s) | s[i] = n }

(b)   The following procedure is an approximate implementation of the specification in part (a) in that it assumes a maximum sequence length. Present an informal but convincing argument that it is otherwise correct with respect to the specification.

```
Const MaxSeqLength = 100;
Type NatSeq = Record
                    value : Array[1..MaxSeqLength] Of Integer;
                    length : Integer
              End;

Procedire X (Var s : NatSeq);
Var swap,pos:Integer;
Begin
  For pos := 1 To s.length Do
    If s.value[pos] < s.value[s.length] Then
    Begin
      swap := s.value[pos];
      s.value[pos] := s.value[s.length];
      s.value[s.length] := swap
    End;
    s.length := s.length - 1
End;
```

Exercise 6.16

(a) Give an informal but clear and precise explanation of the following
     formal specification. Avoid simply translating the symbols into English.

```
max-word-length = 10

Word = Seq of Char
inv-Word(w) △ len w ⩽ max-word-length

X : (w : Word) → 𝔹
X(w) △ w = Y(w)

Y : (w : Word) → Word
Y(w) △ if w = [ ] then w
          else Y(tl w) ⌢ [hd w]
```

(b) The following Pascal code is an implementation of the specification
     given in part (a). Present a convincing informal argument that it is
     correct with respect to the specification.

```
Const MaxWordLength = 10;

Type Word = Record
                length : Integer;
                value : Array [1..MaxWordLength] Of Char
            End;

Function X(w : Word) : Boolean;
Var i, j   : Integer;
    result : Boolean;
Begin
  result := true;
  j := w.length;
  For i := 1 To (w.length + 1) Div 2 Do
```

```
        Begin
            result := result And (w.value[i] = w.value[j]);
            j := j - 1
        End;
        X := result
    End;
```

Exercise 6.17

(a)   Give an informal but clear and precise explanation of the following formal specification. Avoid simply translating the symbols into English.

Y : (s : Seq of $\mathbb{N}$) $\rightarrow$ (r : $\mathbb{N}$)
pre s $\neq$ [ ]
post $\exists$ n $\in$ elems(s) •
       (not ($\exists$ m $\in$ elems(s) •
          Z(s,n) $<$ Z(s,m))
       and
       r = n)

Z : (s : Seq of $\mathbb{N}$, n : $\mathbb{N}$) $\rightarrow$ (r : $\mathbb{N}$)
Z(s,n) $\triangle$ if s = [ ] then 0
         else
            (if hd s = n then 1 else 0) + Z(tl s, n)

(b)   Present a design of an appropriate representation of Seq of $\mathbb{N}$ and an efficient Pascal procedure which implements the specification given in part (a). You may assume an upper limit on the length of the sequence.

Exercise 6.18

(a)   Give an informal but clear and precise explanation of the following formal specification. Avoid simply translating the symbols into English.

Text = Seq of (Seq of Char)

X : (t : Text) $\rightarrow$ (r : $\mathbb{R}$)
pre t $\neq$ [ ]
post r = (Z(Y(t)))/len t

Y : (t : Text) $\rightarrow$ (r : Seq of $\mathbb{N}$)
post len t = len r
    and
      $\forall$ i $\in$ inds(t) • r[i] = len t[i]

Z : (s : Seq of $\mathbb{N}$) $\rightarrow$ (r : $\mathbb{N}$)
Z(s) $\triangle$ if s = [ ] then 0
        else (hd s) + Z(tl s)

(b)   Design an efficient Pascal procedure which implements the specification given in part (a), assuming the Pascal type *Text* to be an adequate representation of the type of the same name in the specification.

SUMMARY

The main emphasis in this chapter was the program design. If the design had been skimped, we might have ended up with a program that resembled the specification, and which had much more complicated data structures and was far less efficient.

The main concepts introduced or reinforced included **equivalence relation**, **data type invariants**, **implication**, **universal** and **existential quantification**, the **file read buffer** and the **For** and **Case** statements.

The following notations were introduced in this chapter.

Specification notation

Distributed union	∪(pdb)
Empty set	{ }
Quantifier	Q i ∈ S • P(i)
For-all	∀ pdb ∈ Parts-database • ∪ (pdb) = Part-number
Exists	∃ s ∈ pdb • p1 ∈ s and p2 ∈ s
Set intersection	ps1 ∩ ps2
Implication	(ps1 ≠ ps2) ⇒ (ps1 ∩ ps2 = { })
Operation parameter	test-parts(p1,p2 : Part-number)
Operation actual parameter	test-parts(hd(input).part1, hd(input).part2)
Set comprehension via function	{ s1 ∪ s2 | s1 ∈ pdb and s2 ∈ pdb . . . }

Pascal notation

For statement	**For** *i* := 1 **To** *MaxPartNumber* **Do** . . .
Writeln integer field specifier	*writeln(part2:1)*
Set constant range	[*'A'* .. *'Z'*, *'0'* .. *'9'*]
File read buffer	*input^*
Write statement	*write(DatabaseFile,database)*
Case statement	**Case** *CommandChar* **Of**
	't','T' : **Begin** . . . **End** ; . . . **End**

LABORATORY EXERCISE – to modify the interchangeable parts system

Purpose

Experience with enhancing a program following the receipt of extra requirements from the customer.

Problem

Up to press, the customer has been very satisfied with the interchangeable parts record system as presented in the case study. However, he has thought of a useful enhancement. He would like to request a list of all the parts that have been recorded as equivalent to each other.

Specification

A formal specification of this new operation is as follows (note that a new output type is needed):

```
Output-type  =  Seq of ( Test-result ∪ Display-result )
Test-result  =  {yes,no}      (*** just as before ***)
Display-result  =  Set of (Seq of Part-number)

display-equivalences

ext rd pdb      : Parts-database
    wr output : Output-type

post output  =  ‾output‾ ⌢
  [ {eq ∈ Seq of Part-number |
        len(eq) > 1
          and
        (∀ i,j ∈ inds eq • i < j ⇒ eq[i] < eq[j])
          and
        elems eq ∈ pdb
    }
  ]
```

Implementation

Write your procedure with the heading

Procedure *DisplayEquivalences*;

TUTORIAL EXERCISE

This exercise gives experience of designing a suitable data structure to satisfy efficiency constraints.

The laboratory exercise above, to display all the equivalences (stored in the interchangeable parts base), typically results in solutions that demonstrate worse-case quadratic, $O(n * n)$, behaviour. That is, the time taken to execute is proportional to $n * n$, where n is the number of items in the parts base.

That exercise illustrates how modifying an existing program with an operation that was not considered when the original data structure was designed can be difficult. This tutorial problem is to consider the interchangeable parts system again, but this time the original operations are extended with display-equivalences. Design a suitable data structure that will enable the operations to be implemented efficiently without using excessive storage. Sketch the implementation of display-equivalences on this new structure.

Key word in context

7

MOTIVATION

This case study covers the development of a fairly large program, and is split into two chapters. The specification and most of the design are presented here, but the discussion of some of the data types used in the program is delayed until the next chapter, where they are used as a vehicle for studying **dynamic data structures.**

Two key topics are presented in this chapter: the **abstract data type approach** to program designs, and the technique of **recursive programming.**

Other concepts introduced include **output parameters** of operations, **lexicographic ordering** of sequences, **cross product** of two types, the design technique of **solving a simpler problem first**, and the pre-declared Pascal procedure ***get.***

As for the story, well we had a lot of difficulty believing Rita this time, but she assures us it's all true!

7.1   Requirements

One evening as Rita walks home past the crowded bus stops, she is intercepted by a stranger on a bicycle.

STRANGER: Excuse me . . .
RITA: Why?
STRANGER: Err, I would like to talk to you.
RITA: Yes?
STRANGER: I work for OK-Corral Software Bureau (SCSS) Limited.
RITA: SCSS?
STRANGER: Supa-Cheap Software Services. Anyway, certain information has come to my attention concerning certain work you indirectly may have done for FMC.
RITA: FMC?
STRANGER: Fordge Motor Company.
RITA: Ah, you mean the interchangeable parts system?
STRANGER: Yes, the IPS.
RITA: Well what about it?
STRANGER: Our PC – that's parent company – have obtained a copy of the program, and are impressed with your expertise.
RITA: (*proudly*) I do my best!
STRANGER: Yes, well they want you to do a job for them.
RITA: No, I'm too busy – I've got a project which is on a tight schedule, and I can't afford to be late with its delivery.
STRANGER: But . . .
RITA: And then there's this book I'm studying. Something to do with KWIC.
STRANGER: KWIC?
RITA: Key word in context.
STRANGER: Our parent company are quite insistent. It's an offer you *cannot* refuse.
RITA: Who are they anyway?
STRANGER: SDI Unlimited.
RITA: SDI?
STRANGER: Err, . . . never mind. Well, what do you think?
RITA: I think if they're that bothered, they should see me themselves. Bye.

The stranger desperately tries to keep up with Rita, but he can't pedal fast enough.

The next day Rita asks her friends what they know about SDI. It seems that everyone either does not know, or will not say. . .

A few days later, she receives a visit at home from a couple of 'heavies'. Rita's visitors insist that she accompanies them on a little journey in their filthy-rich gleaming limo. At first she still refuses, but the sight of an obese wallet marked 'SDI Slush' compromises any thoughts of other work. They take her to a deserted farmhouse several miles outside Minitropolis. There she meets a large gentleman, sporting a King Everard cigar between immaculately polished teeth. His country of origin is not disguised by a several gallon hat that he clearly regards as both uncomfortable and necessary.

    MR BIG: Gee sure. Howdy. Take a seat.

A large hand dislocates Rita's enthusiastically as she politely sits down.

    MR BIG: I guess you know why we're all here. You're quite a hard
           woman to entertain.

He leans forward, adopting a presence comparable with an earth-mover, except that Rita would have settled for a real earth-mover in exchange for his company.

    MR BIG: It's quite simple, Rita. I know your style – you're good.
           You're just what we need for our biggest client.
    RITA: Who's that then? And what does SDI stand for?
    MR BIG: SDI stands for nothing. You don't need to know our client,
           let's just say he has had some influence from time to time.
    RITA: (*sarcastically*) I'm impressed!
    MR BIG: Okay, I'll double the offer.

He produces another wallet, marked 'SDI Contingency'.

    RITA: Hmmmmm . . .
    MR BIG: Now Ronald has a problem.
    RITA: Ronald who?
    MR BIG: Who mentioned Ronald?
    RITA: You did.
    MR BIG: I did? Ah, yes, I did . . . It doesn't matter. This envelope
           contains your instructions. Are you in or not?
    RITA: Well I've got a lot of other work. . . .

Another wallet is placed on the table. On it is written 'SDI – Almost Final Offer'.

    RITA: Hmmm, is there a 'Final Offer'?
    MR BIG: Okay, you can have that when you deliver.
    RITA: Hmmm. . .
    MR BIG: Tax free.

RITA: Okay. I'll do it.

When she arrives home, Rita examines the envelope:

SDI

Top Secret

(not to be taken internally – this isn't the movies)

Inside, scrawled on a note she reads:

Dear Rita

I hope you are well.

Here is my problem. Its my private document collection. I can never find anything because I can't remember where to look in the index. For example, If I'm looking for 'Plan for the Contraction of Future', should I look under Plan, Contraction or Future ?

So it always takes ages to find my favourite reads. Please sort it out at once.

R

P.S. Here is a sample

The Plan

Snow White and the Seven Dwarfs.

The Beano

How to be President in just 10 hours.

The second Plan

Home management and Decorating

The Hamburger Gourmet Guide – Illustrated ed.

S.D.I. – I did it my way

P.P.S. If you need to contact me phone 192 and ask for a Huge Raincoat

– Its a code word.

7.2 Analysis

What the client needs, Rita thinks, is some form of filing system which is flexible enough to cope with searching for items based on different words. The example her client quoted should be locatable under Plan, Contraction *and* Future. Rita supposes that new titles are added only occasionally, in which case it ought to be sufficient to have a program which takes a list of all titles, with some kind of location index, and produces the flexible indexed list. In this list, each title would be somehow found, together with its index, under all the words the client might search on. This sort of system would allow the location indices to be consecutive, based on when the documents were obtained. Thus no shuffling is required when new ones arrive, they are merely added on the end of the shelves. If this is the case, the input title list could be kept in a text file, with one title on each line, and with new items simply being added on the end. The first line in this file is the title of the document in shelf location one, the second line is the title of the document in location two, and so on.

Next Rita considers what words the client is likely to search for, and what form the list should take. The obvious solution here is to assume that the client may search on any word in a title, and that the list contains all word rotations of each title, and the list is sorted for easy searching. For example, with the input list:

> the three little pigs
> the beano
> oxford american dictionary

the output would be as in Figure 7.1. Thus the number of entries in the output equals the number of words in the input. The location indices are obtained simply by counting the input lines.

However, looking at the example again, Rita thinks it is unlikely that the client would wish to look for 'The Beano' using the word 'the'. Certain words should be classed as insignificant, and title rotations beginning with them not included in the index. The collection of insignificant words could also be kept in a file to make it easy for the client to modify which words are considered insignificant. This would be

```
american dictionary oxford  3
beano the   2
dictionary oxford american  3
little pigs the three   1
oxford american dictionary  3
pigs the three little   1
the beano   2
the three little pigs   1
three little pigs the   1
```

Figure 7.1 Example output.

another text file, read by the program when the index is generated, but in which the line structure would not matter as long as the words were separated by at least one space and/or end of line.

Another point which becomes apparent to Rita, is that upper and lower case letters should be treated as the same.

Rita contacts the client via a Huge Raincoat and they discuss the implications of her analysis. His voice seems familiar. . . . Anyway, he is pleased at her understanding of his problem, and likes her suggestions.

Exercise 7.1   The following is a customer's requirement statement for a cross-referencing program. List all the ambiguities, omissions and likely mistakes that you can find in it. Suggest sensible resolutions of ambiguities, possible choices for the omissions, and corrections for the likely mistakes.

A program is required to produce cross-reference listings of various texts. Certain words are to be considered irrelevant noise words and should not be included in the output.

 # 7.3   Specification

The first step of the specification involves Rita formally defining the data types:

Word = Seq of printable characters, upper/lower case insensitive

Word-set = Set of Word

Word-seq = Seq of Word

Word-seq-seq = Seq of (Seq of Word)

Sometimes it is convenient to use the type of natural numbers, but exclude the value zero. We denote this as

$\mathbb{N}1$

In many books it is written as

$\mathbb{N}^+$

Index-entry = Record
                entry : Word-seq
                location : $\mathbb{N}1$
            end

Index-entries = Seq of Index-entry

The program can be specified as an operation called KWIC with three properties:

- The output is sorted into ascending lexicographical (alphabetical) order.
- It contains all significant rotations of each input title.
- It has no extra 'junk', that is, its length is equal to the total number of occurrences of significant words in the input.

Rita specifies the program as an operation with an **output parameter**.

Operations may have **output parameters.** These are written after the brackets round the input parameters, if any. They have no value before execution of the operation, and thus cannot be written in a pre-condition and cannot be hooked in a post-condition. For example, an operation that finds a nearest natural square root and real error of a natural number:

ROOT (n : ℕ) rt : ℕ; err : ℝ

post (err + rt) * (err + rt) = n
    and
      − 0.5 ≤ err ≤ 0.5

Note that there is no fundamental difference between a function and an operation which has exactly one output parameter and no external variables.

KWIC (titles : Word-seq-seq , insig-words : Word-set) kwic-index : Index-entries
pre true
post
    is-sorted(kwic-index)
    and
    has-sig-rotations(titles,insig-words,kwic-index)
    and
    len(kwic-index) = sig-word-count(titles,insig-words)

is-sorted must return true or false, depending on whether the given list of Index-entry records is sorted into **lexicographical order** of the entry fields.

For types that have the ordering relation ≤, such as naturals and characters, there is a corresponding relation, ≼, on sequences of the type, called the **lexicographic ordering,** defined as follows.

3V

An empty sequence is ≤ a non-empty sequence. A non-empty sequence is not ≤ an empty one. Two non-empty sequences with identical heads are ≤ *if and only if* the tail of the first ≤ tail of the second. Two non-empty sequences with different heads are ≤, *if and only if* the head of the first sequence is ≤ the head of the second sequence.

This can be formally written recursively as:

```
_≤_ : (s1 : Seq of some-type , s2 : Seq of some-type) → B
s1 ≤ s2 △
   if s1 = [ ] then true
   else if s2 = [ ] then false
   else
      if hd s1 = hd s2 then
         (tl s1) ≤ (tl s2)
      else
         (hd s1) ≤ (hd s2)
```

This notion extends to sequences of sequences, using the ordering just defined. We also have the other three orderings:

```
A ≥ B  iff  B ≤ A
A < B  iff  A ≤ B and A ≠ B
A > B  iff  B < A
```

For example, the following are all true:

```
[ ] < [0]
[34,25,35] < [34,26,35]
[36,20,35] > [34,37,42]
"abc" ≤ "abd"
"SDI" ≤ "SDI"
"joe" ≤ "joel"
```

And, on sequences of sequences:

```
[ [3,7,2] , [12,9,13] , [56,2,67] ] < [ [3,7,2] , [12,9,14] , [55,2,68] ]
["tom" ,"dick" ,"harry" ] > ["thomas" , "richard", "henry"]
["the" ,"three" ,"little" ,"pigs" ] > ["pigs" ,"the" ,"three" ,"little" ]
```

Exercise 7.2   Which of the following are true?

(a)   "franciscan" < "francise"

(b)   [[246,563] , [ ] , [48,19] , [71]] > [[246,563] , [ ] , [48,19,17] , [70]]

(c)   [[[1] , [1,2,3]] , [[8]]] ≤ [[[1] , [1,2,4]] , [[7,8]]]

To specify is-sorted, it is sufficient to consider all pairs of indices in the given sequence, and ensure that, if they are in ascending order, the elements in the sequence at those positions are in the correct order. In this case, we wish to use an ordering on pairs of Index-entry records, meaning the lexicographic ordering on the entry fields, each of which is a sequence of sequence of characters. Rita writes:

```
less-eq-entry : (ie1 : Index-entry, ie2 : Index-entry) → 𝔹
less-eq-entry(ie1,ie2) △ ie1.entry ⩽ ie2.entry
```

Then she defines is-sorted as:

```
is sorted : (list : Index-entries) → 𝔹
is-sorted(list) △
    ∀ i1,i2 ∈ inds(list) •
        (i1 ⩽ i2) ⇒ less-eq-entry( list[i1], list[i2] )
```

When specifying the next part, has-sig-rotations, Rita must decide whether the empty title is significant. It does not start with an insignificant word because there are no words in it. She decides that an empty title could correspond to a shelf location with no book in it, in which case it should not be significant. To specify has-sig-rotations, Rita must consider all titles in the input, and ensure that each is either empty or, for all significant rotations of it, there is an entry in the output with the rotation and the title's location index. In addition to quantifiers, this specification involves a let expression, as introduced in Chapter 3. She assumes another function, rotate, to specify the rotation of a given Word-seq value a given number of times.

```
has-sig-rotations : (titles : Word-seq-seq , insig-words : Word-set ,
                     kwic-index : Index-entries) → 𝔹

has-sig-rotations(titles,insig-words,kwic-index) △

∀ i ∈ inds(titles) •
    (titles[i] = [ ]
    or
    ∀ j ∈ inds(titles[i]) •
        (let rotation : Word-seq be rotate(titles[i],j) in
            (hd rotation ∈ insig-words
            or
            ∃ some-entry ∈ elems (kwic-index) •
                some-entry = mk-Index-entry(rotation, i)
            )
        )
    )
```

This complicated definition is worth looking at slowly. It says, consider *all* indices, i, of the sequence titles, that is, all values of the set

{1, . . . ,len(titles) }. The title at each of those positions may be empty, in which case it is insignificant and we are not bothered about it being in the index entries. For non-empty titles (and empty ones too, actually!) it says consider all indices, j, of that ith title. Take the jth rotation of that title, and call it rotation. If the head of that rotation is in the set of insignificant words, we are not bothered about that rotation. Otherwise, there must exist an Index-entry value, some-entry, a member of the elements of the sequence kwic-index, such that some-entry consists of the rotation, together with its location. Its location must be the position of the unrotated title in the titles sequence, that is i.

Exercise 7.3

(a)   Is the specification of has-sig-rotations satisfied if rotations beginning with an insignificant word appear in the result?

(b)   Explain why the first disjunct, and hence the disjunction, just inside the outermost quantifier (that is, titles[i] = [ ]) could be removed without changing the meaning of the specification, while making it slightly less clear.

Rita next defines the rotation of a word sequence by a given number of times:

```
rotate : (w : Word-seq , n : N) → Word-seq
rotate(w,n) △
    if n = 0 then w
    else
        rotate((tl(w)) ⌢ [hd(w)], n - 1)
```

Next she turns to the specification of sig-word-count as used in the final part of the conjunction in KWIC. She recognizes the concept as similar to counting chargeable words in a telegram, part of a specification she wrote some time ago when she was still working for May Kit. There she used set comprehension to define the set of all indices of the sequence of words such that the word at that position was not the stop-word, and then took the cardinality of this set. Here she needs to consider the set of all pairs, (i,j), such that the jth word of the ith title is significant. The number of significant word occurrences is the cardinality of this set. Each of the pairs is an element of the **cross product** of the set of natural numbers with itself.

A **cross product** of two types is a set of pairs of values, one value from each of the two types. For example,

ℕ X Char

is the set of all pairs of values, where the first in each pair is a natural number, and the second is a character.

(ℕ X Char) X ℕ = ℕ X (Char X ℕ)

is the set of all triples where the first and third item is a natural number, and the second item is a character. Elements of cross products are written as items separted by commas and surrounded by round brackets (parentheses). For example,

(10, 4) ∈ ℕ X ℕ

---

sig-word-count : (titles : Word-seq-seq , insig-words : Word-set) → ℕ

sig-word-count(titles, insig-words) △
   card (
        { (i,j) ∈ ℕ X ℕ |
          i ∈ inds(titles) and j ∈ inds (titles[i])
          and
          not ((titles[i]) [j] ∈ insig-words)
        }
)

At this point, Rita has completed the specification of the program.

Exercise 7.4

(a)   Give an informal but clear and precise explanation of the following formal specification. Avoid simply translating the symbols into English.

Text = Seq of Line

Line = Seq of Char

X : (F : Text) → ℕ

X(F) △ card { (i,j) ∈ ℕ X ℕ |
                  F[i] [j] ≠ ' '
                  and
                  (j = 1 or F[i] [j − 1] = ' ')
          }

(b)   Assuming the Pascal built-in type *Text* to be an adequate approximation to the type of the same name in part (a), design a procedure that implements the specification.

7.4 Design

Turning her attention to the design, Rita first considers the data structures required. These are sequences and sets, and there are various ways in which they might be implemented. The most obvious is the use of arrays, but she supposes that their finiteness will impose either a serious restriction when they become full, or a large overhead through making them bigger than is ever needed. Some other implementation method is required to allow the structures to grow to exactly the right size without any limit on that size. She knows that this is possible (up to the ultimate limit of the size of the machine that the program runs on!), but is not completely trivial. She could go ahead and make a choice, but since she has not yet designed the program, she does not know precisely which operations on the structures are required. She knows, for example, that sequences are used, but are all the known operations on sequences needed? Concatenation? Index-set? Element-set? The best way to implement the data types may well depend on which operations are going to be used, and how often. She cannot obtain reliable clues from the specification, because the program may look nothing like it. She can only really know what operations are needed after she has designed the program. Thus, she decides to use the **abstract data type** design approach and design the program first.

An **abstraction** focuses on particular aspects of interest while details which could complicate and obscure those basic aspects are ignored.

An **abstract data type** is a type, in the program sense, consisting of a set of values, and an associated collection of operations. However, the type is abstract because its implementation details are hidden from the program during its design (and possibly all its life).

For abstract data types which are quite specific to a single program, it is best to implement the types *after* the design of the program. This is because it is not clear before that point exactly what operations are required, and how frequently, and so on. There is no need to implement operations which are not used, and the frequency of application might influence the choice of representation of the data.

So she turns her attention to the main program. To begin with, she ignores all consideration of converting file representations of the data types to some internal form, because she cannot tell where this is required, and she has not decided what representations to use. Her top level of the design simply splits the program into two parts: one that generates the significant rotations, and one that sorts them:

kwic(titles, insig-words, kwic-index)

var titles : word-seq-seq
    insig-words : word-set
    kwic-index : index-entries

begin
    obtain sig rots of titles using insig-words into kwic-index
    sort kwic-index
end

She is not quite sure which of these two sub-parts is the more complex. On balance, she thinks that the sort operation is harder, so that is the one she will design first. However, both parts of the program are quite complicated, so she decides to construct a specification of each of them. These serve to confirm that she fully understands what each part must do, and also they will be useful later when she designs the other part, and when she checks the final implementations.

7.4.1 Specification of sort

Exercise 7.5 What is wrong with the following proposed specification of the sort operation:

SORT
ext wr kwic-index:Index-entries
post is-sorted(kwic-index) and elems(kwic-index) = elems($\overline{\text{kwic-index}}$)

The two key properties of sorting are that the result sequence is ordered and that it is some permutation of the input sequence. In this case, the input and result sequence are stored in the same variable:

SORT
ext wr kwic-index:Index-entries
post is-permutation(kwic-index,$\overline{\text{kwic-index}}$) and is-sorted(kwic-index)

is-sorted has already been specified with the whole program. Two sequences are a permutation of each other if they have the same elements, and the number of occurrences of each element is the same in each sequence:

is-permutation : (s : Index-entries , ss : Index-entries) → B
is-permutation(s,ss) △
∀ e ∈ elems (s ⌢ ss) •
  no-of-occurrences(e,s) = no-of-occurrences(e,ss)

Finally, the number of occurrences of an element in a sequence is the size of the set of indices that index that element in the sequence. This is formally expressed by:

no-of-occurrences : (t : Index-entry , ts : Index-entries) → N
no-of-occurrences(t,ts) △ card { i ∈ inds ts | ts[i] = t }

7.4.2   Specification of significant rotations

The specification of GET-SIG-ROTATIONS is very similar to that of the whole program itself, except that the resulting index need not be sorted:

GET-SIG-ROTATIONS(titles : Word-seq-seq;
                              insig-words : Word-set) sig-rotations : Index-entries
pre true
post
  has-sig-rotations(titles,insig-words,sig-rotations)
  and
  len(sig-rotations) = sig-word-count(titles,insig-words)

has-sig-rotations and sig-word-count have been defined previously.

Exercise 7.6   Would it be permitted for a correct implementation of GET-SIG-ROTATIONS to produce a sorted list (as specified by is-sorted)?

7.4.3   Design of SORT

Next Rita thinks about the design of the sort algorithm. She decides to solve the problem with a **recursive** procedure.

A **(self) recursive procedure,** like a self-recursive function, is one defined in terms of itself. This means that its statement body will contain at least one procedure call to an instance of itself. For the algorithm to be terminating, there must be a path through the procedure which does not make a recursive call, and arguments to recursive calls must make progress towards the condition under which this path is executed.

In this case, she considers that if she can split the given sequence into two smaller sequences, then recursively sort these, she may merge the sorted parts to form the result. She sketches this roughly:

```
sort(var s : index-entries)
var s1,s2 : index-entries
begin
  if len(s) ≤ 1 then
    already sorted!
  else
  begin
    split s into s1 and s2 { s1 and s2, both shorter than s }
    sort(s1)
    sort(s2)
    merge s1 and s2 into s
  end
end
```

For the recursion to terminate, both s1 and s2 must be shorter than s. This is guaranteed to be *possible* (depending on the split) by the condition of the if statement.

Rita notes that the execution behaviour of this algorithm corresponds to a tree-shaped structure, with the nodes of the tree corresponding to instances of the procedure. The branch nodes correspond to splitting and recursive calls. Leaf nodes correspond to the first part of the procedure where no work is required. Figure 7.2 shows an example of the execution behaviour of the algorithm when sorting a sequence of eight items (which are numbers here), assuming that the split simply cuts the sequence in half.

An algorithm for merging two sorted sequences is not trivial, but perhaps just as difficult is the operation that splits the given sequence in the first place. Rita notes that it would be sufficient for correctness if s1 was simply the first item in s, and s2 was the tail. However, this would not be very efficient.

Exercise 7.7   Why not? Estimate the execution time of such an algorithm, in proportion to the length of the sequence being sorted.

A more efficient approach, she decides, would be to arrange it so that s1 and s2 are approximately half the length of s.

Exercise 7.8   Why? What would be the execution time of this in proportion to the length of the sequence?

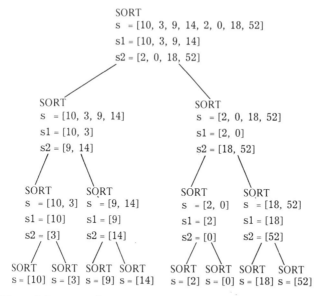

Figure 7.2   Execution behaviour when sorting eight numbers.

At this point Rita notes that s1 and s2 do not have to be **proper
sub-sequences** of s.

A **proper sub-sequence** of a sequence is a sequence which is contained in the second
sequence as consecutive elements. For example:

    [3, 7, 2, 6]

is a proper sub-sequence of

    [1, 8, 2, 3, 7, 2, 6, 1, 8, 9]

On the other hand, the elements of a non-proper sub-sequence are all contained in the
second sequence in the same order, but not as consecutive elements. For example,

    [3, 5, 1, 8]

is a sub-sequence of

    [8, 2, 3, 5, 6, 1, 4, 8]

but not a proper sub-sequence of it.

If she could design it so that all the elements in one sub-sequence are less than or equal to all the elements in the other, the merge operation would simply be concatenation. If the two sub-sequences were the same length on *average* over a number of instances of sort, the average efficiency of this would be the same as if they were always the same length. (This is difficult to prove, but both schemes do indeed have the same average time complexity.) She likes the sound of this, but decides on another refinement: her split operation will produce two sub-sequences and a middle element. She sketches her new design:

```
sort(var s:index-entries)
var smaller,greater : index-entries
      middle : index-entry
begin
  if len(s) > 1 then
  begin
    split s into smaller and greater and middle so that
        len(smaller)<len(s) and len(greater)<len(s)
        and all elements in smaller are ≤ middle
        and all elements in greater are ≥ middle
        and len(smaller) approximately = len(greater) —
            on average over the number of times sort is run
    sort(smaller)
    sort(greater)
    s := smaller ⌢ [middle] ⌢ greater
  end
end
```

To be more sure, she writes a specification of the split operation:

SPLIT (s : Index-entries) smaller,greater : Index-entries; middle : Index-entry

pre   len(s) > 1

post is-permutation(smaller ⌢ [middle] ⌢ greater, s)
    and
    ∀ i ∈ inds(smaller) • smaller[i] ≤ middle
    and
    ∀ i ∈ inds(greater) • middle ≤ greater[i]

The requirement that both resulting sub-sequences are shorter than the original is guaranteed, since one element is taken out and put in middle. The preference that the sub-sequences are about half the length of s does not have to be satisfied every time; only an average is required. (This is quite hard to specify formally.)

In the above specification of split, the pre-condition is more restrictive (that is, more specific) than is required for the post-condition to be satisfiable. However, it is known that the operation is going to be used only when the length of s is greater than one, and this extra information may affect the ease of implementation, or its potential efficiency.

Exercise 7.9   What is the least restrictive pre-condition that makes the post-condition of SPLIT satisfiable? What would be the implication on the efficiency of the implementation if the sort procedure performed the split operation under this condition?

Rita is quite attracted to this design, but how can the split be achieved? Well, assuming that the initial sequence is randomly organized, middle can simply be chosen to be the first element occurring in s, and this will satisfy the preference that the average lengths of the two resulting sub-sequences are approximately the same.

7.4.4   Design of SPLIT

The specification of SPLIT is **non-deterministic,** that is it may be implemented in more than one way.

When an operation (or function) is specified by a post-condition, it might be **non-deterministic** in that it does not tie down precisely what the implementation must do, but instead leaves some freedom of choice. For example, the following operation returns a number below a given one:

SOME-NATURAL-BELOW (n : $\mathbb{N}$1) r : $\mathbb{N}$

post $r < n$

This may not have been a mistake, for there are plenty of contexts where such a number is required, but it is not necessary to state which one. If the implementation language is fully deterministic, the specification should be regarded as defining a class of deterministic implementations, each of which satisfy it. If the implementation language can be non-deterministic (that is, there are some programs which compute different answers at different times for the same input), the specification should be regarded more generally as defining a class of possibly non-deterministic implementations that satisfy it.

The non-determinism comes from elements which are equal to the middle element: do they go in the greater or the smaller sequence? Of course, it does not matter, but if there were likely to be lots of duplicate elements it might be a good idea to alternate where elements equal to the middle one were put, to encourage the two resulting sequences to be of more equal length. However, this likelihood does not apply in the context of the KWIC program.

Thus Rita designs:

```
split(seq:index-entries
        var smaller : index-entries
        var middle : index-entry
        var greater : index-entries)
   begin
     set greater and smaller to empty
     middle := hd seq
     seq := tl seq
     while seq ≠ [ ]
       if less-eq-entry(middle,hd seq)
          greater := greater ⌢ [hd seq]
       else
          smaller := smaller ⌢ [hd seq]
       seq := tl seq
     end-of-while
   end
```

At this stage, Rita has completed the design for SORT, still without considering a representation of the sequences.

She is now ready to start designing the other half of the program.

7.4.5 Design of GET-SIG-ROTATIONS

Referring back to the specification of GET-SIG-ROTATIONS (page 226), Rita realizes that basically its meaning is embedded in has-sig-rotations. The other part simply ensures that there is no extra junk in the result.

```
has-sig-rotations : (titles : Word-seq-seq , insig-words : Word-set,
                     kwic-index : Index-entries) → 𝔹

has-sig-rotations(titles,insig-words,kwic-index) △

∀ i ∈ inds(titles) •
   (titles[i] = [ ]
   or
   ∀ j ∈ inds(titles[i]) •
      (let rotation : Word-seq be rotate(titles[i],j) in
      (hd rotation ∈ insig-words
      or
      ∃ some-entry ∈ elems(kwic-index) •
        some-entry = mk-Index-entry(rotation,i)
      )
      )
   )
```

Thus, examining the specification of has-sig-rotations, she sees that a number of entries may be added to the result for each title in the input. This suggests the use of a loop in the algorithm, with each iteration dealing with a single title. She also notes that nothing is added for empty titles (she knows this from the 'no junk' part of the GET-SIG-ROTATIONS specification). On the other hand, for a non-empty title, an entry is added to kwic-index for each significant word in it. This again suggests the use of a loop, this time dealing with each word in a title.

Thus her initial draft of the design looks like:

```
get-sig-rotations (titles:word-seq-seq; insig-words:word-set;
                   var sig-rotations: index-entries)

var title:wordseq ; word-index:integer

begin
   while titles ≠ [ ]
      title := hd titles
      if title ≠ [ ]
         for word-index := 1 to len(title)
         ⋮
            possible entry in sig-rotations
         ⋮
         end-of-for
      end-of-if
      titles := tl titles
   end-of-while
end
```

After scribbling this down, she realizes that the procedure should set sig-rotations to empty initially. She also notes that, if the title is empty, its length is zero. Hence the if statement is superfluous, because Pascal for loops do nothing if the initial value is already bigger than the final one.

Next she considers what should be done inside the for loop. The specification indicates that each rotation of the title should be considered and entered in the index list together with its location index, if it begins with a significant word. Rita considers that the insertion of location indices is a complication which does not affect the general structure of the solution, so she decides to ignore them for a moment, thus **solving a simpler problem first.**

A potentially helpful method of approaching the design of a solution to a problem, is to **solve a simpler problem first.** Sometimes, one can identify a part of a problem such that, if that part were ignored, the solution to the remainder of the problem would be easier, but have basically the same structure as the full solution. In such cases, it can be helpful to ignore the complication, solve the simpler problem, and then adjust the solution to deal with the full problem.

She notes that, if each iteration of the loop performs one rotation on a title, in total all the rotations will be considered. Thus she extends her design:

```
get-sig-rotations(titles:word-seq-seq; insig-words:word-set;
                  var sig-rotations:index-entries)

var title:wordseq ; word-index:integer

begin
  sig-rotations := [ ]
  while titles ≠ [ ]
    title := hd titles
    for word-index := 1 to len(title)
      if not (hd title ∈ insig-words)
        put title in sig-rotations – with location
      rotate title once
    end-of-for
    titles := tl titles
  end-of-while
end
```

Rotating the title once is achieved by taking the head of it and appending it on the tail.

Having designed the basic solution, she next considers the location indices. Scrutinizing the specification, she sees that the location of a title is exactly its index in the original input sequence. Consequently, if her procedure counts the titles as it processes them in the main loop, the locations will be readily available. Now she is able to make the final additions to the design:

```
get-sig-rotations(titles:word-seq-seq; insig-words:word-set;
                  var sig-rotations:index-entries)

var title:wordseq ; word-index:integer
    location:integer

begin
  sig-rotations := [ ]
  location := 0
  while titles ≠ [ ]
    title := hd titles
    location := location + 1
    for word-index := 1 to len(title)
      if not (hd title ∈ insig-words)
        sig-rotations :=
                 sig-rotations ⌢ [ mk-Index-entry(title, location) ]
      title := (tl title) ⌢ [hd title]
    end-of-for
    titles := tl titles
  end-of-while
end
```

That completes her design of get-sig-rotations.

At this point in the development, she has completed the design of the whole program, still without considering the representation of the data types.

7.5   Design and implementation of abstract data types

If Rita were implementing the program in a language that supported sequences and sets as in her specifications, she would now have completed the design stage of the program. However, Pascal does not offer such data types directly. She considers engaging the services of Timothy Trustworthy, a reliable programmer friend of hers. She would give him the specifications of the data type operations required, and some indication of how often each of them is used, and ask him to implement them. He would not need to see, or even know about, the program she has designed, except perhaps to help him choose an efficient implementation of the types. Assuming that he did the job well, Rita would never need to look at his work. That is the nature of the abstract data type approach.

'Great' she thinks. She rings Timothy. He is out. Out of the country.

Oh, well, she'll have do it herself. She constructs a list of all the operations required for each type and analyses their use. This will enable her to make a sensible choice of representation. Once she has made this choice she will design an implementation of each operation required. Also, she will have to consider input and output of values of the types. This may be required because the program communicates with the world via files, and some of the data types may have to be stored internally for efficiency. Her list of types to be implemented is:

- Word
- Word-set
- Word-seq
- Word-seq-seq
- Index-entry
- Index-entries

She starts with Word.

7.5.1   The data type Word

Word = Seq of printable characters, upper/lower case insensitive.

Titles and index-entries are made up from sequences of words. Although no operations on words are explicitly required by the design, there is an implied use of 'less than or equal' via the ordering on index-entries. This ordering would be readily available in Pascal if the words were stored in **packed arrays** of characters.

Pascal allows the use of all six relations on the type

   Packed Array [1 .. *N*] **Of** *Char*

where *N* is some integer value > 1. (Note: the arrays must be packed, and must be arrays of *Char*, indexed from 1 to something greater than 1.)

Less than or equal is defined similarly to the lexicographic ordering introduced earlier for sequences in our specifications. That is, A <= B if A and B are the same, or the character in A at the first position where they are different is less than the corresponding character in B. (Note: only strings of the same length may be compared in standard Pascal.) The other relational operators are defined as one would expect.

   Deciding to implement words using packed arrays of characters, Rita judges that the restriction imposed by the finiteness of this structure will not be unreasonable if, say, the length is limited to 20 characters, although she will make it easy to change this constant. Words longer than this will be truncated to 20 characters. Words shorter will be filled up to 20 characters by adding spaces on the end.
   Then Rita considers whether using the Pascal less than or equal operator will work correctly when comparing arrays containing words which are shorter than 20 characters. She thinks of an example – the comparison of 'cat' and 'cathy'. Certainly, 'cat' must be less than 'cathy', hence the space that would follow the 't' in 'cat' must be less than 'h'. She reasons that the comparisons will always produce the correct result, as long as the space character is less than any other characters in the word. In the ASCII character set the code for space is 32, and the codes for upper and lower case A are 65 and 97 respectively. However, she cannot assume that the target machine uses the ASCII set, so she rings Huge Raincoat. She is eventually connected to the SDI technical support officer who confirms that it does.

Exercise 7.10   Suppose that Rita had not checked, and that the target machine used some weird character codes, in which the code for space was bigger than the codes for both alphabets. Which of the following comparisons would give a different result depending on whether they were tried on Rita's own ASCII code machine and the weird code target machine?

(a)   *'abcde '* <= *'abcdef '*

(b)   *'xyz   '* <= *'xyy   '*

(c)   *'hello '* <= *'hell   '*

(d)   *'please '* <= *'place '*

Rita also notes that upper and lower case letters in a word are to be treated as the same. One easy way to achieve this is to convert all letters of one case to the corresponding one of the other case (and *not* vice versa!). Given that it is likely that most letters in the input will be lower case, she decides to convert from upper to lower when reading the words.

She writes the Pascal definition of the type:

```
const max-word-length = 20
    ⋮
type word = packed array[1 .. max-word-length] of char
```

Clearly it will be necessary to read words from and write words to text files (for example, reading the insignificant words and writing the KWIC index). Words in the input files are separated by spaces or end-of-lines. These spaces should be skipped between words, but she notes that it should not matter if there is more than one space. One easy way to handle the separating spaces when reading a number of words is to skip them before reading the first word, and then after reading every word. Thus, she decides not to include this skipping inside the procedure to read a word. In any case, end-of-lines are sometimes significant (for example when reading a title an end-of-line marks the end of that title) and sometimes they are not (for example when reading the set of insignificant words). Rita sketches an abstract design for reading a word from a file. She knows it is reasonable to assume that the reading position in the file is not at the end, because of the way she intends to use the procedure: it will only be called when it is known that there is a word to read. Similarly, she can assume that the character at the current position is not a space, as she intends to skip spaces before this procedure is called.

```
read-word(var f : text; var w : word)
{ pre: not eof(f) and f^ ≠ ' ' }

var ch:char
```

```
begin
  while not reached end of the word
    read(f,ch)
    if length of word in w < max-word-length
      if ch ∈ ['A' .. 'Z']
        ch := lower case equivalent of ch
      add ch on end of w
    end-of-if
  end-of-while

  fill up w with spaces
end
```

Then she proceeds to refine this design a little, starting with the loop condition. A word is followed by a space, or an end-of-line. She knows that the procedure only has to look for a space because of the properties of Pascal text files.

In Pascal, for a text file F, when the current position marks the end of a line, the function *eoln*(F) is true. However, at such a point, the current element is a space. That is, $F\char`^ = '$ $'$.

For a non-empty text file, F, the condition *eoln*(F) is always true one character before the condition *eof*(F). In other words, the last character of a Pascal text file, if there is one, is a space corresponding to an end-of-line. Thus a text file cannot end in the middle of a line of text.

To know the length of the word, and where to add each character in the array, she introduces a local variable, length. This will be set to zero at first, and then increased by one each time a character is added to the word. To convert an upper case letter to its lower case counterpart, Rita will use the Pascal **chr** and **ord** functions.

The pre-declared Pascal function **ord** takes a character and returns its ordinal number. The pre-declared function **chr** takes an integer, and returns the associated character, if there is one (otherwise a run-time error occurs).

Thus, the following is true for all values, A and B, of *Char*:

$$A = chr(ord(A))$$
$$(ord(A) < ord(B)) = (A < B)$$
$$chr(0) <= A$$
$$chr(ord('0') + 3) = '3'$$

Rita knows that, in the ASCII character set, the codes for each alphabet are consecutive. So, to convert a capital letter to the same small letter, she can take the code of the capital letter, subtract the code for 'A', add the code for 'a' and turn the result into a character.

So, her refined design for reading a word is:

```
read-word(var f:text; var w:word)
{ Pre: not eof(f) and f^ ≠ ' ' }
{ Reads a word, terminated by a space. The space is not read. }

var length,i:integer; ch:char

begin
  length := 0
  while f^ ≠ ' ' { guaranteed space by pre-condition and eoln
                        before eof }
    length := length + 1
    read(f,ch)
    if length ≤ max-word-length
      if ch ∈ ['A' .. 'Z']
            ch := chr(ord(ch) – ord('A') + ord('a'))
      w[length] := ch
    end-of-if
  end-of-while

  { now space fill: }
  for i := length + 1 to max-word-length
    w[i] := ' '
end
```

She convinces herself that this works, by considering the three possible cases: the length of the word in the file being less than, equal to and greater than max-word-length. Yes, she is convinced.

Exercise 7.11   What is the effect of each of the following Pascal statements?

Var *i:Integer*; *ch:Char*; *b:Boolean*;

(a)   *ch := chr(ord(ch))*;

(b)   *ch := chr(ord('0'))*;

(c)   *i := 8; ch := chr(ord('0') + i)*;

(d)   *b := (ord(ch) < (ord('Z')) **And Not** (ch < 'Z')*;

Next, Rita designs the code to skip spaces between words when they are being read from a file. Sometimes the end of lines are significant and sometimes they are to be treated just like spaces, so her procedure will take a text file and a Boolean value parameter indicating whether ends of lines should be skipped or not. When ends of lines are being skipped, she does not have to look for them separately, as they appear as spaces in the buffer variable anyway. Her design uses the pre-declared Pascal procedure **get**.

There is a pre-declared procedure in Pascal called **get**. This takes a single file as a variable parameter, which must be open for reading. The procedure moves the current read position forward one place, thus updating the buffer variable for that file. The pre-declared procedure *read* (when working on non-text files) is actually not necessary, but is conveniently pre-declared as

> **Procedure** *read*(**Var** f : **File Of** t; **Var** x : t);
> **Begin**
> $x := f\hat{\ }$;
>   *get*(f)
> **End**;

Unfortunately, one may not write procedures with parameters of unspecified types (such as t above) in Pascal. Only the pre-declared procedures are so flexible.

```
skip-space(var f:text; skip-eoln·also:boolean)

var keep-skipping : boolean

begin
  keep-skipping := true
  while keep-skipping
    if eof(f) then
      keep-skipping := false
    else
    if eoln(f) and not skip-eoln-also then
      keep-skipping := false
    else
    if f ^ = ' ' then { includes end-of-lines }
      get(f)
    else
      keep-skipping := false
  end-of-while
end
```

Rita designed the procedure in this way, using a Boolean-valued variable to control the loop, so that she did not fall into a Wally trap (see page 169).

For any file, F, when the condition

> $eof(F)$

is true, the buffer variable, $F\hat{}$ is undefined. Hence it is *never* sensible to write conditions such as:

> $eof(F)$ **Or** $(F\hat{} = '\ ')$

Such conditions are Wally traps.

She might have been tempted to write the loop as:

```
while not eof(f)
        and (not eoln(f) or skip-eoln-also)
        and (f ^ = ' ')
    get(f)
```

However, she knows better!

Finally, she designs the algorithm for writing a word. She does not wish the procedure to write any of the extra spaces stored at the end of the word, so she constructs a loop that stops when it reaches a space or gets to the end of the array:

```
write-word(var f : text; w : word)

var index : integer

begin
  index := 1
  while (w[index] ≠ ' ') and (index ≤ max-word-length)
    write(f,w[index])
    index := index + 1
  end-of-while
end
```

Exercise 7.12 STOP! Before reading on: what is wrong with the procedure Rita has just written?

As always, Rita looks over her design before moving on.

RITA: Oh dear!

Rita has designed a Wally trap in the loop condition. The trap is sprung when the word array contains no spaces. After writing all but the last character of the word, index reaches the value of max-word-length. The condition is still true, and so the last character is written and index is increased by one. When the condition is tested again, the trap springs, as there is no 21st position in the array. Rita alters the design to treat the last character as a special case:

```
write-word(var f : text; w : word)

var index : integer

begin
  index := 1
  while (w[index] ≠ ' ') and (index < max-word-length)
    write(f,w[index])
    index := index + 1
  end-of-while
  if w[max-word-length]≠ ' '
    write(f,w[max-word-length])
end
```

At that she has completed her implementation of the abstract data type Word, with operations to read words from and write words to text files. From her choice of data structure for the type, there is already an existing Pascal operation for 'less than or equal'.

7.5.2 The data type Word-set

Next she considers the data type Word-set, used in the storage of the insignificant words. In her specification, this is defined as

Word-set = Set of Word

The only operation required from the program design is the membership test. However, this operation is required very often, hence it is vital, for any measure of efficiency, to have a representation of the insignificant words stored internally (that is, in the computer's memory) while the program is executing. This also implies that the whole set will need reading from the insignificant words file. However, it does not need writing because the program does not change the set.

Rita goes ahead and designs a Pascal type and implementations of the required operations. However, the story of this development involves many new concepts, for the implementation of **dynamic data structures,** so we have decided to defer it until the next chapter. For the purposes of this chapter, it is sufficient to know what operations she designs, rather than how they work. Although being primarily motivated by the concepts involved, this division is also supportive of the abstract data type approach, the whole point of which is that it is not necessary to know the details of the data type implementation in order to write a program that is based on it.

So here we just list the two operations she designs:

Function *InWordSet*(*w* : *Word*; *ws* : *WordSet*) : *Boolean*
InWordSet(w,ws) △ w ∈ ws

Procedure *ReadWordSet*(**Var** *f* : *Text*; **Var** *ws* : *WordSet*)
Reads the words in the file f into the set ws,
ignoring all spaces and ends of lines.

7.5.3   The data type Word-seq

The type Word-seq is abstractly defined as:

Word-seq = Seq of word

It is used for the titles and rotations of the titles in values of index-entry. From the program design, Rita notes that the operations required for the type are:

- Copying (assignment in get-sig-rotations)
- Length
- Head
- Tail
- Append (where the second item is a sequence of only one element)

There is also an implicit use of 'less than or equal', via the comparison of index-entries in the sort routine.

The nature of these operations imply that the data type must have an internal representation in order to have any measure of efficiency. Hence, the program will also need to read word sequences (terminated by end-of-line in the original input title list) and write word sequences (for the final kwic-index).

Again, the details of this data type are being deferred to the next chapter, and we list here just the operations that Rita designs:

Procedure *CopyWordSeq*(**Var** *CopyWs* : *WordSeq*; *ws* : *WordSeq*)
post CopyWs = ws

This procedure *must* be used instead of the Pascal assignment statement when copying a word sequence. (It is not necessary here to know why this is so, but the reason is explained in the next chapter.) We continue the list:

Function *LengthWordSeq(ws : WordSeq) : Integer*
LengthWordSeq(ws) △ len ws

Procedure *GetHeadWordSeq*(**Var** *h : Word; ws : WordSeq*)
pre ws ≠ [ ]
post h = hd(ws)

Procedure *GetTailWordSeq*(**Var** *t : WordSeq; ws : WordSeq*)
pre ws ≠ [ ]
post t = tl(ws)

Procedure *RightAppendWordSeq*(**Var** *ws : WordSeq; w : Word*)
pre true
post ws = w̄s̄ ⌢ [w]

Function *LessEqWordSeq(w1,w2 : WordSeq) : Boolean*
pre true
post LessEqWordSeq = w1 ≤ w2

Finally, there are procedures to read and write word sequences:

Procedure *ReadWordSeq*(**Var** *f : Text*; **Var** *ws : WordSeq*)
pre not eof(f)
Reads a sequence of words from the first line of f, into ws.
The reading position is left after the end of line.
The words may be separated by any number of spaces.

Procedure *WriteWordSeq*(**Var** *f : Text*; *ws : WordSeq*)
Writes ws to f, on one line. Each word is separated by a single space.
A new line is not produced after the sequence.

Note that the abstract head, tail and concatenate functions are being
implemented by procedures. The reasons for this are discussed in the
next chapter, but here we can examine the implications of that choice of
interface. Consider the following example from the program design:

title := tl(title) ⌢ [hd(title)]

This could be implemented by:

Var *TitleHead:Word;*
　⋮
GetHeadWordSeq(TitleHead,title);
GetTailWordSeq(title,title);
RightAppendWordSeq(title,TitleHead);

7.5.4   The data type Word-seq-seq

This type for modelling the list of titles is defined in the specification as

Word-seq-seq = Seq of Word-seq

Looking at the design of GET-SIG-ROTATIONS, Rita sees that the following operations are required:

- Testing if empty
- Head
- Tail

What is more, the head and tail operations are linked in that there is exactly one application in the design of head for each application of tail. These operations seem to look familiar – they are very similar to those used when reading a file. This leads her to infer that an internal representation of Word-seq-seq is not required in the program, but that the input text file can be processed by reading through it once. So the implementation of this data type is best dealt with by modifying the design.

She plans to implement the operations as follows. Firstly, the file will need to be reset before processing. The operation to test whether the sequence is empty is the end of file function. The head and tail operations are performed together, by the *ReadWordSeq* procedure.

7.5.5   The data type Index-entry

The next data type, Index-entry, is specified as:

Index-entry = Record
                entry : Word-seq
                location : N1
            end

The operations required by the program design for the type are:

- Construction from constituent fields (that is, **mk-Index-entry**(title,location)).
- Less than or equal operation, specified as $\leqslant$ on entry fields.

These operations, and the way they are used by the program, suggest that an internal form is required for this type. Writing of records to external text form is required as part of writing sequences of **index-entry**.

Copying index-entry values is also required. The obvious Pascal implementation of the type is a record:

```
index-entry = record
                 entry : word-seq;
                 location : integer
              end;
```

Firstly Rita studies the operation for record construction. Unfortunately, there is no record construction operator in Pascal. Instead, she has to introduce a local variable of type index-entry, and build the required value using separate assignment statements to the individual fields. To convince herself that this is adequate, she considers a simple example. At one place in the design she has written

sig-rotations := sig-rotations ⌢ [mk-index-entry(title,location)]

In the implementation, she supposes she will write something like

```
Var I:IndexEntry;
    ⋮
I.entry := title;
I.location := location;
RightAppend(SigRotations,I);
```

Next, she focuses her attention on the 'less than or equal' operation. The comparison consists of applying the similar operation on the entry fields of the two arguments. Thus she writes

```
less-eq-entry(ie1,ie2 : index-entry) : boolean
begin
   less-eq-entry := less-eq-word-seq(ie1.entry,ie2.entry)
end
```

Also easy to implement is the operation to copy index-entry values:

```
copy-entry(var copye : index-entry; e : index-entry);
begin
   copy-word-seq(copye.entry,e.entry)
   copye.location := e.location
end
```

Finally, for index-entry, she designs an implementation of the procedure to write the record values. As it was not stated exactly in the original specification, she decides that the records are to be written as one line of text in a file, with the entry field preceding the location field, and separated by two spaces.

```
write-entry(var f : text; ie : index-entry)
begin
  write-word-seq(f,ie.entry)
  writeln(f,' ',ie.location)
end
```

7.5.6 The data type Index-entries

This, the final data type, is abstractly defined as:

Index-entries = Seq of Index-entry

The operations required for it by the program design are:

* Copying
* Testing if empty
* Set to empty
* Length – testing if greater than 1
* Head
* Tail
* Append where second argument is a single item sequence
* Append where either argument may be any length

Rita can see the advantage of having two distinct append operations: it removes the need for an operation that takes an index-entry and turns it into a single item sequence (written as [x]), because the only occurrence of that operator in the design is when appending an index-entry on the back of a sequence of index-entries.

Again, the operations and the way they are used in the program cause her to decide that an internal representation is needed. Thus an operation is required to write values of index-entries, but not one to read them as there are no program input values of this type.

Like some of the previous data types, the details of the implementation of index-entries are considered in the next chapter. We here just list the operations that Rita designs:

Procedure *CopyEntries*(**Var** *CopyIes* : *IndexEntries*; *ies* : *IndexEntries*)
post CopyIes = ies

This must be used instead of the assignment statement.

Function *EmptyEntries*(*ie* : *IndexEntries*) : *Boolean*
EmptyEntries(ie) △ ie = [ ]

Procedure *GetEmptyEntries*(**Var** *ie* : *IndexEntries*)
pre true
post ie = [ ]

Rather than a general length of sequence function, it is sufficient for the program to have a function that tests whether a given sequence has at least two elements (see the design of sort):

Function *AtLeast2Entries*(*ie* : *IndexEntries*) : *Boolean*
AtLeast2Entries(ie) △ len ie > 1

Like those for Word-seq, some abstract functions are implemented as procedures:

Procedure *GetHeadEntries*(**Var** *h* : *IndexEntry*; *ies* : *IndexEntries*)
pre ies ≠ [ ]
post h = hd ies

Procedure *GetTailEntries*(**Var** *t* : *IndexEntries*; *ies* : *IndexEntries*)
pre ies ≠ [ ]
post t = tl ies

Procedure *RightAppendEntries*(**Var** *ies* : *IndexEntries*; *ie* : *IndexEntry*)
pre true
post ies = $\overline{\text{ies}}$ ⌢ [ie]

Procedure *AppendEntries*(**Var** *ie1* : *IndexEntries*; *ie2* : *IndexEntries*)
pre true
post ie1 = $\overline{\text{ie1}}$ ⌢ ie2

Finally, there is a procedure to write the entry list to a text file:

Procedure *WriteEntries*(**Var** *f* : *Text*; *ie* : *IndexEntries*)
Rewrites the file, f, and then
writes the elements of ie to it, one entry per line.

7.6   Implementation

Even though we have not yet seen all of them, Rita has designed the various data type operations at the same level of abstraction as Pascal – now they must be translated into syntactically correct Pascal. Implementing the program designs requires a little more effort, but even this is not too strenuous. Rita starts with the top level of the program. The program heading must contain the file names for the titles, and the external representation of insig-words and kwic-index:

Program *kwic*(*titles,InInsigWords,OutKwicIndex*)

Then she writes all the type definitions, including the equivalence of *WordSeqSeq* and *Text*:

> *WordSeqSeq* = *Text*

The variables required are the same as in the abstract design, except that there are also the *Text* file representations of the input insignificant words and the output KWIC index:

```
Var titles                     : WordSeqSeq;
    InInsigWords,OutKwicIndex  : Text;
    InsigWords                 : WordSet;
    KwicIndex                  : IndexEntries;
```

The main body of the program is also the same as the abstract, except that it is required to read the insignificant words and write the KWIC index:

```
Begin
    ReadWordSet(InInsigWords,InsigWords);
    GetSigRotations(titles,InsigWords,KwicIndex);
    sort(KwicIndex);
    WriteEntries(OutKwicIndex,KwicIndex);
End.
```

Then Rita considers the *GetSigRots* procedure. She recalls the design:

```
get-sig-rotations(titles:word-seq-seq; insig-words:word-set;
                  var sig-rotations:index-entries)

var title:word-seq ; word-index:integer ; location:integer

begin
    sig-rotations := [ ]
    location := 0
    while titles ≠ [ ]
        title := hd titles
        location := location + 1
        for word-index := 1 to len(title)
            if not (hd title ∈ insig-words)
                sig-rotations := sig-rotations ⌢
                                    [ mk-Index-entry(title, location) ]
            title := (tl title) ⌢ [hd title]
        end-for
        titles := tl titles
    end-of-while
end
```

Rita notes that titles was a value parameter in the design, but must be a variable parameter in the implementation, because Pascal does not allow files to be value parameters.

Pascal does not allow value parameters which are files. Neither does it allow value parameters which contain files (for examples record, array of files). This is because value parameters are implemented by copying the actual parameter value when the procedure is called. This would mean copying the entire file!

Also associated with the implementation of *WordSeqSeq* is the requirement that the procedure must reset the file before processing it.

Further consideration of the implementation leads her to change the algorithm slightly, so that the local variable title is of type *IndexEntry*. This will make the implementation of the part that constructs the *IndexEntry* record a little easier. Rita also notes that a local variable is required to hold the head of the title, as the head operation is implemented as a procedure. Otherwise, the implementation consists of replacing the abstract operations by the corresponding concrete ones:

```
Procedure GetSigRots(Var titles : WordSeqSeq; InsigWords : WordSet;
                     Var SigRotations : IndexEntries);

Var title                : IndexEntry;
    WordIndex,location   : Integer;
    HeadOfTitle          : Word;

Begin
  reset(titles);
  GetEmptyEntries(SigRotations);
  location := 0;
  While not(eof(titles)) Do
  Begin
    ReadWordSeq(titles,title.entry); { including eoln }
                              { head and tail combined }
    location := location + 1;
    title.location := location;
    For WordIndex := 1 To LengthWordSeq(title.entry) Do
    Begin
      GetHeadWordSeq(HeadOfTitle,title.entry);
      If Not InWordSet(HeadOfTitle,InsigWords) Then
        RightAppendEntries(SigRotations,title);
      RightAppendWordSeq(title.entry,HeadOfTitle);
      GetTailWordSeq(title.entry,title.entry);
    End;
  End;
End;
```

The implementation of the sort procedure requires a similar process. It is being left as a Laboratory Exercise. Having completed *sort*, all that remains is the implementation of the various data type procedures from their designs. Once this is done, the program is ready to be tested.

Exercise 7.13   Study the following specification of the sorting of a hand of cards:

```
hand-size  = 13
Val-no     = { 1 , . . . , 13 }
Suit-no    = { 1 , . . . , 4 }

Playing-card = Record
                    value : Val-no
                    suit : Suit-no
               end

Hand = Seq of Playing-card
inv-Hand(h) △ len h ⩽ hand-size
                and card elems h = len h

SORT (h : Hand) sh : Hand
post same-elems(h,sh) and is-sorted(sh)

is-sorted : (h : Hand) → 𝔹
is-sorted (h) △ ∀ i1,i2 ∈ inds h • i1 > i2 ⇒ greater(h[i1],h[i2])

same-elems : (h : Hand , sh : Hand) → 𝔹
same-elems(h,sh) △ elems h = elems sh

greater : (c1 : Playing-card , c2 : Playing-card) → 𝔹
greater(c1,c2) △ (c1.suit > c2.suit)
                    or
                 (c1.suit = c2.suit) and (c1.value > c2.value)
```

(a)   Explain the meaning of the invariant inv-Hand.

(b)   Define a Pascal data type to implement the data type Hand in the specification, then design a Pascal procedure to sort a hand of cards.

7.7   Huge Raincoat . . .

Having tested the program, Rita telephones her client and tells him that she's ready to install it. Within minutes, a helicopter arrives and, blindfolded, she is taken on board, where she suddenly feels drowsy. . . . Some time later, she finds herself, without blindfold, on a Concorde flying over lots of water. Waiting for her at the other end of the flight is a similar helicopter trip to a secret place. When finally the blindfold is again removed, she is in a large room with a beefy security guard. All round the room there are hundreds of documents on shelves. It's just like she anticipated! Then she is shown the 'machine'. There is a label on it:

TRS 80

On loan from:

Computer Science,
Manchester University

So, she types in the program and tries it. Of course, it works. Just as she is completing it, the security guard goes to the toilet. Being a person of high moral fibre, her curiosity gets the better of her after a whole second. Rita rushes to the nearest shelf, and grabs the first document she finds. By some amazing quirk of fate, written on the front cover she sees:

SDI: The Plan

Top Secret

Do NOT read (applies especially to Rita)

Well, she is tempted. Rita's heart is pounding... She opens the cover... and reads:

NEW! from MacDoughnuts [†]

SPACE BURGERS!

Yes, 100% Beef PACKED! into TINY capsules

- Bursting with taste!
- Bursting with calories!

Try them with
SPACE CHIPS
– they're out of this world!

"Just suck 'em, 'n' see!"
Ronald MacDoughnut

[†]MacDoughnuts is a trade mark of Superlative Digestions Incorporated.

SUMMARY

This chapter introduced two key topics: the **abstract data type approach,** and **recursive programming.** Abstract data types are reinforced in Chapters 9 and 10, with the specification and use of a strings package. Further examples of recursion in programs appear in Chapters 8 and 12.

Other concepts introduced include **output parameters** of operations, **lexicographic ordering** of sequences, **cross product** of two types, the design technique of **solving a simpler problem first,** and the pre-declared Pascal procedure *get*.

The next chapter is concerned with the details of the data type implementations omitted from this one. These are used as a vehicle for studying **dynamic data structures.**

The following notations were introduced in this chapter.

Specification notation

Natural numbers from 1 upwards $\mathbb{N}1$
Lexicographic ordering $\leqslant$
Cross product $(i,j) \in \mathbb{N} \times \mathbb{N}$

Pascal notation

Ordinal code of characters   *chr(ord(ch) – ord('A') + ord('a'))*
File read position increment   *get(titles)*
Relations on strings $<, <=, >=, >, =, <>$

LABORATORY EXERCISE – to implement the sort procedure

Problem

Write a Pascal procedure to perform a recursive sort of sequences of Index-entry, as designed in the text for this case study. (This algorithm is called 'quick-sort'.)

Specification

The formal specification of the operation is:

Index-entry = { some type with a $\leqslant$ ordering }

Index-entries = Seq of Index-entry

SORT
ext wr s : Index-entries
post is-permutation(s,s̄) and is-sorted(s)

is-sorted : (s : Index-entries) $\rightarrow$ $\mathbb{B}$
is-sorted(s) $\triangle$
$\forall$ i1,i2 $\in$ inds s $\bullet$ i1 $<$ i2 $\Rightarrow$ s[i1] $\leqslant$ s[i2]

is-permutation : (s1 : Index-entries , s2 : Index-entries) $\rightarrow$ $\mathbb{B}$
is-permutation(s1,s2) $\triangle$
$\forall$ e $\in$ elems (s1 $\frown$ s2) $\bullet$ no-of-occurrences(e,s1) = no-of-occurrences(e,s2)

no-of-occurrences : (t : Index-entry , ts : Index-entries) $\rightarrow$ $\mathbb{N}$
no-of-occurrences(t,ts) $\triangle$ card { i $\in$ inds(ts) | ts[i] = t }

Implementation

Your procedure must have the following heading:

Procedure *sort*(**Var** *seq:IndexEntries*);

You should split the procedure into sub-procedures as appropriate.

Your implementation may make use of the following declarations and operations, and not assume any other properties of the types (for example, you may not use assignment on them):

Type *IndexEntry* = { *of no concern, but has a less-than ordering* }
        IndexEntries = { *of no concern* }

Function *LessEqEntry*(*ie*1,*ie*2:*IndexEntry*):*Boolean*;
{ *post LessEqEntry* = *ie*1 $\leqslant$ *ie*2 }

Procedure *CopyEntries*(**Var** *CopyIes:IndexEntries*; *ies:IndexEntries*);
{ *post CopyIes* = *ies* }

Function *EmptyEntries*(*ie:IndexEntries*):*Boolean*;
{ *post EmptyEntries* = ([ ] = *ie*) }

Procedure *GetEmptyEntries*(**Var** *ie:IndexEntries*);
{ *post ie* = [ ] }

Function *AtLeast2Entries*(*ies:IndexEntries*):*Boolean*;
{ *post AtLeast2Entries* = *len*(*ies*) $>$ 1 }

Procedure *GetHeadEntries*(**Var** *h:IndexEntry*; *ies:IndexEntries*);
{ *pre ies* $\neq$ [ ] }
{ *post hd ies* = *h* }

Procedure *GetTailEntries*(**Var** *t:IndexEntries*; *ies:IndexEntries*);
{ *pre ies* $\neq$ [ ] }
{ *post tl ies* = *t* }

Procedure *RightAppendEntries*(**Var** *ies:IndexEntries*; *ie:IndexEntry*);
{ *post* $\overline{ies}$ $\frown$ [*ie*] = *ies* }

Procedure *AppendEntries*(**Var** *ie*1:*IndexEntries*; *ie*2:*IndexEntries*);
{ *post* $\overline{ie1}$ $\frown$ *ie*2 = *ie*1 }

Dynamic data types of KWIC

MOTIVATION

This chapter presents the development of the implementations for the abstract data types omitted from the discussion in Chapter 7. There are three of these, and they are all implemented using **dynamic data structures**. In particular their implementation is based on **linked lists**.

8.1 Design and implementation of the abstract data types

Imagine you are the proud owner of a spanking new time machine. You appreciate that in the abstract data type approach one can use operations of a data type without knowing about their implementation. Right now, however, you would really like to study the implementations of the abstract data types which were omitted from the previous chapter. Have you got that much imagination? Okay, suppose you were to cast your time machine back to the moment when Rita was developing those types, and this time witness them for yourself – that's what this chapter is about.

The three data types for which we omitted the discussion of development are

- Word-set
- Word-seq
- Index-entries

Let's start with Word-set. Whoooosh (that was your time machine casting back).

8.1.1 The data type Word-set

This data type is defined as

Word-set = Set of Word

The only operation required from the KWIC program design is the membership test. However, this operation is required very often, and that's why Rita knows she must have an efficient representation of the insignificant words stored internally (that is, in the computer's memory) while the program is executing. This also implies that the whole set needs reading from the insignificant words file. However, it does not need writing because the program does not change the set.

She considers using an array structure for the internal storage, but rejects this on the grounds that either there would be a large overhead on the program, or there would soon come a point when it would not be possible to add new words to the set without recompiling the program with a larger array. Even though this would not present a massive inconvenience to the customer (if she supplied explicit instructions as to how it could be done), there is no real justification for it. Instead, she intends to use a **dynamic structure**.

A **dynamic data structure** is one that does not have a fixed size, but which is allowed to grow (and contract) as the requirements of the program change during its execution. This is achieved in many languages (for example in Pascal) by asking the system for more, new, variables, known as **dynamic variables**.

A normal variable name (such as *length*) can be thought of as a **static reference**, in that it always refers to the same variable (or an instance of it, in the case of a local variable of a recursive procedure). The space for such a variable can be allocated by the compiler and hence it is called a **static variable**. A **dynamic variable** is one which is actually created at run-time, usually for use in some dynamic data structure. The space for such variables cannot be allocated at compile-time, because it is generally impossible to predict how many are needed. The name of a dynamic variable is not an identifier, as with static variables, but is a **dynamic reference** or **pointer**. A dynamic reference may be thought of as an address, perhaps the memory address where the variable actually resides (although that is implementation dependent). Dynamic references are values and may be stored in other variables (either dynamic or static) and may be copied, and so on. When a (static or dynamic) variable, X, contains as its value the dynamic reference of some dynamic variable, we say that X **points to** that dynamic variable.

(Dynamic references cannot be printed or used in calculations because their concrete form is implementation dependent.)

To implement the Word-set data type, Rita chooses to employ a **linked list**.

A list is a sequence. A **linked list** is a list implemented by a chain of dynamic variables. Each dynamic variable in the list is called a **node** and contains a value, which is an element of the list, plus a pointer to the next variable in the list. Figure 8.1 shows an individual node, and Figure 8.2 shows an example linked list of natural numbers. To mark the end of the chain of nodes, the reference field of the final dynamic variable holds a special value indicating that it points to nothing. (In Pascal, this special value is called **Nil**.) The nodes are usually implemented using records for the value and reference pair.

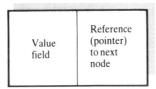

Figure 8.1   A linked list node.

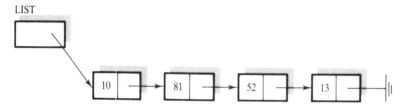

Figure 8.2   Linked list representation of [10,81,52,13].

Dynamic references are values, and all values have a type in Pascal. The types of references are known as **pointers** and are denoted by ˆ followed by the type of the variables that may be referenced. For example,

ˆ *Integer*

denotes the type **pointer to** *Integer*, and is the set of all possible references of dynamic variables which have the type *Integer*. (A space between the ˆ symbol and the name of the type is not needed. Its presence or not is a matter of style.)

Rita writes the Pascal type definition for the word sets:

word-set = ˆ word-set-rec ;

word-set-rec = record
               this-word : word ;
               next : word-set { nil marks the end of the
                             chain }
     end

A static variable of type word-set will point to the first node in a linked list. Each node in that list will be a dynamic variable of type word-set-rec. Hence the type of the static variable must be a pointer to word-set-rec. Similarly, the next field in each node must be a pointer to word-set-rec.

The only place in Pascal where one may write a type name textually before its definition is within the definition of a pointer type. This relaxation of the normal restriction is required because of the inherently recursive nature of dynamic type definitions.

The next task on her list is the design of an implementation for the membership test operation. Assuming that the linked list has been built

and contains all the insignificant words, the membership test involves
starting at the front of the list and working along until the word being
searched for is found, or the end of the list is reached. Rita's draft design
is:

```
in-word-set(w:word; ws:word-set) : boolean

var found:boolean

begin
  found := false
  while not found and (ws ≠ nil)
    found := this-word of node pointed to by ws = w
    move ws onto the next node
  end-of-while
  in-word-set := found
end
```

The routine thus needs to access each dynamic variable from the variable
that points to it.

In Pascal, to access the variable pointed to by some other variable, *X*, one writes:

$$X\char`^$$

The routine also needs to copy pointers, so that it can move along the list
in the loop.

Pointer values may be assigned from one variable to another, but note that it is the
reference which is being copied, and not the actual value of the dynamic variable
referenced by the pointer (if there is one!). Figure 8.3 illustrates the distinction between
copying references, and copying values of dynamic variables. Consider the linked list in
part (a) of the figure. Part (b) shows the resulting structure after the execution of:

$$x := y$$

Part (c) shows the result after executing

$$x\char`^ := y\char`^$$

on the same initial structure.

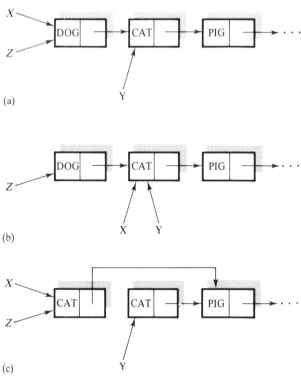

Figure 8.3 Copying references (a) initially : X, Y and Z are pointers to the nodes in the list (b) after $X := Y$ (c) after $X\hat{} := Y\hat{}$.

Rita then refines her design to:

```
in-word-set(w:word; ws:word-set) : boolean

var found:boolean

begin
  found := false
  while not found and (ws ≠ nil)
    found := ws ^.this-word = w
    ws := ws ^.next
  end-of-while
  in-word-set := found
end
```

The behaviour of the above function may be studied with the aid of Figure 8.4. This shows how the pointer ws moves along the list one place for each iteration of the loop. By the end, ws has the value nil, but that does not matter as it is a value parameter of the function.

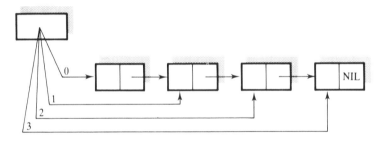

Figure 8.4   Scanning a linked list.

Exercise 8.1   The following specification defines a function which evaluates a polynomial represented as a sequence of coefficients for a given value of X:

```
poly-eval : (co-effs : Seq of ℝ , X : ℝ) → ℝ
poly-eval(co-effs,X) △
    if co-effs = [ ] then
      0
    else
      hd co-effs + (X * poly-eval(tl co-effs , X))
```

Assume that the following data structure is a valid representation of Seq of ℝ:

$$SeqOfReal = {}^{\wedge}SeqOfRealRec;$$

$$SeqOfRealRec = \textbf{Record}$$
$$ThisCoEff : Real;$$
$$rest : SeqOfReal$$
$$\textbf{End}$$

Implement the poly-eval function twice as a Pascal function, first recursively and then non-recursively. Discuss the comparative advantages and disadvantages of these two solutions.

As stated earlier, to use the insignificant words in the program they need to be read from the text file where they are stored and placed in a linked list. This involves creating a **new variable** to store each word as it is read, and chaining that variable on to the list.

In Pascal, the pre-declared procedure **new** takes as a variable parameter, a variable P, of type $^{\wedge}T$, for some type T. It creates a new variable, of type T, and sets P to reference it. The value of the new variable is undefined. The new variable is unique in that it does not coincide with any existing variable accessible dynamically or statically before the call to *new*.

For example, suppose we had the static variable

$x : {}^{\wedge} Integer$

Execution of the statement

$new(x)$

would cause a new variable of type *Integer* to be created, and *x* would be left pointing to it. The value of the new variable, that is of

$x^{\wedge}$

would be undefined.

The easiest place to add a new variable to a linked list is at the front, because that place is readily accessible. In the case of word-set, the order in which the words are stored in the list does not matter, so they may be added at the front. Rita's first design of read-word-set is:

```
read-word-set(var f : text ; var ws : word-set)

var new-w : word-set { for referencing the new variable }

begin
  reset(f)
  ws := nil

  while not eof(f)
    new(new-w)
    read-word(f,new-w ^.this-word)
    chain new-w variable on front of ws
  end-of-while
end
```

To chain the new variable on to the front of the list, the procedure must make the next field of the new variable point to the first item in the list; and then make ws point to the new variable. Thus:

```
new-w ^.next := ws
ws := new-w
```

The procedure must also skip spaces and end-of-lines before the first word and after each word. Rita's refined design is:

```
read-word-set(var f : text ; var ws : word-set)

var new-w : word-set { for referencing the new variable }

begin
```

```
      reset(f)
      ws := nil
      skip-space(f,true)

      while not eof(f)
         new(new-w)
         read-word(f,new-w ^.this-word)
         skip-space(f,true)
         new-w ^.next := ws
         ws := new-w
      end-of-while
   end
```

That completes the design of the implementation of the abstract data type word-set with the membership test function and reading a word set from a text file.

Exercise 8.2   Design a procedure that adds a new value to the end of a linked list.

8.1.2   The data type Word-seq

The type Word-seq is abstractly defined as:

    Word-seq = Seq of word

It is used for the titles and rotations of the titles in values of **index-entry**. From the program design, Rita notes that the operations required for the type are:

- Copying (assignment in **get-sig-rotations**)
- Length
- Head
- Tail
- Append (where the second item is a sequence of only one element)

There is also an implicit use of the 'less than or equal' operation, via the comparison of **index-entries** in the sort routine.

The nature of these operations implies that the data type must have an internal representation in order to have any measure of efficiency. Hence, the program will also need to read word sequences (terminated by end-of-line in the original input title list) and write word sequences (for the final KWIC index).

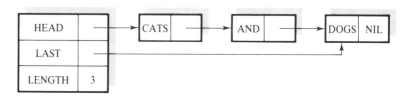

Figure 8.5   A non-empty word sequence.

Rita decides to use a dynamic structure to store word sequences. She notes that she could use an identical representation to the one chosen for word-set. However, some of the operations, such as length and append, would require scanning the linked lists to count the elements or find the end, and this would be inefficient. To avoid this she considers a structure which has a linked list to store the sequence, but also has an explicit length count, and a direct pointer to the last node in the list. These three items will be grouped together using a record type. Thus, these records will have three fields: a head, pointing to the linked list; a last, pointing to the last node in the linked list; and a length, being a count of the number of nodes in the list. An empty list will have a value of nil for both the head and last fields, and a length of zero. Figure 8.5 illustrates the representation of a non-empty list. Rita writes the Pascal type definitions for the representation:

```
word-seq-list  = ^ word-seq-list-rec;

word-seq  =  record
                  head,last : word-seq-list
                  length    : integer
             end
{ Empty list represented by: head = nil; last = nil;
   length = 0 }

word-seq-list-rec = record
                         head : word
                         tail  : word-seq-list
                    end
{ End of list marked by tail = nil }
```

The first operation she considers is that for copying word sequences. She realizes that it is generally unsound to allow a linked list to be shared by two sequences, because subsequently changing one of them would also change the other! Hence, to copy a sequence, the program must actually copy the linked list by making new nodes, rather than just copying the pointer to the head of it. Copying a linked list is most elegantly achieved by a recursive algorithm. She will design another procedure, copy-word-seq-list, which will take a linked list as its first parameter and produce a copy of it in its second, and return a pointer to the last node in the copy in its third parameter, so that this can be put in the the last field. Rita writes:

```
copy-word-seq(var copy-ws : word-seq; ws : word-seq)
{ copy-ws := ws }
begin
  copy-ws.length := ws.length
  copy-word-seq-list(copy-ws.head,copy-ws.last,ws.head)
end
```

It is copy-word-seq-list which will be recursive. It must copy the given linked list by creating new nodes and copying the words. Rita has an idea of how the list may be copied: if it is nil, it is easy. Otherwise the procedure may copy the head, and then recursively copy the tail. A complication to this is the pointer to the last item in the new list, so Rita decides to ignore this at first. Thus, she sketches:

```
copy-word-seq-list(var copy-list : word-seq-list;
                       list : word-seq-list)
{ copy-list := list, ignore pointer to last for the moment }
begin
  if list = nil then
    copy-list := nil
  else
    new(copy-list)
    copy the head from list to head of copy-list
    copy the tail from list to tail of copy-list
end
```

She then makes this more concrete:

```
copy-word-seq-list(var copy-list : word-seq-list;
                       list : word-seq-list)
{ copy-list := list, ignore pointer to last for the moment }
begin
  if list = nil then
    copy-list := nil
  else
    new(copy-list)
    copy-list ^.head := list ^.head
    copy-word-seq-list(copy-list ^.tail, list ^.tail)
end
```

Having solved this simpler problem, she next considers the third parameter, which she calls copy-last. This must be set to point to the last node in the copy, or nil if there are no nodes. By examination, she sees that the stage where the pointer to the last node is known is just after the recursive call, and then under the condition that the tail of the new list is nil. In addition, the recursive calls must be passed the copy-last parameter unchanged, and it must be set to nil if list is nil. Her completed design is:

```
copy-word-seq-list(var copy-list,copy-last : word-seq-list;
                                    list : word-seq-list)
{ copy-list := list, copy-last := pointer to last node in copy-list }
begin
  if list = nil then
    copy-list := nil
    copy-last := nil
  else
    new(copy-list);
    copy-list ^.head := list ^.head
    copy-word-seq-list(copy-list ^.tail, copy-last, list ^.tail)
    if copy-list ^.tail = nil
      copy-last := copy-list
  end-of-if
end
```

The next operation Rita considers is the length function. The length of
a word sequence is readily available in the representation as the length
field of the word-seq record. Nevertheless, for elegance and future
maintainability, she provides a function to access this value:

```
length-word-seq(ws : word-seq) : integer
begin
  length-word-seq := ws.length
end
```

The head function is also fairly simple, although not quite as obvious as
length. Unfortunately, it cannot be implemented in Pascal as a function
because the result is a word, which is an array.

Results of functions in Pascal may not be structured items, such as arrays, records and
files. They may only be simple types, such as *Integer*, *Real*, *Boolean*, or pointer types. This
is an idiosyncratic restriction due to the technique used to implement Pascal function
calls when the language was first designed and implemented.

Instead, she designs a procedure to get the head of a sequence.

```
get-head-word-seq(var h : word; ws : word-seq)
{ pre ws ≠ [ ]
  post h = hd(ws)}
begin
  h := ws.head ^.head
end
```

Similarly, the tail function returns a word-seq value, which is a record, and thus she has to implement it as a Pascal procedure. Another point she notes is that this procedure must copy the tail of the sequence to avoid any sharing problems. She can use the same procedure to copy the tail of the linked list as she designed for the full copy operation. Thus the design is similar to that of the copy procedure, except that the length of the copy is one less than the length of the original, and the linked list copied is the tail of the original:

```
get-tail-word-seq(var t : word-seq; ws : word-seq)
{ pre ws ≠ [ ]
  post t = tl(ws)}
begin
  t.length := ws.length - 1
  copy-word-seq-list(t.head,t.last,ws.head ^.tail)
end
```

Now she considers the append function. She has already noted that the second argument is always a single item in the design. She concludes that no sequence copying is required if her operation appends an item on to the back of an *existing* sequence. In places where this is not what is required, the program implementation would have to precede the operation by an explicit copy.

The basic method, then, is to create a new variable, link it on the end, place the appended item in it, and set the last pointer to reference it. When linking the new variable on the end of the existing sequence, there are two cases to consider, depending on whether or not the original sequence is empty. Rita's design is:

```
right-append-word-seq(var ws : word-seq; w : word)
{ post ws = ws ⌢ [w] }
var new-w : word-seq-list
begin
  new(new-w)
  new-w ^.head := w
  new-w ^.tail := nil { since last in new list }
  if ws.head = nil then
    ws.head := new-w
  else
    ws.last ^.tail := new-w
  ws.last := new-w
  ws.length := ws.length + 1
end
```

Next she examines the 'less than or equal' operation, which is required implicitly from the design. This involves comparing two sequences, element by element, until they are different or the end of one of them is reached. This can be solved in an iterative manner, using a loop to scan through the sequences while the corresponding elements of each are the same. Because the result of the operation is a Boolean, she decides to implement it using a Pascal function:

```
less-eq-word-seq(w1,w2 : word-seq) : boolean
{post less-eq-word-seq = w1 ≤ w2}
var equal-so-far : boolean; w1-list-pos, w2-list-pos : word-seq-list
begin
  equal-so-far := true
  w1-list-pos := w1.head
  w2-list-pos := w2.head
  while (w1-list-pos ≠ nil) and (w2-list-pos ≠ nil)
          and equal-so-far
    if w1-list-pos ^.head ≠ w2-list-pos ^.head
      equal-so-far := false
    else
      w1-list-pos := w1-list-pos ^.tail
      w2-list-pos := w2-list-pos ^.tail
  end-of-while

  if w1-list-pos = nil
    less-eq-word-seq := true
  else
  if w2-list-pos = nil
    less-eq-word-seq := false
  else
    less-eq-word-seq := w1-list-pos ^.head ≤ w2-list-pos ^.head
end
```

As already stated, the word sequences must be read from text files. Initially they consist of a single line of text, with words separated by spaces. Spaces before and between words must be skipped. Obviously, end-of-lines must not be skipped when reading the words in a word sequence, as these separate consecutive word sequences in the list of titles. However, it is sensible to skip the end-of-line once the word sequence has been read. Rita observes that the textual form of a word sequence is another representation of it. Thus the read procedure should be very similar to that designed for copying, except that there are two different representations involved, and it is necessary to count the words to obtain the length.

```
read-word-seq(var f : text; var ws : word-seq)
{ pre not eof(f)
  Reads a sequence of words from the first line of f, into ws.
  The reading position is left after the end of line.
  The words may be separated by any number of spaces. }
begin
  skip-space(f,false) {that is, not ends of lines}
  read-word-seq-list(f,ws.head,ws.last,ws.length)
```

```
  get(f) { skips end of line }
end
```

Rita's design for the recursive **read-word-seq-list** is:

```
read-word-seq-list(var f : text; var list,last : word-seq-list;
                   var length : integer)
{ pre   not eof(f) and (f^ ≠ ' ' or eoln(f) )
  post word-seq-list-viewed-as-seq-of-char(list) ⌢ f = f̄
        and last points to last variable in list
        and length = len(list) }
begin
  if eoln(f) { end of list }
     list := nil
     last := nil
     length := 0
  else
     new(list)
     read-word(f,list ^.head)
     skip-space(f,false)
     read-word-seq-list(f,list ^.tail,last,length)
     length := length + 1

     if list ^.tail = nil
        last := list
  end-of-if
end
```

To convince herself that this is correct, she observes that reading a list is equivalent to reading the head, followed by reading the tail; unless the list is empty. Also, the length of an non-empty list is the length of its tail, plus one. Spaces must be skipped after reading a word. Otherwise eoln(f) is not an accurate test for the end of the sequence because there might be spaces after the last word on the line.

Exercise 8.3   Would it be correct in the above design of read-word-seq-list to move the line that adds one to the length to before the recursive call?

Finally she designs the procedure to write word sequences. The procedure is used as part of writing an index entry, and must write all the words on one line, separated by one space. Rita does not want to have a leading or trailing space before the first word or after the last. The operation can be easily implemented iteratively, because appending on the back of a file is simply achieved by writing to it. She decides that all words except the first will have a space written before them. However, if the sequence is empty, there is no first word.

```
write-word-seq(var f : text; ws : word-seq)
var list-pos : word-seq-list
begin
  if ws.head ≠ nil
    write-word(f,ws.head ^.head) {that's right!}
    list-pos := ws.head ^.tail
    while list-pos ≠ nil
      write(f,' ')
      write-word(f,list-pos ^.head)
      list-pos := list-pos ^.tail
    end-of-while
  end-of-if
end
```

At this point, she has completed the design of the word sequence data type implementation.

Exercise 8.4   Design an efficient program to print the longest line from a text file. There must be no arbitrary limit on the length of this line.

To resolve any ambiguity in the requirements, here is a formal specification of the problem:

Text = Seq of (Seq of Char)

LONGEST-LINE:(input : Text) → (output : Seq of Char)

pre   true

post ∃ line ∈ (elems(input) ∪ { [ ] }) •
          (not ∃ other-line ∈ (elems(input) − {line}) •
                  len other-line > len line
)
          and
          line = output

Exercise 8.5

(a)   Give an informal but clear and precise explanation of the following formal specification. Avoid simply translating the symbols into English.

X (i : ℤ)
ext wr s : Seq of ℤ
pre ∀ j ∈ {1 , . . . , len s − 1} • s[j] < s[j + 1]
post elems s ∪ {i} = elems s
        and
        ∀ j ∈ {1 , . . . , len s − 1} • s[j] < s[j + 1]

(b)   Argue informally, yet convincingly, why the following procedure is a correct implementation of the above specification.

```
Type SeqOfInteger = ^ SeqRec;
     SeqRec = Record
                     head : Integer;
                     tail  : SeqOfInteger
              End;

Procedure X (Var ThisList : SeqOfInteger; ThisValue : Integer);

   Procedure Rec (Var S : SeqOfInteger);
   Var NewInt : SeqOfInteger;
       here    : Boolean;
   Begin
     If S = Nil Then
       here := true
     Else
       here := S^.head > ThisValue;
     If here Then
     Begin
       new(NewInt);
       NewInt^.head := ThisValue;
       NewInt^.tail := S;
       S := NewInt
     End
     Else
     If S^.head <> ThisValue Then
       Rec (S^.tail)
   End; {Rec}
Begin
  Rec(ThisList)
End; {X}
```

8.1.3 The data type Index-entries

Whooshing your time machine forward over the development of the data
types which were discussed in Chapter 7, you would soon arrive at
Index-entries. Let's look inside . . .

    Index-entries = Seq of Index-entry

The operations required for it by the program design are:

- Copying
- Testing if empty
- Set to empty
- Length – testing if greater than 1
- Head

- Tail

- Append where second argument is single item sequence

- Append where either argument may be any length

Rita can see the advantage of having two distinct append operations: it removes the need for an operation that takes an index-entry and turns it into a single item sequence (written as [x]), as the only occurrence of that operator in the design is when appending an index-entry on the back of a sequence of index-entries.

Again, the operations and the way they are used in the program cause her to decide that an internal representation is needed. Thus an operation is required to write values of index-entries, but not one to read them because there are no program input values of this type.

Rita observes that a suitable implementation could be very similar to that chosen for word-seq. However, in this case, a general length operation is not required, because it is relatively easy to check whether a sequence has a length which is greater than 1, and that can be provided instead. Consequently her Pascal data type for the implementation is:

```
index-entries-list  =  ^ index-entries-list-rec;

index-entries  =  record
                    head, last : index-entries-list
                  end;

index-entries-list-rec  =  record
                             head : index-entry;
                             tail  : index-entries-list
                           end;
```

Here note that index-entries-list-rec is an example of a record which has a field that is also a record. index-entry was another example. This is allowed in Pascal, and may be perfectly natural. You have already seen several examples of records which have an array as one field.

Rita starts with the procedure to copy index-entries. This is similar to the one designed for word-seq.

In fact, the whole data type is similar, so we have left its development as a laboratory exercise!

When a variable is supplied as the actual parameter for a formal **value** parameter of a procedure, the procedure cannot alter the value of that variable outside it (except by a direct global access). However, when the variable is of a pointer type, the procedure is able to alter the value of the dynamic variable referenced by the pointer, if there is one. For example:

```
Type IntegerList = ^IntegerListRec;
      IntegerListRec = Record
                          head : Integer;
                          tail  : IntegerList
                       End;

Procedure ChangeHead(ThisList : IntegerList; NewHead : Integer);
{ pre ThisList <> Nil }
{ ThisList := [NewHead] ⁀ tl ThisList }
Begin
    ThisList^.head := NewHead
End;
```

This is technically alright, as the pointer itself is not being changed, just the variable that it points to. However, somebody looking at the procedure heading may be given the impression that the abstract value of *ThisList* is not altered, as *ThisList* is a value parameter, particularly if the heading is used in an abstract specification (in terms of sequences) of the procedure. Pascal has no formal mechanism for indicating the fact that a change may occur to some dynamic variable accessible by following the pointer.

However, when we write a specification of a procedure by giving its heading and then pre- and post-conditions in terms of the abstract values of any parameters which are actually implemented by pointers, the value parameters do not have their abstract values altered outside the procedure. Thus the example above would be abstractly specified with *ThisList* as a variable parameter.

A generalization of this applies to parameters which are not themselves pointers, but which contain pointers (that is, an array of pointers, or a record containing a field which is a pointer).

8.1.4   Issues not addressed

Although the implemented program is correct, there are two related issues which have not been addressed, concerning the implementation of the dynamic data types. One is that there has been no attempt to minimize the amount of copying undertaken. It is certainly true that the program copies some data structures which do not need copying. Related to this is that the program makes no attempt to reclaim the memory allocated to dynamic variables that it no longer requires. Unfortunately this **garbage collection** is not automatic in Pascal. A consequence of these two points is that the machine running the program will run out of dynamic variable memory sooner than it needs to. We are assuming in this case study that this does not present a problem, that is, that the machine has sufficient memory to hold all the dynamic variables created during execution.

The strings package implementation in Chapter 12 deals with both of these problems.

Exercise 8.6   Study the following specification of a palindrome checker (that is, a checker for words which are spelt the same in reverse, for example 'adooda'):

Word = Seq of Char

Palindrome : (w : Word) $\rightarrow$ $\mathbb{B}$
Palindrome (w) $\triangle$ $\forall$ i $\in$ inds(w) • w[i] = w[len w − i + 1]

The following Pascal function is an attempt to implement the above specification, assuming a simple linked list of words. However, there is a (deliberate) mistake. Identify the mistake, propose a correction for it and then present a convincing informal argument that the corrected function implements the specification. Diagrams will probably help your argument.

Type *Word* = ^*Wordrec*;
        Wordrec = **Record**
                        head : *Char*;
                        tail : *Word*
                    End;

Function *Palindrome* (*ThisWord* : *Word*) : *Boolean*;
Var *IsPalindrome* : *Boolean*;

    Procedure *Check*(**Var** *left* : *Word*; *right*: *Word*);
    Begin
      If *right* <> **Nil Then**
      Begin
        check(*left*, *right*^.*tail*);
        left := *left*^.*tail*;
        If *left*^.*head* <> *right*^.*head* **Then**
          IsPalindrome := *false*
      End;
    End;

    Begin
      IsPalindrome := *true*;
      Check(*ThisWord*,*ThisWord*);
      Palindrome := *IsPalindrome*
    End;

Exercise 8.7   Describe three different ways in which one might implement a sequence of integers in Pascal, based on arrays, linked lists and files respectively. Give the Pascal type declarations, and some simple examples.

    Discuss reasons that would affect the suitability of each implementation.

SUMMARY

This chapter was concerned with the implementation of the abstract data types omitted from Chapter 7. These were used as a vehicle to introduce **dynamic data structures** and in particular **linked lists**. More advanced uses of linked lists can be seen in Chapter 12.

The following notations were introduced in this chapter.

Pascal notation

Pointer type   *IndexEntriesList* = ˆ *IndexEntriesListRec*
New dynamic variables   *new*(*NewW*)
Dynamic variable access   *CopyList*ˆ.*head*

TUTORIAL EXERCISE

This tutorial is intended to draw out the relationship between iterative and recursive algorithms.

The following is a specification of a sequence reversal operation:

REVERSE-SEQ
ext wr s : Seq of ℕ
post s = reverse($\overleftarrow{s}$)

reverse : (s : Seq of ℕ) → Seq of ℕ
reverse (s) △
    if s = [ ] then [ ]
    else
        reverse(tl s) ⌢ [hd s]

A recursive implementation of REVERSE-SEQ follows. It assumes a simple linked list implementation of sequences. Note that no new dynamic variables are created. This is adequate, as the resulting sequence is stored in the same variable as the original, and thus no list-sharing problems will occur.

Type *Seq* = ˆ *SeqRec*;

   SeqRec =
      Record
         head : *Integer*;
         tail : *Seq*
      End;

Procedure *ReverseSeq*(**Var** *s* : *Seq*);
{ *s* := *reverse*(*s*) }

Var *HeadOfS* : *Seq*;

```
Procedure append (Var s1 : Seq; s2 : Seq);
{ s1 := s1 ⌢ s2 }
Begin
  If s1 = Nil Then
    s1 := s2
  Else
    append(s1 ^.tail, s2)
End;

Begin { of ReverseSeq }
  If s = Nil Then { nothing }
  Else
  Begin
    HeadOfS := s;
    s := s^.tail;
    HeadOfS^.tail := Nil;
    ReverseSeq(s);
    append(s,HeadOfS)
  End
End;
```

1

Propose a non-recursive implementation of REVERSE-SEQ. The simplest way to do this is to have a loop that strips off the head of the sequence and adds it to the front of another. The loop ends when the sequence is empty. Initially the sequence being built up must be set to empty. After the loop, this sequence contains the reverse of the original.

2

What are the advantages of each of the implementations of REVERSE-SEQ?

3

The following procedure recursively copies a linked list:

```
Procedure CopySeq(Var copy : Seq; s : Seq);
{ post copy = s }
Begin
  If s = Nil Then
    copy := Nil
  Else
  Begin
    new(copy);
    copy^.head := s^.head;
    CopySeq(copy^.tail,s^.tail)
  End
End;
```

Propose a non-recursive alternative to the above procedure. This can be done by treating the first item as a special case, and copying it into the result. From then on, a local pointer to the last item in the new sequence can be used in a loop, which strips off the head of the remaining sequence and puts it on the end of the copy being built. Thus, the inside of the loop is similar to the right-append operation on word sequences in the KWIC case study. To facilitate this, the procedure must discriminate between the conditions of the original sequence being empty or not.

4

Attempt a non-recursive solution for the quick-sort procedure in the KWIC case study. Why is it difficult?

LABORATORY EXERCISE – to implement Index-entries

Purpose

To implement an abstract data type.

Problem

Write Pascal procedures and functions to implement the Index-entries abstract data type.

Specification

The type is specified as:

Index-entry = {some type}

Index-entries = Seq of Index-entry

The following procedures and functions must be implemented:

Procedure *CopyEntries*(**Var** *CopyIes* : *IndexEntries*; *ies* : *IndexEntries*);
{ *post CopyIes* = *ies* }

Function *EmptyEntries*(*ie* : *IndexEntries*) : *Boolean*;
{ *post EmptyEntries* = ([ ] = *ie*) }

Procedure *GetEmptyEntries*(**Var** *ie* : *IndexEntries*);
{ *post ie* = [ ] }

Function *AtLeast2Entries*(*ies* : *IndexEntries*) : *Boolean*;
{ *post AtLeast2Entries* = (*len*(*ies*) > 1) }

Procedure *GetHeadEntries*(**Var** *h* : *IndexEntry*; *ies* : *IndexEntries*);
{ *pre ies* ≠ [ ] }
{ *post hd ies* = *h* }

Procedure *GetTailEntries*(**Var** *t* : *IndexEntries*; *ies* : *IndexEntries*);
{ *pre ies* ≠ [ ] }
{ *post tl ies* = *t* }

Procedure *RightAppendEntries*(**Var** *ies* : *IndexEntries*; *ie* : *IndexEntry*);
{ *post* $\overline{ies}$ ⌢ [*ie*] = *ies* }

Procedure *AppendEntries*(**Var** *ie*1 : *IndexEntries*; *ie*2 : *IndexEntries*);
{ *post* $\overline{ie1}$ ⌢ *ie*2 = *ie*1 }

Procedure *WriteEntries*(**Var** *f* : *Text*; *ie* : *IndexEntries*);
{ *Opens f via rewrite, and then writes the elements of ie, in the form
    produced by 'WriteEntry'* }

Implementation

You must use the following Pascal types for the implementation:

IndexEntriesList = ^ *IndexEntriesListRec*;

IndexEntries = **Record**
                    head, last : *IndexEntriesList*
              End;

IndexEntriesListRec = **Record**
                            head : *IndexEntry*;
                            tail : *IndexEntriesList*
                      End;

You will need to use the following procedures and functions, which have
already been implemented:

Procedure *CopyEntry*(**Var** *CopyE* : *IndexEntry*; *e* : *IndexEntry*);
{ *post CopyE* = *e* }

Procedure *WriteEntry*(**Var** *f* : *Text*; *ie* : *IndexEntry*);
{ *Writes ie to the end of f, which must be open for writing.* }

Testing the implementation

How are you going to test your implementation? You should write a *simple*
test program that tests all of the operations. The program should be simple,
otherwise it is not clear how adequate the testing is. It does not matter what
the program does, or, indeed, whether it does anything sensible, as long as it
tests your implementation.

One problem is the type *IndexEntry*. To test your routines, it is
sufficient to use a simple type for this, rather than the complicated one in the
case study. Similarly, you should use simple definitions of the two assumed
procedures *CopyEntry* and *WriteEntry*. (This is called **stubbing**.) For example,
your test program might contain:

```
     ...
Type
     ...
     IndexEntry  =  Integer;

  ...

Procedure CopyEntry(Var CopyE : IndexEntry; e : IndexEntry);
{ post CopyE  =  e }
Begin
  CopyE :=  e
End;

Procedure WriteEntry(Var f : Text; ie : IndexEntry)
{ Writes ie to the end of f, which must be open for writing. }
Begin
  writeln(f,ie)
End;
```

String search – a simple software tool

MOTIVATION

The main purpose of this short case study is to stress further the abstract data type (ADT) approach to program design. It shows, over and above the previous KWIC example, how an ADT may be a reusable component rather than specific to just one program development.

The chapter also illustrates how programmers can be their own customers. That is, programmers need tools, just as electrical engineers need soldering irons, oscilloscopes, and so on, to make their work more efficient. Everyone is familiar with the two most common software tools – the text editor and the compiler. In this case study we hope to show how it is worthwhile developing other simple, single-functionality tools for the programmer.

9.1   Requirements

Cynthia Cynical works for Robustic Recipe – a large, but not very successful software house. Her job is to maintain the company's main database product. It's called Master Plaster, because it's meant to be a cure-all for data storage and retrieval problems. It's big, and, perhaps not entirely coincidentally, it doesn't work. Cynthia's job entails fixing an endless stream of reported bugs, and at the same time introducing more bugs, which will eventually get reported to her endless list.

> CYNTHIA: It's a living.

Her problem is that the software is indeed very large, and consists of 347 programs, each residing in a separate file. Cynthia originally authored none of it, and the programmer documentation is far from ideal. So it always takes her days to fix small bugs, never mind the more serious ones. Her boyfriend is convinced that she is becoming more and more like her name since she started the job three months ago. She gets most frustrated when she is trying to find a string, such as a file name, which she knows should occur in a few of the programs, but has no idea which. She gets tired of entering and exiting the text editor 347 times, just to search for a string.

> CYNTHIA: Yes – you should try it. (It's bad for your finger nails!)

The problem is one of trying to pierce an ear with a pile-driver. The editor is big and unwieldy because it has many functions built in, not just string search, and it must take a copy of the file just in case the user decides to change it. It can have no 'knowledge' of the fact that only a single search is to be performed.

Cynthia eventually complains to her boss, William Wise-Guy:

> WILLIAM: Oh! Why don't you write a utility program just to search for occurrences of a string in a file?
> CYNTHIA: I haven't got time to do that! I'm far too busy fixing the bugs! Can't somebody else do it?
> WILLIAM: It'll be worth spending the time, to save time later. You could even wrap the program in a simple command script so that it's applied to all your files.

Cynthia gets the impression that William will check to see if she has done what he suggested, so she decides she'd better do it. She writes down a requirement statement:

A program is required which, given a string and a text file, prints all lines from the file that contains the string, if any. There can be no assumptions about the maximum length of the string or the number or length of lines in the file.

(It may not surprise those readers who have never encountered a similar program that such utilities already exist on most reasonable operating systems. However, Robustic Recipe is a little detached from the real world.)

The requirement that no maximum length can be assumed is due to Cynthia's cynical disposition. She has heard of Sod's law.

> CYNTHIA: In any case, if a job is worth doing, it should be done properly or not at all.

9.2 Analysis

Some aspects of the requirements are still ambiguous, for example:

- Is the empty string always present in a line or always absent?
- If a line is exactly the search string does it still 'contain' it?
- If the string occurs more than once on a line should the line be printed a corresponding number of times?
- Where does the program obtain the string to search for, and the text to be searched?

Cynthia constructs a formal specification which records her resolutions of these ambiguities.

Exercise 9.1 The following is a customer's requirement statement for a spelling checker program. List all the ambiguities, omissions and likely mistakes that you can find in it. Suggest sensible resolutions of ambiguities, possible choices for the omissions, and corrections for the likely mistakes.

A program is required to check the spelling of documents. It should report all words, from a document, not present in any dictionary. Obvious grammatical rules, such as plurals, '-ing' endings, and so on, should also be dealt with.

9.3 Specification

The first step of the specification is concerned with defining the data types:

∃∀

String = Seq of Char

Text = Seq of String

The program can be specified as an operation SEARCH with one auxiliary function called matching-lines:

SEARCH

ext wr input   : Text *** search string obtained from first line ***
     wr output   : Text *** matching lines written to output ***
     rd search-text : Text *** the text to be searched ***

pre (input ≠ [ ])

post let search-string:String be hd($\overleftarrow{\text{input}}$) in
          output = matching-lines(search-string, search-text)
          and
          input = tl($\overleftarrow{\text{input}}$)

Now is a good time finally to introduce the formal definition of the **sub-sequence** operator in specifications. (This will help with your answer to the exercise coming shortly.)

The formal definition of the **sub-sequence** selection operator is:

$-[-, \ldots, -]$: (s : Seq of X, i : $\mathbb{N}$, j : $\mathbb{N}$) → (rs : Seq of X)

pre $0 < i \leq j + 1$ and $j \leq$ len(s)

post ∃ s1,s2:Seq of X •
        len(s1) = i – 1
        and
        len(s2) = len(s) – j
        and
        s1 ⁀ rs ⁀ s2 = s

The pre-condition has been chosen to permit extracting an empty sequence when

$i = j + 1$

and a singleton sequence when

$i = j$

```
matching-lines(search-string:String , search-lines:Text) → Text
matching-lines(search-string,search-lines) △
   if search-lines = [ ] then
      [ ]
   else
   if ∃ i,j ∈ inds(hd search-lines) •
         (i ≤ j and search-string = (hd search-lines)[i, . . . , j]) then
      [hd search-lines ] ⌢ matching-lines(search-string, tl(search-lines))
   else
      matching-lines(search-string, tl(search-lines))
```

The first line of the input file will be the string to be searched for. The file to be scanned is called search-text, and the results, if any, are to be written to the output file.

Most of the specification is contained in the recursive function matching-lines. If the search-lines parameter is empty, the result is the empty sequence. Otherwise, if the search string occurs in the first line of the text to be searched, the result is that line appended with the result of matching the rest of the text. Finally, if the search string is not present in the first line, the result is simply the value of matching-lines applied to the rest of the text.

Exercise 9.2   How have the first three ambiguities in the requirements statement given in the previous section been resolved, according to the specification? That is, is the empty string always or never present in a line, is the search string contained in itself, and how are multiple occurrences of a string on one line dealt with?

9.4 Design

Using top-down stepwise refinement, Cynthia constructs an abstract design:

```
program search
begin
   read search-string from input
   reset(search-text)
   while not eof(search-text)
      read a line from search-text
      if search-string is in the line then
         write the line
   end-of-while
end
```

Cynthia next asks herself whether Pascal has all the data types she needs for this problem. Sadly the answer is No! The program requires exactly the same string abstraction (Seq of Char) as used in the specification. She remembers that Pascal has only fixed-length strings; that is, for each string variable it is necessary to declare its length as a constant integer. Such fixed-length strings can neither grow nor contract as the program execution might demand. She wants **unbounded** strings.

A problem may be **unbounded** in its requirement for data. This means that, although every instance of the problem has a finite requirement, there is no upper bound on the requirement. That is, there is *always* the possibility of an instance that requires more than the one which has required the most so far. Such problems need data types which are unbounded. An unbounded data type has no upper limit on the size of data which can be stored, even though every value has a finite size.

Exercise 9.3 Pascal does directly have a type resembling an unbounded sequence of characters, but for pragmatic reasons it is too costly to use for this, and similar, applications. What is it?

Just as Cynthia is supposing that she will have to do some work to implement unbounded strings, she hears one of her colleagues talking to another about a 'strings package', or something. She asks them about it. They explain that the company has just recently purchased an abstract data type for unbounded strings of characters in Pascal from a small, but successful software house called Slow-Haste Software Services. Everyone at Robustic Recipe was reinventing the wheel by implementing un-bounded strings in every application program that needed them. Now, they are all very pleased that a better solution has been found.

An **abstract data type** may be so generally applicable, that it is a desirable thing to make an implementation of it available to many programs and programmers. Most computer installations have a software library, in which widely useful routines can be kept. An abstract data type implementation is an example of a **package** of such routines associated with one or more data types.

Cynthia doubts that this package will help her – how can it? Whoever it was that wrote it cannot possibly have known what she wants!

However, she decides to take a look at the documentation anyway. To Cynthia's amazement, she discovers that the package offers exactly what she wants, and more! Here are the three operations she can use:

Procedure *ReadlnSTRING*(**Var** *TextFile* : *Text*; **Var** *result* : *String*);

Procedure *WritelnSTRING*(**Var** *TextFile* : *Text*; *ThisString* : *String*);

Function *PosOfStringInSTRING*(*ThisString*,
                        PossibleSubString : *String*) : *Nat0*;

Nat0 is a type defined by the package to be the set of whole numbers between 0 and the largest integer, inclusive. The documentation tells Cynthia what these operations do. The first of the three operations reads a line from the text file into the given string variable. The second writes the value of the given string variable as a line to the file. The third operation locates the position of the second given string within the first, or, more to the point, returns zero if it is not found. If the second string is empty, the result is zero.

Exercise 9.4   What other string operations might be useful in a general-purpose string-handling package?

Cynthia hastily implements her design.

9.5   Implementation

She fills in the names of the operations, and types the program in.

```
Program search(input,output,SearchText);
Var SearchString, SearchLine : String;
     SearchText : Text;
Begin
    ReadlnSTRING(input,SearchString);
    reset(SearchText);
    While Not eof(SearchText) Do
    Begin
        ReadlnSTRING(SearchText,SearchLine);
        If PosOfStringInSTRING(SearchLine,SearchString) <> 0 Then
            WritelnSTRING(output,SearchLine);
    End;
End.
```

She tries it: it does not compile. From the error messages produced, Cynthia thinks that the Pascal compiler does not know anything about the strings package operations she has used. Looking at the package documentation again, she sees that she is supposed to use a **source inclusion directive** in the program.

A feature that is not strictly part of the Pascal language, but is found in most compilers and program development environments, is the facility of a **source inclusion directive**. This enables one to refer to a source file, by name, from within another program's source file. In Berkeley UNIX Pascal, this is written as

#include "filename"

The Pascal compiler switches to reading the named file on encountering the *#include* directive, and, on reaching the end of that file, returns to compiling from the line immediately following the *#include*. The syntax of such a mechanism differs from Pascal, system to system, but is seldom totally absent. It is so essential (and simple) that we should feel no guilt at using it, even though it is a non-standard Pascal language extension.

Rather than embed the details of the strings implementation in an application program that should not be concerned with them, the package has all the details that the Pascal compiler needs contained in a file called *strings.h*. Thus Cynthia adds the line

#include "strings.h"

in the appropriate place and tries again. This time the program compiles. Yippee! She then runs it. It crashes with a "pointer value out of range" error.

CYNTHIA: I knew it wouldn't work!

At that moment, William Wise-Guy steps into Cynthia's office.

WILLIAM: Hello. I hear you've decided to use the new strings package. What do you think of it?
CYNTHIA: It doesn't seem to work. I think I'll write my own routines.
WILLIAM: Let me see.

After looking at the program, William suggests that Cynthia ought to read the section on initialization and finalization in the package documentation. This she does and discovers that every string variable, *S*, must be initialized via the statement

InitSTRING(S)

before its first use, and finalized via

FinalSTRING(S)

after its last use, otherwise the package will not work. She is *convinced* that the author of the package is an awkward person with nothing better to do than catch people out. She certainly can't see any good reason for these rules, even though William assures her it is not uncommon with abstract data types for there to be some rules, such as initialization, which must be adhered to for them to work correctly.

She adds these lines to obtain the final program:

```
Program search(input, output, SearchText);

#include "strings.h"

Var SearchString, SearchLine : String;
    SearchText : Text;
Begin
  InitSTRING(SearchString);
  InitSTRING(SearchLine);
  ReadlnSTRING(input, SearchString);
  reset(SearchText);
  While Not eof(SearchText) Do
  Begin
    ReadlnSTRING(SearchText, SearchLine);
    If PosOfStringInSTRING(SearchLine, SearchString) <> 0 Then
      WritelnSTRING(output, SearchLine)
  End;
  FinalSTRING(SearchLine);
  FinalSTRING(SearchString)
End.
```

When she tries it this time, it works! Very soon she is whizzing through the bugs in Master Plaster, but she still thinks that the strings package author is awkward, and has a good mind to tell him so.

Exercise 9.5

(a)   Give an informal but precise explanation of the following formal specification:

F : (L : Seq of ℕ) → (R : Seq of ℕ)

post (∀ i ∈ {1 , . . . , len R − 1} • R[i] < R[i + 1])

    and

    elems L = elems R

(b)   Design a procedure to implement the specification in part (a). Your design should assume the abstract data types *SeqOfNat* and *SetOfNat* as defined below:

Type *SeqOfNat* = *some implementation of Seq of* ℕ
       SetOfNat = *some implementation of Set of* ℕ

Procedure *SetEmpty*(**Var** *S* : *SeqOfNat*);
post S = [ ]

Procedure *GetElems*(*SeqN* : *SeqOfNat*; **Var** *SetN* : *SetOfNat*);
post SetN = elems SeqN

Procedure *ExtractLargest*(**Var** *SetN* : *SetOfNat*; **Var** *largest* : *Integer*);
pre SetN ≠ { }
post largest ∈ $\overleftarrow{SetN}$
    and
    (not ∃ other ∈ $\overleftarrow{SetN}$ • other > largest)
    and
    SetN = $\overleftarrow{SetN}$ − { largest }

Procedure *FrontAppend*(*This* : *Integer*; **Var** *SeqN* : *SeqOfNat*)
post SeqN = [This] ⌢ $\overleftarrow{SeqN}$

Function *Cardinality*(*SetN* : *SetOfNat*) : *Integer*
Cardinality(SetN) △ Card(SetN)

Exercise 9.6 The following is a specification of an abstract type Queue:

Queue = Seq of Qel

with operations

newQ
ext wr qu : Queue
post [ ] = qu

enQ (e : Qel)
ext wr qu:Queue
post $\overleftarrow{q}$ ⌢ [e] = q

deQ
ext wr qu : Queue
    wr e : Qel
pre qu ≠ [ ]
post [e] ⌢ qu = $\overleftarrow{qu}$

is-emptyQ : Queue → 𝔹
is-emptyQ(qu) △ [ ] = qu

(a)   Propose an adequate Pascal data type representation of Queue. Discuss any advantages and/or limitations of your chosen representation.

(b)   Write a procedure or function in Pascal for each of the above Queue operations.

SUMMARY

This short chapter reinforced the abstract data type approach to program design. In this case, the abstract data type was a general-purpose package which can be used in many programs. The next chapter presents the full description of the strings package (and explains the need for those 'awkward' rules!). The implementation of the package is described in Chapter 12.

The following notations were introduced in this chapter.

Pascal notation

Source inclusion directive   *#include "strings.h"*

Specification of the strings package

MOTIVATION

This chapter presents the specification of the whole strings package. As well as being an example of how one might write the user guide for such a package, it is also a source of many formal specifications which have *not* been discussed in detail before you see them. Thus, reading this chapter gives you practice at understanding formal specifications. The implementation of the package is covered in Chapter 12.

The specification concept of **set difference** and the Pascal concepts of ***maxint*, procedural parameters** and **conformant arrays** are introduced.

The notation used is an appropriate mixture of Pascal and VDM. Pascal headings are given for each of the functions and procedures, together with an implicit or explicit specification.

10.1 Scenario

Cynthia gets more cynical about the motives of the author of the strings package.

> CYNTHIA: How dare he be so awkward!

She decides to visit Slow-Haste Software Services to demand an explanation! She takes a copy of the package documentation with her. It is written by a Mr R.U. Rigorous. When she arrives at the place, she meets a well dressed, red-haired woman.

> CYNTHIA: I'd like to see Mr Rigorous, please.
> RITA: I think you mean me!
> CYNTHIA: Are you R.U. Rigorous? Oh, errr... well, there are, that is, there seem to be some silly rules, well rules, in the strings package, the one you sold to Robustic Recipe. I've used it, I work for them, and, don't get me wrong, I think it's good, but well, there are these rules and I don't see why, and some of the other parts seem odd, and I've brought the documentation and, err, am I making sense?
> RITA: Hello. Sit down and perhaps we can work through it?
> CYNTHIA: Yes please.
> RITA: Right – let's make a coffee.

10.2 The strings package

So, over a cup of coffee, Cynthia and Rita read the documentation together. . . .

The Strings Package – User Guide
by
R.U. Rigorous

Introduction

The strings package described in this user guide implements a powerful string abstract data type which allows the user to perform many operations on unbounded variable length strings within a Pascal program. The usual Pascal definition,

    Packed Array [1 .. *n*] **Of** *Char*

gives strings of a fixed length which are not suitable in applications requiring variable, and in particular, unbounded length character sequences. In this documentation we refer to the usual Pascal strings as **static strings** and those implemented by the package as **dynamic strings.**
    The operations provided for dynamic strings include all those provided by Pascal for static strings. There are the six relational operators (= ,≠,>,≥,<,≤); the construction of string constants; the selection of an element at a particular position in a string; updating a string in a particular position and assignment of one string to another. The strings package also offers other useful operations, including finding the length of a string; reading strings from and writing strings to files; constructing the empty string; converting a character to a string; concatenating two strings together; replicating a string, say *n* times, to form a longer string, *n* times the length of the original; extracting a sub-string; converting between static and dynamic strings; and finding the position of a given sub-string in another string.

    CYNTHIA: Surely it wasn't necessary to have so many operations?
    RITA: Well, if the package is to be versatile and widely useful, it must have a wide range of operations. There is an almost endless range of possibilities. Did it have what you wanted?
    CYNTHIA: Hmmm. Carry on.

Special features

String values are shared between variables whenever possible. Thus, for example, in the case of concatenating two strings together, if there are no references to the first string, that string is reused in the result of the concatenation, rather than it being copied to a new area of memory. In addition to this sharing of strings by variables, once there are no variables at all referencing a string, the memory it takes up is reclaimed by the system.

Specification

Abstract data type

The string type may be regarded as an implementation of

> **Type** *String* = *Seq of Char { unbounded }*

The package regards the Pascal built-in type *Text* as an implementation of

> **Type** *Text* = *Seq of String*

where each line of text is a separate element, of type *String*.

The built-in Pascal type **Integer** is not infinite, and the cardinality of the type is language implementation dependent. However, there is a pre-declared constant called ***maxint*** which is defined as the highest positive integer, and the lowest negative integer for the particular Pascal implementation. In other words, *maxint* is defined as some value (usually a power of 2, minus 1) and *Integer* is defined as:

> **Type** *Integer* = - *maxint* .. *maxint*

In addition, the strings package defines two convenient natural number types as follows:

> **Type** *Nat0* = 0 .. *maxint*;
> *Nat*1 = 1 .. *maxint*

CYNTHIA: I suppose those look useful.

RITA: I included them really because I wanted to use them in the operations.

CYNTHIA: Hmmmm. It's the next bit that I thought was completely unnecessary.

Initialization and finalization

String variables (including elements of arrays of strings, string fields of records, and so on) *must* be initialized exactly once before they are first used, and *should* be finalized exactly once after they are no longer required. (If the variables are not finalized, the package will run out of memory sooner than it needs to.)

A string variable is initialized by the *InitSTRING* procedure, and finalized by the *FinalSTRING* procedure. Note that local variables must be initialized and finalized for *every* *instance* of the procedure or function in which they are defined.

CYNTHIA: I can't see why the variables should be initialized and finalized.

RITA: Okay, I'll tell you. The strings are stored in a dynamic structure and the package implements semi-automatic garbage collection. When a string variable is assigned a new value, the space occupied by the previous value is recovered so that it can be reused.

CYNTHIA: So?

RITA: Well, at the start of execution of a Pascal program, all the variables are undefined. If there were no initialization, what would happen when a string variable was assigned a value for the first time?

CYNTHIA: Err, I don't know.

RITA: Well, the package would try to recover the space occupied by the existing value, but there isn't one; at least, not a sensible one. There's no way of knowing if a variable has been given a value or is undefined. Not in Pascal.

CYNTHIA: So the program would crash?

RITA: Yes, the error message would probably be something like "Pointer variable out of range".

CYNTHIA: (*cough*) Hmmm, yes it probably would be. Err, what about finalization?

RITA: That is needed to recover the memory used by the value of a variable after that variable is no longer required. The package cannot know on its own whether a variable is finished with.

CYNTHIA: I see. Carry on.

In addition, there are other cases of initialization and finalization to be undertaken. Formal value parameters which are strings must be initialized within the procedure or function accepting the parameter *before* their *first* reference. This is done via *InitValParamSTRING*. Such parameters should also be finalized via *FinalSTRING* after their last reference within the procedure or function.

CYNTHIA: This is even stranger – but I suppose there's a good reason.

RITA: Yes, the package implements structure sharing. When a string is assigned to a variable, the value isn't actually copied. Instead, the variable assumes a pointer to the string.

When it comes to collect the memory used in a string (for example in finalization), it is important to know that there are no other pointers to it.

CYNTHIA: I see, but what's that got to do with value parameters?

RITA: A value parameter is given a copy of the actual parameter when the procedure or function is called. This means there is then an extra pointer to the string given as the actual parameter. The initialization here just tells the package that fact.

CYNTHIA: I half understand!

RITA: Well, if you want to know more, I suggest you read Chapter 12.

CYNTHIA: Hmmm. Carry on.

Lastly, there is a finalization that must be used when constructing the result of a function that returns a string. The value of the result should be built in a local variable of the function. This variable must be initialized. When the result is complete, it should be assigned to the name of the function through a special finalization primitive called *AssignFuncResultSTRING*. This *also* finalizes the variable used to build the result, which must not be referenced again, and must *not* be finalized via *FinalSTRING*. The following skeleton function illustrates this:

```
Function f(. . .) : String;
Var ResultVar : String;
  . . .
Begin
  InitSTRING(ResultVar);
  . . .
  { statements to build the result into ResultVar }
  . . .
  f := AssignFuncResultSTRING(ResultVar)
End;
```

There is a real example of a user defined function in the section on assignment of strings (next but one).

CYNTHIA: Well, explain this if you can!

RITA: Okay. It's all to do with the number of references to a string. The result of a function has no references to it – but that doesn't mean the value isn't needed. It might be that the result is going to be assigned to a variable, or used as a value parameter to another function. In both cases, there will be one reference to the string at that time. In other places, such as ordinary finalization and assignment, when the package-

discovers that there are no references left to a string value, it collects the memory occupied by it. That would be a disaster for function results!

CYNTHIA: Okay, you've convinced me. I might read Chapter 12 sometime to get more details.

RITA: Yes, I'd recommend that, but remember you don't need to know why these rules are important to use the package. You just need to obey them.

CYNTHIA: Okay, carry on.

If any of the above rules are violated, the strings package will not work correctly. (In particular, if the initializations are not performed, the package will cause run-time errors and, if the finalizations are not performed, the package will require considerably more memory.)

These, then, are the operations to perform initialization and finalization:

Procedure *InitSTRING*(**Var** *ThisString* : *String*);

post ThisString = [ ]

Procedure *InitValParamSTRING*(**Var** *ThisString* : *String*);
{
* *Initializes ThisString, which must be a value parameter of the*
* *procedure or function calling InitValParamSTRING, to be safely usable*
* *within the current procedure or function.*
* *Every value parameter must be initialized in this way.*
}

Procedure *FinalSTRING*(**Var** *ThisString* : *String*);
{
* *Reclaims the storage associated with the string ThisString.*
* *Every string variable should be finalized exactly once after its last use.*
}

Function *AssignFuncResultSTRING*(**Var** *ThisString* : *String*) : *String*;
{
* *Returns the value of the string ThisString and finalizes the variable*
* *ThisString.*
* *A string value should be assigned to a function result via this*
* *'function'.*
}

Exercise 10.1 Although *AssignFuncResultSTRING* is technically a Pascal function, why is it not a true function?

Exercise 10.2   Can you guess what data type is used to implement the type *String*?

String length

There is a function that yields the length of a string:

Function *LengthOfSTRING(ThisString* : *String*) : *Nat0*;

LengthOf STRING(ThisString) △ len (ThisString)

CYNTHIA: At least that's straightforward.

Assignment of strings

The normal Pascal assignment statement (: =) *must not* be used for assigning string values, otherwise the package will have unpredictable effects. The following operation must be used instead.

Procedure *AssignSTRING*(**Var** *lhs* : *String; rhs* : *String*);

pre true
post rhs = lhs

CYNTHIA: I thought this was very inconvenient indeed! Is it necessary?

RITA: I'm afraid so. The package allows string values to be shared between many variables by pointers. This works okay as long as the package knows about it.

CYNTHIA: So?

RITA: Imagine that two variables, *X* and *Y*, share the same string, and the package does not know because the normal Pascal assignment was used. What would happen if *X* was altered using an operation that updates in place?

CYNTHIA: Ah! The value of *Y* would get updated too!

RITA: Exactly. Now it would be nice to be able to redefine the usual assignment statement, or at least make its use a compile-time error. But that cannot be done in Pascal, so the responsibility stays with the programmer.

CYNTHIA: Oh. Carry on.

The exception to this is when assigning the result of a string-yielding function. This must be done via the *AssignFuncResultSTRING* primitive on the right-hand side of the assignment (: =) operation. For example, the following is a user-defined function to convert all capital letters in a string to the corresponding lower case letters (assuming the character set has contiguous alphabetic characters).

```
Function UpperToLower(ThisString : String) : String;
{ converts all upper to lower case in ThisString to give result }
Var result : String;
     ch : Char;
     index : Nat1;
Begin
   InitValParamSTRING(ThisString);
   InitSTRING(result);
   AssignSTRING(result,ThisString);
   FinalSTRING(ThisString);      { *** ThisString finalized here *** }
   For index := 1 To LengthOf STRING(result) Do
   Begin
      ch := IndexSTRING(result,index);
      If ch In ['A' .. 'Z'] Then
         ChangeCharInSTRING(result, index,
                              chr(ord(ch) - ord('A') + ord('a')))
   End;
   UpperToLower := AssignFuncResultSTRING(result);
End;
```

CYNTHIA: Hmmm. I've only just noticed – why is *ThisString* finalized so early on?

RITA: I'm glad you mentioned that, because I'm now thinking I should have brought attention to it in the guide. A string variable should be finalized after it is no longer required, such as here. If in doubt, or for the wary, it could be left to the end of the function.

CYNTHIA: Yes, that's what I would do.

RITA: That's fine, but there is an efficiency advantage to finalizing it earlier. The *ChangeCharInSTRING* operation must take a copy of the string if there is more than one reference to it. If *ThisString* is finalized after the loop, there certainly are at least two pointers to the value the first time the loop is executed. If it is finalized before the loop, there *might* be only one reference, depending on where the string came from outside the function.

CYNTHIA: So finalizing *ThisString* as soon as possible might save making an unnecessary copy of the string once it is in *result*?

RITA: You're getting the hang of it, but it's quite subtle and not so important to worry about at first. Should we go on?

Reading and writing strings to/from text files

When writing to a text file, the last line may be incomplete, but this is not so during reading. Consequently, the abstract view of *Text* as a sequence of strings is not quite appropriate for writing strings, unless one assumes the following abstract behaviour of the pre-declared procedures *rewrite*, *reset*, *write* and *writeln*:

- *rewrite* creates a sequence containing only one item, which is the empty string (line).

- Closing a file which is open for writing, by either ending the program or effecting a *reset* on it, discards the last item (line) if and only if it is an empty string.

- *write* adds its output to the last line, while *writeln* does this and then also adds on an empty line.

Bearing this abstract behaviour in mind, the following operations are provided for reading strings:

Procedure *ReadlnSTRING*(**Var** *TextFile* : *Text*; **Var** *result* : *String*);

pre   TextFile open for reading and not eof(TextFile)

post result = hd(TextFile) and TextFile = tl (TextFile)

CYNTHIA: So this reads the whole line into *result*.

RITA: Exactly. The next operation is more general and allows the user to pass a function as a parameter to define where the string ends.

A **parameter** to a procedure or function may itself be a **procedure** or **function**. These are declared in Pascal by giving a formal parameter name to the procedure or function, and specifying its parameters (and the result type for a function). The actual procedure or function passed as a parameter in a call does not have to have the same name, but its parameters (and result type for a function) must match in order, type and whether variable, value, or themselves procedure or function parameters. For example, there follows the skeleton of a sort procedure for arrays of *Integers* which can be given a function providing any non-reflexive total order relation on pairs of *Integers* (for example < or >):

```
Procedure sort(Var s : IntegerArray;
            Function order(i, j : Integer) : Boolean
            );
    Var pos : Integer . . .
        . . .
    If order(s[pos], s[pos + 1]) Then
        . . .
    . . .
    End
```

The *ReadSTRING* procedure is similar to *ReadlnSTRING*, except that it may stop reading *before* the end of a line, depending on a function parameter.

Procedure *ReadSTRING*(**Var** *TextFile* : *Text*;
                               Var *result* : *String*;
                               Function *stop*(*c* : *Char*) : *Boolean*);

pre   TextFile open for reading and not eof(TextFile)

post   let first-line : String be hd (TextFile) in
          (∃ n ∈ ℕ •
                stop (first-line[n])
                and (not ∃ m ∈ ℕ •
                            m < n and stop(first-line[m])
)
                and result = first-line [1 , . . . , n − 1]
                and TextFile = [first-line[n , . . . , len first-line]] ⌢ tl(TextFile)
)
          or
          ((not ∃ n ∈ ℕ • stop(first-line[n]))
            and result = first-line
            and TextFile = [ ] ⌢ tl(TextFile)
)

CYNTHIA: Wow! This is a bit more complicated.

RITA: True, but nevertheless a very useful operation.

CYNTHIA: Let's see – it's given a function, hmmm, yes. I'll see it in the end – I must admit I skipped this one when I read it.

RITA: Okay – try splitting it into bits. You see there are two main parts of the post-condition? Look at the last part first, as that seems easier.

CYNTHIA: There does not exist a position in the first line so that the *stop* function is true for the character at that position. So then it reads the whole line, just like *ReadlnSTRING*.

RITA: Yes, but there is a subtle difference.

CYNTHIA: I see it. Now what about the other case?

RITA: That's when there is a position at which the *stop* function is true.

CYNTHIA: And there does not exist an earlier position – ah I see, it must be the first place where it's true.

RITA: Yes.

CYNTHIA: Then it reads the first line up to that point, no, one place before it.

RITA: You've got it.

Exercise 10.3 What is the subtle difference that Cynthia noticed? Why do you think this difference is justified?

There are two operations provided for writing strings to text files. *WriteSTRING* writes a string to a text file, appending it to the last line in the file:

Procedure *WriteSTRING*(**Var** *TextFile* : *Text*; *ThisString* : *String*);

pre TextFile open for writing

post TextFile = $\overline{\text{TextFile}}$[1 , . . . , len($\overline{\text{TextFile}}$) – 1]
         $\frown$ [$\overline{\text{TextFile}}$[len($\overline{\text{TextFile}}$)] $\frown$ [ThisString]]

CYNTHIA: Hmmm, one has to be careful with the square brackets in these post-conditions.

WritelnSTRING appends a string on to the end of the last line in a text file, and then appends an empty line on to the end of the file:

Procedure *WritelnSTRING*(**Var** *TextFile* : *Text*; *ThisString*: *String*);

pre TextFile open for writing

post TextFile = $\overline{\text{TextFile}}$ [1 , . . . , len($\overline{\text{TextFile}}$) – 1]
         $\frown$ [$\overline{\text{TextFile}}$[len($\overline{\text{TextFile}}$)] $\frown$ [ThisString]] $\frown$ [[ ]]

CYNTHIA: I can see now why we have to assume that strange abstract behaviour of *write* and *writeln*.
RITA: Yes – I couldn't think of another way of specifying it all.

Construction of strings

Now the operations concerned with constructing strings are specified. There is a function that yields the empty string:

Function *EmptySTRING* : *String*;

EmptySTRING $\triangle$ [ ]

CYNTHIA: Why wasn't this declared as a constant?
RITA: Well, Pascal doesn't allow what I needed. But it doesn't really make any difference.

Another function converts a single character into a string:

Function *CharToSTRING*(*ThisChar* : *Char*) : *String*;

CharToSTRING(ThisChar) $\triangle$ [ThisChar]

The function *ConcatSTRING* appends two strings together to yield a string result:

Function *ConcatSTRING(s1, s2 : String) : String;*

ConcatSTRING(s1, s2) △ s1 ⌢ s2

There is a function to replicate a string a number of times, concatenating all the replicas together.

Function *ReplicateSTRING(RepString : String;*
                          RepCount : Nat0) : String;

post len(ReplicateSTRING) = RepCount * len(RepString)
    and
    ∀ i ∈ inds ReplicateSTRING •
        ReplicateSTRING[i] = RepString[((i − 1) mod len(RepString)) + 1]

CYNTHIA: Hmmm, I always have to think about these. Why do you subtract one before the mod, and then add one after? Don't they just cancel out?

RITA: It wouldn't be needed if string indices started at zero, but they start at one. Think about, say, when i is 4 and the length of *RepString* is also 4.

CYNTHIA: Errr, ahh. Yes – I see now.

The function *ChangeCharInSTRING* replaces the character at a given position in a string by another given character. The position may be beyond the end of the string, in which case it is first appended with enough spaces to make its length up to the position. First, we define a max auxiliary function.

max : (i : ℕ , j : ℕ) → (m : ℕ)
post (m = i or m = j)
    and
    (m ⩾ i) and (m ⩾ j)

A set may be subtracted from another set by the **set difference** operator. This yields another set which has exactly all the elements of one set, which are not members of the other.

_ – _ : (s1 : Set of X , s2 : Set of X) → (r : Set of X)

post (∀ e ∈ s1 •
            if e ∈ s2 then not(e ∈ r)
            else e ∈ r)
)
    and
    (∀ e ∈ r • r ∈ s1)

∃∀ For example,

$$\{ 12, 34, 5, 6, 13 \} - \{ 74, 13, 82, 34, 123 \} = \{ 12, 5, 6 \}$$

Procedure *ChangeCharInSTRING*(**Var** *UpdateString* : *String*;
UpdatePos : *Nat* 1;
UpdateChar : *Char*);

post len UpdateString = max(UpdatePos, len($\overleftarrow{\text{UpdateString}}$))
   and
    ∀ i ∈ inds($\overleftarrow{\text{UpdateString}}$) − { UpdatePos } •
    UpdateString[i] = $\overleftarrow{\text{UpdateString}}$[i]
    and
    UpdateString[UpdatePos] = UpdateChar
    and
      ∀ i ∈ (inds(UpdateString) − inds($\overleftarrow{\text{UpdateString}}$)) − { UpdatePos } •
      UpdateString[i] = ' '

CYNTHIA: Why did you pick such an obscure way of writing it?
RITA: Oh − I thought it was nice. How would you write it?
CYNTHIA: Hmmm, I'd obviously divide it into the two parts, corresponding to whether the update position is beyond the end of the string, or not. Like this:

post if UpdatePos ⩽ len ($\overleftarrow{\text{UpdateString}}$) then
    UpdateString[UpdatePos] = UpdateChar
  else
    UpdateString = $\overleftarrow{\text{UpdateString}}$
         ⌢ spaces(UpdatePos − len $\overleftarrow{\text{UpdateString}}$ − 1)
         ⌢ [UpdateChar]

CYNTHIA: Assuming spaces(n) returns a string of n spaces.
RITA: Oh − that's not quite right. What you need is . . .

Exercise 10.4 What is wrong with Cynthia's post-condition? How would Rita correct it?

Indexing and sub-string extraction

There are two functions provided for extracting sub-parts of a string. *IndexSTRING* yields the character at a given position in a given string:

Function *IndexSTRING(ThisString : String; i : Nat 1) : Char;*

pre i ≤ LengthOfSTRING(ThisString)

IndexSTRING(ThisString, i) △ ThisString[i]

GetSubSTRING yields a sub-string of a given string, between two positions. It is similar to the sub-sequence of specifications, but has no pre-condition.

Function *GetSubSTRING(ThisString : String; FromPos : Nat 1;*
                              ToPos : Nat 0) : String;

GetSubSTRING(ThisString,FromPos,ToPos) △
    if FromPos ≤ ToPos ≤ len ThisString then
        ThisString[FromPos , . . . , ToPos]
    else
        [ ]

Conversion between static and dynamic strings

Operations are provided to convert between static and dynamic strings.

It is often required to have a procedure or function which can accept arrays of various sizes as a parameter. Although each Pascal array has a fixed size, the language allows parameters to be defined as **conformant arrays.** A conformant array is a formal parameter which is an array, for which the element type and the index type are defined, but for which the lower and upper bounds of the indices are left unspecified. The array may be packed, and may be a variable or value parameter. For example:

```
Procedure sort(Var list : Array [lo .. hi : Integer] Of Integer);
Var scan,pos,max,swap : Integer;
Begin
  For scan := 1 To hi – lo Do
  Begin
    max := hi – scan + 1;
    For pos := lo To hi – scan Do
      If list[pos] > list[max] Then
        max := pos;
    swap := list[max];
    list[max] := list[hi – scan + 1];
    list[hi – scan + 1] := swap
  End
End;
```

This procedure takes an array of integers, indexed by integers as a variable parameter.

The index range has not been fixed, but instead the lowest and highest index values are called *lo* and *hi* respectively. This enables the procedure to sort the array by referring to *lo* and *hi* as variables. It may be applied to any array of *Integer* indexed by any sub-range of *Integer*.

A restriction is placed on the use of formal conformant arrays as actual parameters to other procedures, based on the need for the Pascal compiler to be able to predict statically the exact size of each actual conformant array parameter. The restriction is that a formal conformant array value parameter may not be passed on as an *actual* value parameter. (However, it may be passed as an actual variable parameter).

(Conformant arrays are available in level 1 standard Pascal, but not in level 0.)

A function is provided to convert a static string into a dynamic string:

Function *MakeSTRING*(
        static : **Packed Array**[*lo* .. *hi* : *Integer*] **Of** *Char*) : *String*;

Similarly, a dynamic string may be turned into a static string. This will cause truncation if the static string is too small, or space filling if it is too big:

Procedure *MakeStaticSTRING*(
        dynamic : *String*;
        Var *static* : **Packed Array**[*lo* .. *hi* : *Integer*] **Of** *Char*);

```
post let static-len be hi - lo + 1 in
        if static-len > len(dynamic) then
           ( ∀ i ∈ { lo , . . . , lo + len(dynamic) - 1 } •
             static[i] = dynamic[i - lo + 1]
           )
           and
           ( ∀ i ∈ { lo + len(dynamic) , . . . , hi } •
             static[i] = ' '
           )
        else
           ( ∀ i ∈ { lo , . . . , hi } •
             static[i] = dynamic[i - lo + 1]
           )
```

CYNTHIA: Why did you choose to space fill it? Why not use some other character?
RITA: Yes, indeed. What other character did you have in mind?
CYNTHIA: Hmmmm.

String matching

The function *PosOfStringInSTRING* takes two strings and returns the position of the second in the first as a proper sub-sequence, or zero if such a position does not exist.

Function *PosOfStringInSTRING(ThisString,*
                     PossibleSubString : String) : Nat0;

post (∃ i,j ∈ inds(ThisString) •
          (i ≤ j and ThisString[i , . . . , j] = PossibleSubString
          and not (∃ k, l ∈ inds(ThisString) •
                    (k < i and ThisString[k , . . . , l] = PossibleSubString))
          and PosOfStringInSTRING = i))
     or
     (not ∃ i,j ∈ inds(ThisString) •
          (i ≤ j and ThisString[i , . . . , j] = PossibleSubString
          and PosOfStringInSTRING = 0))

CYNTHIA: It took me a little while to see if the empty string is considered as a sub-string for this operation, when I used it.

RITA: Yes, I suppose I could have pointed out in the text that it isn't.

Exercise 10.5

(a) What part of the post-condition of *PosOfStringInSTRING* tells Cynthia that the empty sequence is not considered present in another string?

(b) What change could one make to the post-condition so that the empty sequence is considered as present?

(c) Suppose *PossibleSubString* occurs more than once in *ThisString*. Which position is returned?

String comparisons

Finally, the package provides six comparison functions, each taking two strings and returning a Boolean result. These are defined in terms of the lexicographical ordering relation on sequences of characters:

Function *EqualSTRING(left,right : String) : Boolean*;

EqualSTRING(left,right) △ left = right

Function *NotEqualSTRING(left,right : String) : Boolean*;

NotEqualSTRING(left,right) △ left ≠ right

Function *GreaterSTRING(left,right : String) : Boolean*;

GreaterSTRING(left,right) △ left > right

Function *GreaterOrEqualSTRING(left,right : String) : Boolean*;

GreaterOrEqualSTRING(left,right) △ left ⩾ right

Function *LessSTRING(left,right : String) : Boolean*;

LessSTRING(left,right) △ left < right

Function *LessOrEqualSTRING(left,right : String) : Boolean*;

LessOrEqualSTRING(left,right) △ left ⩽ right

The Pascal operators = and <> *must not* be used on strings, even though they would not cause a compile-time error.

Exercise 10.6 Using the strings package, design and implement a Pascal function to count the number of lines in a given text file in which the string 'sob story' occurs.

Using the strings package

The strings abstract data type package is made available to an application program by including the compiler directive

   #include "strings.h"

and compiling the program together with the pre-compiled package object code. All the operations described in this guide may be used in the applications program by calling the appropriate **Procedure** or **Function** in the usual way, as if it had been declared in the program by the user.

Example

The following program illustrates how the package is used. The program concatenates consecutive pairs of input lines of a text file and outputs them to another text file. If the number of input lines is odd, the last line written to the output file is simply the last line of the input file.

   Program *ConcatLines(InText, OutText)*;
   {
   * *Concatenates consecutive pairs of input lines of a text file and*
   * *outputs them to another text file. If the number of input lines is odd,*
   * *the last line written to the output file is simply the last line of the*
   * *input file.*
   }

   #include "strings.h"

```
Var InLine1, InLine2, OutLine : String;
    InText, OutText : Text;
Begin
  InitSTRING(InLine1);
  InitSTRING(InLine2);
  InitSTRING(OutLine);
  reset(InText);
  rewrite(OutText);
  While not eof(InText) Do
  Begin
    ReadlnSTRING(InText, InLine1);
    If eof(InText) Then
      AssignSTRING(OutLine,InLine1)
    Else
    Begin
      ReadlnSTRING(InText,InLine2);
      AssignSTRING(OutLine,ConcatSTRING(InLine1,InLine2))
    End;
    WritelnSTRING(OutText,OutLine)
  End;
  FinalSTRING(InLine1);
  FinalSTRING(InLine2);
  FinalSTRING(OutLine)
End. { ConcatLines }
```

RITA: Well, we've got to the end.

CYNTHIA: Thanks. I do feel a lot better about it, but I can't really see it being used very widely. It doesn't let you, say, replace all occurrences of one string by another.

RITA: Not directly, but that can be written fairly easily.

Exercise 10.7 Write a function that takes three dynamic strings and returns a dynamic string result. The result is the first string with all non-overlapping occurrences of the second string replaced by the third. An efficient version would be iterative and make use of *PosOfStringInSTRING*. A recursive specification is:

```
string-replace : (main : String , replace : String , replacement : String)
            → String

pre replace ≠ [ ]

string-replace(main,replace,replacement) △
  If len main < len replace then main
  else
    if main[1 , ... , len replace] = replace then
      replacement
        ⌢ string-replace (main[len replace + 1 , ... , len main],
                          replace, replacement)
    else
      [hd main]
        ⌢ string-replace(tl main, replace, replacement)
```

Exercise 10.8   You have been commissioned to write an application program requiring the manipulation of integers in the range $-\infty$ (minus infinity) to ∞ (infinity). Pascal integers have only values between negative and positive *maxint* inclusive. Pascal reals are similarly inadequate, because of the limitation on the number of significant figures.

   The application requires the operations: add, subtract, multiply, div and mod. It also requires assignment of large integers, and input from and output to text files.

   Describe how you would tackle the problem using the abstract data type approach. Write Pascal type definitions that would constitute an adequate representation of the type. Describe, perhaps with examples, how this representation relates to the corresponding abstract values. Write a procedure or function for each of the required operations.

Exercise 10.9   The operations add, remove1 and remove2 are specified as follows:

```
add (x : ℕ)
ext wr s : Seq of ℕ
pre true
post s = [x] ⁀ s̅

remove1 r : ℕ
ext wr s : Seq of ℕ
pre s ≠ [ ]
post s̅ = [r] ⁀ s

remove2 r : ℕ
ext wr s : Seq of ℕ
pre s ≠ [ ]
post s̅ = s ⁀ [r]
```

The abstract data type X is defined to be

   Seq of ℕ

together with the operations add and remove1. The abstract data type Y is defined to be

   Seq of ℕ

together with the operations add and remove2.

(a)   Many 'real-life' (non-computing) situations can be modelled by use of the data types X and Y. Give examples for each.

(b)   Describe a Pascal data structure to represent the values of the abstract data type X and provide implementations for its operations. (You may not assume that the sequences are bound in length.)

(c)   Describe any difficulties that would arise in implementing the abstract data type Y using the above Pascal data structure. Suggest an alternative data structure that alleviates these difficulties.

SUMMARY

This chapter served as an example of how one might write the user guide for an abstract data type package. It should also have been useful to study the formal specifications, as they were not discussed in detail before they were presented. The implementation of the strings package is covered in Chapter 12.

The specification concept of **set difference** and the Pascal concepts of *maxint*, **procedural parameters** and **conformant arrays** were presented.

The following notations were introduced in this chapter.

Specification notation

Set difference   inds(UpdateString) – {UpdatePos}

Pascal notation

Largest integer	*maxint*
Procedure parameter	**Procedure** *ReadSTRING*(... **Function** *stop* ...)
Conformant array	**Function** *MakeSTRING*(
	static : **Packed Array** [*lo* .. *hi*] **Of** *Char*)
	: *String*

TUTORIAL EXERCISE

This exercise attempts to reinforce your knowledge of the following areas:

(a)   The abstract data type (ADT) approach to program design.

(b)   The use of the String ADT.

(c)   Implementing the ADT Set of String, using dynamic data structures.

Imagine a program that checks the spelling of a document against a collection of words. This collection of words consists of two 'dictionaries', one fixed and the other alterable. The fixed dictionary would be very large, and would be stored on the machine in some library, but accessible by every user. The other dictionary would be smaller and privately owned by the user of the program. The private dictionary would contain words specific to the user's requirements, for example, names of people and technical jargon. The input to the program is a document, and the output is the same document, but with some words corrected. Any words in the input document which do not occur in either of the dictionaries are displayed on the standard output. The user may then enter the correct spelling of that word, or state that it is spelt correctly. The correct spelling of the word is added to the private dictionary. The main dictionary is not altered by the program.

The dictionaries are stored in text files, and thus need to be read by the program and stored in the Set of String abstract data type. Each word in the document needs to be searched for in the dictionaries, to check whether the word is spelt correctly. New words are added only occasionally to the private dictionary, and never to the main dictionary. The private dictionary needs to be written back to the text file when the program ends, if it has changed.

The set of string operations needed by the program are:

SetOfString = Set of String

initSS
ext wr ss : SetOfString
post { } = ss   (* initialize, always first op *)

isemptySS: (ss : SetOfString) → Boolean
isemptySS(ss) △ { } = ss   (* true iff ss is the empty set *)

ismemberSS: (s : String,ss : SetOfString) → Boolean
ismemberSS(s, ss) △ s ∈ ss   true iff s is in the set ss *)

chooseSS : (ss : SetOfString) → (any : String)
pre ss ≠ { }
post any ∈ ss   (* pick a string from a non-empty set *)

insertSS(s : String)
ext wr ss : SetOfString
post {s} ∪ s̄s̄ = ss   (* add s to the set ss *)

deleteSS(s : String)
ext wr ss : SetOfString
post ss = s̄s̄ – {s}   (* delete s from the set ss *)

1

Suggest various different representations of SetOfString, and associated algorithms for the operations, together with their appropriateness for the spelling program in terms of time and space efficiency.

2

Propose a simple, yet adequate representation and write the bodies of some of the seven operations.

Birds and bees

(All you ever wanted to know and were too afraid to ask)

MOTIVATION
The main emphasis in this case study is the importance of requirements analysis, in the domain of an unfamiliar discipline, and the use of **two-dimensional arrays** and the concepts of **error recovery** and **error routines**. Some subtle aspects of run-time efficiency are exposed in the implementation. Of course, the case study provides lots of experience of program specification and design, and hard work for Rita!

11.1   Scenario

Rita is commencing a new contract as a programmer in the biology department of Bell-Fruit University, Upper Middle Hampton (UK). She likes the new department – everyone seems so nice, including her immediate boss, Professor Rosemary Pollen. Thus Rita is not worried that she knows nothing about biology. That is, until the *afternoon* of her first day!

 ## 11.2   Requirements

PROFESSOR POLLEN: Right – as your first assignment, I want you to write a population behaviour simulation program.

RITA: Eh?

PROFESSOR POLLEN: Yes, we will use it to demonstrate population behaviour to first-year undergraduates.

RITA: I can't do that! Can I?

PROFESSOR POLLEN: It must be possible for the user to set the data governing the behaviour.

RITA: Err...

PROFESSOR POLLEN: And there'll be two types of beasts – let's say birds and bees. Birds eat bees. Yes, I like that. The birds eat the bees. They all live in the forest, but birds eat bees. The students will like the puerility.

RITA: Err..

PROFESSOR POLLEN: Of course, it doesn't really matter what they're called.

A feeling of panic almost overwhelms Rita – how on earth can she undertake such a task? What does she know about birds and bees (that could be printed here!)? Then she remembers all about requirements analysis. Thank goodness!

RITA: (*with confidence*) Okay, we'll have to sort out the more specific requirements.

PROFESSOR POLLEN: Oh. Yes, I suppose so.

After a time, Rita has extracted a list of informal requirements as follows:

The forest consists of a number of cells of equal size. Each cell is capable of supporting at most one bird. It may also support a number of bees, up to a maximum. The bird in a cell eats a fixed percentage of the bees in the cell. The bees in a cell multiply by a fixed amount per generation. A bird has a fitness, which is increased by the number of bees it eats. A bird spends a fixed percentage of its fitness per generation, simply living. With a fitness at or above some fixed level (the fertile level), a bird is fertile and will reproduce eight birds, enough to fill all the neighbouring cells which do not contain a bird. A reproducing bird loses the fixed fertility level of fitness in the reproduction process. A bird with a fitness of zero is not alive.

The program must graphically show the forest, updating the display after each generation. The simulation ends if static equilibrium is obtained. (This means that a subsequent generation would not alter the forest.) Otherwise the simulation continues forever.

She takes these requirements away to analyse them. Certainly, it seems, Rita needs some more information and clarification. She formulates a list of questions which she presents to Rose, who patiently supplies the answers.

RITA: Can fitness be less than zero?

PROFESSOR POLLEN: No.

RITA: Is it the case that a dead bird does not eat bees? (The requirements suggest that they do!)

PROFESSOR POLLEN: Yes, dead birds do not eat bees.

RITA: Is exactly one point of fitness added to a bird for each bee eaten by it?

PROFESSOR POLLEN: Yes.

RITA: Is there a difference between a cell containing a dead bird and a cell not containing a bird (assuming the bees are the same)?

PROFESSOR POLLEN: No.

RITA: How often do birds reproduce? – What is a generation?

PROFESSOR POLLEN: A bird reproduces at most once per generation. A generation is the period of time during which a bird may, if fit enough, reproduce once.

RITA: Where do these fixed percentages and levels come from?

PROFESSOR POLLEN: The fixed factors are only fixed during a simulation. They are actually obtained from the user at run-time.

RITA: What is the initial state of the forest?

PROFESSOR POLLEN: The initial forest should be set up by the user, along with the fixed factors.

RITA: How is the forest to be displayed?

PROFESSOR POLLEN: Any method that allows a visual interpretation of the forest state, with actual bird and bee distributions and fitness.

RITA: How big is the forest?

PROFESSOR POLLEN: The bigger the better, but perhaps limited by the size of the screen and the chosen method of display.

RITA: What sort of machine, and what language is to be used?

PROFESSOR POLLEN: Ah, good point. It must run on the departmental Bozo 1.001 microcomputers using Pascal. By the way, these have no graphics facilities.

Rita studies these replies in the context of the original requirements, in the hope of finding more ambiguities. However, her lack of knowledge of biology deprives her of an intuitive understanding of the problem, so she starts to construct the formal specification.

Exercise 11.1   The following is a customer's requirement statement for a hospital's nurse's shift rota program. List all the ambiguities, omissions and likely mistakes that you can find in it. Suggest sensible resolutions of ambiguities, possible choices for the omissions, and corrections for the likely mistakes.

> A program is required to manage the shift rota of the nursing staff on a hospital ward. A shift must comprise within one half of the total number of staff available. Student nurses must not be more than twice the qualified staff. There must be at least one SRN per shift. All staff must not work more than three weekends from four.

11.3   Specification

Rita starts by attempting to formalize all the informal rules that transform the forest between successive generations. She postulates that the forest is a **matrix** of cells, x-max by y-max big:

x-max:ℕ   y-max:ℕ

These will be constants based on the screen size and the display method, and will be chosen later.

As you have already seen, an **array** is a bounded structure of elements, each accessed by an index in some range. They have been largely used in Pascal so far to implement short sequences. In general, an N-dimensional array is a bounded structure requiring N indices, in N ranges, to access an element. All the elements are the same type. In principle, the index types could be anything, but in Pascal they must be **scalar**, which means that they have a notion of successor. (For example, *Integer, Boolean, Char*: given one value there is, in general, a next one. This is not true of *Real*.) In particular, a two-dimensional array is often called a **matrix**.

For example, a chess board could be defined in Pascal, assuming the type *Piece* as

Var *ChessBoard* : **Array**[1..8, 1..8] **Of** *Piece*;

The indices do not have to be the same size, or indeed sub-ranges of the same type.

She constructs a type specification of the forest, borrowing notation from Pascal:

```
Forest = Array [1..x-max, 1..y-max] of Cell

Cell = Record
           bees : N { count of bees }
           bird : N { fitness of bird, 0 = dead }
        end
```

The program essentially applies certain rules to the matrix, to obtain the new forest after a generation. First Rita considers the birds eating. Living birds consume a fixed percentage of the bees in their cell. In this transformation, the final value of each cell is a simple function of the initial value of the corresponding cell. All cells can be considered via all pairs x, y indexing them:

```
birds-eating : (before : Forest , bird-efficiency : N)
                  → (after : Forest)
{bird-efficiency = percentage of bees that birds eat}

post
    ∀ x ∈ {1,...,x-max}, y ∈ {1,...,y-max} •
       (if before[x,y].bird = 0 then
           after[x,y] = before[x,y]
        else
           let feed : N be ( (before[x,y].bees) * bird-efficiency) div 100 in
               after[x,y] = mk-Cell(before[x,y].bees - feed ,
                                     before[x,y].bird + feed)
```

Rita notes the assumption she has made concerning the rounding errors of the div operator. At a convenient time (before implementation!) she must check with Professor Pollen that this is acceptable.

Next she considers birds spending fitness by living. A living bird loses a fixed percentage of fitness each generation. Again, there is a direct correspondence between initial and final cells:

birds-living : (before : Forest , bird-energy-use : $\mathbb{N}$)
            → (after : Forest)
{ bird-energy-use = percentage fitness spent living }

post
  ∀ x ∈ {1 , . . . , x-max}, y ∈ { 1 , . . . , y-max } •
    (let loss : $\mathbb{N}$ be ((before[x,y].bird) * bird-energy-use) div 100 in
      after[x,y] = mk-Cell(before[x,y].bees , before[x,y].bird − loss)
)

Again she makes a note to check that the rounding implied here is acceptable.

Thirdly she considers bees breeding. They increase by a fixed multiple each generation, up to a maximum fixed level. Attempting to formalize this makes her realize its ambiguity: if by breeding the bees would be bigger than the maximum, do they still breed at all? Rita decides that it is probable that they do, that is, bees breed by the multiplier, but the number of them is truncated to the maximum number. However, this assumption must be checked later.

bees-breeding : (before : Forest , fertility : $\mathbb{N}$, maximum : $\mathbb{N}$)
            → (after : Forest)

{ fertility = multiplication of bees due to breeding }

post
  ∀ x ∈ {1,...,x-max}, y ∈ {1,...,y-max} •
    after[x,y] = mk-Cell(min(before[x,y].bees * fertility, maximum) ,
                    before[x,y].bird)

The specification of min is trivial.

Exercise 11.2   Famous last words! Try writing the specification of the min function: it takes two natural numbers and returns the smaller of them. Once you've done that, write it again in a completely different way.

Finally she specifies the reproduction of birds. This is more difficult, as a fertile bird will give birth to a new bird in all the vacant squares round it. Consequently, there is not a functional correspondence between the value of a cell in the final forest and the corresponding cell in the initial forest alone. As she studies the transformation in more detail, she realizes that the requirements did not state how fit a newborn bird is! Well, this won't affect the specification too much, so she just adds this to her list of questions.

The bees are unaffected by this transformation. Also, living but infertile birds are not changed. Cells without a bird (bird value is zero)

have a newborn bird if the cell has a fertile neighbour. Fertile birds lose
the 'fertile-level' of fitness. Rita makes use of an auxiliary function to
determine whether a cell is a neighbour of another:

is-neighbour : (x : $\mathbb{N}$, y : $\mathbb{N}$, xn : $\mathbb{N}$, yn : $\mathbb{N}$) → $\mathbb{B}$

is-neighbour(x,y,xn,yn) △
   - 2 < x - xn < 2
  and
   - 2 < y - yn < 2
  and
  not ((x,y) = (xn,yn))

Then she specifies the birds breeding as:

birds-breeding : (before : Forest, fertile-level : $\mathbb{N}$)
              → (after : Forest)

post
  ∀ x ∈ {1, . . . , x-max} , y ∈ {1, . . . , y-max} •
  (after[x,y].bees = before[x,y].bees
  and
  let fitness : $\mathbb{N}$ be before[x,y].bird in
    (fitness > 0 and fitness < fertile-level ⇒ after[x,y].bird = fitness)
    and
    (fitness ⩾ fertile-level ⇒
      after[x,y].bird = (fitness - fertile-level)
      and
      ∀ xn ∈ {1, . . . , x-max} , yn ∈ {1, . . . , y-max} •
        is-neighbour(x,y,xn,yn) and before[xn,yn].bird = 0
        ⇒ after[xn,yn].bird = ? *** newborn level ***
)
    and
    (fitness = 0
     and
    (not ∃ xn ∈ {1, . . . , x-max} , yn ∈ {1, . . . , y-max} •
      is-neighbour(x,y,xn,yn) and before[xn,yn].bird ⩾ fertile-level
) ⇒ after[x,y].bird = 0
)
)

Having completed the above specification, she notes that a more succinct
version can be constructed, in which the rule considers each cell of the
result in turn. This is because the rule is equivalent to saying that all
fertile birds lose the fertile level of fitness, and a bird is born in a vacant
cell if and only if the cell has a fertile neighbour.
    Before rewriting the specification, she checks with her boss about
the fitness of a newborn bird, the use of the div operator, and her
interpretation of the maximum number of bees in a cell. Perhaps not

surprisingly, a newborn bird has a fitness of 1, and her truncation of bee multiplication was a correct assumption.

> RITA: Another thing – I'm not sure about the percentage calcula-
> tions, whether to use div or not?
> PROFESSOR POLLEN: Eh? Is it expensive?
> RITA: Ahh, sorry. I'll explain what I mean ...

Rita finds out that downward rounding of the amount of feed is appropriate for birds-eating, because (she is told) it is important that a bird does not eat all the bees in its cell, unless its efficiency is 100%. (That is, even if the bird-efficiency is 99%, a bird will always leave at least one bee uneaten.) This means that her assumption for the use of div was correct in this case.

On the other hand (she is told) it must be possible for a bird to die by losing its fitness due to living. Thus, for example, for a 20% bird energy-use and a fitness of 2, rather than losing 20% of 2 (which equals 0 via div) the bird should *retain* a fitness of 80% of 2 (which equals 1 via div). Hence, with a fitness of 1 and a positive fitness loss, a bird will die. Thus her assumption about the use of div in birds-living was wrong.

Rita goes away to amend the specifications.

birds-living : (before : Forest , bird-energy-use : $\mathbb{N}$)
                    $\rightarrow$ (after : Forest)
{ bird-energy-use = percentage fitness spent living }

post
    $\forall$ x $\in$ {1,...,x-max} , y $\in$ {1,...,y-max} $\bullet$
       after[x,y] = mk-Cell(before[x,y].bees ,
                                (before[x,y].bird * (100 – bird-energy-use)) div 100)

Exercise 11.3   If a bird has a fitness of 4, and the bird-energy-use is 60%, what will be its fitness after living for that generation (ignoring breeding and eating)?

After this, she rearranges and completes the specification of birds breeding:

birds-breeding : (before : Forest , fertile-level : $\mathbb{N}$)
                      $\rightarrow$ (after : Forest)

post
    $\forall$ x $\in$ {1, . . . , x-max} , y $\in$ {1, . . . , y-max} $\bullet$
       after[x,y].bees = before[x,y].bees
       and

```
(let fitness : ℕ be before[x,y].bird in
    (fitness > 0 and fitness < fertile-level
        ⇒ after[x,y].bird = fitness)
    and
    (fitness ⩾ fertile-level
        ⇒ after[x,y].bird = fitness − fertile-level)
    and
    (fitness = 0 ⇒
        if has-fertile-neighbour(before,x,y) then after[x,y].bird = 1
        else after[x,y].bird = 0
    )
)
```

has-fertile-neighbour : (f : Forest , x : ℕ , y : ℕ) → 𝔹

has-fertile-neighbour(f,x,y) △
    ∃ xn ∈ {1, . . . , x-max} , yn ∈ {1, . . . , y-max} •
        is-neighbour(x,y,xn,yn) and f[xn,yn].bird ⩾ fertile-level

At this point Rita notes how the simple specifications she has written enabled her to spot many inadequacies in the original requirements (or at least her understanding of them). The study has also afforded her a greater understanding of the relationships involved, particularly the alternative ways of expressing birds breeding.

However, to check that what she has obtained so far is correct, she discusses the consequences of the rules with Rose. She does this by going over a number of examples, with Rita indicating what transformations will occur.

Exercise 11.4 It's a good idea for you to do that now – think of some simple example forests (keep them small!) and apply the various transformations to them.

One implicit assumption that she has made, which only comes to light at this meeting, and which by chance is correct, is that if a bird dies by giving birth, a new bird cannot be born into that cell in the same generation. (Perhaps this is just as well – if it were not the case, it would be more difficult to specify the rule. We would either incorporate an intermediate stage, in which all the birds that breed have lost their fitness but no birds are yet born, or add an extra condition to the case for a new bird being born, that the bird previously there had a fitness of exactly the fertility level.)

The next stage is to combine the four rules into a single function specifying the total transformation between generations. The obvious way to achieve this is to compose them functionally. Rita's first attempt at this is:

```
generate : (before : Forest , bees-fertility : ℕ , bees-maximum : ℕ,
             bird-efficiency : ℕ , bird-fertility-level : ℕ,
             bird-energy-use : ℕ) → (after : Forest)

generate(before,bees-fertility,bees-maximum,bird-efficiency,
          bird-fertility-level,bird-energy-use) △

birds-breeding(
   bees-breeding(
      birds-living(
         birds-eating(before,bird-efficiency),
         bird-energy-use),
      bees-fertility,bees-maximum),
   bird-fertility-level)
```

But then Rita realizes that the order in which the functions are composed might (it usually does!) make a difference to the result. Perhaps there is a specific order that Professor Pollen requires? Rita discusses this with her. Rose asks Rita if she can think of some examples where the order would make a difference. So, Rita studies the specifications trying various combinations. After a little while she finds that if a new bird is born and then loses fitness through living it will immediately die, unless it eats in between! Also, if a bird dies, and then one nearby gives birth, a new bird takes its place. This does not happen if the order is reversed. Rita shows these examples to her boss who, having now appreciated the discrete nature of the simulation, wishes to give the matter some thought.

The next day, Rose has it all worked out. She tells Rita what order is required in a generation:

(1)   First all the birds breed (and lose fitness due to breeding) if they are fit enough.

(2)   Next, all the bees breed.

(3)   Thirdly, all the birds eat the bees.

(4)   Finally, all the birds lose fitness due to living.

Rose feels that this will give the appropriate simulations she wants. Rita notes that her first attempt was wrong, but that the general idea of functional composition was right. The correct specification is:

```
generate : (before : Forest , bees-fertility : ℕ , bees-maximum : ℕ ,
             bird-efficiency : ℕ , bird-fertility-level : ℕ ,
             bird-energy-use : ℕ) → (after : Forest)

generate(before,bees-fertility,bees-maximum,bird-efficiency,
          bird-fertility-level,bird-energy-use) △

birds-living(
   birds-eating(
```

```
              bees-breeding(
                   birds-breeding(before,bird-fertility-level),
                   bees-fertility,bees-maximum),
              bird-efficiency),
         bird-energy-use)
```

The entire simulation consists of outputting a series of these forests until either a generation does not change or forever. Abstractly regarding the output as a sequence of forests, each together with a generation count, the simulation is specified by a possibly non-terminating recursive function as follows:

```
simulation : (count : ℕ , before : Forest , bees-fertility : ℕ,
                   bees-maximum : ℕ , bird-efficiency : ℕ ,
                   bird-fertility-level : ℕ , bird-energy-use : ℕ)
                → (output : Seq of (Forest X ℕ))

simulation(count,before,
                   bees-fertility,bees-maximum,bird-efficiency,
                   bird-fertility-level,bird-energy-use) △

let after : Forest be
              generate(before,bees-fertility,bees-maximum,bird-efficiency,
                   bird-fertility-level,bird-energy-use)
in
   [(before, count)] ⌢
    (if before  =  after then
       [(after, count  +  1)]
     else
       simulation(count  +  1,after,bees-fertility,bees-maximum,bird-efficiency,
                   bird-fertility-level,bird-energy-use)
   )
```

11.3.1   Output representation

Having completed the specification of the actual transformations required, Rita next concentrates on the choice of display to be employed. Although both the birds and the bees are to be continually displayed, she postulates that it would be best to show them separately on the same screen, rather than interleaved as they are in the forest. This would show more clearly the separate behaviour of the birds and bees, while it would still be easy to compare and relate the two. Rita checks this with the boss: she thinks it's a great idea!

So how should she represent each cell with its corresponding value? Remembering that the intention is to allow the user to monitor the overall behaviour of the forest, rather than see the values corresponding to a particular cell, she suggests that a cell's value could be represented by a single character. The entire forest could be represented by a sequence of lines of such characters. Perhaps a space would represent zero, '1' would represent 1, '2' would represent 2, and so on.

> PROFESSOR POLLEN: And what about 10?
> RITA: Well, another character.

But clearly it is limited, and Rita is told that the values can become rather big. Then inspiration strikes:

> RITA: Suppose the output is displayed in a small number of ranges, with an associated scaling factor. This factor would change to suit the maximum value to be displayed.
> PROFESSOR POLLEN: Excellent. This has the added advantage that the overall trends in bee and bird fitness could be seen by watching the scaling factor change.

Thus it is decided that each cell is to be represented by a character, which corresponds to a range, multiplied by a scaling factor. Zero will be represented by a space, otherwise there will be ten ranges, corresponding to 1 to 10 times the scaling factor. The following ten characters are to be used for the ten ranges:

123456789#

Thus, with a scaling factor of 100, the value 473 would be represented by the character '5', as that is the nearest range value. The scaling factor is to be based on the maximum value to be displayed, and should be the smallest number such that the maximum value can be represented. Professor Pollen agrees:

> PROFESSOR POLLEN: Ah, but you must distinguish between a value which is actually zero, and a value which is smaller than half the scaling factor (that is, one that would round down to zero).

Rita suggests that such values, close to zero, should be represented by a full stop ('.'). Rose indicates that there should be two different scaling factors, one for the birds and one for the bees, as they may have vastly different values, depending on the simulation factors.

Rita makes a note to arrange the implementation so that future changes in the representation characters used and the number of ranges are easily possible.

The output of a forest will comprise the following. Firstly the birds values, as a matrix of characters, each line corresponding to a row of the forest. This will be followed by the birds' scaling factor, and then a similar representation of the bees' values. Lastly, the generation count will be displayed.

11.3.2 Output specification

Rita constructs a specification of various parts of the output mechanism. Firstly, the scaling factor is a function of the maximum value and is a natural number greater than zero:

```
least-scale-needed : (max : N) → (scale : N1)

post 10 * scale ⩾ max
     and not ∃ other ∈ N1•
               10 * other ⩾ max and other < scale
```

The next part of the output mechanism that Rita specifies is the relationship between a value, the scale factor and the character used to represents the value in that scale. For this she needs to use the Pascal *round* function.

Pascal has two pre-declared functions for locating integer values near to a real value. (Often inappropriately called type conversions.) One of these returns the integer furthest from zero but which is no further from zero than the real argument. Formally, this is specified as:

```
trunc : (a : Real) → (r : Integer)

post a ⩾ 0 and 0 ⩽ a − r < 1
     or
     a < 0 and −1 < a − r ⩽ 0
```

The other function returns an integer which is (one of) the closest to the real argument:

```
round : (a : Real) → (r : Integer)

post a ⩾ 0 and r = trunc(a + 0.5)
     or
     a < 0 and r = trunc(a − 0.5)
```

```
output-rep-char : (value : N , scale : N) → Char
output-rep-char(value,scale) △
if value = 0 then ' '
else
   strength-chars(round(value/scale))
```

strength-chars : (n : ℕ) → Char
strength-chars(n) △ ".123456789#" [n + 1]

Exercise 11.5 What are the values of the following expressions?

(a)   trunc(3.6)

(b)   trunc(− 3.6)

(c)   trunc(7.5)

(d)   round(7.5)

(e)   round(− 7.5)

(f)   round(− 3.6)

(g)   round(3.6)

A forest of either bees or birds is displayed as a sequence of lines, each corresponding to (say) a Y row of the array. This can be abstractly viewed as a two-dimensional array of characters, with the same index structure as the forest. A one-to-one correspondence exists between values of the cells in the forest and the characters on the screen. The relationship is easily specified using the output-rep-char function.

Exercise 11.6 Specify the relationship between a forest, and its output representation as a matrix of characters.

11.3.3 Input data

Having achieved an appropriate measure of formalism in the output mechanism study, Rita next concentrates on the input data before commencing with the program design. There are five numeric pieces of information (factors) and the initial forest state to be entered to the program. Given that the user is likely to run the program many times with the same data, or to change the data only slightly, she concludes that the best way of presenting it all is as a file which can be edited by the user, and read by the program. The program must perform some reasonable validation checks on the data. For example, the specification of the generation assumes that the factors are not less than zero, whereas the user might put any values (possibly not even numbers) in the data file. The initial forest will be represented using exactly the same representation as on the output, with the bees and birds presented separately and each with a scale factor. Thus, with a scale factor of 175, a '2' represents 2 * 175 = 350. A full stop ('.') in the input forest represents a value of 1. Rita also thinks that it would be nice to allow textual comments to be embedded in the input data. These will include blank lines and lines beginning with a '!' character, and will be completely ignored by the program. To aid the use of a screen text editor, the lines that make up the representation of the forest will end with a '!' character. This is because it is difficult to see trailing spaces on a line of text, but these are valid representation characters in the initial forest. Numeric factors will be presented on a line, with any trailing text on the line ignored. Rita decides on the following order for the data:

- Bees' fertility ($\geqslant 0$)
- Bees' maximum count ($\geqslant 0$)
- Bird efficiency (%)
- Bird energy use (%)
- Bird fertility level ($\geqslant 0$)
- Bird scale (> 0)
- Bird fitness matrix
- Bee scale (> 0)
- Bee matrix

11.3.4   Specification of input

The only aspect of the input mechanism that Rita considers worth formalizing is the relationship between forest cell values and their initial representation. She notes that the output representation of a value corresponding to an input character is the same as that input character, assuming the same scale. Thus, for legal characters other than space or dot, it is sufficient to say that the value represented is a multiple of the scale, and that the character is the same as that which would be used to represent the value on output, in the same scale.

input-char-value : (in-char : Char , scale : $\mathbb{N}$) → (value : $\mathbb{N}$)

pre in-char ∈ { ' ', '.', '#' } ∪ { '1' ,..., '9' }

post (in-char = ' ' and value = 0) or (in-char = '.' and value = 1)
    or
    (not(in-char ∈ { ' ', '.'})
    and
    (value mod scale = 0)
    and
    (output-rep-char(value,scale) = in-char)
)

Note that, unlike the above specification, the whole program will not assume that the characters in the initial forest matrices are legal, it will validate them. The above specification serves merely to state the relationship between legal characters and the value they represent.

11.4 Design

Having adequately specified the behaviour of the program, Rita next considers its design, commencing the process at the top level. The algorithm basically involves reading the factors and the initial forest, and then continually generating a new forest until a generation has no effect. The most naive interpretation of the specification would lead her to a solution that actually maintains a sequence of forests, each item in the sequence being the generation after the previous item. But, of course, the sequence of forests corresponds to the history of output on the display during execution. The program need only maintain approximately one forest internally, this being the value of the forest at the current stage of the simulation. However, as generating a new forest results in a forest, each cell of which is not a direct function of the corresponding cell in the old one (compare with birds breeding), the program must keep a copy of the old forest when producing the new one after each generation. So the program will have a 'before' and 'after' forest and will be designed so that the effect

    after := generate(before)
    swap after and before

is continually effected, until there is no change in the forest. This will be achieved by a **repeat loop**.

The **repeat loop** has a **termination condition** which is tried *after* the loop body is executed. If the condition is false, the body of the loop is repeated and then the condition is tried again, and so on. When the condition is tried and is true, the loop execution stops. The general form is

    repeat
      actions of the loop
    until termination-condition

Because the condition is tested after execution of the loop body, the body will always be executed at least once.

Thus Rita's draft of the top-level of the program is:

```
program birds-and-bees(output,bb-data)

const x-max = ?
      y-max = ?
type cell = record
                bees : 0 .. maxint
                bird : 0 .. maxint
            end

    forest = array [1..x-max, 1..y-max] of cell

var bb-data : text { factors and initial forest }
    before,after : forest

    { various factors and so on. }

    generation-no : integer
    changed : boolean
    data-error : boolean { true iff error in input data }
begin
  { initialization }
  read-the-factors { sets data error if error in data }
  read-initial-birds(before)
  read-initial-bees(before)

  if not data-error
    generation-no := 0
    clear-screen
    display(before)
    repeat
      generation-no := generation-no + 1
      generation(before, after)
      display(after)
      changed := before ≠ after { Note: can't do this directly in
                                        Pascal }
      before := after
    until not changed
    writeln('Stability achieved')
  end-of-if
end
```

The most complex part of the program yet to be refined is the generation procedure, so Rita heads for this next.

One method of implementing this task, perhaps the most obvious from the specification, is to divide it into four sub-tasks, corresponding to the four transformations formalized in the specification. Assuming this to be the case, the procedure design would be:

```
generation(before : forest; var after : forest)
var birds-bred,bees-bred,birds-eaten : forest
begin
   birds-breeding(before,birds-bred)
   bees-breeding(birds-bred,bees-bred)
   birds-eating(bees-bred,birds-eaten)
   birds-living(birds-eaten,after)
end
```

As suggested by the universal quantifier in the specifications of the above transformations, their implementations may be achieved via nested for loops, over x and y in the appropriate ranges. Before proceeding any further, however, Rita notes that at least three of these transformations can be implemented by one set of nested loops because, for each, the final value of a cell is a direct function of the initial value of the same cell, and nothing else. These transformations are: bees-breeding, birds-eating and birds-living.

The other transformation, birds-breeding, requires reference to the value of neighbouring cells before the transformation when comput-ing the final value of a cell. This is more difficult to combine with the others, as the order in which cells are processed may then affect the final result. To avoid that, one would have to keep a version of each cell just before the birds breed (that is, an intermediate forest). But then she notes that, by chance, this transformation is applied before the others, and hence that the required intermediate forest is actually the initial forest before each generation. Consequently, if the procedure produces a new forest from the previous one, but keeps the previous one while this is being done, all four transformations can be combined in one pair of nested for loops. Rita judges that this relationship is worth exploiting, because it will contribute to the speed of the simulation, which is important, but does not involve excessive development time. Hence, she carefully redesigns and refines the procedure:

```
generation(before : forest; var after : forest)
var x,y : integer
    new-bird,new-bees,feed : integer
begin
   for x := 1 to x-max
     for y := 1 to y-max
       new-bird := before[x,y].bird
       new-bees := before[x,y].bees

       { first the birds breed: }
       if new-bird = 0
       begin
         if has-fertile-neighbour(before,x,y)
            new-bird := 1 { Congratulations: it's a bird }
       end
```

```
        else
        if new-bird ⩾ fertilitylevel
            new-bird := new-bird − fertilitylevel

        { now the bees breed: }
        new-bees := new-bees * fertility
        if new-bees > bees-maximumcount
            new-bees := bees-maximumcount

        { now birds feed: yummy }
        if new-bird > 0
            feed := (new-bees * bird-efficiency) div 100
            new-bird := new-bird + feed
            new-bees := new-bees − feed
        end-of-if

        { finally, bird loses energy just living: }
        new-bird := (new-bird * bird-energy-left) div 100
            { Note: bird-energy-left = 100 − bird-energy-use }

        after[x,y].bees := new-bees
        after[x,y].bird := new-bird
    end-of-for-loops
end
```

Before proceeding, she ensures that the design does in fact implement the function generate, assuming a correct implementation of has-fertile-neighbour. This she does by observing each transformation separately, and ensuring that they are composed in the correct order.

Rita moves on to the design of has-fertile-neighbour. She reasons that each cell has eight neighbours:

```
has-fertile-neighbour(this-forest : forest; x,y : integer) : boolean
{ iff x,y has a fertile neighbour in this-forest }
var fertile-neighbour-found : boolean
    neighbour-no : integer
begin
  fertile-neighbour-found := false
  neighbour-no := 1
  while not fertile-neighbour-found and (neighbour-no ⩽ 8)
    fertile-neighbour-found :=
      neighbour-fitness(this-forest,x,y,neighbour-no)
        ⩾ bird-fertility-level
    neighbour-no := neighbour-no + 1
  end-of-while
  has-fertile-neighbour := fertile-neighbour-found
end
```

This algorithm looks at each of the neighbours in turn, stopping when a fertile one is found or when all eight have been considered. But then it dawns on Rita that cells on the edge of the forest have only five

1 x – 1, y – 1	2 x, y – 1	3 x + 1, y – 1
4 x – 1, y	x, y	5 x + 1, y
6 x – 1, y + 1	7 x, y + 1	8 x + 1, y + 1

Figure 11.1   Cell neighbour numbering scheme.

neighbours, and those on a corner have only three. Apart from making the program more complex, these special cases are going to slow down the execution, if each cell has to be checked to see how many neighbours it has. Then she has a *brilliant* idea: if the forest has an extra band of cells all round it, which are guaranteed never to have a fertile bird residing therein, then every cell in the real forest has exactly eight neighbours, and the effect will be as required! Thus, she alters her top-level design as follows:

$$\vdots$$

type forest = array[0 .. x-max + 1, 0 .. y-max + 1] of cell
   {Note: can't write x-max + 1 directly like this in Pascal }

$$\vdots$$

begin

$$\vdots$$

   initialize-forests(before, after) { set the band around the forest }

$$\vdots$$

end

Then she returns her attention to the **has-fertile-neighbour** function, to the design of the sub-function **neighbour-fitness**. This must compute the fitness of the bird in the neighbouring cell to (x,y), corresponding to **neighbour-no**, in the forest. It may use any neighbouring number scheme she wishes, as long as each neighbour has one unique number between 1 and 8 inclusive. Rita decides to number the neighbours as in Figure 11.1. Thus, she must find the relationship between x, y and **neighbour-no**; and the corresponding x and y coordinates of the neighbour. After some thought, she supposes that the discontinuity in the numbers at the centre of the square is going to cause some problems. So she decides that the function will subtract one from **neighbour-no** if it is less than five. This effectively gives the adjusted numbering scheme of Figure 11.2. In this, the value 4 corresponds to the original cell, but 4 cannot be a value of **neighbour-no** because if it is greater than or equal to 5 it is not changed, but if it is less than or equal to 4, it is decremented. Now, the address of each neighbour is found by adding an X-offset and a Y-offset to x and y respectively. Each offset is either – 1, 0 or 1.

0	1	2
x − 1, y − 1	x, y − 1	x + 1, y − 1
3	(4)	5
x, y − 1	x, y	x + 1, y
6	7	8
x + 1, y − 1	x, y + 1	x + 1, y + 1

Figure 11.2 Adjusted cell neighbour numbering scheme.

Considering the Y-offset Rita draws up the table shown in Figure 11.3. From this, she is able to deduce the relationship:

> Y-offset = (neighbour-no div 3) − 1

Similarly, for the X-offset she draws the table of Figure 11.4, and deduces the relationship:

> X-offset = (neighbour-no mod 3) − 1

Rita is now able to design the function:

```
neighbour-fitness(this-forest : forest;
                  x,y,neighbour-no : integer) : integer
{pre 0 < neighbour-no < 9}

var xn,yn : integer
begin
  if neighbour-no < 5
    neighbour-no := neighbour-no − 1 {now: 0, ..., 8}
  yn := y + (neighbour-no div 3) − 1
  xn := x + (neighbour-no mod 3) − 1
  neighbour-fitness := this-forest[xn,yn].bird
end
```

Y-offset	Neighbour numbers
−1	{0, 1, 2}
0	{3, (4), 5}
1	{6, 7, 8}

Figure 11.3 Y-offset and neighbour number relationship.

X-offset	Neighbour numbers
−1	{0, 3, 6}
0	{1, (4), 7}
1	{2, 5, 8}

Figure 11.4   X-offset and neighbour number relationship.

Now that she has completed this branch of the design refinement, she decides to jot down the design of the procedure that initializes the edges of the forests. Both the 'before' and 'after' forests need treating in this way, as the generation procedure and the initial reading procedures will never change these parts.

```
initialize-forests(var f1,f2 : forest)
var x,y : integer

    initcell(x,y : integer)
    begin
      f1[x,y].bird := 0
      f1[x,y].bees := 0
      f2[x,y] := f1[x,y]
    end

begin
  for x := 0 to x-max + 1
    initcell(x, 0)
    initcell(x, y-max + 1)
  for y := 1 to y-max
    initcell(0, y)
    initcell(x-max + 1, y)
end
```

11.4.1   Design of the output mechanism

Having had a large mug of tea, Rita next tackles the design of the part of the program that displays a forest. This involves outputting the representation of the birds, then the bees and the generation number. The previous contents of the screen should be overwritten: thus the screen cursor should be sent home (that is, to the first position on the screen).

```
display(f : forest)
begin
  cursor-home
  display-birds
  display-bees
  writeln('Generation ',generation-no)
end
```

Displaying the birds involves calculating the scaling factor and then outputting a character for each bird fitness cell value (y-max lines of x-max characters) such that the xth character of the yth line represents the bird fitness of cell x,y. Calculating the scaling factor involves finding the maximum bird fitness to be displayed. This relatively simple task comprises scanning through all the cells in the forest. Rita observes that this could easily be done (for efficiency reasons) as a by-product of the generation procedure. Thus she invents two new variables at the top level of the program:

```
maximum-bees,
maximum-bird : integer
```

and includes some simple additions at the beginning of the generation procedure and at the end of the loop inside it:

```
begin
  maximum-birds := 0
  maximum-bees := 0
  ⋮
  for ...
    for ...
      ⋮
      if new-bird > maximum-bird
        maximum-bird := new-bird
      if new-bees > maximum-bees
        maximum-bees := new-bees
    end-of-for-loops
end
```

The design of the procedure display-birds is simply:

```
display-birds
var x,y,scale : integer
begin
  calculate-scale(maximum-birds,scale)
  for y := 1 to y-max
    for x := 1 to x-max
      write(output-rep-char(f[x,y].birds,scale))
    writeln
  writeln('Birds, scale = ',scale)
end
```

Displaying the bees is similar.

Exercise 11.7 Design a Pascal procedure to initialize a two-dimensional array of characters all to have the value ' '. Make it general for any size of array, indexed by integers.

Next she studies the function that yields the output character corresponding to a particular value and a scale. She decides that the number of output ranges should be a program constant, rather than always 10. This will offer flexibility, which assists future maintenance. Also, for both efficiency and flexibility, she decides that the output character corresponding to each range should be stored in an (unpacked) array, indexed by that range. Rita adds the following declarations to the top level of the design:

    const range-count = 10

    var strength-chars : array[0..range-count] of char

Her design of output-rep-char is:

    output-rep-char(strength,scale : integer) : char
    begin
      if strength = 0
        output-rep-char := ' '
      else
        output-rep-char := strength-chars[round(strength/scale)]
    end

The characters stored in the **strength-chars** array will require initializing. Rita adds the line:

    initialize-strength-chars

to the start of the top level, and then designs the following procedure:

    initialize-strength-chars
    var packed-strength:packed array[1..range-count + 1] of char
        { Note: can't write range-count + 1 as here in standard
          Pascal }
        i : integer
    begin
      packed-strength := '.123456789#'
      for i := 0 to range-count
        strength-chars[i] := packed-strength[i + 1]
    end

Finally for display, she considers the operation of calculating the scale. From the specification she sees that the scale must be the smallest number greater than zero such that, when multiplied by the range count, it is greater than or equal to the maximum value represented. One way of implementing this is:

```
calculate-scale(max : integer; var scale : integer)
begin
  scale := max div range-count
  if scale * range-count < max
    scale := scale + 1
  else
  if scale = 0
    scale := 1
end
```

At this point, she has completed the design of the parts of the program to display the forest (apart from trivial bits such as clearing the screen).

While Rita is looking again at the (modified) top-level design, to see what should be refined next, the part where the 'before' and 'after' forests are compared catches her eye. The only way to achieve this in Pascal would involve comparing the two arrays, element by element, because the language does not permit the comparison of whole arrays directly.

General array comparison (such as equality) is not permitted in Pascal. Shame. Neither is record comparison. However, packed arrays of char may be compared.

However, it strikes her that the generation procedure could detect whether the forest has altered as yet another by-product. Going back to this procedure, she adds:

```
changed := false
```

at the front, and at the end of the loop within it:

```
if not changed
  if new-bird ≠ before[x,y].bird
    changed := true
  else
  if new-bees ≠ before[x,y].bees
    changed := true
```

Rita also crosses out the line:

    changed := before ≠ after

from the top-level program design.

11.4.2   Design of the input mechanism

The remaining parts of the program are concerned with reading and
validating the data. To the front of the top level of the program, just
before the call to **read-the-factors**, Rita adds:

```
data-error := false
reset(bb-data)
```

And just after **read-initial-birds** she inserts:

```
check-eof
```

This will check that the end of the data file has been reached when all the
data has been read.

Then she designs the procedure to read the simulation factors:

```
read-factors
var bird-energy-use:integer
begin
  read-non-neg-number(bees-fertility)
  read-non-neg-number(bees-maximum-count)
  read-percentage(bird-efficiency)
  read-percentage(bird-energy-use)
  read-non-neg-number(bird-fertility-level)

  bird-energy-left := 100 - bird-energy-use
end
```

Rita also adds the following variables to the top-level design (replacing
the 'various factors' comment!).

```
bees-fertility,
bees-maximum-count,
bird-efficiency,
bird-energy-left,
bird-fertility-level : integer
```

Reading a non-negative number involves skipping any comments in the
input, reading a number and checking that it is greater than or equal to
zero. Reading a percentage involves reading a non-negative number and

ensuring that it is greater than zero, and less than or equal to 100. To exploit the maximum amount of generality of such low-level read procedures, she decides to leave their design until after designing the other higher level read procedures, namely: read-initial-birds and read-initial-bees.

Like the corresponding display procedures, these two are obviously similar to each other. Rita notes that for the initial display of the forest to work correctly, the procedures must also compute the initial maximum values of bird fitness and bee count. Reading an initial forest of bird fitnesses comprises reading the scale, and then the y-max lines. Each of these lines consists of x-max characters, followed by a '!'. Each line could also be preceded by comments.

```
read-initial-birds(var initial : forest)

var x,y : integer
    scale : integer
    new-bird : integer

begin
  maximum-bird := 0
  read-pos-number(scale)
  for y := 1 to y-max
    comment-skip
    for x := 1 to x-max
      read-char-value(new-bird,scale)
      initial[x,y].bird := new-bird
      if new-bird > maximum-bird
        maximum-bird := new-bird
    end-of-for
    read-end-of-line
  end-of-for
end
```

Reading the initial bees is similar. Finally, Rita must design the lower level reading routines. These are:

- Comment-skip

- Read-non-neg-number

- Read-pos-number

- Read-percentage

- Read-char-value

- Read-end-of-line

- Check-eof

Some of these may use others in their implementation. Rita decides that the program should handle errors in the input data by means of **error recovery**.

Error recovery is a technique of dealing with errors in input data by reporting the error and then attempting to correct it. This involves choosing a sensible default value for the data which can be used in place of erroneous input. In this way, the exponential effect of one early error condition on later parts of the program can be avoided. That is, each part of a program need only be concerned with possible errors that may be detected during execution of that part, and not with errors arising in previously executed parts of the program.

On encountering an error, the flag data-error will be set to true, but the routines should also report an error message. She decides to use a simple **error routine** for this.

For programs that have to deal with a variety of possible errors in input data, it is often useful to use a single **error routine**. This is given some error value, usually from an enumerated type, as a parameter, and writes a corresponding message. In this way, it is easy to control the format and perhaps the frequency of error messages. For example, it may be desired only to report the first three messages, all other calls on the routine being ignored. Error routines are very often used in conjunction with error recovery.

Once Rita has designed each low-level read routine, she will have a list of all possible input data errors that have to be dealt with. She starts with the procedure to skip comments. This must skip all blank lines, and lines starting with an exclamation mark, until another line or the end of file is reached. Rita designs the procedure in her usual professional manner, avoiding the obvious Wally trap. However, we seem to have misplaced it.

Exercise 11.8   Never mind – we're sure you could have a bash at doing it, but watch out for that Wally trap. You might like to look at the skip-space procedure of Chapter 7 for a hint.

Reading a non-negative number comprises skipping comments, checking that a number is present, reading it and ensuring that it is

greater than or equal to 0. Rita arbitrarily decides to return the value 1
if an error is detected:

```
read-non-neg-number(var n : integer)
begin
  n := 1
  comment-skip
  if eof(bb-data)
    error(non-neg-num-error)
  else
  if not bb-data ^ in ['0'..'9']
    error(non-neg-num-error)
    readln(bb-data)
  else
    readln(bb-data,n)
end
```

Reading a positive number entails reading a non-negative number and
checking that it is greater than zero:

```
read-pos-number(var n : integer)
begin
  read-non-neg-number(n)
  if n = 0
    error(pos-num-error)
    n := 1
end
```

Reading a percentage involves an extra check:

```
read-percentage(var n : integer)
begin
  read-pos-number(n)
  if n > 100
    error(percent-error)
    n := 100
end
```

Reading a character representing a value is similar to displaying a
character representation of a value:

```
read-char-value(var n : number; scale : integer)
var ch : char
    i : integer
    found : boolean
begin
  n := 1 { default result if an error is detected }
  if eof(bb-data)
    error(char-val-error)
```

```
         else
         if eoln(bb-data)
            error(char-val-error)
         else
         begin
            read(bb-data,ch)
            if ch = ' '
               n := 0
            else
            if ch = strength-chars[0]
               n := 1
            else
            begin
               found := false
               i := 1
               while not found and (i < range-count)
                  if ch = strength-chars[i]
                     found := true
                  else i := i + 1
               end-of-while
               if ch = strength-chars[i]
                  n := i * scale
               else
                  error(char-val-error)
            end
         end
      end
```

Reading an end-of-line in the forest involves checking that the current character is an exclamation mark. This must be followed immediately by an end-of-line:

```
read-end-of-line
begin
   if eof(bb-data)
      error(eoln-error)
   else
   begin
      if bb-data ^ = '!'
      begin
         get(bb-data)
         if not eoln(bb-data)
            error(eoln-error)
      end
      else
         error(eoln-error)
      readln(bb-data)
   end
end
```

Finally, for these low-level read routines, the procedure which checks for
end-of-file:

```
check-eof
begin
  if not eof(bb-data)
     error(eof-error)
end
```

This just leaves the error procedure and the associated enumerated
type of errors. To the top level, Rita adds:

```
type error-kind = (non-neg-num-error,pos-num-error,
                   percent-error,char-val-error,
                   eoln-error,eof-error)
```

The error procedure must set the flag **data-error** and produce an error
message associated with the given error. However, she decides that only
the first error should be reported, otherwise a proliferation of unhelpful
messages can result from, say, just one piece of missing data. Hence, the
procedure must do nothing if **data-error** is already set:

```
error(this-error : error-kind)
begin
  if not data-error
    case this-error of
      non-neg-num-error
                    : writeln('Non-negative number expected')
      pos-num-error : writeln(' ... ')
      percent-error : writeln(' ... ')
      char-val-error : writeln(' ... ')
      eoln-error    : writeln(' ... ')
      eof-error     : writeln(' ... ')
    end-of-case
    data-error := true
  end-of-if
end
```

At last she has completed the program design, except for the odd bits that
she considers as trivial. Phew!

Exercise 11.9   Propose modifications to the design that would cause the
program to report the line number of the line in the data file where an error
is detected, in addition to the error message.

11.5   Implementation

Now she is ready to embark on the final mission – the implementation.

11.5.1   Efficiency issues

Firstly, she looks through all the designs with a view to identifying any efficiency improving changes she could make, because, in this case, speed of the final code (up to a point) improves its usefulness. One very simple thing that strikes her is that several of the procedures and functions require a forest as a **value parameter.**

Value parameters to procedures and functions in Pascal are implemented at run-time by actually copying the value when the procedure or function is called. For large items, this copying might have some significant effect on the efficiency of the execution. This effect can be removed by using variable parameters instead, as these are not copied but are referenced by an implicit pointer. However, in such cases, the programmer should include a comment to the effect that this is merely an optimization, and must always ensure that the parameter is not unintentionally changed.

Of course, there is a trade-off. If the large item is accessed from within the procedure or function very many times, the extra time taken to follow the implicit pointer for each access could add up to more time than that taken to copy the whole value.

As an optimization, Rita decides to implement most of the value parameters of type forest as variable parameters. The likely exceptions are the procedures generation and display, which access every element of the given forest.

Similarly, she notices that the 'after' forest is explicitly copied to the 'before' forest between generations in the design. Rita decides to avoid this large copying by having an array of two forests, with before and after being implemented as two indices in the array. That way, only the indices need to be swapped. This involves replacing the variable declarations:

    before,after : forest

with:

    forests : **Array**[1..2] **Of** Forest;
    before,after : 1..2

The index variables need to be initialized at the start of the program:

> *before* := 1;
> *after* := 2

All references to before and after need to be replaced by *forests*[*before*] and *forests*[*after*], respectively; except for the swapping assignment. This is replaced by:

> *before* := *after*;
> *after* := 3 − *before*;

11.5.2   Clearing the screen

Another aspect of the implementation is the trivial procedures to clear the screen and send the cursor home. Rita looks up in the Bozo 1.001 User Manual for the character sequences required to achieve this. To send the cursor home, the sequence

> escape [H

is needed, and to clear the screen from the cursor onwards:

> escape [J

The escape character has code 27. Thus, the two procedures are implemented as:

```
Const EscapeCharCode = 27;
⋮
Procedure CursorHome;
Const home = '[H';
Begin
    write(chr(EscapeCharCode), home);
End;

Procedure ClearScreen;
Const clear = '[J';
Begin
    CursorHome;
    write(chr(EscapeCharCode), clear);
End;
```

Rita works out the values for the constants x-max and y-max, based on the size of the screen to be used. In the design she made use of the expression x-max + 1

in a type declaration, and similar uses. However, this cannot be written in such places in Pascal, so she defines another constant instead. That is:

Const *xMax* = 79;
     xMaxPlusOne = 80;

The second constant is used in the implementation, instead of the expression in the design.

The rest of the implementation is merely concerned with ordering the various procedures and functions into an appropriate sequence and nesting; and filling in all the **Begin**s and **End**s, crossing the 'i's and dotting the 't's. The main body involves a **repeat loop.**

In Pascal, one form of loop construct is the **Repeat** statement, which tests a condition after executing the iterative part. It involves the keywords **Repeat** and **Until**. The rules of Pascal do *not* insist that the loop body is a single statement:

Repeat
     statement-1;
     statement-2;
     ...
Until

Having tested the program, Rita shows it to Rose. Rose tries it with some very interesting data which causes some very nice patterns to appear on the display. Rita does not hide her fascination. Rose proclaims her immense satisfaction, and insists that Rita help her as a demonstrator in the Biology laboratories from now on.

RITA: But, I don't know *anything* about biology!

Exercise 11.10

(a)   Give an informal but clear and precise explanation of the following formal specification. Avoid simply translating the symbols into English.

Periods = { 9 , . . . , 17}
Day = Set of Periods
Desk-diary = Seq of Day
inv-Desk-diary(d) $\triangle$ len d = 5

profs-meeting : (prof1 : Desk-diary , prof2 : Desk-diary , prof3 : Desk-diary)
         → (free-times : Desk-diary)

post

   ∀ week-day ∈ inds free-times •
     (free-times[week-day] ∩
       (prof1[week-day] ∪ prof2[week-day] ∪ prof3[week-day])) = { }
     and
     (free-times[week-day] ∪ prof1[week-day]
       ∪ prof2[week-day] ∪ prof3[week-day]) = {9 ,..., 17}

Note that a professor's desk diary records when a professor is busy; not when she (or he) is free.

(b)   Write Pascal type declarations and a procedure that implements the specification in part (a).

Exercise 11.11

(a)   Give an informal but clear and precise explanation of the following formal specification. Avoid simply translating the symbols into English.

square-size = 50

Matrix = Array[1..square-size , 1..square-size] of ℕ

Direction = { –1 , 0 , 1}

magic : (M : matrix) → 𝔹
magic(M) △
   let magic-sum be sum-tlbr-diag(M) in
     sum-bltr-diag(M) = magic-sum
     and
     (∀ i ∈ {1 , . . . , square-size} •
     sum-row(M,i) = sum-column(M,i) = magic-sum
)

sum-tlbr-diag : (M : matrix) → ℕ
sum-tlbr-diag(M) △ sum(M, 1, 1, 1, 1)

sum-bltr-diag : (M : matrix) → ℕ
sum-bltr-diag(M) △ sum(M, 1, square-size, 1, –1)

sum-row : (M : matrix , i : ℕ) → ℕ
sum-row(M,i) △ sum(M, 1, i, 1, 0)

sum-column : (M : matrix , i : ℕ) → ℕ
sum-column(M,i) △ sum(M, i, 1, 0, 1)

sum : (M : matrix , x : ℕ , y : ℕ
       dx : direction , dy : direction) → ℕ
sum(M,x,y,dx,dy) △
   if not (x ∈ {1 , . . . , square-size})
   or not (y ∈ {1 , . . . , square-size})
   then 0
   else M[x,y] + sum(M, x + dx, y + dy, dx, dy)

(b)   Given the specification in part (a), choose a suitable Pascal type to implement the matrix, and design either a Pascal function or procedure which implements the function magic.

SUMMARY

This chapter was primarily emphasizing the importance of requirements analysis and formal specification. Rita was able to produce the product that Rose wanted, despite not knowing about the subject area. In addition, we saw the use of **two-dimensional arrays** and the concepts of **error recovery** and **error routines**.

The following notations were introduced in this chapter.

Pascal notation

Two-dimensional array	**Type** *forest* = **Array**[1..*XMax*,1..*YMax*] **Of** *Cell*
Trunc and round	*OutputChar* := *StrengthChars*[*round*(*strength*/*scale*)]
Repeat statement	**Repeat**...**Until Not** *changed*

TUTORIAL EXERCISE

This tutorial involves *writing* some simple specifications. Some of the exercises may require you to identify a pre-condition to eliminate any awkward or meaningless cases. Also, the English requirements may deliberately have ambiguities or inaccuracies in them. You should note any that you spot, and make what you consider to be sensible interpretations. (Of course, in the real world, you would have to consult the customer.)

1 – Square root

Specify an operation that approximates the square root function by finding a number whose square is within 10^{-6} of a given real number.

2 – Lower case letters count

Write an **explicit** function that, given a sequence of characters, returns the number of lower case letters in the sequence. Is a pre-condition necessary?

3 – String search

Given:

String = Seq of Char

Specify a function that returns the position of a string, S, in another string, T, or returns zero if S is not in T.

4 – Sequence merging (a challenge!)

Specify an operation that takes two sequences of integers and generates a merged sequence. That is, the first element is from the first sequence, the second from the second, the third from the first sequence, and so on.

5 – Average sized set (a real challenge!)

Specify an operation that given a Set of (Set of X), returns a member of that set, which has a cardinality equal to the mean average cardinality of all the member sets (assuming such a set exists).

Implementation of the strings package

12

MOTIVATION

This case study exposes some more sophisticated dynamic data structures, although still based on the idea of a linked list. The data structures used are very complex indeed by novice standards (Rita *is* an expert) and, unlike some of the previous case studies, have not been chosen as a compromise between what is ideal and what can be grasped in an introductory book. The reader may well be excused from studying this chapter until after having gained a little more experience of programming.

The specification of the strings package was presented in Chapter 10. Thus, unlike most of the previous chapters, which were separated into the four stages of programming, this is just concerned with various interesting parts of the strings package design. The entire strings package implementation is given in Appendix C.

The discussion also introduces the Pascal concepts of the ***dispose*** statement, the **With** statement and **variant records**. More general design issues covered are **reference counts**, **state indicators** and the employment of an **unbounded sum of bounded sub-problems** to solve an **unbounded problem**.

12.1   The strings package design

The package is presented here in the form of algorithm designs of the most interesting parts. All the Pascal details can be found in Appendix C. The most critical design decision was the choice of data structure used to store string values, so that is described first.

12.1.1   The data structure

The three main criteria affecting the design of the package, in order of decreasing priority, are: unboundedness, efficiency and ease of use.

Unboundedness considerations

The strings must be unbounded, as that is the purpose of the package. This means that, apart from the possibility of using all the available memory in the computer, there must be no maximum length of any string. The two unbounded data structuring techniques available in Pascal are files and dynamic variables. Storing string values in files would be far too inefficient because files are usually stored on some slow magnetic media (such as disks) and limited operations are available on them (one can't efficiently alter a value in the middle of a file, for example). So a data structure based on dynamic variables and pointers was Rita's only choice.

Efficiency considerations

The package must be efficient. This includes both time and space, although there is often a conflict between the two. It must be possible to implement the operations required on strings in an acceptable time efficiency, while the space occupied by the string values should not be excessive.

Recomputation of often used information should be avoided – for example, the length of a string. Instead, such frequently needed data should be stored explicitly in the structure.

For both time and space efficiency, it should be possible to share string values between several variables, whenever it is sound to do so. For example, if a user's program design requires the value of one string variable to be assigned to another, it may be that the structure can be shared between the two. Only the pointer to the structure need be copied in such cases, instead of creating a completely new copy of it (as was done in Chapter 8).

For space efficiency, Rita thought about the overhead caused by the pointers themselves. For example, she considered it unacceptable for there to be a pointer for every character in a string (as there would be in a simple linked list) because that would have doubled the space requirements (assuming that a character and a pointer occupy the same space).

Finally, for space efficiency, it must be possible to reuse the memory allocated to string values which are no longer required, otherwise programs will run out of space much sooner than necessary, if indeed they ever need to.

Ease of use considerations

Considering the ease of use of the package affected the way in which the other criteria were satisfied. The programmer using the package has enough to worry about without being expected to consider the soundness of string value sharing, and the reuse of string memory. Thus Rita considered it desirable to have automatic sharing of string values whenever possible, and automatic **garbage collection** of unwanted string values. Rita thinks these facilities are so valuable that they are worth the cost of insisting that the programmer initializes and finalizes string variables, though this is an inconvenient requirement.

12.1.2   The chosen structure

Rita chose a linked list as the basis of the structure. However, rather than have a link pointer for every character in the string, the nodes of the list each contain several characters, or, as Rita calls it, a 'chunk'. This enables an optimization in the amount of space needed to store a string, as discussed shortly. Abstractly, the string value represented by a linked list of chunks is formed by scanning from the front of the list and concatenating all the chunks together. The linked lists used in Chapter 8 are exactly like those used here, except that in Chapter 8 the chunk size was always one.

Rita decided to represent strings as pointers, so that they may be returned as the results of functions. An empty string is represented by a nil pointer, as shown in Figure 12.1.

To implement automatic disposal and sharing, it is necessary to have a **reference count** in the data structure.

Figure 12.1 The empty string.

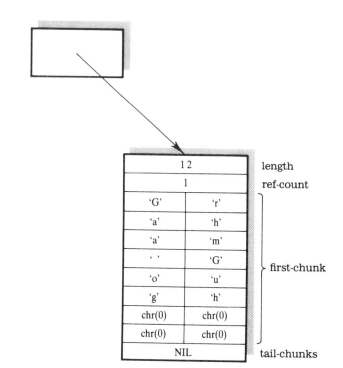

1 2		length
1		ref-count
'G'	'r'	
'a'	'h'	
'a'	'm'	
' '	'G'	first-chunk
'o'	'u'	
'g'	'h'	
chr(0)	chr(0)	
chr(0)	chr(0)	
NIL		tail-chunks

Figure 12.2   A string of length 12.

A **reference count** is a counter, attached to a particular data item, which keeps a tally of how many variables point to that data item. Whenever a new variable references the item, its reference count is incremented. Whenever a variable ceases to point to the item, the reference count is decremented. A variable ceases to point to an item by changing its value so that it points elsewhere, or nowhere (that is assuming the value **Nil** in Pascal) or by being no longer required.

Reference counters are very often used in automatic garbage collection schemes, so that the space occupied by a value may be safely reused when its reference count is zero.

Without a reference count, the package would not know when it is safe to share string values and when it is safe to reuse the memory occupied by a string value.

A non-empty string is implemented as a pointer to a dynamic record containing the length of the string (to avoid its recomputation), the reference count (for automatic disposal and sharing of strings), the first chunk of characters, and a tail pointing to a linked list of the remaining chunks, or nil if there are none. A chunk is implemented by a packed array of characters. The last chunk of the string might not be completely used, and Rita chose to fill it up with null characters, that is, *chr(0)*. (This choice was not entirely arbitrary – see Section 12.1.14). Figures 12.2 and 12.3 show pictorial representations of typical string values.

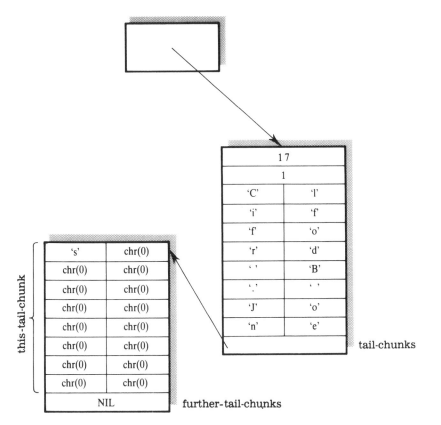

Figure 12.3   A string of length 17.

12.1.3 The Pascal data types for strings

The types that are defined in the strings package (corresponding to the
informal description and example diagrams) are:

```
      const chunk-size = 16; { any length > 0 will work }

      type nat0 = 0 .. maxint;
           nat1 = 1 .. maxint;

           string = ^ string-rec;

           string-tail = ^ string-tail-rec;

           string-rec = record
                        length       : nat1; { never 0 as NIL
                                                 represents '' }
                        ref-count    : nat0; { number of current
                                                 references }
                        first-chunk : packed array [1 .. chunk-size]
                                         of char;
                        tail-chunks : string-tail
                      end;
```

:=

```
string-tail-rec = record
              this-tail-chunk      : packed array
                                     [1..chunk-size] of
                                     char;
          further-tail-chunks : string-tail
        end;
```

Figure 12.4 shows a longer string, with a more complicated structure.

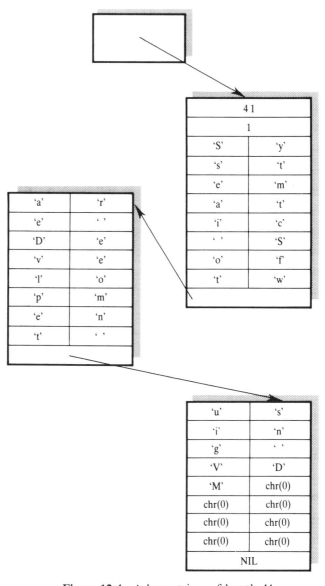

Figure 12.4   A long string, of length 41.

12.1.4   Choice of chunk size

Rita realized that there is a trade-off for space efficiency concerning the optimal size of the chunks. If they are big, the number of links required is small, and hence the overall space used tends to be reduced. However, the last chunk in the string will most often not be full. On average, approximately half the space in the last chunk will be wasted. The best chunk size depends on how much space a pointer and a character occupy, and also on the expected distribution of the lengths of the strings. For example, in an application where the strings package is used for a word processor so that each line is stored in a string, it would be sensible to choose a chunk size of 80 characters, because it is likely that very many of the lines would be nearly that in length. That would mean that pointers are only needed on the few lines that are longer than 80 characters, and yet very little space would be wasted.

For more random applications, it is best to consider the sizes of the components of the structure. On a typical 32-bit word-addressed computer (that is, one that has 32 binary digits per memory word), a character occupies 8 bits, and a pointer needs 32 bits! However, a single character would be stored in 32 bits, with 24 bits wasted. So, if the chunk size were 1 on such machines, the space requirement would be eight times the absolute minimum! A packed array of 4 characters would typically occupy 32-bits with no wastage, so a chunk size of four would use only twice as much space as the minimum in full chunks. A chunk size of 100 would use 1.04 times the minimum space in full chunks, but an average of 49.5 characters per string would be wasted. It should be clear that the chunk size should be such that the array occupies a whole number of words. This means that it should be a multiple of four on most 32-bit computers. Rita chose 16, but arranged it so that the size may be easily altered by changing just one constant declaration.

We asked Rita why she put the first chunk of a string in the head record, instead of having a linked list for all the chunks.

> RITA: I did give that a lot of thought. I knew it would mean having two different types that store parts of the value of the string, and that that would lead to more complicated code. However, I decided it was worth it so that, in applications where many of the strings are nearly the same length, those strings could be stored in just one dynamic record by choosing an appropriate chunk size. That would make them more efficient.
>
> US: Oh, right.

12.1.5   When do we share?

Rita also gave the subject of sharing some considerable thought – when is it safe to share, and when not? It was already clear to her that a reference count would be needed. The only possible problem with sharing is unwanted side-effects. For example, suppose that the value of the variable Y is assigned to the variable X so that they then share the value. Suppose subsequently that an operation is applied to Y which alters its value (for example, *ChangeCharInSTRING*). This must not have an effect on X, so the variables must first be separated. Thus the rule is that whenever the package is about to alter an existing string value, if the reference count for it is not one, then it must first create a new copy of it and work on that instead. At all other times it can safely share string values, as long as it keeps track of the reference count. So if three variables share a value, and one of them has its version updated, the result will be an updated *copy* of the original string, and the other two variables will still share the original. (Of course, the reference count of the original must be decremented.)

12.1.6   Initialization and finalization primitives

As was described in Chapter 10, the rules for correct use of the strings package insist that all string variables are initialized and finalized, and similarly for string value parameters. This is to maintain the reference counting mechanism, enabling strings to be both shared and disposed of safely. The following procedure initializes a string:

```
init-STRING(var this-string: string)
begin
   this-string := nil
end
```

The finalization is done by the final-STRING procedure. This takes a string variable as a variable parameter and, if it is not nil, decrements the reference count of the string value it points to. If then there are no references left to that value, it is **disposed** of.

In Pascal, the pre-declared procedure ***dispose*** is the inverse of *new*. It takes one variable parameter, of type $^\wedge T$, for some type T. When applied to some pointer variable, P, it assumes that P points to a dynamic variable, of type T, previously created via *new*. The memory occupied by that dynamic variable is returned to the operating system, and the variable no longer exists. The value of the variable P is *undefined* afterwards, thus it is an error to attempt to use its value (for example, by assignment or $P^\wedge$). It is also an error to attempt to access the dynamic variable that was disposed (for example, by another pointer variable that was pointing to it).

For example, consider the following:

new(*p*);
q := *p*;
dispose(*q*);

After executing these, the values of both *q* and *p* are totally undefined, and thus *p*^ does not exist.

The disposal can be done in a loop, working along the linked list of chunks. However, it is necessary to use a local variable, next-tail-chunks, temporarily to store a pointer to the next item to be disposed, because it is erroneous to (attempt to) access the value of a dynamic variable after it has been disposed.

```
final-STRING(var this-string: string)

var this-tail-chunk, next-tail-chunks: string-tail

begin
  if this-string = nil
    { Do nothing }
  else
    this-string ^.ref-count := this-string ^.ref-count – 1
    if this-string ^.ref-count < 1 { Was the only ref. to this
                                                    string }
      this-tail-chunk := this-string ^.tail-chunks
      dispose(this-string)
      while this-tail-chunk ≠ nil
        next-tail-chunks := this-tail-chunk ^.further-tail-chunks
        dispose(this-tail-chunk)
        this-tail-chunk := next-tail-chunks
      end-of-while
    end-of-if
    this-string := nil
  end-of-if
end
```

Rather than repeat the phrase this-string^., Rita actually used a **With** statement instead.

The Pascal **With** statement enables access to the fields of a record without having to specify the record for each access. This is most useful when there are to be several accesses to fields of the same record during some part of the program. The format is:

With *some-record-variable* **Do**
  statement

:= Within the statement, the fields of the given record may be referenced by name, without preceding them by the record variable and a dot.

As with other structured Pascal statements, the body of the **With** statement must be a single statement, and hence it is often compound. For example, with the record variable

> *ThisStudent* : **Record** *sex:(male,female)*; *age:Integer* **End**

the statements

> *ThisStudent.sex* := *female*;
> *ThisStudent.age* := 18

are equivalent to

> **With** *ThisStudent* **Do**
> **Begin**
>   *sex* := *female*;
>   *age* := 18
> **End**

Rita actually wrote the following to update the reference count:

```
with this-string ^ do
    ref-count := ref-count – 1
```

More complicated cases of initialization and finalization arose as a result of using strings as parameters to procedures and functions, and returning them as results from functions. If a string is used as a value parameter to a procedure or function, this causes an implicit copying of the string, and thus the reference count of the string needs to be incremented. The init-val-param-STRING operation does just this:

```
init-val-param-STRING(this-string: string)
begin
    if this-string ≠ nil
        with this-string ^ do
            ref-count := ref-count + 1
end
```

As described in Chapter 10, assign-func-result-STRING is called when a function returns a string as its result. The return value should be constructed into an initialized local variable and then assigned to the function identifier (using the ordinary Pascal assignment operator) via assign-func-result-STRING. For example, if the name of the function was func-name and the local variable containing the result was result-var, the assignment would be effected by:

    func-name := assign-func-result-STRING(result-var)

Once the function identifier points to the string, this assign-func-result-STRING dereferences the local variable from the string. Note that, in this case, if the reference count of the string becomes zero, the storage space should *not* be reclaimed because the string is still needed as the result of the function it has now been assigned to.

```
assign-func-result-STRING(var this-string:string):string
begin
  if this-string ≠ nil
    with this-string ^ do
      ref-count := ref-count – 1
  assign-func-result-STRING := this-string
  this-string := nil
end
```

This is one of the rare examples of a legitimate use of a function with a side-effect. Although it is not very elegant, it is the cleanest way to assign the value of the function result to the function identifier. None of the more general primitives can be used; for example, the value could not be assigned using the assign-STRING procedure because of the Pascal rule that function results can only be given by assignment statements. The local variable could not be finalized using final-STRING because that would dispose of the value if the reference count was zero. Rita could have invented a finalize-variable-which-is-a-function-result-STRING procedure and insisted that it be applied to the result variable after it has been assigned to the function result, but that would have meant the programmer writing two statements.

12.1.7 Implementation of main strings package operations

The implementation details of the strings package operations are hidden from the user of the package. When she implemented them, the obvious question Rita asked herself was whether they should be hidden from each other. Certainly it can help when implementing a complicated string operation to use other, perhaps less complicated, operations of the package. If the former does not assume how the latter work, the final package will be more easily maintained. This is because changing the method of implementation, but not the functional definition, of an operation will not affect any other operation that uses it. However, there may be cases where it is only sensible on the grounds of efficiency to exploit knowledge of how an operation works within the package. Rita adopted the philosophy that the implementation of each operation should be hidden from the others, except where that would lead to unacceptable inefficiency. Whenever there was an assumption about how an operation worked, it would have to be clearly documented.

So, in this respect, the package uses itself in much the same way as a program which uses it. A consequence of this is that the operations of the strings package must obey the rules regarding initialization and finalization of any parameters and local variables that are strings.

12.1.8 Assignment of strings

The assignment operation is specified as

> **Procedure** *AssignSTRING*(**Var** *lhs*: *String*; *rhs*: *String*);
>
> pre true
> post rhs = lhs

When assigning one string to have the same value as another, there is no need for a copy to be made. All that the operation must do is copy the pointer to the string and increment the reference count of the string value. It may be that the parameter which is assuming the new value already points to a string. If this is so, the reference count of that old string must be decremented and the value disposed of if the count becomes zero. In fact, that is precisely what is done when a string variable is finalized:

```
assign-STRING(var lhs: string; rhs: string)
begin
  init-val-param-STRING(rhs)
  final-STRING(lhs) { to dereference any existing value }
  if rhs = nil { Empty string }
    lhs := nil
  else
    lhs := rhs  { Ref. copy }
    with rhs ^
      ref-count := ref-count + 1
  end-of-if
  final-STRING(rhs)
end
```

Figure 12.5 illustrates the result of the statement

> assign-STRING(string2,string1)

where **string1** is as in Figure 12.2.

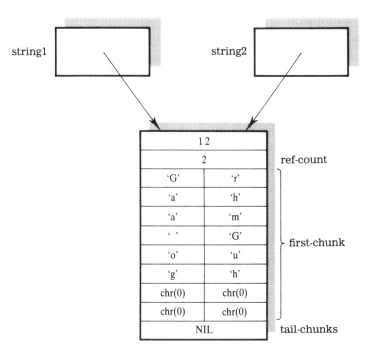

Figure 12.5 The results of assign-STRING(string2,string1), where string1 was as in Figure 12.2.

12.1.9 Length of a string

The operation to return the length of a string is specified as

> **Function** *LengthOfSTRING(ThisString : String):Nat0;*
>
> LengthOfSTRING(ThisString) △ len(ThisString)

The required value is readily obtained from the string data structure:

```
length-of-STRING(this-string : string):nat0
begin
  init-val-param-STRING(this-string)
  if this-string = nil
    length-of-STRING := 0
  else
    length-of-STRING := this-string ^.length
  final-STRING(this-string)
end
```

Rita freely admits that she was tempted not to bother with the initialization and finalization of this-string here, because the body does not use any of the operations of the package. However, it was not just pedantic application of her adopted philosophy that made her put it in. No, just as she had decided to write them solely because of her pedantic application of the philosophy, she realized why they were important! Consider the following statement:

```
length-I-need := 
      length-of-STRING(some-function-of-mine(some-arguments))
```

The string passed to the length function has a reference count of zero, because it is the result of some other function. If there was no finalization at the end of the length function, the string would never be disposed! This would result in a loss of useful memory, which could be critical if this or similar statements were executed a lot. Rita was tempted to omit the initialization and finalization because she mistakenly considered them as the dual of each other: one increments the reference count, and the other decrements it. However, the finalization may also dispose the string, whereas the init-val-param-STRING does not create it. As the code is written, init-val-param-STRING increments the reference count to one, and then final-STRING decrements it to zero and disposes the memory used. Rita is firmly convinced that pedantic adoption of sensible rules is sensible, unless one can *prove* otherwise.

12.1.10 Indexing strings

The operation to access a particular element of a string is specified as

Function *IndexSTRING(ThisString : String; i : Nat1):Char;*

pre i ≤ LengthOfSTRING(ThisString)

IndexSTRING(ThisString,i) △ ThisString[i]

This function returns the character occurring at a given index position in a particular string. It is implemented by looping through the linked list, until it finds the chunk that contains the required character:

```
index-STRING(this-string : string; i : nat1):char

var j : 2..maxint; chunk : string-tail

begin
  init-val-param-STRING(this-string)
  with this-string ^
    if i ≤ chunk-size
      index-STRING := first-chunk[i]
    else
```

```
            chunk := tail-chunks
            for j := 2 to (i – 1) div chunk-size
                chunk := chunk ^.further-tail-chunks
            index-STRING := chunk ^.this-tail-chunk[
                                         (i – 1) mod chunk-size + 1 ]
        end-of-if
    final-STRING(this-string)
end
```

Note that the procedure will cause a run-time error if its pre-condition is violated. We asked Rita what she thought about that:

> RITA: Obviously, I could have put a test in and defined the operation to do something if the position was beyond the end of the string. However, that would make the operation less efficient when the position is not beyond the end of the string. In particular, in applications where the nature of the program ensures that the position is in range, the added test would be just wasted time – over-engineering. Users of the package should read the specifications, and if they wish to use this operation in places where the position *might* be out of range, they should provide their own test for it.

12.1.11   Possible improvement of index-STRING

One possible problem with Rita's implementation of indexing is the need to search from the beginning of the string for the chunk containing the position required. This problem is caused by the data structure being a linked list.

Coming back to the current implementation, it's interesting to see an example here of the disadvantage of abstract data types. Many applications of indexing need to index every position in a string; for example, to count the number of upper case letters. Scanning once through a linked list is a linear problem: the time taken is proportional to $N \times M$, for a list of length N nodes each containing M values. However, with the above implementation, such an algorithm would take time proportional to $N^2 \times M$, because it is necessary to go back to the beginning of the list before looking at each position. So it would be much faster if the program used the linked list structure directly, rather than have it hidden through the abstract data type.

Given that such forward scans may be common, a possible improvement, which would not affect the functionality or interface of the package, would be to add an intermediate linked list pointer to the string head record. This new pointer would point to one of the chunks in the linked list. It would be accompanied by a natural number corresponding to the first string position in the chunk pointed to. The intermediate pointer would be used as a starting point for searching, if the required position was not before it. The intermediate pointer would be set after all searches. Thus scanning through a string in a forwards direction would be efficient (but not so in a backwards direction!). This fact would be documented as a behavioural characteristic of the package.

12.1.12   Converting dynamic to static strings

Converting a dynamic string to a packed array representation involves scanning through each element in the string and putting it into the array, until either the array is full or the end of the string is reached. This form of scanning is needed many times within the package, and thus Rita designed two auxiliary operations (not advertised to users of the package) and another data type to help. The data type enables a position within a string to be recorded. One of the auxiliary operations, set-to-first-pos-STRING, sets a position to the first of a given string. The other, move-to-next-pos-STRING, moves a given position forward one place within a string.

The data type that records a position in a string is a record with two fields: a pointer to a node of the string, and an index into the chunk in that node. The pointer must reference either a string-rec record, or a string-tail-rec record, depending on whether the position represented is in the first chunk of the string or a subsequent one. So the pointer is either of type string or of type string-tail. This means that the data type must be a **variant record.**

We sometimes wish to represent data that has more than one possible form. This is done in Pascal through the **record** concept, but with alternative or **variant** field names. The alternatives are based on a special field known as a **tag**, and are expressed via a case structure.

For example, the following variant record type might be found in an order processing program for True-Blue-Trendy-Togs, a made-to-measure clothing workshop:

```
garment = Record
              customer : String;
              material : (Denim, StretchDenim, RippedDenim, StoneWashedDenim);
              colour   : (Blue, DarkBlue, LightBlue, StreakyBlue);
              Case GarmentKind : (trousers, jacket, skirt, blouse) Of
                  trousers : (InsideLeg, TrouserWaist : Integer;
                              TrouserFit : (LoosePants, TightPants, SopranoPants));
                  jacket : (Chest, JacketArmLength, JacketLength : Integer;
                            JacketStyle : (SingleBreasted, DoubleBreasted,
                                MachoBreasted));
```

```
       skirt : (SkirtHem, SkirtWaist : Integer;
                Split : (NoSplit, SmallSplit, BigSplit,
                         EyePopperSplit);
                Pleated : Boolean);
       blouse : (Bust, BlouseLength, BlouseWaist,
                 BlouseArmLength : Integer;
                 BlouseNeck : (HighNeck, PlungeNeck, NavelDisplayNeck);
                 pockets : Boolean);
   End;
```

A record value from this type has the fields *customer*, *material*, *colour* and the tag field *GarmentKind*, and has three, four, four or six other fields depending on the value of the tag being *trousers*, *jacket*, *skirt* or *blouse* respectively. Note that the fields corresponding to a particular variant do not exist unless the tag field has the appropriate value for that variant.

The type of the positions within a string is called pos-in-string and is defined as

```
pos-in-string = record
                  index-in-chunk: 1 .. chunk-size;
                  case in-first-chunk:boolean of
                    true: (head-chunk-containing-pos: string);
                    false: (tail-chunk-containing-pos: string-tail)
                end;
```

The procedure set-to-first-pos-STRING initializes a pos-in-string so that it refers to the first position in the given string. Although the procedure does not change the string parameter, it is implemented as a variable parameter to ensure that it actually is a string *variable*, rather than the result of a function.

```
set-to-first-pos-STRING(var first-pos:pos-in-string;
                        var this-string: string)

begin
  with first-pos
    in-first-chunk := true
    head-chunk-containing-pos := this-string
    index-in-chunk := 1
end
```

The move-to-next-pos-STRING procedure returns the character at the given position in the string and moves the position along to the next one. There are two cases, depending on whether the position is still in the head chunk or in a tail chunk. The procedure assumes that the position is a legal position, and is not at the end of the string.

:=

```
              move-to-next-pos-STRING(var this-pos: pos-in-string;
                                   var char-at-this-pos: char)
     var next-chunk: string-tail
     begin
       with this-pos
         if in-first-chunk
           { header record }
           char-at-this-pos : =
             head-chunk-containing-pos ^.first-chunk[index-in-chunk]
           if index-in-chunk ≠ chunk-size
             index-in-chunk : = index-in-chunk + 1
           else
             index-in-chunk : = 1
             next-chunk : = head-chunk-containing-pos ^.tail-chunks
             { change variant }
             in-first-chunk : = false
             tail-chunk-containing-pos : = next-chunk
           end-of-if
         else
           { tail record }
           char-at-this-pos : =
             tail-chunk-containing-pos ^.this-tail-chunk[index-in-chunk]
           if index-in-chunk ≠ chunk-size
             index-in-chunk : = index-in-chunk + 1
           else
             index-in-chunk : = 1
             tail-chunk-containing-pos : =
               tail-chunk-containing-pos ^.further-tail-chunks
           end-of-if
         end-of-if
     end
```

Now, returning to the conversion from dynamic to static strings, the
operation is defined as

Procedure *MakeStaticSTRING(dynamic: String;*
Var *static:* **Packed Array** [*lo. .hi:Integer*] **Of** *Char*);

```
post let static-len = hi − lo + 1 in
    if static-len > len(dynamic) then
        (∀ i ∈ { lo , . . . , lo + len(dynamic) − 1 } •
        static[i] = dynamic[i − lo + 1]
        )
        and
        (∀ i ∈ { lo + len(dynamic) ,. . . , hi } •
        static[i] = ' '
        )
    else
        (∀ i ∈ { lo , . . . , hi } •
        static[i] = dynamic[i − lo + 1]
        )
```

This is implemented by moving from the beginning to the end of the
static array, extracting the characters from the dynamic string and
copying them into the static. If the dynamic string is shorter than the
static one, the static array is padded out with space characters.

```
make-static-STRING(
                dynamic: string;
                var static: packed array[lo. .hi:integer] of char)

var pos-in-static: integer
    length-copied-so-far: nat1
    length-of-dynamic: nat0
    ch : char
    pos-in-dynamic: pos-in-string

begin
  init-val-param-STRING(dynamic)

  length-copied-so-far := 0
  length-of-dynamic := length-of-STRING(dynamic)
  if length-of-dynamic ≠ 0
    set-to-first-pos-STRING(pos-in-dynamic, dynamic)
  for pos-in-static := lo to hi
    if length-copied-so-far < length-of-dynamic
      move-to-next-pos-STRING(pos-in-dynamic, ch)
      static[pos-in-static] := ch
      length-copied-so-far := length-copied-so-far + 1
    else
      static[pos-in-static] := ' '
  end-of-for
  final-STRING(dynamic)
end
```

12.1.13   Reading strings

As described in Chapter 10, there are two procedures for reading a line
from a text file into a string variable. One of these, readln-STRING,
reads the whole line into the string variable such that the file read
position is left pointing after the end of the line.

Procedure *ReadlnSTRING*(**Var** *TextFile* : *Text*; **Var** *result* : *String*);

pre   TextFile open for reading and not eof(TextFile)

post result = hd($\overline{\text{TextFile}}$) and TextFile = tl($\overline{\text{TextFile}}$)

In the design of this procedure, Rita exploited the fact that an unbounded
problem can be solved by an **unbounded sum of bounded sub-problems.**

Programming often requires the solution of problems that handle unbounded data. This can lead to inefficiency, as often the most efficient data structure in a particular programming language is bounded (for example, arrays versus linked lists). One route round this stems from the fact that an unbounded problem can be the **unbounded sum of bounded sub-problems.** This can be applied by recognizing the sum (for example, concatenation of strings) and achieving the unbounded sum by iteration or recursion.

The string to be read from the file is unbounded. This could be read by repeatedly reading a single character, and concatenating that on to a dynamic string, initially set to empty. Reading a single character is a bounded problem, so such an algorithm would be an unbounded sum of bounded problems. However, it would not be very efficient. Rita's solution reads a number of characters into an array, until the array is full or the end of the string is reached. That array is then converted to a dynamic string by the make-limited-STRING procedure. This is similar to the make-STRING procedure described in Chapter 10, but it converts only a leading portion of the array rather than all of it (since the array might not be full). Then, if the end of the string to be read was not reached, the procedure recursively reads the rest of the string and concatenates the result on to the end of that already read. Thus, the problem has been split up into the concatenation of a bounded string with an unbounded string, which may itself be the concatenation of a bounded and an unbounded string (and so on). This approach is sufficiently efficient, as long as the array is large enough that the recursion is not needed very often.

```
readln-STRING(var text-file: text; var result: string)

const buffer-length = 120

var rest-of-line : string
    partial-line-length : nat0
    partial-line : packed array [1. .buffer-length] of char
      { maybe all }
begin
  init-STRING(rest-of-line)
  partial-line-length := 0
  while not eoln(text-file) and
          (partial-line-length ≠ buffer-length)
      partial-line-length := partial-line-length + 1
      read(text-file, partial-line[partial-line-length])
  end-of-while
```

```
    if partial-line-length = 0
      assign-STRING(result, empty-STRING)
    else
      assign-STRING(result,
                      make-limited-STRING(partial-line,
                                            partial-line-length))
    end-of-if
    { Check for more characters on the input line }
    if not eoln(text-file)
      { Get the rest }
      readln-STRING(text-file, rest-of-line)
      assign-STRING(result, concat-STRING(result, rest-of-line))
    else
      get(text-file) { move past the end-of-line }
    end-of-if
    final-STRING(rest-of-line)
  end
```

The other read procedure, **read-STRING**, has an extra function parameter, stop, which returns a Boolean value. This procedure also reads a string from a text file, but, in this case, the string is terminated, either by coming to the end of the line, or by the stop function returning a value of true when it is applied to the character currently being read, whichever occurs first. In either case, the file read position is left at (rather than after) the terminator.

Procedure *ReadSTRING*(**Var** *TextFile*: *Text*;
                    Var *result*: *String*;
                    Function *stop*(*c*:*Char*):*Boolean*);

pre   TextFile open for reading and not eof(TextFile)

post let first-line: String be hd($\overleftarrow{\text{TextFile}}$) in
        ($\exists$ n $\in$ $\mathbb{N}$ •
            stop(first-line[n])
            and (not $\exists$ m $\in$ $\mathbb{N}$ •
                        m < n and stop(first-line[m])
)
            and result = first-line[1 , . . . , n − 1]
            and TextFile = [first-line[n , . . . , len first-line]] $\frown$ tl ($\overleftarrow{\text{TextFile}}$)
)
        or
        ((not $\exists$ n $\in$ $\mathbb{N}$ • stop(first-line[n]))
          and result = first-line
          and TextFile = [ ] $\frown$ tl($\overleftarrow{\text{TextFile}}$)
)

The design is similar to the previous one. The differences are in the conditions of the while loop, the if statement guarding the recursion, and the absence of the get to skip the terminator.

```
read-STRING(var text-file: text; var result: string;
                    function stop(c:char):boolean)

const buffer-length = 120

var rest-of-line : string
    partial-line-length : nat0
    partial-line : packed array [1..buffer-length] of char
begin
  init-STRING(rest-of-line)
  partial-line-length := 0
  while not eoln(text-file)
        and (partial-line-length ≠ buffer-length)
        and not stop(text-file ^ )
    partial-line-length := partial-line-length + 1
    read(text-file, partial-line[partial-line-length])
  end-of-while
  if partial-line-length = 0
    assign-STRING(result, empty-STRING)
  else
    assign-STRING(result,
                  make-limited-STRING(partial-line,
                                      partial-line-length))
  { Check for more characters on the input line }
  if not stop(text-file ^ ) and not eoln(text-file)
    { Get the rest }
    read-STRING(text-file, rest-of-line, stop)
    assign-STRING(result, concat-STRING(result, rest-of-line))
  final-STRING(rest-of-line)
end
```

Rita is aware that she could have implemented readln-STRING by using read-STRING, but she decided not to in the interests of run-time efficiency.

12.1.14   Comparison of strings

The six comparison operations are very similar to each other. One of them is specified as

Function *EqualSTRING(left,right: String):Boolean*;

EqualSTRING(left,right) △ left = right

Because of the similarity, Rita decided to use an auxiliary general string comparison function. This returns one of three possible values as its result, corresponding to the first given string being less than, equal to or greater than the second.

string-compare-result =
    (string-less-than, string-equal, string-greater-than)

The compare-STRING operation is implemented by a loop which compares the strings, chunk by chunk. The loop has a complicated exit condition, depending on results of comparisons or lengths of strings. This is controlled by a **state indicator.**

Some problems require the design of a loop with a complicated exit condition consisting of several possible states. One way to achieve this is to have a **state indicator.** This is a variable, usually of an enumerated type, which can have one of several values, each corresponding to one of the possible exit conditions. The typical use of a Boolean typed flag can be regarded as a special case of the general concept of a state indicator.

```
compare-STRING(left, right: string):string-compare-result

var left-length, right-length: nat0
    left-tail, right-tail: string-tail
    state: (go-on, less, greater, stop)
begin
  init-val-param-STRING(left)
  init-val-param-STRING(right)

  left-length := length-of-STRING(left)
  right-length := length-of-STRING(right)
  { Do trivial cases first }
  if left-length = 0
    if right-length = 0
      compare-STRING := string-equal
    else
      compare-STRING := string-less-than
  else
  if right-length = 0
    compare-STRING := string-greater-than
  else
    { Non-trivial cases – both left and right are non-empty }
    left-tail := left ^.tail-chunks
    right-tail := right ^.tail-chunks
    if left ^.first-chunk < right ^.first-chunk
      state := less
    else
    if left ^.first-chunk > right ^.first-chunk
      state := greater
    else
      state := go-on
```

```
                    { Check tails if necessary }
                    while state = go-on
                      if left-tail = nil or right-tail = nil
                        state := stop
                      else
                      if left-tail ^.this-tail-chunk < right-tail ^.this-tail-chunk
                        state := less
                      else
                      if left-tail ^.this-tail-chunk > right-tail ^.this-tail-chunk
                        state := greater
                      else
                        left-tail := left-tail ^.further-tail-chunks
                        right-tail := right-tail ^.further-tail-chunks
                    end-of-while

                    { Final check for differing lengths (and so on) }
                    case state of
                      less: compare-STRING := string-less-than
                      greater: compare-STRING := string-greater-than
                      stop: if left-length < right-length
                              compare-STRING := string-less-than
                            else
                            if left-length > right-length
                              compare-STRING := string-greater-than
                            else
                              compare-STRING := string-equal
                    end-of-case
                  end-of-if {not left-length = 0 and not right-length = 0}
                  final-STRING(left)
                  final-STRING(right)
                end
```

The compare-STRING procedure makes use of the fact that the last chunk of a string is filled up in the unused positions with the smallest character, *chr(0)*. This enables the procedure to compare even the last chunks of a string in one go, rather than comparing individual characters, because

$$\forall\ c \in Char \bullet chr(0) \leqslant c$$

and

$$\forall\ s \in Seq\ of\ Char,\ c \in Char \bullet s < (s \frown [c])$$

Each of the six comparison operations uses compare-STRING to rank the strings, and sets its Boolean result accordingly:

```
equal-STRING(left,right: string):boolean
begin
  init-val-param-STRING(left)
  init-val-param-STRING(right)
  equal-STRING := compare-STRING(left, right) = string-equal
  final-STRING(left)
  final-STRING(right)
end
```

The other five comparisons are similar.

12.1.15 Concatenation of strings

The concatenate operation takes two strings and returns their concatenation.

Function *ConcatSTRING(s*1, *s*2: *String):String*;

ConcatSTRING(s1,s2) △ s1 ⌢ s2

Rita's algorithm creates a new string, copies s1 on to it and then adds s2 on to that. s1 can be copied in whole chunks, but s2 needs to be copied as individual characters. Rita spotted an optimization: if the reference count of s1 is zero when the concatenate is called, then there is no need to make a fresh copy of it. This would be the case if it was the result of some other function. She uses an auxiliary procedure copy-STRING to make a copy of s1 otherwise. A similar optimization applies if either of the strings are empty. In these cases the result is obtained by assigning the other string, rather than copying it.

```
concat-STRING(s1, s2: string):string

var null: char { set to chr(0) }
    result:string
    length-of-s1:integer
    extra-tail-chunk-count:integer
    extra-tail-chunk-list:stringtail
    next-result-chunk:stringtail

begin { of concat-STRING }
  null := chr(0)
  init-val-param-STRING(s1)
  init-val-param-STRING(s2)
  init-STRING(result)

  { Deal with trivial cases first }
  if s1 = nil
    assign-STRING(result,s2)
  else
  if s2 = nil
    assign-STRING(result,s1)
```

:=

```
else

  { Both s1 and s2 are non-empty }

  { Obtain convenient copy of length of s1 }
  length-of-s1 := s1 ^.length

  { If there were no references to s1 beforehand, we can
    reuse that string in the answer }
  if s1 ^.ref-count = 1 { Note: it has been incremented by
                                  init-val-param-STRING }
    assign-STRING(result,s1)
  else
    copy-STRING(result,s1)

  { Now fill in the answer }
  with result ^
    { Set length }
    length := length-of-s1 + s2 ^.length

    build-extra-chunks(extra-tail-chunk-list,extra-tail-chunk-count)
    { builds enough tail chunks to store s2 on the end of
      result }

    { Append new chunks on end of result }
    append-tail-on-result(extra-tail-chunk-list,next-result-chunk)
    { Adds on chunk-list to result, and finds
      next-result-chunk, = pointer
      to first tail chunk to contain a char after the old s1 }

    { At this stage, result contains (a copy of) s1, and
      enough chunks for s2. next-result-chunk points to the
      tail chunk to be next used for copying s2 }

    copy-s2-to-result(next-result-chunk)
  end-of-if {not s1 = nil and not s2 = nil}

  final-STRING(s1)
  final-STRING(s2)
  concat-STRING := assign-func-result-STRING(result)
end
```

The implementations of the sub-procedures build-extra-chunks, append-tail-on-result and copy-s2-to-result can be found in Appendix C.

Rita has noted a possible future extension which could help the efficiency of many programs that use concatenation. She feels that statements like

```
assign-string(this-string,
              concat-STRING(this-string, some-string))
```

are quite common. In principle, it should be possible to avoid copying the value of **this-string** if there are no other references to it. Unfortunately, this information is contained only outside the strings package, and so the string will always be copied. To facilitate the optimization, Rita is considering extending the package with a procedure that concatenates a string value on to the end of a string variable. Such an apparently trivial consideration could make a vast difference to the speed of a program that, say, built a string by adding on a single character at a time inside a loop.

12.2   Robustness

One issue that has not been addressed is that of the robustness of the strings package; that is, how easy it is to cause it to crash. Quite correctly, Rita's view is that it is the responsibility of the programmer to ensure that the rules of the package and all the pre-conditions of the operations are satisfied. Otherwise, the code would have to be less efficient. However, there are times when a programmer makes a mistake, and some of those times the mistake is hard to find. In such circumstances, it would be nice to have a version of the package that is robust, and helps the programmer discover the mistake, rather than just crashing. This version would check all the pre-conditions and report an error if any were violated. The main cause of problems is the inadvertent omission of initialization and finalization of string variables. The latter causes no functional problems, merely one of using more memory. However, the former causes a crash in the real package when an uninitialized variable is assigned a value. One way of preventing this problem in the inefficient robust version would be simply to omit the finalization of the left-hand side in an assignment, in case the variable had never been initialized.

Exercise 12.1

(a)   Give an informal but clear and precise explanation of the following formal specification. Avoid simply translating the symbols into English. Suggest meaningful names for L, D, n, i and o.

$$L = \text{Seq of Char}$$
$$\text{inv-L(list)} \triangleq \text{len(list)} \leqslant 100$$

$$D$$
$$\text{ext rd i:L}$$
$$\qquad \text{rd c:Char}$$
$$\qquad \text{wr o:L}$$

$$\text{pre   true}$$

post not (c ∈ elems o)
    and
    (∀ x ∈ elems o ∪ elems i – {c} • n(x,o) = n(x,i))
    and
    (∀ j,k ∈ inds o •
        j < k ⇒ ∃ p,q ∈ inds i • i[p] = o[j]
                     and
                     i[q] = o[k]
                     and
                     p > q
)

n : (c : Char , list : L) → (r : ℕ)
pre   true
post card { i ∈ inds(list) | list[i] = c } = r

(b)   Write a program to implement the above specification. Make sensible assumptions about the form of the input and output.

(c)   What would be the impact on the implementation if the expression

$$p > q$$

on the last line of the specification of D were altered to

$$p < q$$

Exercise 12.2

(a)   Give an informal but clear and precise explanation of the following formal specification. Avoid simply translating the symbols into English. (Suggest better names for func, argument and result.)

func : (argument : Seq of Char) → (result : array['a' .. 'z'] of ℝ)
pre   true
post ∀ i ∈ {'a' , . . . , 'z' } •
        result[i] * card { j ∈ inds argument | argument[j] ∈ { 'a' , . . . , 'z' } }
        =
        card { j ∈ inds argument | argument[j] = i }

(b)   Design an efficient Pascal procedure that implements the specification given in part (a). The argument in the specification is to be implemented as a text file, and must be a variable parameter of the procedure. The result in the specification is to be implemented as a second variable parameter. You should choose appropriate names for these, and any other identifiers you use (including the name of the procedure).

Exercise 12.3   The function D is specified as follows:

D : (s : Seq of ℝ) → (s1 : Seq of ℝ)
pre s ≠ [ ]
post s1 = if len s = 1
        then [0]
        else d(tl s , 1)

d : (s : Seq of ℝ , n : ℕ) → Seq of ℝ
d(s,n) △ if s = [ ] then [ ]
            else [n * hd s] ⌢ d(tl s , n + 1)

(a)   Give an informal but clear and precise explanation of the above formal
       specification. Avoid simply translating the symbols into English. What
       well known mathematical operation is being modelled by D?

(b)   Assume the following Pascal data structure:

SeqOfReal = ^ *SeqOfRealRec*;

SeqOfRealRec = **Record**
                        head : *Real*;
                        tail   : *SeqOfReal*
                   End;

Give a non-recursive implementation of the function D.

Exercise 12.4

(a)   Give an informal but clear and precise explanation of the following
       formal specification. Avoid simply translating the symbols into English.

            wild-card = '*'

            matches (this-string : Seq of Char) result : B
            ext rd pattern:Seq of Char
            pre true
            post result = ∃ wild-card-substitution ∈ Seq of Seq of Char •
                            this-string

                            =

                    fill-in-wild-cards(pattern,wild-card-substitution)

            fill-in-wild-cards : (pattern : Seq of Char,
                                substitution : Seq of Seq of Char) → Seq of Char
            fill-in-wild-cards(pattern,substitution) △
                if pattern = [ ] then [ ]
                else
                    if hd pattern = wild-card then
                        hd substitution ⌢ fill-in-wild-cards(tl pattern , tl substitution)
                    else
                        [hd pattern] ⌢ fill-in-wild-cards(tl pattern , substitution)

(b)   The following procedure (with its associated declarations) is an
       approximate implementation of the specification in part (a), in that it
       assumes an implementation of sequences of characters with a
       maximum length. Present an informal but convincing argument that it
       is otherwise correct with respect to the specification. Diagrams will
       probably assist your argument. Comment on the efficiency of the
       algorithm.

Const *MaxSeqLength* = 100;

Type *SeqOfChar* = **Record**
                        value : **Array**[1. .*MaxSeqLength*] **Of** *Char*;
                        length : 0. .*MaxSeqLength*
                   End;

```
Var pattern : SeqOfChar;

Procedure matches(ThisString : SeqOfChar; Var result : Boolean);

  Procedure MatchRemaining(ThisStringPos, PatternPos : Integer);
  Var AfterWildEndPos : Integer;
  Begin
    If PatternPos > pattern.length Then
      result := result Or (ThisStringPos > ThisString.length)
    Else
    Begin
      If pattern.value[PatternPos] <> '*' Then
      Begin
        If ThisStringPos <= ThisString.length Then
          If ThisString.value[ThisStringPos] =
             pattern.value[PatternPos] Then
             MatchRemaining(ThisStringPos + 1, PatternPos + 1)
      End
      Else
      Begin
        For AfterWildEndPos := ThisStringPos To
                               ThisString.length + 1 Do
          MatchRemaining(AfterWildEndPos, PatternPos + 1)
      End;
    End;
  End;

Begin
  result := false;
  MatchRemaining(1,1)
End;
```

SUMMARY

This chapter has described the major features of interest in the design of the strings package. If you are interested (and feel strong enough) to see the implementation of the entire strings package, it is listed in Appendix C.

The chapter has been a vehicle for studying some more sophisticated dynamic data structures, although they were still based on the idea of a linked list.

It also introduced the Pascal concepts of the *dispose* statement, the **With** statement and **variant records.** More general design issues presented included **reference counts, state indicators,** and the employment of an **unbounded sum of bounded sub-problems** to solve an **unbounded problem.**

The following notations were introduced in this chapter.

Pascal notation

dispose statement	*dispose*(*ThisString*)
With statement	**With** *ThisString*^ **Do** *RefCount* := *RefCount* + 1
Variant records	**Record** ... **Case** ... **Of** ... **End**

TUTORIAL EXERCISE

The following tutorial exercises refer to the whole strings package (given in full in Appendix C). They test not only understanding of Chapter 12, but also the ability to understand code which has not been previously explained.

1

Write a function, *TextToString*, which converts a text file into a string by concatenating all the lines. For example, if the file *f* contains

        ABCD
        EFGHI
        JK

then

        EqualSTRING(*TextToString*(*f*),*MakeSTRING*('*ABCDEFGHIJK*'))
            = *True*

2

Write a procedure that, given an array of strings, sorts them into ascending lexicographic (normal dictionary) order.

3

(a)   What problems can arise if a user of the strings package ignores the advice to copy strings only via the *AssignSTRING* procedure?

(b)   Why is *MakeSTRING*('!') illegal?

(c)   In the operation *ChangeCharInSTRING*, why is *CopySTRING*(*UpdateString,UpdateString*) not equivalent to a dummy statement?

(d)   What is the advantage of making most of the string operations functions rather than procedures?

(e)   Under what circumstances can the reference count of a string value be zero?

Appendix A
Collected concepts

The concepts introduced throughout this book are reproduced here in an order more suited to perusal of related items. Entries in the main index at the back of the book refer to the place in the text where a concept is defined and also its appearance in this appendix.

A.1 General concepts

A.1.1 The four stages of programming

The programming process is concerned with producing a program to solve a problem. It may be divided into four stages of development: requirements analysis, specification, design and implementation.

- *Requirements* The requirements of the user are expressed informally, ambiguously and often incompletely in English. Requirements analysis is intended to give the programmer a full understanding of the problem.

- *Specification* With the insight and understanding gained from the requirements analysis, the specification part of the process produces a precise and complete statement of the program behaviour, as the basis of a contract between the customer and the programmer. Unambiguous, formal mathematical concepts are used to define the *effect*, but *not* the method of the program.

- *Design* This informal process produces an algorithm for solving the problem described in the specification.

- *Implementation* This stage is the (relatively straightforward) task of converting the design into a program written in some formal computer programming language, and testing it on a computer.

The requirements analysis stage of programming

The requirements are initially put forward by the customer. They are written (or spoken!) informally in English and are not always complete. This can be because the customer has not considered the problem deeply enough, or, more usually, simply does not have a sufficient appreciation of computer programming to be aware of the absolute exactness needed. It is the task of the person normally called the **systems analyst** to discuss the requirements with the originator of the problem and make them more precise. This is often difficult because not only may the user not know about programming, but also the systems analyst may not know about the user's application area.

Another source of defects is that natural language is not formal, and therefore is not always precise. Consequently, anything written in natural language can be interpreted in different ways by different people, or by the same person at different times. A change of wording can sometimes improve the precision of the requirements statement, but in many cases it is not possible to write the requirements precisely until the formal specification stage.

The specification stage of programming

A specification is a formal description of the required program using notation based on logic and mathematics. This describes the data and program operations in an abstract manner, without any stipulations about how these should be implemented. The specification should be complete and unambiguous. It may form the basis of a contract between the customer and the programmer. It should then later be possible to verify whether the program (which is also formal) does in fact implement the specification, and thus whether the contract has been satisfied.

The design stage of programming

Program design is the activity of transforming a formal specification, which defines the *effect* of a program, into some other notation (similar to a formal programming language) which defines *how* this effect is going to be achieved.

Data structures implementing the data types, and algorithms which produce the effect of the operations defined in the specification, must be designed.

Program designs are expressed in an informal notation, usually quite closely resembling the implementation programming language, but with the finer details omitted. This allows the programmer to concentrate on the often difficult process of algorithm construction.

The purpose of the design process is to produce an algorithm that correctly implements the specification. The clearer the algorithm, the more likely it is to be understood. Thus a simple algorithm which is thought to be correct is more likely to be correct than a complex one. Related to this is the fact that very often a program is altered after it is completed, because of changes in the requirements of the customer. Modifying a program is likely to introduce errors, unless the program is very clear to understand. (A program is most often modified by a programmer who did not write it originally.)

On the other hand, efficiency of space and time can be important, as the program must produce results within an acceptable period, and must be able to run on the resources available. There is no point, however, in having a fast solution that produces the wrong answer. There is usually a trade-off between the clarity and simplicity of the method used, and its efficiency. When considering how efficient an algorithm needs to be, the programmer must bear in mind the cost of the design and implementation process, and that of future modifications. It may be that a very efficient algorithm is possible, but would take a long time to develop, and hence cost more. This may be justified, if say the application is time critical. But a program that runs occasionally, and that can be left running overnight, does not need to be very fast.

The implementation stage of programming

Once the design of the program has been formulated, the implementation stage is the relatively straightforward phase of translating the design into the syntax of the programming language being used (in our case, Pascal). The programmer must then ensure that the resulting program actually implements the specification. This is done both by comparing the program with the specification and by running the program and testing all the different logical paths. (The relationship can be proved *formally*, but that is beyond the scope of this book.)

Idealization (approximate implementations)

Often a specification may be regarded as an idealization of the actual requirements, such that an **approximate implementation** is sufficient. For example, in specifications we regard integer (or natural) numbers as being the full infinite set, but it is usually sufficient (and hence appropriate) to implement them using the Pascal type *Integer*, which is bounded. It is quite common, for another example, to specify some structured data using unbounded sequences, when in fact a bounded array implementation is acceptable.

A.1.2   The process of abstraction

An **abstraction** focuses on particular aspects of interest while details which could complicate and obscure those basic aspects are ignored.

A.1.3   Programming errors (bugs)

A **bug** is a term for an error in a program.

A.1.4   Computer data and program files

A computer **file** is a unit of information in a computer system. A file has a beginning and an end, and may be written and read like a book (or even a ring-file). A file may contain **data** (for example, the information concerning all employees of a certain business) or a **program.**

A.1.5   Recovery from errors in input data

Error recovery is a technique of dealing with errors in input data by reporting the error and then attempting to correct it. This involves choosing a sensible default value for the data which can be used in place of erroneous input. In this way, the exponential effect of one early error condition on later parts of the program can be avoided. That is, each part of a program need only be concerned with possible errors that may be detected during execution of that part, and not with errors arising in previously executed parts of the program.

Error routine

For programs that have to deal with a variety of possible errors in input data, it is often useful to use a single **error routine.** This is given some error value, usually from an enumerated type, as a parameter, and writes a corresponding message. In this way, it is easy to control the format and perhaps the frequency of error messages. For example, it may be desired only to report the first three messages, all other calls on the routine being ignored. Error routines are very often used in conjunction with error recovery.

A.1.6   Unbounded problems

A problem may be **unbounded** in its requirement for data. This means that, although every instance of the problem has a finite requirement, there is no upper bound on the requirement. That is, there is *always* the possibility of an instance that requires more than the one which has required the most so far. Such problems need data types which are unbounded. An unbounded data type has no upper limit on the size of data that can be stored, even though every value has a finite size.

A.1.7   Equivalence relations

A **relation** is something that relates two objects (arguments). If R is a relation then

    R(X,Y)

is either true or false. For example, 'less than' (<) on integers is a relation. For any two integers, X, Y, the expression

    X < Y

is either true or false.

An **equivalence relation** is a relation that also has the three following properties. Firstly, an equivalence relation is **reflexive**, that is all objects are related to themselves:

    R(X,X) = true

regardless of X. An equivalence relation is also **symmetric,** that is:

    R(X,Y) = R(Y,X)

regardless of X and Y. Finally, an equivalence relation is **transitive**. This means:

    if R(X,Y) and R(Y,Z) then R(X,Z)

'Less than' on integers is not an equivalence relation, whereas equality is. A more illustrative example comes from hypothetically ideal beasts called white mice, and the relation 'is nice to'. This relation is an equivalence relation on pairs of idealized white mice, due to the following invariant principles of their conduct: all mice are nice to themselves (reflexive); all mice are nice to every mouse that is nice to them (symmetric); and all mice are nice to every mouse that is nice to some mouse that they are also nice to (transitive). This does not stop mice being horrible. In some colonies, mice are only nice to themselves, but the relation is still an equivalence relation. In most colonies, there are gangs of mice such that the members of each gang are really nice to each other, but each gang is pretty nasty to each other gang. 'Is nice to' is still an equivalence relation in these places.

A.1.8 Reference count

A **reference count** is a counter, attached to a particular data item, which keeps a tally of how many variables point to that data item. Whenever a new variable references the item, its reference count is incremented. Whenever a variable ceases to point to the item the reference count is decremented. A variable ceases to point to an item by changing its value so that it points elsewhere, or nowhere (that is, assuming the value **Nil** in Pascal) or by being no longer required.

Reference counters are very often used in automatic garbage collection schemes, so that the space occupied by a value may be safely reused when its reference count is zero.

A.1.9 Wally trap

A **Wally trap** happens when the programmer has written a condition which is apparently sensible, but which may cause a run-time error, because some part of it has an undefined value. There are two usual forms, based respectively on the **And** operator and the **Or** operator.

In an **And-based Wally trap,** one part of the **And** (conjunct) may be undefined when the other part is false. For example, assuming the variables

x : **Array** [1 .. 10] **Of** *Integer*
i : *Integer*

the following condition is an **And**-based Wally trap:

(i **In** [1 .. 10]) **And** (x[i] = 100)

When the first conjunct is true, the expression is evaluated to true or false depending on the value of $x[i]$. The problem is that, if the first conjunct is false, the second one is undefined. This happens, for example, when the value of i is 11. The mistake occurs when the programmer expects the **And** operator to be generous and return a false result when one of its conjuncts is false, regardless of whether the other is undefined. However, in Pascal (and similar languages) such undefined expressions cause a run-time error when they are detected. So, at best, the computer will evaluate both conjuncts of the expression (even though this is not optimally efficient) and always give a run-time error. At worst, the computer that the program is tested on might evaluate the first conjunct, find that it is false and not look at the second one, but return false as the result. This is disastrous, since sooner or, worse still, later the program will be run on a computer that always computes both conjuncts or computes the second one first! So the program you tested and found to be working does not run on the customer's machine! Don't you feel a Wally?

An example of an **Or-based Wally trap,** based on the same variables as above, is

$$(i > 10) \textbf{ Or } (x[i] = 20)$$

This problem does not occur in specifications, because there the operators are defined more generously to return a result whenever possible. That is, and returns false when either of its conjuncts is false (even if the other would be undefined) and or returns true if either of its disjuncts is true. Jones (1990) gives a more detailed discussion of this for the interested reader.

A.2   Specification concepts

A.2.1   Named constants

It is possible to give a meaningful name to a constant value. Such a name can then be used instead of the constant value, thus aiding the clarity of the specification. Such associations also make a specification easier to change, should that be necessary. For example:

basic-tax-rate = 25.0

A.2.2   Data types

A **data type** in specifications is a collection (set) of values. For example, the set of all natural numbers (that is, whole numbers greater than or equal to 0).

Alias names for data types

Sometimes it is helpful to give an alternative name to a type that is already defined. This can greatly aid the clarity of the specification. We write:

A = B

to indicate that the type A is the same as B. For example:

Employee = $\mathbb{N}$

Data type invariant

Sometimes when defining a type we know more about it than can be deduced from standard constructions, such as Seq of .... These additional characteristics are called **invariants,** as they are extra things which are always true about the type. Invariants can be written explicitly after a type definition.

In specifications a data type invariant may be written formally by defining a predicate function associated with the type. The name of the function is **inv-** followed by the name of the type. The function always takes a value of the type as one parameter, and yields true or false as the result. For example, for a type called S, the associated invariant predicate could be:

inv-S : (s : S) → (p : $\mathbb{B}$)
pre ...
post ...

Or the function could be defined explicitly:

inv-S : (s : S) → (p : $\mathbb{B}$)
inv-S(s) $\triangle$ ...

The names of the parameter and the result (s and p in the above example) are not fixed by any convention, whereas the name of the function (inv-S) is. The function expresses formally the extra properties that are true for all members of the type.

Data type invariants are actually a convenient form of set comprehension, as illustrated by the following example:

S = Seq of $\mathbb{N}$
inv-S(s) $\triangle$ (len s = 10)

is equivalent to:

S = { s ∈ Seq of ℕ | len s = 10 }

Equality (on data types)

All types in specifications have an **equality operator**, denoted:

=

This takes two values from the same type and gives true if they are the same value, and false otherwise. It is an **infix** operator (that is, the operator symbol is written between the two arguments). Thus in an expression we write:

x = y

to mean true if and only if x and y have the same value.

The opposite of equality, not-equality, is denoted:

≠

and is used in the same way.

Basic types

The basic types are

𝔹 ℕ ℝ ℤ Char

Boolean type

There is a type assumed to exist in specifications known as **Boolean** and written 𝔹. This has only two values, **true** and **false**. Actually, pre- and post-conditions are expressions of this type. Such expressions are also known as **truth-valued expressions** or **predicates**.

Boolean functions (and, or, not) There are various Boolean operators which can be used to combine Boolean expressions. One of these is **conjunction**, otherwise known as **and**. This takes two Boolean expressions, called **conjuncts,** and returns one Boolean result.

It can be described by way of a table called a **truth table**.

and:		
p	q	p and q
T	T	T
F	T	F
T	F	F
F	F	F

Another Boolean operator which takes two values is **disjunction** otherwise called **or**. This takes two **disjuncts** and is defined as:

or:		
p	q	p or q
T	T	T
F	T	T
T	F	T
F	F	F

A third operator on the Boolean type is **negation** otherwise called **not**. This takes one Boolean value and gives a Boolean result:

not:	
p	not(p)
T	F
F	T

not has a higher precedence than and, which has a higher precedence than or.

Implication   Another function on Booleans is **implication,** written

$$\Rightarrow$$

This takes two Boolean arguments and returns a Boolean result:

$$\_ \Rightarrow \_ : (p : \mathbb{B} , q : \mathbb{B}) \rightarrow \mathbb{B}$$

The result of $p \Rightarrow q$ is always true, unless q is false and p is true.

$\Rightarrow$:		
p	q	$p \Rightarrow q$
T	T	T
F	T	T
T	F	F
F	F	T

For example,

$$(3 < 5) \Rightarrow (\text{len}([1,0]) = 2)$$

is true.

It is often used with variables (for example, quantified or function arguments) to express a dependency of some value on another. For example,

$$\forall x \in \mathbb{N} \bullet x < 10 \Rightarrow x + 1 < 11$$

Natural number type

We assume the existence of some elementary types when writing specifications. Among these is

$$\mathbb{N}$$

which contains all the natural numbers: $0, 1, 2, \ldots$.

Sometimes it is convenient to use the type of natural numbers, but exclude the value zero. We denote this as

$$\mathbb{N}1$$

In many books it is written as

$$\mathbb{N}^+$$

Mod and div (on naturals)   Another operation over $\mathbb{N}$ is the infix **mod**. This takes two arguments, divides the first by the second, and returns the remainder. **div** is the operator that returns the result of the division, hence the following is always true for every n,m : $\mathbb{N}$:

$$(n \text{ div } m) * m + (n \text{ mod } m) = n$$

For example,

$$17 \text{ mod } 4 = 1$$
$$17 \text{ div } 4 = 4$$

Integer number type

Another elementary data type used in specifications is

$$\mathbb{Z}$$

which contains all the whole numbers, including negative ones:

$$\ldots, -2, -1, 0, 1, 2 \ldots$$

The set of natural numbers, ℕ, is a sub-set of ℤ.

Real type

Another assumed type in specifications is

    ℝ

This contains all the **real** numbers between negative and positive infinity. For example, 3.141 592 6.

Char type

Another data type which is usually assumed to exist in specifications is **Char**. This is the set of characters, such as 'A', 'b', '2', '?', and so on. The exact contents of the set is context dependent. In this book we consider it as being the same as the corresponding type in Pascal.

Set type

We have already said that a data type is a set of values. A **set** is an unordered collection of distinct objects – there is no order of the elements in a set. What is more, a value cannot be an element of some set more than once – it is either in the set, or it is not. For example, the set containing only 4, 6, 2, 4 and 2 is the same as the set containing only 4, 2 and 6.

Empty set

In general, a set may be **empty**, that is contain no elements. The empty set is denoted:

    { }

Set enumeration

In specifications, a set may be denoted by simply listing all of its elements separated by commas within curly brackets. For example,

    { 6,2,90,12 }

This of course is the same as:

    { 12,2,90,6 }

and:

    { 12,2,12,90,2,6 }

and so on.

Enumerated set type

In specifications, a new type may be constructed by simply listing the values as a set, written between curly brackets and separated by commas. The values may be part of another type defined elsewhere, or be completely new values. For example:

Player = { human, computer }

Sub-range (interval) of Integer

In specifications, a set may be defined as a **sub-range** or **interval** of the set of integers, $\mathbb{Z}$. The sub-range is the set of integers between two given values, inclusive. These limits are written as two expressions separated by dots. For example,

{ 5 , . . . , 12 }

is the same as:

{ 5,6,7,8,9,10,11,12 }

The formal specification of the notation is given below. In such descriptions of **infix** (two arguments with the operator between) or, as in this case, **mixfix** or **distfix** (a mixture of arguments and operator symbols) operators, underscores are used to mark the argument places in the signature.

$$\{\_,\ldots,\_\} : (i : \mathbb{Z} , j : \mathbb{Z}) \to (rs : \text{Set of } \mathbb{Z})$$
$$\{i,\ldots,j\} \triangleq \{k \in \mathbb{Z} \mid i \leqslant k \leqslant j\}$$

This means that the set is empty if i is greater than j.

Set membership

Another function on sets is a test for **membership** of a set, written as

$\in$

This returns true if a given value is an element of a given set. For example,

c $\in$ { a,b,c }

is true, but not

d $\in$ { a,b,c }

Cardinality of sets (card)

card is a function that says how many elements there are in a (finite) set, that is it yields the **cardinality** of a given set. For example,

card ({ a,d,c,a,e,e }) = 4

Set comprehension

A general way of specifying the elements in a set is by what is called **set comprehension.** This defines a set that contains all elements from another set which satisfy some property. One form involves a logical variable from a given type, which is a typical member of the set being constructed. For example,

{ i ∈ ℕ | 1 ≤ i ≤ 3 }

This means the set ({) of *all* elements, i, from the set ℕ, such that (|) 1≤i≤3. It is the same as the set {1,2,3}. One could imagine constructing the set by taking all the natural numbers, and removing those for which the property is *not* true. Another example is:

{ s ∈ Seq of { 1,2,3 } | len(s) = 2 and s[1] < s[2] }

This is the same as:

{ [1,2] , [2,3] , [1,3] }

Set comprehension is, of course, most useful for denoting very large (or even infinite) sets, or sets dependent on an unknown, such as a function argument or operation external variable.

There is an alternative form for writing set comprehensions. Rather than say the members of the set are the values of some logical variable satisfying a given property, it is often more convenient to state that the members of the set are the values yielded after applying some function to all the values of one or more logical variables having certain properties.

For example, the set of factorials of all prime numbers can be specified, assuming definitions of fact and is-prime, as:

{ fact(i) | i ∈ ℕ and is-prime(i) }

More generally, the elements of the set being defined are all the possible values of some expression, written before the |, involving some functions and/or operators applied to each other and to some logical variables. The types of these logical variables are given on the right-hand side of the |, together with their other properties.

For example, the set of squares of all distances from the origin in integer coordinate geometry is:

{ x * x + y * y | x ∈ ℤ and y ∈ ℤ }

Set difference

A set may be subtracted from another set by the **set difference** operator. This yields another set which has exactly all the elements of one set, which are not members of the other.

_ _ _ : (s1 : Set of X , s2 : Set of X) → (r : Set of X)

post (∀ e ∈ s1 •
   if e ∈ s2 then not (e ∈ r)
   else e ∈ r
)
  and
  (∀ e ∈ r • r ∈ s1)

For example,

{ 12, 34, 5, 6, 13 } − { 74, 13, 82, 34, 123 } = { 12, 5, 6 }

Set intersection

A function on sets that is similar to union is **intersection.** This takes two sets and returns the set of elements that are in *both* sets. For example:

{2,7,8,2,5} ∩ {4,2,9,8,3} = {2,8}

and

{ [2,4], [ ], [5] } ∩ { [4,2], [0,5] } = { }

Set union

A function on sets (and thus on specification types) is **set union**. This takes two sets and produces the set containing all values that were in either of the two given. In specifications we use the infix ∪ operator for union. For example:

{4,3,10,1} ∪ {25,10,2,1,15} = {4,10,25,3,15,1,2}

Distributed union (of set of sets)

The **distributed union** of a set of sets is the union of all the element sets. For example,

$$\cup (\{ \{3,5,10\} , \{4,10\} , \{9,3,2\} \})$$
$$= \{3,5,10\} \cup \{4,10\} \cup \{9,3,2\}$$
$$= \{2,3,4,5,9,10\}$$

Sequence type

A **sequence** is a list of elements, possibly with duplicates, where the order
in which they occur is important. When we write:

Y-seq = Seq of Y

we are defining a type called Y-seq. This contains all possible sequences
such that each element of those sequences is one of the values of type Y.
  A sequence may be **empty**, that is contain no elements. Whatever
the type of sequence, the empty sequence is denoted in specifications as:

[ ]

Non-empty sequence values may be written by listing the elements,
separated by commas and inside square brackets.
  Example elements of the type

Seq of $\mathbb{N}$

are the sequences

[ ]
[153]
[5 , 1 , 8 , 1]

Note that 1 occurs twice in the last example.

Constants of type Seq of char

In specifications, we often write a sequence of characters as a string inside
quotes (''). This is an abbreviation for the full format written with
individual characters. For example,

''fred''

is an abbreviation for

['f','r','e','d']

Head and tail of sequences (hd, tl)

Two simple functions on sequences are:

hd : (s : Seq of X) $\rightarrow$ (h : X)
tl : (s : Seq of X) $\rightarrow$ (t : Seq of X)

where **hd** returns the first item in the given sequence and **tl** returns all but the first item. For example,

hd ([3,1,2]) = 3
tl ([3,2,1]) = [2,1]

Length of sequences

There exists a function in specifications called **len** which can be applied to all sequence values and which gives the length of the sequence, that is, the number of elements in it. Thus, for example, if S is a sequence from the type:

Seq of $\mathbb{R}$

then the meaning of:

len(S)

is the number of real numbers in the sequence S. If S is the sequence

[1.3 , 2.4 , 8.1 , 0.2]

then

len(S) = 4

Note that a sequence length is always a natural number, and that

len([ ])

is zero.

Concatenation (on sequences)

A function on sequences, **concatenation,** written

$\frown$

takes two sequences and joins them together in order. It is an associative infix operator, that is:

$$(s1 \frown s2) \frown s3 = s1 \frown (s2 \frown s3)$$

for all sequences s1, s2 and s3. For example:

$$[4,1,3] \frown [5,3] \frown [2] = [4,1,3,5,3,2]$$

Index and element sets of sequences (inds, elems)

Two more functions on sequence data types are **inds** and **elems**. They are both functions from a sequence to a set. inds yields the set of indices of the elements in a given sequence and elems yields the set of elements in a sequence:

inds : (s : Seq of X) → (i : Set of ℕ)
inds (s) is the set of all naturals from 1 to len(s)

elems : (s : Seq of X) → (e : Set of X)
elems (s) is the set of all elements of s

For example, if s = [a,b,b,c], inds(s) = {1,2,3,4} and elems(s) = {a,b,c}.

Indexing sequences

There exists a function which may be applied to any sequence, S, and a natural number, i, which returns the ith element in S, counting from 1 upwards. The value of i must be in the range 1 to the length of S. The function is applied by following the sequence with square brackets enclosing the value of i. For example, for a sequence X of type

Seq of ℕ

containing the natural numbers

$$[1,7,9,3,8]$$

the value of

X[4]

is the fourth element in the sequence X, that is, the natural number 3.

Sub-sequences

All sequence types have a function to extract a (proper) **sub-sequence** of a sequence. The function takes a sequence and two indices, and returns the sub-sequence occurring between the two indices inclusive. The function is denoted as:

s [i1 , . . . , i2]

where s is a sequence, and i1 and i2 are the two indices.
    Thus, for example, if s was the sequence

    [A, B, C, D, E, F, G]

then s[3 , . . . , 6] would be the sequence

    [C, D, E, F]

The formal definition of the sub-sequence selection operator is:

    _ [_ , . . . , _] : (s : Seq of X , i : $\mathbb{N}$, j : $\mathbb{N}$) → (rs : Seq of X)

    pre $0 < i \leqslant j + 1$ and $j \leqslant len(s)$

    post ∃ s1,s2:Seq of X •
        $len(s1) = i - 1$
        and
        $len(s2) = len(s) - j$
        and
        s1 ⌢ rs ⌢ s2 = s

The pre-condition has been chosen to permit extracting an empty
sequence when

    $i = j + 1$

and a singleton sequence when

    $i = j$

Proper sub-sequences

A **proper sub-sequence** of a sequence is a sequence which is contained in
the second sequence as consecutive elements. For example:

    [3, 7, 2, 6]

is a proper sub-sequence of

    [1, 8, 2, 3, 7, 2, 6, 1, 8, 9]

On the other hand, the elements of a non-proper sub-sequence are all
contained in the second sequence in the same order, but not as
consecutive elements. For example,

    [3, 5, 1, 8]

is a sub-sequence of

[8, 2, 3, 5, 6, 1, 4, 8]

but not a proper sub-sequence of it.

Lexicographic ordering of sequences

For types that have the ordering relation ≤, such as naturals and characters, there is a corresponding relation ≤ on sequences of the type, called the **lexicographic ordering,** defined as follows.

An empty sequence is ≤ a non-empty sequence. A non-empty sequence is not ≤ an empty one. Two non-empty sequences with identical heads are ≤ if and only if the tail of the first ≤ tail of the second. Two non-empty sequences with different heads are ≤ if and only if the head of the first sequence is ≤ the head of the second sequence.

This can be formally written recursively as:

```
_ ≤ _ : (s1 : Seq of some-type , s2 : Seq of some-type) → 𝔹
s1 ≤ s2 △
    if s1 = [ ] then true
    else if s2 = [ ] then false
    else
        if hd s1 = hd s2 then
            (tl s1) ≤ (tl s2)
        else
            (hd s1) ≤ (hd s2)
```

This notion extends to sequences of sequences, using the ordering just defined. We also have the other three orderings:

```
A ≥ B    iff    B ≤ A
A < B    iff    A ≤ B and A ≠ B
A > B    iff    B < A
```

For example, the following are all true:

```
[ ] < [0]
[34,25,35] < [34,26,35]
[36,20,35] > [34,37,42]
"abc" ≤ "abd"
"SDI" ≤ "SDI"
"joe" ≤ "joel"
```

And, on sequences of sequences:

```
[ [3,7,2] , [12,9,13] , [56,2,67] ] < [ [3,7,2] , [12,9,14] , [55,2,68] ]
["tom" ,"dick" ,"harry" ] > ["thomas" ,"richard" ,"henry" ]
["the" ,"three" ,"little" ,"pigs" ] > ["pigs" ,"the" ,"three" ,"little" ]
```

Cross product type

A **cross product** of two types is a set of pairs of values, one value from each of the two types. For example,

ℕ X Char

is the set of all pairs of values, where the first in each pair is a natural number and the second is a character.

(ℕ X Char) X ℕ = ℕ X (Char X ℕ)

is the set of all triples where the first and third items are natural numbers, and the second item is a character. Elements of cross products are written as items separated by commas and surrounded by round brackets, for example

(10, 4) ∈ ℕ X ℕ

Record type

A **record** is a value consisting of several separate items collected together. The items are called **fields** of the record. A **record type** is a data type (that is, a set) containing all the record values of a particular form. The types of the fields might not be the same as each other, but they are fixed for a given record type.

The fields of a record type each have a name. Record types are defined in our specifications by listing these names, and, with each, the type of the values which may occupy the field. For example,

```
Personal-details = Record
                     first-name : Seq of Letter
                     surname : Seq of Letter
                     age : ℕ
                     sex : {female , male}
                   end
```

This defines the type Personal-details, as the set of all possible records with those fields described.

Make (constructor) functions (on records)

In specifications we **construct** a **record value** by making use of an automatically defined function based on the name of the record type. Every record type, for example

```
Rtype = Record
            field1 : Type1
            field2 : Type2
            . . .
        end
```

has an associated function, for example mk-Rtype, with a signature of

```
mk-Rtype : (field1 : Type1 , field2 : Type2 , . . .) → Rtype
```

This takes an argument from each of the appropriate types and produces the corresponding record value.

For example, with the record type

```
Pencil-sharpener = Record
                       diameter : ℕ
                       blade-angle : ℕ
                       material : {plastic , steel}
                       colour : { silver, red, blue, yellow, green }
                   end
```

the value of

```
mk-Pencil-sharpener (10, 20, plastic, blue)
```

is a record of type Pencil-sharpener with diameter of 10, blade-angle of 20, material of plastic and colour of blue.

Field selection (on records)

Fields of a record are selected in our specifications by means of a **field access** function. There is one of these functions for each field in a record. The name of the function is a dot (.) followed by the field name. The result type of the function is the type of the field. For example, if we have the type and variable:

```
Car = Record
          make : Seq of Char
          wheels : ℕ
          colour  : {red, blue, yellow, pink}
          sun-roof : 𝔹
      end

SOME-OP
ext rd my-car : Car
. . .
```

then, assuming that the variable my-car contains the details of my car, its colour, its number of wheels and whether it has a sun-roof are respectively:

```
my-car.colour
my-car.wheels
my-car.sun-roof
```

A.2.3   Operation

An **operation** is some action which is part of a user's requirements. An operation has a name and generally has a **state** consisting of external entities (variables) which it may access and/or update. It also may have a **pre-condition** and a **post-condition.** A specification of an operation typically looks like the following:

```
NAME

ext  . . . *** external variables ***

pre  . . . *** pre-condition ***

post . . . *** post-condition ***
```

Explicit operations

An operation may be specified by giving an algorithm for it, similar to a program, but not as pedantic on syntax. The algorithm may call other operations as commands. Such a definition is called an **explicit** specification of an operation (or, less formally, an **explicit operation).** A typical skeleton explicit operation is

```
NAME
ext . . .
pre . . .
begin
   . . .
end
```

Implicit operations

An operation may be defined solely by its pre- and post-conditions. This is called an **implicit** (or **input/output) specification** of an operation (or, less formally, an **implicit operation),** because, in general, absolutely no indication is given as to how it might be implemented.

External variables

The **external** variables in the state of an operation are listed at the beginning of the operation specification, each with its type. These types denote the set of values that the variables may possess. The variables have different access modes depending on whether they are **read only** (rd), indicating that the operation may not change the value, or **read and write** (wr), indicating that it *may* both access the value and change it.

Pre-condition

An operation may have a **pre-condition**. This is an expression, either true or false, that characterizes all the assumptions the operation may make concerning the values of its state before the operation executes.

true **pre-condition**

The pre-condition of an operation or function may be written as simply

    true

A pre-condition characterizes all that may be assumed to be true before the operation executes or the function is applied. Thus, if a pre-condition is merely true, this means that *nothing* may be assumed.

Violation of pre-condition

An operation specification gives no hint as to what the operation will do if the pre-condition is not satisfied before the operation executes. This is because an implementor is *free* to assume that the condition is satisfied. For example, one implementation might never stop, another might stop with a run-time error, a third might give the wrong answer, and so on.

Post-condition

An operation **post-condition** characterizes all the things that must be accomplished by the operation by the time it has finished executing, provided that the pre-condition is satisfied before its execution.

Initial value of variable in post-condition

In the post-condition of an operation we often wish to refer to the external state occurring before the operation was executed. To differentiate between the state before and after execution of the operation, the value of any variable before execution is referred to by the variable name **hooked** with a back-pointing arrow drawn above it. For example, the value of the variable

    input

before execution of an operation is written

$$\overline{\text{input}}$$

Note that it is never necessary to hook a variable that has read only access mode, because the final value and the initial value must be the same.

Non-deterministic operations

When an operation (or function) is specified by a post-condition, it might be **non-deterministic** in that it does not tie down precisely what the implementation must do, but instead leaves some freedom of choice. For example, the following operation returns a number below a given one:

SOME-NATURAL-BELOW (n : $\mathbb{N}1$) r : $\mathbb{N}$

post r < n

This may not have been a mistake, as there are plenty of contexts in which such a number is required, but it is not necessary to state which one. If the implementation language is fully deterministic, the specification should be regarded as defining a class of deterministic implementations, each of which satisfies it. If the implementation language can be non-deterministic (that is, there are some programs that compute different answers at different times for the same input), the specification should be regarded more generally as defining a class of possibly non-deterministic implementations that satisfy it.

Operation input parameters

Operation specifications may be given (value) **parameters** in a similar way to function arguments. Operations cannot change the values of these parameters.

Actual parameters

In explicit operations, when the algorithm calls another operation that requires value parameters, the actual values passed are written in brackets after the called operation name.

Output parameters of operations

Operations may have **output parameters.** These are written after the brackets around the input parameters, if any. They have no value before execution of the operation, and thus cannot be written in a pre-condition and cannot be hooked in a post-condition. For example, an operation that finds a nearest natural square root and real error of a natural number:

ROOT (n : ℕ) rt : ℕ; err : ℝ

post (err + rt) * (err + rt) = n
    and
        − 0.5 ≤ err ≤ 0.5

Note that there is no fundamental difference between a function and an operation that has exactly one output parameter and no external variables.

A.2.4   Function

A **function** is a mapping or correspondence between sets of values. A function is **applied** to values, called the **arguments** of the function, and yields a value called the **result** of the function. The types of the arguments is called the **arity** (sometimes called the domain – but see later) and the type of the result is called the **value sort** (sometimes called the range – see later). When a function is applied to different arguments it may yield the same result but it is not possible to yield different results for different applications of the function to the same arguments. For example:

multiply (4,2)   = 8
multiply (8,1)   = 8
multiply (7,3)   = 21
multiply (8,1)   = 8 (still!)

From the point of view of specification, it is extremely useful to state the arity and value sort of a function. This information, together with the function name, is presented in the function **signature**. For example, len is a function that takes a sequence and returns a natural:

len : (s : Seq of X) → (l : ℕ)

s is being used here as a name for the argument, within the function; and l as a name for the result.

The arity of a function of more than one argument is given as a list of all the argument sets separated by commas. For example:

multiply : (x : ℕ , y : ℕ) → (m : ℕ)

A function can only be applied to the set of values specified in its arity and will always yield a result in the value sort. Note that a function does not have external variables (state).

Total and partial functions

If a function is defined for *all* the values in its arity, it is said to be a **total function**. If it is only defined for some of the values, it is a **partial function**. For example, the function div over two natural numbers is a partial function, because it is not (usually) defined for dividing by zero. A function that has a pre-condition of true is a total function, because it assumes nothing about the values of its arguments, and hence must be defined for all values in its arity. The **domain** of a function is the sub-set of its arity, for which it is defined. Thus, the domain of a total function is exactly its arity. (Sometimes the arity is called the domain, even for partial functions.)

Similarly, the **range** of a function is the sub-set of its value sort, containing the elements yielded by the function for at least one argument in its domain. (Sometimes the value sort is called the range.)

Recursive functions

A **(self) recursive function** is one which is defined in terms of itself. For example the well-known factorial function:

```
fact : (n : ℕ) → ℕ
fact (n) △
    if n = 0 then 1
    else n * fact (n − 1)
```

For a finite recursive function to be well defined, there must be a **base case** involving no recursion, and each recursive application must be applied to an argument value that 'gets nearer' the base case value (in some sense). The base case for the above factorial example is the value zero, and the function can be shown to be well defined because, given a number greater than zero, the argument for the recursive application is nearer to zero.

It is possible to have infinite recursive functions, which do not need a base case. The most typical examples act over an infinite sequence, yielding a corresponding infinite sequence. For example:

```
increment : (Seq of ℕ) → Seq of ℕ
increment (s) △ [hd s + 1] ⁀ increment (tl s)
```

Pre-condition

A function specification may include a **pre-condition**. This true or false expression characterizes all things that an implementation of the function may assume about its arguments (that is, its input).

Post-condition

A function may be specified via a **post-condition**. This characterizes all
required things about the relationship between the function arguments
and the function result.

Implicit functions

Like operations, functions may be completely specified using pre- and
post-conditions. Such a definition is called an **implicit specification** of a
function (or, less formally, an **implicit function**), because it (generally)
gives no hint as to how the function might be implemented. If no
pre-condition is given for an **implicit** function specification, the pre-
condition true is assumed.

Explicit functions

Functions may be defined explicitly by presenting an expression in terms
of the arguments, as the function result. This is *instead* of a post-
condition. Such a definition is called an **explicit specification** of a
function (or, less formally, an **explicit function**). The result expression is
written after the symbol

$$\triangle$$

which may be read as 'is defined to be'. For example,

increment : (i : $\mathbb{N}$) $\rightarrow$ $\mathbb{N}$
increment (i) $\triangle$ i + 1

Note that the name of, and the parentheses round, the result in the
signature *may* be omitted.

An explicit function may also be given a pre-condition. However, if
a pre-condition is omitted, then, rather than assuming simply true, the
actual pre-condition is deduced from the result expression, and is exactly
the weakest pre-condition (the one that assumes the least) required for the
result expression to be defined. The weakest possible pre-condition is true.

Function specification

Sometimes it is convenient to specify a program, or part of a program,
as a **function** rather than a more general operation. This is merely a
specification technique, and should not affect the approach taken to the
implementation.

A.2.5   Expressions

An **expression** is a structured sequence of symbols, consisting of **operators** (such as +, −), **variables,** function names and curly brackets. An expression has a value which depends on the value of any variables occurring in it.

Operators

An **operator** is something that combines expressions to form larger expressions. Examples are addition of natural or real numbers (+), subtraction (−), multiplication (*) and so on. Operators have a **precedence,** indicating how powerful they are at competing with other operators for their arguments. For example, without precedence, it would not be possible to say whether the expression

    34 + 16 − 56

meant

    (34 + 16) − 56

or

    34 + (16 − 56)

Luckily, the value of both expressions is − 6, and so the two operators have been defined to have the same precedence. However, this is not true for expressions like

    34 + 16 * 56

which has the value 2800 or 930 depending on which operator is applied first. In specifications and in programs, multiplication has higher precedence than addition. Division has the same precedence as multiplication and, likewise, subtraction has the same precedence as addition.

Conditional expression (if–then–else)

In specifications, we can write an **if–then–else** (or **conditional**) expression to denote two alternative expressions depending on a condition. The general form is

    if b then e1 else e2

where b is any **predicate** (condition) and e1 and e2 are expressions of the same type. The type of the if–then–else is the same as the type of e1 and e2. The meaning of the expression is e1 if b is true, or e2 otherwise. This is similar to the Pascal if–then–else statement, but should not be confused with it.

Let expression (let–be–in)

As a convenience and/or to aid clarity, when we write expressions in a specification, we can give a simple name to some sub-expression, and then use that name rather than the sub-expression. This might avoid repetition of a lengthy term, or simply give some intuitive name to a part of an expression.

The format is:

    let X : X-type be sub-expression in expression

For example:

    let quotient : ℝ be total / count
    in quotient * quotient – total

This is equivalent to

    (total / count) * (total / count) – total

Quantified expressions

In specifications we often wish to express the truth of some proposition (Boolean expression) applied to some or all values of a certain set (type). The general form of such expressions is:

    Q i ∈ S • P(i)

where Q is a **quantifier,** i is a **logical variable,** S is a set and P(i) is a proposition involving i. Such expressions are themselves propositions, either true or false. There may be more than one logical variable, from more than one set. The two most common quantifiers are the **universal quantifier** (for all) written

    ∀

and the **existential quantifier** (exists), written

    ∃

The quantifiers have a lower precedence than the logical operators and, or
and not.

Existential quantifier (exists)

The **existential quantifier,** called **exists**, expresses the truth of a proposition for at least one member of a set. For example,

   ∃ s ∈ Seq of ℕ • s[3] = s[4]

is true. (There does exist at least one sequence of natural numbers having
the third and fourth elements the same.) On the other hand,

   ∃ i,j ∈ ℕ, s ∈ Seq of {1,3,5} • s[i] = j * 2

is false. (There do not exist two natural numbers and a sequence of {1,3,5}
such that the ith element is 2 times j.)
      If the set of values for the logical variable (or one of the logical
variables) is empty, the expression is defined to be false. For example:

   let s : Seq of ℕ be [ ] in
      ∃ i ∈ inds(s) • s[i] = 10

is false. (There does not exist an element of the empty sequence such that
its value is 10!)

Universal quantifier (for all)

The **universal quantifier,** written as

   ∀

and pronounced **for all**, expresses the truth of some proposition for every
member of a set. For example:

   ∀ i ∈ ℕ • i ⩾ 0

is true. (Every natural number is greater than or equal to zero.) On the
other hand,

   ∀ i,j ∈ ℕ, s ∈ Seq of ℕ • s[i] = s[j]

is false. (It is not true that for every pair, i and j, of natural numbers and
sequence, s, of natural numbers, the ith and jth elements of s are the
same.) Note the small extension allowing more than one logical variable
(i,j) to be quantified in the same expression.
      If the set of values for the logical variable (or one of the logical
variables) is empty, the expression is defined to be true. For example:

```
let s : Seq of ℕ be [ ] in
    ∀ i ∈ inds(s) • s[i] = 10
```

is true. (All the elements of the empty sequence are 10!)

A.3   Design concepts

A.3.1   Top-down stepwise refinement

Designing a program is no different from any other difficult task –
generally, it cannot be done in one go. The designer of a motor car does
not start by drawing the front bumper, then working through in every
detail until the back bumper is drawn. There is too much complexity to
be contained in the mind all at once. So the job is split into meaningful
parts – first the overall shape, with labels for the various sub-parts, such
as 'engine'. Then each sub-part can be designed in the same manner –
engine split into combustion part, cooling part, transmission part . . . .

   Similarly, in program design, one can **control the complexity** by
abstracting away from the unnecessary detail early on. This is called
top-down stepwise refinement (TDSR) because the process starts at the
top level of the problem and works downwards, refining each step.

   It is just another form of the age-old axiom 'divide and conquer'.

Refining complex steps first

As a general guide in TDSR designs, when faced with the choice of which
step to refine next, it is usually a good idea to pick the one that looks
most complex. This is because there may be some influence between the
steps which becomes apparent only when you examine them in more
detail. These dependencies could affect the appropriateness of the choice
of steps you have made, thus it is preferable that they show up early.
They are more likely to show up in complex steps.

A.3.2   Abstract data type

An **abstract data type** is a type, in the program sense, consisting of a set
of values and an associated collection of operations. However, the type
is abstract, because its implementation details are hidden from the
program during its design (and possibly all its life).

Abstract data type design approach

Like top-down stepwise refinement, the **abstract data type approach to program design** is a way of employing abstraction, thus making the overall task easier. It is of most use when a problem solution naturally uses some complex data type(s) which can be implemented in a number of ways, or at least the implementation of which is not immediately obvious. The design process is made easier by the programmer initially pretending that the data types are actually built in to the programming language. This leads to a design of the program which is independent of the actual implementation of these types. Then, separately, the data type implementations can be considered, by choosing a suitable representation and implementing the various operations. In this way, the total design process is divided into logical chunks. Of course, TDSR is still used in the design of the program and the algorithms for the data type operations.

Program specific abstract data type

For abstract data types which are quite specific to a single program, it is best to implement the types *after* the design of the program. This is because it is not clear before that point exactly what operations are required, and how frequently. There is no need to implement operations which are not used, and the frequency of application might influence the choice of representation of the data.

Abstract data type package

An abstract data type may be so generally applicable that it is a desirable thing to make an implementation of it available to many programs and programmers. Most computer installations have a software library, in which widely useful routines can be kept. An abstract data type implementation is an example of a **package** of such routines associated with one or more data types.

A.3.3 The 'how would I do it' approach to design

Sometimes, a good way to approach a problem is to ask yourself how you would do it if you, not the computer, had to do it. This can cause you to think of a good and simple solution – since humans seem to have an instinct for avoiding doing more than is required!

A.3.4   Solving a simpler problem first

A potentially helpful method of approaching the design of a solution to a problem is to **solve a simpler problem first**. Sometimes, one can identify a part of a problem such that, if that part were ignored, the solution to the remainder of the problem would be easier, but have basically the same structure as the full solution. In such cases, it can be helpful to ignore the complication, solve the simpler problem, and then adjust the solution to deal with the full problem.

A.3.5   Data and program structure

Many algorithms are primarily concerned with processing some form of structured data. In such cases, the most natural solution is often one which has the same structure as the data. So, if the data involves the repetition of some form (for example a sequence), the algorithm would have a loop to process that repetition. If the items of data involved alternative forms, then the algorithm would have alternative parts to process each of the forms. Thus, identifying the structure of the data that an algorithm must process can often lead to the most appropriate structure for the algorithm itself.

A.3.6   State indicators

Some problems require the design of a loop which has a complicated exit condition consisting of several possible states. One way to achieve this is to have a **state indicator.** This is a variable, usually of an enumerated type, which can have one of several values, each corresponding to one of the possible exit conditions. The typical use of a Boolean typed flag can be regarded as a special case of the general concept of a state indicator.

A.3.7   Unbounded sum of bounded sub-problems

Programming often requires the solution of problems that handle unbounded data. This can lead to inefficiency, as often the most efficient data structure in a particular programming language is bounded (for example, arrays versus linked lists). One route round this stems from the fact that an unbounded problem can be the **unbounded sum of bounded sub-problems.** This can be applied by recognizing the sum (for example, concatenation of strings) and achieving the unbounded sum by iteration or recursion.

A.3.8   General programming language concepts

Procedure

A **procedure** is a programming concept. It is a sub-part of a program, designed to achieve some part of the overall task performed by the program. Procedures have a name and a body consisting of statements to be executed. They are referenced by a **procedure call** statement. When such a call is executed, the computer executes the body of the procedure, and then continues execution from the point after the call. (Thus it behaves as though the body of the procedure was written in place of the procedure call.) Large programs should *always* be split into procedures, as this is the only way to make their design and implementation a manageable task. This fits in extremely well with the TDSR method of program design, because the various design steps can be refined as separate procedures. An added benefit, but which is only a *secondary* motive, is that procedures can be called from different places in a program, thus removing the need for great textual repetition of code. In designs we normally indicate where a procedure is to be called by simply inserting its name as a statement.

Procedure parameter

Although well-named and suitably sized procedures contribute greatly to the clarity of a program, it is not always immediately clear what interaction an individual procedure has with the rest of the program. For example, a procedure might be given some value which is stored in a variable in the main program, or might return some value in some variable, or both. A comment in the procedure that describes the interface can help, but many languages provide a formal mechanism for stating at least part of it. A **parameter** is such a mechanism and is rather like a function argument. The two kinds of parameters most frequently used in Pascal are **value** and **variable** parameters. The first is a value passed to the procedure by the piece of program that calls it. The second is a variable which is similarly passed.

Procedure by-value parameter   A procedure **value parameter** is a value which is explicitly presented to a procedure when it is called. The principle is the same as that of function arguments in our specifications, where a function is applied to a value. For consistency with Pascal, parameters in our designs are defined within brackets in the procedure heading and the values actually applied to the procedure are written in brackets after the procedure name in the procedure call. For example, the procedure

```
write-money-with-leading-asterisks(number : Real;
                                   field-width : Integer)
begin
  . . .
  { loop to write the lead chars }
  . . .
    write(output,'*')
  . . .
  { write the number with two decimal places }
  write(output,number:1:2)
  . . .
end
```

is designed to take two value parameters (in the following order): a *Real* number, which will be displayed with two decimal places, and an *Integer* field which will be filled up with leading asterisks. We can write the statement

```
write-money-with-leading-asterisks(tax-rate * taxable-pay, 10)
```

assuming that tax-rate and taxable-pay are *Real* variables. This statement will execute the body of the procedure write-money-with-leading-asterisks, which will act on the values supplied.

Suppose that later during the design it became clear that sometimes asterisks, sometimes spaces and sometimes zeros were needed as the leading character. The above procedure could be altered to

```
write-money-with-leading-char(number : Real;
                              field-width : Integer;
                              lead-char : Char)
begin
  . . .
  { loop to write the lead chars }
  . . .
    write(output,lead-char)
  . . .
  { write the number with two decimal places }
  write(output,number:1:2)
  . . .
end
```

Then the same effect as before would be achieved by

```
write-money-with-leading-char(tax-rate * taxable-pay, 10, '*')
```

(As another example, the Pascal pre-declared procedure *writeln* takes value parameters which are displayed on the output file.)

Procedure variable parameter   In contrast to procedure value parameters, through a **variable parameter,** a procedure may be given a variable from which it can read a value, and to which it can write a value. A variable parameter is similar to an external variable with read/write access in our specifications, except that the actual variable referenced may be different, depending on the call of the procedure. For consistency with Pascal, variable parameters are defined within brackets after the word var in the procedure heading in our designs. Similarly, the variables to which the procedure is actually applied are written in brackets after the procedure name in the procedure call. For example, suppose we wished the write-money-with-leading-char procedure to write the result to a different file in different parts of the program. The file to be used could be passed to the procedure as a variable parameter. Thus, the heading could be

```
write-money-with-leading-char(var result-file : Text;
                        number : Real;
                        field-width : Integer;
                        lead-char : Char)
begin
   . . .
   { loop to write the lead chars }
   . . .
      write(result-file,lead-char)
   . . .
   { write the number with two decimal places }
   write(result-file,number:1:2)
   . . .
end
```

Then a call to the procedure might be

```
write-money-with-leading-char(audit-file, tax-rate, 5, '0')
```

(As another example, the Pascal pre-declared procedure *readln* takes variables as parameters and places values in them from the input file.)

Recursive procedures

A **(self) recursive procedure,** like a self-recursive function, is one which is defined in terms of itself. This means that its statement body will contain at least one procedure call to an instance of itself. For the algorithm to be terminating, there must be a path through the procedure which does not make a recursive call, and arguments to recursive calls must make progress towards the condition under which this path is executed.

Function

In many languages, a programmer may define **functions** algorithmically. These are used to split a program into parts in a similar way to procedures. However, rather than being sub-routines executed as one statement, they are used in program expressions as functions taking a number of arguments and returning a value result. A program function has a body of statements which is executed during the evaluation of each program expression containing an application of the function.

For consistency with Pascal, in our designs the result of the function is returned by assigning the desired value to the name of the function. For example, the design of a function which returns the largest of two given integers is

```
largest-number(n1,n2 : Integer) : Integer
begin
  if n1 > n2
     largest-number := n1
  else
     largest-number  := n2
end
```

With this design, a statement to write the largest of three given integer exam marks might be

```
write(output,largest-number(CS110-exam-mark,
                    largest-number(CS120-exam-mark,
                               CS130-exam-mark)))
```

assuming that CS110-exam-mark, CS120-exam-mark and CS130-exam-mark are declared as *Integer* variables.

Function definition

Program functions are defined via an algorithm that actually computes the result. For consistency with Pascal, in our designs the result is performed by an assignment statement treating the function name as a variable. Function algorithms generally should not directly access or update variables defined outside the function. For clarity, all input to a function should be through its value parameters, and all output from it through its result value.

Dynamic data structures

A **dynamic data structure** is one that does not have a fixed size, but which is allowed to grow (and contract) as the requirements of the program change during its execution. This is achieved in many languages (for example, in Pascal) by asking the system for more, new, variables, known as **dynamic variables.**

Dynamic variables and references

A normal variable name (length, for example) can be thought of as a **static reference,** in that it always refers to the same variable (or an instance of it, in the case of a local variable of a recursive procedure). The space for such a variable can be allocated by the compiler and hence it is called a **static variable.** A **dynamic variable** is one which is actually created at run-time, usually for use in some dynamic data structure. The space for such variables cannot be allocated at compile-time, because it is generally impossible to predict how many are needed. The name of a dynamic variable is not an identifier, as with static variables, but is a **dynamic reference** or **pointer.** A dynamic reference may be thought of as an address, perhaps the memory address where the variable actually resides (although that is implementation dependent). Dynamic references are values and may be stored in other variables (either dynamic or static) and may be copied. When a (static or dynamic) variable, x, contains as its value the dynamic reference of some dynamic variable, we say that x **points to** that dynamic variable.

(Dynamic references cannot be printed or used in calculations because their concrete form is implementation dependent.)

Linked lists

A list is a sequence. A **linked list** is a list implemented by a chain of dynamic variables. Each dynamic variable in the list is called a **node** and contains a value, which is an element of the list, plus a pointer to the next variable in the list. Figure 8.1 (page 257) shows an individual node, and Figure 8.2 (page 258) shows an example linked list of natural numbers. To mark the end of the chain of nodes, the reference field of the final dynamic variable holds a special value indicating that it points to nothing. (In Pascal, this special value is called **Nil.**) The nodes are usually implemented using records for the value and reference pair.

Assignment of pointers

Pointer values may be assigned from one variable to another; but note that it is the reference which is being copied, and not the actual value of the dynamic variable referenced by the pointer (if there is one!). Figure 8.3 (page 260) illustrates the distinction between copying references, and copying values of dynamic variables. Consider the linked list in part (a) of that diagram. Part (b) shows the resulting structure after the execution of:

$$x := y$$

Part (c) shows the result after executing

$$x^\wedge := y^\wedge$$

on the same initial structure.

Statements

A programming language **statement** is an instruction telling the computer to *do* something.

Conditional statement

A **conditional statement** is a programming concept that involves some action or sequence of actions which must be executed if and only if a certain condition is satisfied (true) just beforehand. In designs we tend to write, for example:

```
if a = b
   c := d
   e := f
```

This means that the two assignment statements will be executed if and only if a = b when execution reaches the conditional statement. (Note that Pascal insists on the use of the word **Then** in **If** statements.) An extension of the concept of a conditional statement involves *two* alternative actions or sequences of actions. The first must be executed if a certain condition is true just beforehand, otherwise the second must be executed. For example:

```
if x > y
   write x
else
   write y
```

This would cause the largest value of x and y to be output.

Iteration (looping)

A **loop** is a programming concept involving the repeated execution of some actions. This iteration is usually controlled by some true or false condition involving the values of program variables. The loop stops when the condition becomes true or false, depending on the kind of loop.

While loop   One particular form of loop is called the **while loop**. This has a **continuation condition** and a body of actions. The condition is evaluated (tested) *before* the loop body is executed. If the value of the condition is true, the actions in the body of the loop are executed and then the condition is tried again, and so on. When the condition is evaluated and is false, the loop execution stops. For example, the following loop reads and processes all the remaining elements of a sequence:

> while the sequence is not empty
>   remove the next element from the front of the sequence
>   process the removed element
> end-of-while

Note that, if the condition is false to begin with, the body of the loop will not be executed at all.

For loop The **for loop** executes a controlling statement ('the body') a number of times with the aid of a **control variable** and a range of values. Each time the body of the loop is executed, the control variable assumes one value from the range, in ascending order, until each value has been thus used. If the range is empty (the start value is greater than the end value) the loop body is not executed at all. For loops should (only) be used where the required number of iterations can be computed *before* the loop starts. The body should *not* explicitly change the value of the control variable. The use of for loops is often suggested by the occurrence of a universal quantifier in a specification.

Repeat loop The **repeat loop** has a **termination condition** which is tried *after* the loop body is executed. If the condition is false, the body of the loop is repeated and then the condition is tried again, and so on. When the condition is tried and is true, the loop execution stops. The general form is

> repeat
>   actions of the loop
> until termination-condition

Because the condition is tested after execution of the loop body, the body will always be executed at least once.

Variable

A program **variable** is a named object which contains a value from a specified type (for example, a real number) during execution of the program. (It may be thought of rather concretely as being similar to a labelled pigeonhole, in which only a specified type of pigeon may be placed.) A variable represents a unique entity of the problem being solved by the program, and this should be reflected in its name. For example, in a program that controls a model train on a track, one may expect a variable called train-position, which might contain the number of a sensor that the train has just passed. A program may explicitly examine and change the value of its variables during execution. A good design rule is that the value of a variable should *always* reflect the meaning of the entity its represents. For example, every time the train passes a sensor, the program should change the value of train-position accordingly.

Local variable

A **local variable** in a procedure is one defined and used only within that procedure. It has no meaning outside the procedure. Local variables are good for reducing the complexity of a program, because entities related to only one procedure can be hidden from the rest of the program, thus reducing overall the number of entities at the top level of the program.

A.4   Pascal concepts

A.4.1   Program

A **program** is a formal and executable description of a method to undertake some task, written as a set of instructions. During **execution** of the program, the computer pedantically obeys these instructions regardless of whether this results in the behaviour expected or desired by the programmer. In Pascal, a program consists of a **heading,** various **declarations** and a **program body.** The heading introduces the name of the program and specifies the domain of its interaction with the outside world. The declarations define the names and characteristics of various objects in the program. The statement body contains instructions for execution of the program.

Program parameter

The identifiers enclosed within brackets after the program name specify the limit of the program's interaction with the outside world. The occurrence of the identifier ***input*** states that the program may accept data from the standard input list (usually the keyboard). The occurrence of the identifier ***output*** states that the program may send data to the standard output (usually the display). The occurrence of other names indicates that the program can access and/or update items (usually files) of that name. In order for it to be known what kind of objects these are, they must be declared as variables later in the program. This is not required for *input* and *output*. For example, the program

Program *double(input,output)*

may accept data from the standard input, and write data to the standard output.

Program body

The algorithm of a Pascal program is contained in the **program body**. This is a statement sequence occurring between the reserved words **Begin** and **End**, and followed by a full stop (.).

A.4.2 Identifier

An **identifier** is a word used to name an object (for example, a program). In Pascal, identifiers start with a letter and contain only letters and digits. Upper and lower case letters are interchangeable throughout Pascal. For example:

*EmployeeDetails*1988

A.4.3   Reserved word

A **reserved word** is a word, consisting only of letters, which is used as part of the Pascal language, (**Program**, for example) and may not be used as an identifier. The complete list of Pascal reserved words appears in Appendix B.

A.4.4   Comment

A **program comment** is a piece of text which is part of a program, but which is ignored by the computer during execution. Its purpose is to help to document the program, so that humans (programmers) looking at the text may have a better understanding of what it does and how it does it. Every program should have a comment near the front which states what it does, and in various places throughout explaining interesting parts. In Pascal, comments occur between left and right curly brackets: { }. They may extend over many lines, and may be placed anywhere in a program. The computer treats each comment as a space. For example:

```
{ This is a
  comment in
  Pascal }
```

A.4.5   Indentation (program layout)

A program can be very large indeed, and thus quite difficult for humans to read. One excellent way of improving the clarity of the program is to use **indentation** to make the structure more obvious. This involves laying out the program text very carefully, so that, for example, **Begin**s and **End**s line up vertically. There are many different styles in common use, but, in this book, all Pascal programs (and designs) are indented in one style. However, all successful styles are based on the principle that the more the structure of the program is nested, the more the lines are indented. Thus here, for example, we indent inwards after a **Begin** and outwards before an **End**. We also indent within such things as while loops and if statements even if the body is not compound. There are other places where we use indentation to add to the clarity, as you will see. At least two spaces should be used, although more than four causes the lines to become too short if they are to still fit on a reasonably sized page. It is well worth indenting programs as they are implemented, rather than as a final step, because the clarity added will help greatly with the implementation process itself (in particular, with finding typing mistakes).

A.4.6   Source-file inclusion

A feature that is not strictly part of the Pascal language, but is found in most compilers and program development environments, is the facility of a **source inclusion directive.** This enables one to refer to a source file, by name, from within another program's source file. In Berkeley UNIX Pascal, this is written as

```
#include "filename"
```

The Pascal compiler switches to reading the named file upon encountering the #include directive, and, on reaching the end of that file, returns to compiling from the line immediately following the #include. The syntax of such a mechanism differs from Pascal system to system, but is seldom totally absent. It is so essential (and simple) that we should feel no guilt at using it, even though it is a non-standard Pascal language extension.

A.4.7   Constant

As in specifications, the ability to declare entities which have a constant value in a program greatly increases its readability. This may be done in

Pascal via a **constant declaration.** The name given to the constant value is written in place of the constant wherever it is needed in the program. It also means that, if the value of the constant is ever changed, a simple change to the constant declaration is all that is needed, rather than looking through the program to change each occurrence of that particular value. For example,

> **Const** *BasicTaxRate* = 25.00;

Constant declarations in Pascal may not employ an expression to produce the value. This is an unfortunate deficiency in the current version of standard Pascal, which is remedied in the proposed new standard for Extended Pascal.

A.4.8   Type

A **program type,** like the types used in specifications, is a set of values. However, program types also have an associated collection of functions defined on them. In Pascal, types are named by identifiers. There are a few built-in types including one containing all the whole numbers (between two implementation dependent limits) above and below zero, and zero. This is identified as *Integer.* The real type (subject to implementation dependent precision and bounds) is also built in and identified as *Real.* The operators on integers and reals include addition (+), subtraction (–), multiplication (*), division (/) giving a real number result, and the usual comparisons.

Type declaration

A **type declaration** in Pascal associates a name with a type definition. The name is an identifier. The form is:

> **Type** *Weekday* = (*monday,tuesday,wednesday,thursday,friday*)

This defines a type with five values as listed, and calls the type *Weekday.*

Alias name (for type)

Just as in specifications, we may assign an alternative name to an existing type in Pascal. For example

> **Type** *Century* = *Integer*;

Equality

Most Pascal data types allow an **equality comparison** operation, denoted = . For these types, there is also the converse not-equality comparison, denoted <>. The result of such comparisons is of type *Boolean*.

Standard types

The standard types are all pre-declared, and include:

> *Integer   Real   Boolean   Char*

Integer type

The built-in Pascal type ***Integer*** is not infinite, and the cardinality of the type is language implementation dependent. However, there is a pre-declared constant called ***maxint*** which is defined as the highest positive integer, and the lowest negative integer for the particular Pascal implementation. In other words, *maxint* is defined as some value (usually a power of 2, minus 1) and *Integer* is defined as:

> **Type** *Integer* = $-$ *maxint . . maxint*

Relational operators (on arithmetic expressions)   In addition to equality and not-equality, Pascal allows the normal four comparison operators for the *Integer* (and *Real*) data type. These are written as the normal symbols for **less than** and **greater than** (< and >) and as an approximation to the normal symbols for **less than or equal** and **greater than or equal** (<= and >=).

Integer divide   The operator **Div** in Pascal takes two integer arguments and returns an integer. The second argument *must* not be zero. The result is the value of the first argument divided by the second, rounded towards zero to the nearest integer. Thus, where ***abs*** means absolute value (ignore the sign):

> $abs(i) - abs(j) < abs((i \text{ } \mathbf{Div} \text{ } j) * j) <= abs(i)$

The sign of the result will be positive if the signs of the arguments are the same, otherwise negative.

Integer remainder after division   The operator **Mod** in Pascal takes two integer arguments and returns an integer. The second argument *must* be greater than zero. If the first argument is non-negative, the result is the remainder when the first argument is divided by the second (exactly as our notion of mod in specifications). (A more general interpretation applies if the first argument is negative.) The following is *always* true of the result:

$$0 \leqslant i \text{ Mod } j < j$$

Truncation and rounding to integers Pascal has two pre-declared functions for locating integer values near to a real value (often inappropriately called type conversions). One of these returns the integer furthest from zero but which is no further from zero than the real argument. Formally, this is specified as:

```
trunc : (a : Real) → (r : Integer)

post a ⩾ 0 and 0 ⩽ a – r < 1
    or
    a < 0 and –1 < a – r ⩽ 0
```

The other returns an integer which is (one of) the closest to the real argument:

```
round : (a : Real) → (r : Integer)

post a ⩾ 0 and r = trunc(a + 0.5)
    or
    a < 0 and r = trunc(a – 0.5)
```

Boolean type

As seen in specifications, the **Boolean** data type, $\mathbb{B}$, has two values for true and false respectively and there are various associated functions. In Pascal, this type is called ***Boolean***, and is pre-declared in the same way as *Integer*. All conditions of **While** loops and **If** statements are in fact expressions of type *Boolean*. The two values are the pre-declared identifiers ***true*** and ***false***. The result of comparisons, such as < on integers, is of the *Boolean* type. For example, the value of

$$(sum > 0)$$

is either *true* or *false*.

Boolean negation (**Not**) There is a built-in operator in Pascal which takes a true or false value and negates it. That is, if it is given true, it returns false, and vice versa. It is called **Not**. Thus, for example,

Not *eof* (*f*)

is true when the file *f* has *not* had all of its data read.

Boolean operators (**And**, **Or**)   There is a built-in operator on the Pascal *Boolean* data type called **And**. This takes two arguments and returns true if both are true, and false otherwise. Another is **Or**. This takes two Boolean arguments and returns true if at least one of the arguments is true, and false if both of them are false.

And and **Or** are reserved words (as is **Not**). For example,

$(sum < 0)$ **And** $(sum > 0)$

always has the value *false*.

Char type

There is another built-in data type in Pascal called *Char*, which contains characters. The character set may vary from one computer to another but they include the upper case and lower case alphabets, 'A'..'Z' and 'a'..'z', the decimal digits '0'..'9' and the space character, ' '.

A character constant is represented by writing it enclosed in single (close) quotes. For example

$'a'$, $'B'$, $'*'$, $'8'$

Ordering of characters   The values of the Pascal type *Char* are ordered. Each character has an **ordinal number,** sometimes called a **character code,** which start from 0 and go up to the cardinality of the character set, minus one. Each distinct character has a distinct ordinal number. The actual value associated with each character is implementation dependent, as is the actual set of characters supported. However, in a standard implementation, the codes for the digits, '0' to '9' are guaranteed to be ascending and consecutive. The codes for each of the two alphabets, 'A' to 'Z' and 'a' to 'z' are guaranteed to be ascending, but not necessarily consecutive (for example, the code for 'B' is greater than the code for 'A', but not necessarily just one more). Most, but not all, computers nowadays use the **ASCII** character set and codes, in which the digits and also each of the alphabets are consecutive.

The relational operators $<$, $>$, $\leqslant$, $\geqslant$ on characters are supported in Pascal, and are defined as the corresponding relation on integers acting on the ordinal numbers of the characters.

Char functions (ord, chr)   The pre-declared Pascal function *ord* takes a character and returns its ordinal number. The pre-declared function *chr* takes an integer and returns the associated character, if there is one (otherwise a run-time error occurs).

Thus, the following is true for all values, A and B, of *Char*:

$$A = chr(ord(A))$$
$$(ord(A) < ord(B)) = (A < B)$$
$$chr(0) <= A$$
$$chr(ord('0') + 3) = '3'$$

Sub-range types

Pascal allows the definition of **sub-range** types, denoted similarly to sub-ranges of sets in our specifications. Any of the Pascal types with the notion of successor may be sub-ranged. These include: *Integer, Char* and *Boolean* (false is less than true), but not *Real*. (Real numbers do not have a unique successor.)

Array index descriptions in the form $v1..v2$ are actually sub-range types.

Enumeration types

In Pascal, an **enumerated type** is a new type defined by a programmer, for which all the values are explicitly listed as identifiers. These values are written between parentheses ( ) and are separated by commas. There are few operations associated with enumerated types. For example:

(*monday,tuesday,wednesday,thursday,friday*)

This defines a type with five values, as listed.

Structured types

There are four kinds of **structured types** in Pascal: **arrays, records, sets** and **files.**

Packed types

Any Pascal structured type (record, array, set, file) may be declared as **Packed** by simply adding that word in front of the type construction. This may cause values of the type to occupy less space, at the cost of execution taking a little longer. However, the behaviour of the type is not affected *except* for arrays of *Char* indexed from 1 upwards. These have more operations available than their unpacked counterparts, in that they may be compared.

Record types

Just as in specifications, we may define record types in Pascal. The fields are listed by name and type, and the field access operations may be used in a similar way to those seen in specifications.

However, Pascal offers no operation to construct record values from the collection of values for the fields (the mk-Blah-blah functions in our specifications). Hence it is not possible to have a constant record value written in a program, and all record values have to be stored in variables, constructed by assignment to the individual fields.

Records may be copied completely in one assignment statement, but, in standard Pascal, two record variables may not be compared for equality.

Record field selection   As in our specifications, fields of a record are referenced in Pascal by suffixing the record variable with a dot followed by the field name.

Comparison of records   Unfortunately, in standard Pascal it is not permitted to compare two record values to see whether they are the same. Instead, one must explicitly compare all or a sufficient sub-set of the fields of the records.

Variant records   We sometimes wish to represent data that has more than one possible form. This is done in Pascal through the **record** concept, but with alternative or **variant** field names. The alternatives are based on a special field known as a **tag**, and are expressed via a case structure.

For example, the following variant record type might be found in an order processing program for True-Blue-Trendy-Togs, a made-to-measure clothing workshop:

```
garment = Record
              customer : String;
              material  : (Denim, StretchDenim, RippedDenim,
                          StoneWashedDenim);
              colour    : (Blue, DarkBlue, LightBlue, StreakyBlue);
              Case GarmentKind : (trousers, jacket, skirt, blouse) Of
                 trousers : (InsideLeg, TrouserWaist : Integer;
                            TrouserFit : (LoosePants, TightPants,
                                                        SopranoPants));
                 jacket : (Chest, JacketArmLength, JacketLength :
                                                        Integer;
                          JacketStyle : (SingleBreasted, DoubleBreasted,
                                          MachoBreasted));
                 skirt : (SkirtHem, SkirtWaist : Integer;
                         Split : (NoSplit, SmallSplit, BigSplit,
                                 EyePopperSplit);
                         Pleated : Boolean);
```

> *blouse* : (*Bust, BlouseLength, BlouseWaist,*
> *BlouseArmLength* : *Integer*;
> *BlouseNeck* : (*HighNeck, PlungeNeck,*
> *NavelDisplayNeck*);
> *pockets* : *Boolean*);

End;

A record value from this type has the fields *customer, material, colour* and the tag field *GarmentKind*, and has three, four, four, or six other fields depending on the value of the tag being *trousers, jacket, skirt* or *blouse* respectively. Note that the fields corresponding to a particular variant do not exist unless the tag field has the appropriate value for that variant.

Array type

An **array** type is a structured Pascal data type. Each array value comprises a fixed number of separate components or **elements.** These elements are values from another Pascal data type. Each element of an array has an **index**, distinct from the indices of the other elements. The indices are chosen from another Pascal data type, and are often integers.

An array is typically declared as follows:

Type *column* = **Array** [1..10] **Of** *Integer*;

In this example, each value of the type *column* is an array consisting of ten separate integers. These ten elements are indexed from 1 to 10.

Arrays indexed from 1 upwards are very similar to sequences in our specifications, but it is important not to confuse the two concepts.

Unlike a file, elements of an array may be accessed randomly. In Pascal, it is possible to alter particular components of an array without having to update all the elements in the array.

Array indexing   To select an element of an array, the array is subscripted by an **index** in a similar way to the selection of an element from a sequence in our specifications. For example,

InputBuffer [5]

denotes the element indexed by the value 5 in the array *InputBuffer*.

Multi-dimensional array   As you have already seen, an array is a bounded structure of elements, each accessed by an index in some range. They have been largely used in Pascal so far to implement short sequences. In general, an **N-dimensional array** is a bounded structure requiring *N* indices, in *N* ranges, to access an element. All the elements are the same type. In principle, the index types could be anything, but in Pascal they must be **scalar**, which means that they have a notion of successor. (For example, *Integer, Boolean, Char*: given one value there is, in general, a next one. This is not true of *Real*.) In particular, a two-dimensional array is often called a **matrix**.

For example, a chess board could be defined in Pascal, assuming the type *Piece* as

Var *ChessBoard* : **Array**[1..8, 1..8] **Of** *Piece*;

The indices do not have to be the same size, or indeed sub-ranges of the same type.

Comparison of arrays   General array comparison (equality, for example) is not permitted in Pascal. Shame. Neither is record comparison. However, packed arrays of *Char* may be compared.

Character string types   There is a standard way of manipulating *fixed* length strings of characters in Pascal. This is through an array of *Char* indexed from 1 to some number greater than 1, which is also packed. These packed arrays (may) occupy less space than unpacked ones, but, more importantly, Pascal offers more facilities, such as comparison, simply because they are packed.

Character string constant   Character string constants can be written in Pascal as a sequence of characters surrounded by single quotes ('). The type of such a string with *N* characters in it is:

Packed Array [1 .. *N*] **Of** *Char*

(Consequently, string constants may be assigned into string arrays of the same size.)

String operations (relational)   Pascal allows the use of all six relations on the type

Packed Array [1 .. *N*] **Of** *Char*

where *N* is some integer value > 1. (Note that the arrays must be packed, and must be arrays of *Char*, indexed from 1 to something greater than 1.)

Less than or equal is defined similarly to the lexicographic ordering introduced earlier for sequences in our specifications. That is, *A* <= *B* if *A* and *B* are the same, or the character in *A* at the first position where they are different is less than the corresponding character in *B*. (Note that only strings of the same length may be compared in standard Pascal.) The other relational operators are defined as one would expect.

Set type

Set types may be used in Pascal, although the type of elements and the size of sets is restricted. Membership test is implemented as an infix operation, called **In**. Set constants are written in a notation slightly divergent from traditional mathematics, using square rather than curly brackets. (Unfortunately, these look rather like the sequences we write in specifications – do not confuse them!) For example,

[1,3,5,7,8,10,12]

denotes a value of type **Set of** *Integer*, containing only the elements listed.

Defining a set by sub-ranges   When denoting a set value in Pascal, as well as enumerating the elements, one may specify **ranges** of elements which are members of the set. For example:

[3 .. 21 , 50, N + 1, 105]
[$'A'$ .. $'Z'$, $'a'$ .. $'z'$, $'0'$ .. $'9'$, $'$ $'$]

File type

The **sequential file** is the basis of all input and output in Pascal. A sequential file may be created by adding new elements, one at a time, to the end of an originally empty file. An already existing sequential file may be read, an element at a time, starting at its beginning. A file type is denoted:

File Of X

where X is the type of the items in the file.
      (Note that there is no Pascal operator to test for equality between two files.)

Reset and rewrite statements   There are two pre-declared procedures, **reset** and **rewrite**, which initialize files so that they are in the correct state for reading from or writing to respectively. *reset(f)* causes the next read statement to file f to read the first element in that file. *rewrite(f)* sets f to be the empty file so that any previous contents of the file are discarded.

End of file   There is a pre-declared function in Pascal which takes a file and returns as its result true or false depending on whether the file is at its end point, that is whether there is no more data to be read from the file. It is written:

$$eof(f)$$

where f is the file.

File input buffer   When reading a file in Pascal, one may examine the element at the current reading position without moving on to the next element. This is because Pascal associates with each file a **buffer variable.** For a file, F, the buffer variable is called

$$F\char94$$

and it contains the element at the current position. This is most useful if one wishes to read the file conditionally, when the condition is based on the value that would be read. When the file is opened for reading (*reset*), the buffer variable contains the first element, if there is one.

The buffer variable associated with the standard input file,

$$input\char94$$

is initially set to the first character of the input, if there is one. However, to allow for sensible use of interaction, the language implementation usually delays the association of keyboard characters until the value is needed in the program.

For any file, F, when the condition

$$eof(F)$$

is true, the buffer variable, $F\char94$ is undefined. Hence it is *never* sensible to write conditions such as:

$$eof(F) \textbf{ Or } (F\char94 = '\ ')$$

Such conditions are Wally traps.

Read statement   A **read** statement is a program statement that causes data to be taken from a file and copied into program variables. In Pascal, one of the ways of accomplishing this is via the pre-declared procedure *read*. This reads data from a file variable and places the value read in another variable. The format is:

$$read\,(\,file\text{-}variable,\ result\text{-}variable)$$

Get statement   There is a pre-declared procedure in Pascal called **get**. This takes a single file as a variable parameter, which must be open for reading. The procedure moves the current read position forward one place, thus updating the buffer variable for that file. The pre-declared procedure **read** (when working on non-text files) is actually not necessary, but is conveniently pre-declared as

> **Procedure** *read*(**Var** *f*: **File Of** *t*; **Var** *x*:*t*);
> **Begin**
>   *x* := *f* ^;
>   *get*(*f*)
> **End**;

Unfortunately, one may not write procedures with parameters of unspecified types (for example, *t* above) in Pascal. Only the pre-declared procedures are so flexible.

Write statement (on non-text files)   There is a pre-declared procedure in Pascal, called **write**. When used with non-text files, it takes a file variable and an expression, evaluates the expression and writes the value on to the end of the file. The expression must be of the correct type for the file, and the file must be open for writing (a *rewrite* must have been performed on it).

Text type   Pascal **text files** are sequential files whose elements are of type *Char*. They are a pre-declared type called **Text**. For example,

> **Var** *x* : *Text*;

They are not quite the same as **File Of** *Char*, because they are structured into lines.

Actually, the files *input* (usually keyboard) and *output* (usually display) are pre-declared variables of type *Text*.

Readln statement   There is a pre-declared procedure in Pascal, called **readln**. This is used to read items of data from a text file, such as *input*, placing the values in named variables. After this any data following on the same line is ignored, and the read position is arranged to be the start of the next line (if there is one). For example:

> *readln*(*input*, *pile*)

This would read the next item of data from the input file, and place the value in the variable *pile*. Spaces preceding the data are ignored. Any text after the data up to the end of the line are also ignored. An error occurs if the data is not compatible with the type of the variable.

End of line condition (eoln)   There is a pre-declared Pascal function called **eoln**. This takes a file of type *Text* which has been opened for reading, and returns a Boolean result. The result is true when the current reading position in the file is at the end of a line, and is false otherwise.

For a non-empty text file, F, the condition $eoln(F)$ is always true one character before the condition $eof(F)$. In other words, the last character of a Pascal text file, if there is one, is a space corresponding to an end-of-line. Thus a text file cannot end in the middle of a line of text.

In Pascal, for a text file F, when the current position marks the end of a line, the function $eoln(F)$ is true. However, at such a point, the current element is a space. That is, $F^\wedge = '\ '$.

Writeln and write on text files   **writeln** is a procedure which is pre-declared in Pascal. It takes an arbitrary number of parameters, separated by commas. If the first parameter is a text file variable, the output is written to that file. Otherwise it is written to the file *output*. The other parameters are expressions which are evaluated and then output in the order they appear in the statement. The expressions may be of mixed types. In particular they may be string constants or integer values. A new line is produced on the output file after the data is written. For example:

> *writeln(output,' The date today is ',date, ' of ',month)*

Pascal has a pre-declared procedure called **write** which is used to write items to files. When used with text files, such as *output*, it is exactly like *writeln*, except that a new line is not written after the data.

Field specifier for write and writeln   Items to be written by the *writeln* statement (and *write* on text files) can be suffixed by an integer **field specifier** indicating how many characters the representation of that value should occupy. Field specifiers must always be greater than zero. They are written in the program after a colon (:) following the item to which they refer.

Field specifier for string values   In the *write* and *writeln* statements, the field specifier of an item which is a character, or a string of characters (packed array of *Char*), defines the exact number of characters that will be written for that item. If the field specifier is less than the length of the string, the string is truncated on the right. (If the field specifier is N, only the first N characters are written.) If the field specifier is greater than or equal to the length of the string, a number of spaces are written before the string. For example:

> *write('A':7)*

This writes six spaces and then the letter 'A'.

> *writeln(CurrentWord:10)*

This writes the first ten characters of *CurrentWord* followed by a new line, if *CurrentWord* is a packed array of *Char*, indexed from 1 to some value greater than or equal to 10.

Field specifier for integer values   For integer items in the *writeln* (or *write* on text files) statement, the field specifier is interpreted as follows. If the decimal representation of the integer being written requires fewer characters than the width specifies, the representation is space filled on the left to make it up to the width. Otherwise, the representation is written using as many characters as are required for the value without any space filling. For example:

> *writeln(count:7)*

If, say, count has the value 57, the output for the above statement would be five spaces followed by the string '57'.

> *writeln(MaxPartNumber:1)*

The value 1 as a field specifier causes the number to be written using exactly as many characters as required by its decimal representation, without any spaces.

> *writeln(salary:MaxWidth + 2)*

The above example illustrates that the field specifiers may be expressions involving program variables.

Pointer types

Dynamic references are values, and all values have a type in Pascal. The types of references are known as **pointers** and are denoted by ^ followed by the type of the variables that may be referenced. For example,

> *^ Integer*

denotes the type **pointer to** *Integer*, and is the set of all possible references of dynamic variables which have the type *Integer*. (The space between the ^ symbol and the name of the type is not needed, but its presence or not is a matter of style.)

The only place in Pascal where one may write a type name

textually before its definition is within the definition of a pointer type. This relaxation of the normal restriction is required due to the inherently recursive nature of dynamic type definitions.

Indirect access to variable (via pointer)

In Pascal, to access the variable pointed to by some other variable, X, one writes:

$X\hat{\ }$

New statement

In Pascal, the pre-declared procedure **new** takes as a variable parameter, a variable P, of type $\hat{\ }T$, for some type T. It creates a new variable, of type T, and sets P to reference it. The value of the new variable is undefined. The new variable is unique in that it does not coincide with any existing variable accessible dynamically or statically before the call to *new*.

For example, suppose we had the static variable

$x : \hat{\ }Integer$

Execution of the statement

new (x)

would cause a new variable of type *Integer* to be created, and x would be left pointing to it. The value of the new variable, that is, of

$x\hat{\ }$

would be undefined.

Dispose statement

In Pascal, the pre-declared procedure ***dispose*** is the inverse of *new*. It takes one variable parameter, of type $\hat{\ }T$, for some type T. When applied to some pointer variable, P, it assumes that P points to a dynamic variable, of type T, previously created via *new*. The memory occupied by that dynamic variable is returned to the operating system, and the variable no longer exists. The value of the variable P is *undefined* afterwards, thus it is an error to attempt to use its value (for example, by assignment or $P\hat{\ }$). It is also an error to attempt to access the dynamic variable that was disposed (by another pointer variable that was pointing to it).

For example, consider the following:

new (*p*);
q := *p*;
dispose(*q*);

After executing these, the values of both *q* and *p* are totally undefined, and thus *p*^ does not exist.

A.4.9   Variable declaration

A **variable declaration** in Pascal defines a new variable, by giving its name and type. The name of a variable is an identifier. For example, the declarations

> **Var** *sum* : *Integer*;
>   *mean* : *Real*;

define two variables – *sum* of type *Integer* and *mean* of type *Real*.

A.4.10   Procedure declaration

A **procedure declaration** defines a procedure used elsewhere in the program via procedure calls. It starts with a **procedure heading** which names the procedure with an identifier (and defines any parameters – see later). The procedure heading is followed by the procedure's statement body. Every procedure should contain a comment after the heading, explaining what it does. Like all declarations, a procedure must be declared textually before it is used. For example:

```
Procedure XthPowerOfY;
{ pre x >= 0 }
{ power := y to the power x; x := 0 }
Begin
  power := 1;
  While x > 0 Do
  Begin
    power := power * y;
    x := x - 1
  End
End;
```


Local variable

Local variables can be defined within procedures just as in the main program. They exist only when the procedure is being executed and cannot be referenced by the main program. They do *not* retain their value between calls of the procedure defining them.

Local declaration

As well as declaring local variables, a procedure or function may locally declare constants, types, procedures and functions. The declared items may only be used within the declaring procedure.

Value parameters

Pascal procedure or function value parameters are declared in the procedure or function heading after the procedure name, and between brackets. For each parameter, a name is given followed by the type of the value expected for that parameter. The names given here are called **formal value parameters,** and are used to reference the value throughout the body of the procedure or function.

For example, the following function has two formal value parameters called *ThisYear* and *ThisMonth*.

> **Function** *MonthSize(ThisYear : Year*; *ThisMonth : MonthNo) : Integer*;
> **Begin**
> ...
> ... *ThisMonth* ...
> ... *ThisYear* ...
> ...
> **End**

A procedure or function may have a mixture of both value and variable parameters. For example, the following procedure heading defines three variable parameters, *a*, *b* and *e*; and three value parameters, *c*, *d* and *f*:

> **Procedure** *MixtureOfValueAndVariable* (**Var** *a,b*: *Integer*; *c,d* : *Boolean*;
>   **Var** *e* : *Real*; *f* : *Char*)

Procedure or function value parameters actually passed to a procedure are written as expressions within brackets after the name of the procedure in the procedure call. These values are called **actual value parameters,** and are associated with the procedure's formal parameters by the order in which they are written. The type of an actual parameter must be compatible with the type of the corresponding formal parameter. There is no relationship between the name of a formal parameter and any variable or constant involved in the associated actual parameter.

For example, assuming the function *MonthSize*, which takes two value parameters, one might construct the expression:

> 10 * *MonthSize*(89,7)

Value parameters in Pascal behave like pre-initialized variables, in the sense that they are given a value by the statement that calls the

procedure; but that procedure may change the value during its execution. However, such a change does *not* affect anything outside the
procedure.

Value parameters to procedures and functions in Pascal are
implemented at run-time by actually copying the value when the
procedure or function is called. For large items, this copying might have
some significant effect on the efficiency of the execution. This effect can
be removed by using variable parameters instead, because these are not
copied but are referenced by an implicit pointer. However, in such cases,
the programmer should include a comment to the effect that this is
merely an optimization, and must always ensure that the parameter is
not unintentionally changed.

Of course, there is a trade-off. If the large item is accessed from
within the procedure or function very many times, the extra time taken
to follow the implicit pointer for each access could add up to more time
than that taken to copy the whole value.

Pascal does not allow value parameters which are files. Neither
does it allow value parameters which contain files (record, array of files,
for example). This is because value parameters are implemented by
copying the actual parameter value when the procedure is called. This
would mean copying the entire file!

When a variable is supplied as the actual parameter for a formal
value parameter of a procedure, the procedure cannot alter the value of
that variable outside it (except by a direct global access). However, when
the variable is of a pointer type, the procedure is able to alter the value
of the dynamic variable referenced by the pointer, if there is one. For
example:

```
Type IntegerList = ^IntegerListRec;
     IntegerListRec = Record
                           head : Integer;
                           tail : IntegerList
                      End;

Procedure ChangeHead(ThisList : IntegerList; NewHead : Integer);
{ pre ThisList <> Nil }
{ ThisList := [NewHead] ⌢ tl ThisList }
Begin
   ThisList^.head := NewHead
End;
```

This is technically alright, because the pointer itself is not being changed,
just the variable it points to. However, somebody looking at the
procedure heading may be given the impression that the abstract value of
ThisList is not altered, because *ThisList* is a value parameter, particularly
if the heading is used in an abstract specification (in terms of sequences)

of the procedure. Pascal has no formal mechanism for indicating the fact that a change may occur to some dynamic variable accessible by following the pointer.

However, when we write a specification of a procedure by giving its heading and then pre- and post-conditions in terms of the abstract values of any parameters actually implemented by pointers, the value parameters do not have their abstract values altered outside the procedure. Thus the example above would be abstractly specified with *ThisList* as a variable parameter.

A generalization of this applies to parameters which are not themselves pointers, but which contain pointers (an array of pointers, or a record containing a field which is a pointer).

Variable parameters

Pascal procedure or function variable parameters are declared in the procedure or function heading after the procedure name, and between brackets. For each parameter, a name is given, followed by the type of the variable expected for that parameter. To distinguish a variable parameter from a value parameter, the word **Var** is written before it. The names given in the heading are called **formal variable parameters,** and are used to reference the variable throughout the body of the procedure or function.

For example, the following procedure has one formal variable parameter, called *current*:

```
Procedure GetTime(Var current : Time);
Begin
    . . .
    current := . . .
    . . .
End;
```

Procedure variable parameters actually passed to a procedure are variables written within brackets after the name of the procedure in the procedure call. These are called **actual variable parameters,** and are associated with the procedure's formal parameters by the order in which they are written. The type of the actual parameters must be compatible with the type of the formal parameters. Note that actual variable parameters are not expressions – they are variables. There is no relationship between the names of the formal parameters and the names of the corresponding actual parameters.

For example, the procedure which has the heading:

```
Procedure GetTime (Var current : Time);
```

might be called as:

GetTime(TimeNow)

Conformant array parameters

It is often required to have a procedure or function which can accept arrays of various sizes as a parameter. Although each Pascal array has a fixed size, the language allows parameters to be defined as **conformant arrays.** A conformant array is a formal parameter which is an array, for which the element type and the index type are defined, but for which the lower and upper bounds of the indices are left unspecified. The array may be packed, and may be a variable or value parameter. For example:

```
Procedure sort(Var list : Array [lo .. hi:Integer] Of Integer);
Var scan,pos,max,swap:Integer;
Begin
  For scan := 1 To hi - lo Do
  Begin
    max := hi - scan + 1;
    For pos := lo To hi - scan Do
      If list[pos] > list[max] Then
        max := pos;
    swap := list[max];
    list[max] := list[hi - scan + 1];
    list[hi - scan + 1] := swap
  End
End;
```

This procedure takes an array of integers, indexed by integers as a variable parameter. The index range has not been fixed, but instead the lowest and highest index values are called *lo* and *hi* respectively. This enables the procedure to sort the array by referring to *lo* and *hi* as variables. It may be applied to any array of *Integer* indexed by any sub-range of *Integer*.

A restriction is placed on the use of formal conformant arrays as actual parameters to other procedures, based on the need for the Pascal compiler to be able statically to predict the exact size of each actual conformant array parameter. The restriction is that a formal conformant array value parameter may not be passed on as an actual value parameter. (However, it may be passed as an actual variable parameter.)

(Conformant arrays are available in level 1 standard Pascal, but not in level 0.)

Procedural parameters

A parameter to a procedure or function may itself be a procedure or function. These are declared in Pascal by giving a formal parameter name to the procedure or function, and specifying its parameters (and the result type for a function). The actual procedure or function passed as a parameter in a call does not have to have the same name, but its parameters (and result type for a function) must match in order, type and whether variable, value, or themselves procedure or function parameters. For example, there follows the skeleton of a sort procedure for arrays of *Integers* which can be given a function providing any non-reflexive total order relation on pairs of *Integers* (for example, $<$ or $>$):

```
Procedure sort(Var s:IntegerArray;
               Function order(i, j:Integer):Boolean
               )
Var pos:Integer ...

    .  .  .
    If order(s[pos],s[pos + 1]) Then
       . . .
    . . .
End
```

A.4.11   Function declaration

A **function declaration** defines a program function consisting of a heading, local declarations and a body. The heading defines the name of the function, the formal value (or variable) parameters and the result type. Within the body of the function, the name is treated as a *write-only* variable, in order to assign the function result. For example:

```
Function factorial (n : Integer) : Integer;
{ Assumes n >= 0 }
Var result : Integer;
Begin
  result := 1;
  While n > 0 Do
  Begin
    result := result * n;
    n := n - 1;
  End;
  factorial := result
End;
```

Note that it is necessary to have a local variable in the above example. This is because the name of the function is treated as a write-only variable for assigning the result. It is not allowed to replace the variable *result* with the function name *factorial*, that is to have the statement:

factorial : = *factorial* * *n*;

because that would be reading the value associated with *factorial*. (The reason for this is clear when one considers that Pascal allows functions that have no parameters, and also allows functions to be recursive.)

A final note about variable parameters of functions. Pascal allows this, but there are few cases where their use is justified. The main reason for this is that functions should have all their input through their parameters (arguments) and all their output through their result. Variable parameters, on the other hand, are an explicit means for allowing a procedure or function to change the value of a variable. As hinted, though, there are cases for exception to this general principle, but they are rather subtle.

Results of functions in Pascal may not be structured items, such as arrays, records and files. They may only be simple types, such as *Integer*, *Real* and *Boolean*, or pointer types. This is an idiosyncratic restriction due to the technique used to implement Pascal function calls when the language was first designed and implemented.

A.4.12   Statements

Condition

A **condition** is a program expression having either a true or false value when evaluated. Like all program expressions, these conditions may contain variables, constant values and operations. The values of such variables are used when the expression is evaluated, thus it is possible (in fact, likely!) that sometimes the condition is true, and sometimes false.

Empty statement

Pascal has a statement that has no spelling, and no effect. It is called the **empty** statement. For example, if one places a semicolon immediately before an **End**, there is said to be an empty statement between them. This is because a semicolon is used as the statement separator.

Statement sequence

A **statement sequence** is a list of program statements, which are executed by the computer in the order in which they textually appear. In Pascal the statements in the list are separated by semicolons (;).

Compound statement

A **compound** statement is a sequence of statements which is treated as a single statement. This can sometimes help the clarity of the program, but is mostly used for writing a statement sequence in places where only a single statement is syntactically legal. In Pascal a compound statement is constructed by surrounding the sequence with the reserved words **Begin** and **End.**

Assignment statement

An **assignment** statement contains a variable and an expression. When executed, the expression is evaluated, and its value is placed in the named variable. (Hence the types of the named variable and that of the expression must be compatible.) In Pascal, the variable name and the expression are separated by the : = symbol. For example:

    sum := sum + next

In this example, *sum* has the value of *next* added to it.

Procedure call statement

In Pascal, a (parameterless) procedure is **called** by a statement consisting simply of the name of the procedure. For example, the statement

    HumanMove;

executes the body of the procedure *HumanMove.*

If statement

In Pascal, the standard conditional statement is the **If** construct. The syntax rules of the language insist that the conditional part is a single statement. In cases where more than one statement is to be conditionally executed, those statements are formed into a compound statement with **Begin** and **End** round them. The **If** construct involves the reserved words **If** and **Then**. For example:

    If x > y Then
    Begin
      swap := x;
      x := y;
      y := swap
    End

An extension of the Pascal **If** statement is the **If–Else** statement. This involves *two* alternative conditional statements and the reserved words **If**, **Then** and **Else**. The first statement is executed if the condition is true just beforehand, otherwise the second is executed. For example:

```
If x > y Then
   max := x
Else
   max := y
```

Case *statement*

The Pascal **Case** statement is a specialized form of alternatives command (like if–then–else), based on the value of a single expression. It comprises an expression (called the **case-index**) of some ordinal type (*Integer*, *Char*, *Boolean*; but not *Real*); and a collection of non-overlapping lists of distinct values from the same type, each list associated with an action (statement). The general form is:

```
Case e Of
   c1,c2,c3 : st1;
   c4 : st2;
   . . .
End
```

where e is an expression, $c1$, $c2$, ... are constants of the same type, and $s1$, $s2$, ... are single statements (perhaps compound, with **Begin** and **End**). On execution of a **Case** statement, the given expression is evaluated and the value compared with the lists of constants. If the value of the expression occurs in one of the lists, the action associated with it is performed. If the value of the expression does not appear in one of the lists, a run-time error occurs. It is for this reason that a **Case** statement is often written inside an **If** statement, the latter checking that the value of the expression is one of those covered by the former. (Some non-standard implementations of Pascal allow a very convenient addition to the **Case** statement which enables the programmer to state what should be done if the value of the expression does not occur in any of the lists. This usually involves the keyword **Otherwise**. Of course, the disadvantage of using non-standard features is that the program can only be run on that, or similarly non-standard implementations.)

While *statement*

In Pascal, one form of loop construct is the **While** statement, which tests a condition before executing the iterative part. It involves the keywords

While and **Do**. The syntax rules of Pascal insist that the loop body is a single statement. Thus, in cases where a sequence of statements is required for the body, a compound statement is used. For example

```
While next <> 0 Do
Begin
   sum := sum + next;
   next := next - 1
End
```

For *statement*

The for loop concept is used in Pascal by the **For** statement. This involves the reserved words **For**, **To** and **Do**. The rules of the language insist that the loop body is a single statement, so in practice it is often a compound statement, with a **Begin** and **End**. The control variable must be declared within the same program block (procedure) as the one in which the statement occurs. The value of the control variable must not be altered by assignment inside the loop body (which would be bad practice anyway). Also, the value of the control variable is *undefined* after the loop execution terminates.

Repeat *statement*

In Pascal, one form of loop construct is the **Repeat** statement, which tests a condition after executing the iterative part. It involves the keywords **Repeat** and **Until**. The rules of Pascal do *not* insist that the loop body is a single statement:

```
Repeat
   statement-1;
   statement-2;
   . . .
Until condition
```

With *statement*

The Pascal **With** statement enables access to the fields of a record without having to specify the record for each access. This is most useful when there are to be several accesses to fields of the same record during some part of the program. The format is:

> **With** *some-record-variable* **Do**
>   *statement*

Within the statement, the fields of the given record may be referenced by name, without preceding them by the record variable and a dot.

As with other structured Pascal statements, the body of the **With** statement must be a single statement, and hence it is often compound. For example, with the record variable

> *ThisStudent* : **Record** *sex*:(*male, female*); *age*:*Integer* **End**

the statements

> *ThisStudent.sex* := *female*;
> *ThisStudent.age* := 18

are equivalent to

> **With** *ThisStudent* **Do**
> **Begin**
>   *sex* := *female*;
>   *age* := 18
> **End**

Appendix B
Pascal reserved words and syntax

B.1   Reserved words

The 35 Pascal reserved words are:

And	**End**	**Nil**	**Set**
Array	**File**	**Not**	**Then**
Begin	**For**	**Of**	**To**
Case	**Function**	**Or**	**Type**
Const	**Goto**	**Packed**	**Until**
Div	**If**	**Procedure**	**Var**
Do	**In**	**Program**	**While**
Downto	**Label**	**Record**	**With**
Else	**Mod**	**Repeat**	

B.2   Syntax

Letter

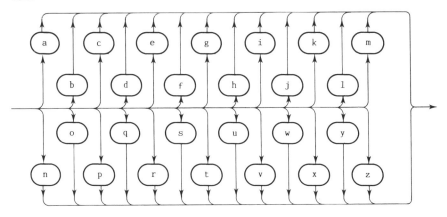

Digit

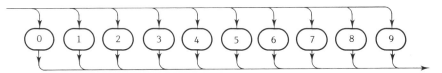

455

Identifier and Directive

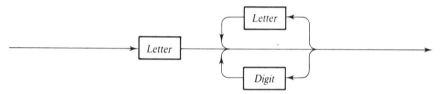

UnsignedInteger

UnsignedNumber

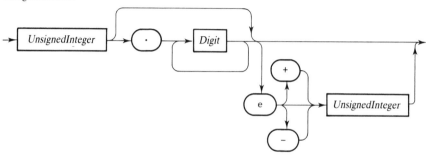

CharacterString

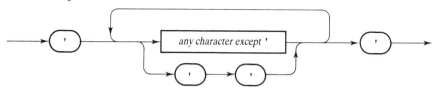

ConstantIdentifier, VariableIdentifier, FieldIdentifier, BoundIdentifier
  TypeIdentifier, ProcedureIdentifier and FunctionIdentifier

UnsignedConstant

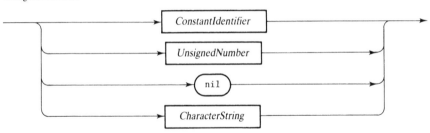

Constant

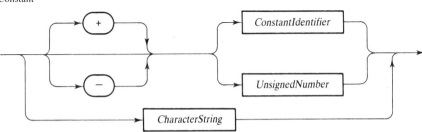

Variable

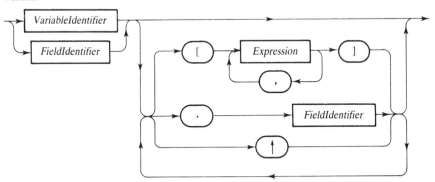

Factor

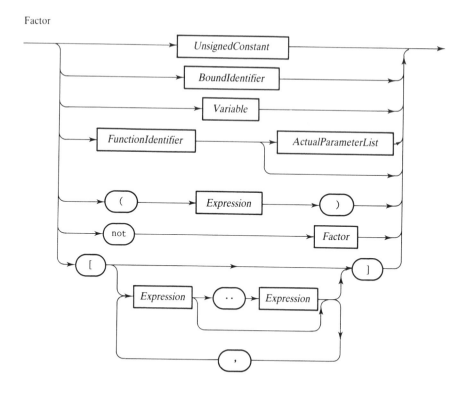

Term

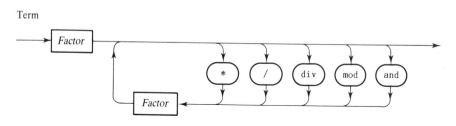

SimpleExpression

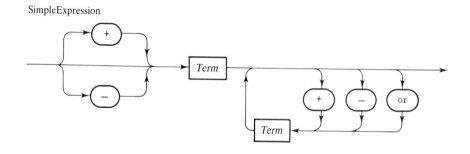

Expression

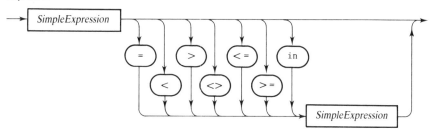

ActualParameterList

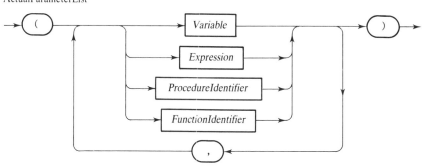

WriteParameterList

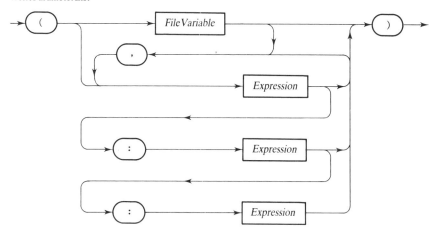

IndexTypeSpecification

ConformantArraySchema

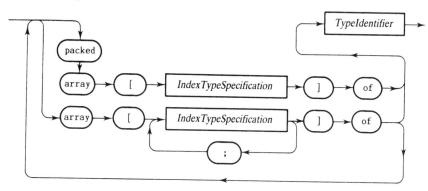

FormalParameterList

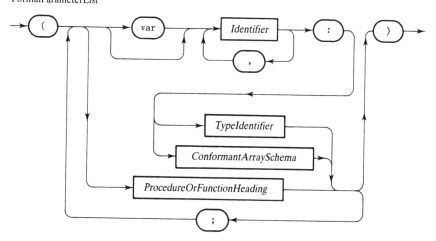

ProcedureOrFunctionHeading

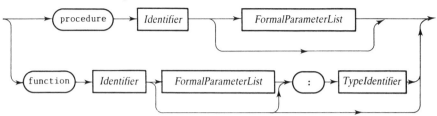

OrdinalType

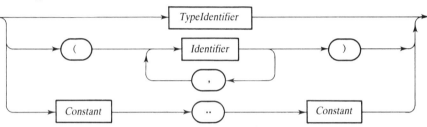

Type

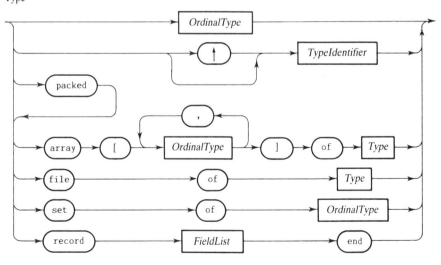

FieldList

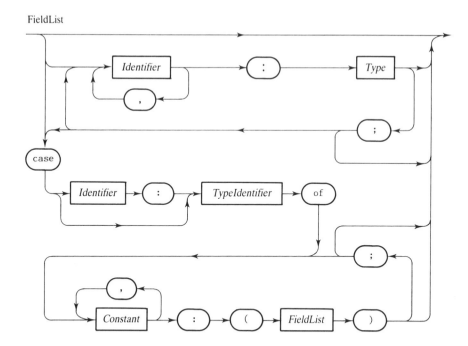

Statement

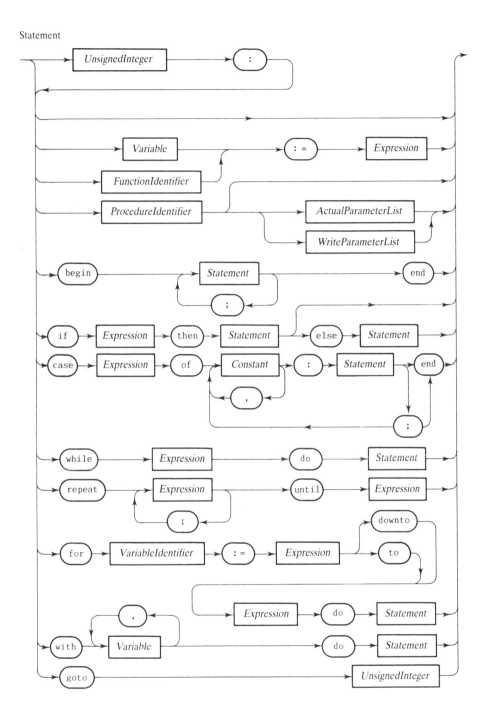

Block

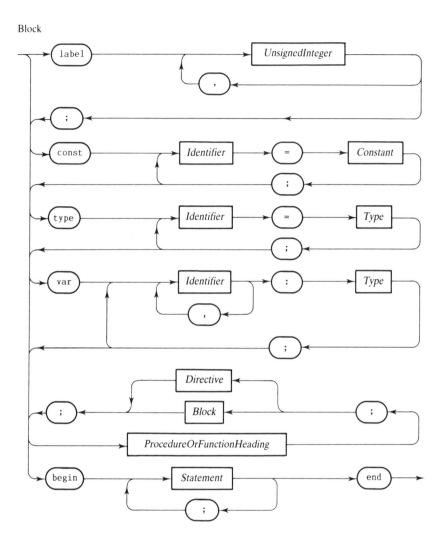

Program

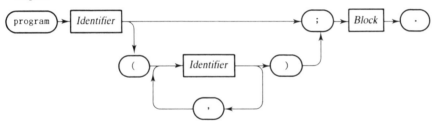

Appendix C
Full implementation of the strings package

This appendix contains the Pascal code for all the procedures and functions of the strings package, the designs for some of which were presented in Chapter 12. For the benefit of readers with standard Pascal compilers, possibly not supporting a mechanism for separate compilation, the code is presented in the order dictated by the ISO Pascal Standard and may be simply edited in with any application code that requires it.

```
Program StringsPackageInISOLevel1Pascal(input, output);

{ String chunk length – any length > 0 will work }
Const ChunkSize = 16;

Type Nat0 = 0 .. maxint;
     Nat1 = 1 .. maxint;

     String = ^StringRec;
     StringTail = ^StringTailRec;
     StringRec = Record
                     length    : Nat1; { Note: no 0 as Nil represents '' }
                     RefCount : Nat0; { The number of references to
                                        this string. Note: only = 0
                                        when string is the result of a
                                        function, since there are no
                                        program variable references to
                                        it at the time the function
                                        terminates }
                     FirstChunk : Packed Array [1..ChunkSize] Of
                                                             Char;
                     TailChunks : StringTail
                 End;

     StringTailRec = Record
                         ThisTailChunk: Packed Array [1..ChunkSize]
                                                         Of Char;
                         FurtherTailChunks: StringTail
                     End;
```

467

{ *Result of string comparison – internal to ADT at the moment* }
StringCompareResult = (*StringLessThan, StringEqual, StringGreaterThan*);
{ *Type for sequencing through strings – internal to ADT at the moment* }
PosInString = **Record**
      IndexInChunk: 1. .*ChunkSize*;
      Case *InFirstChunk:Boolean* **Of**
        true: (*HeadChunkContainingPos*: *String*);
        false: (*TailChunkContainingPos*:
                        StringTail)
      End;

Procedure *InitSTRING*(**Var** *ThisString*: *String*);
{
* *Initialize ThisString to be the empty or null string* ''
}
Begin
  ThisString := **Nil**
End{ *InitSTRING* };

Procedure *FinalSTRING*(**Var** *ThisString*: *String*);
{
* *Dereference ThisString, and reclaim the storage if last reference*
}

Var *ThisTailChunk, NextTailChunks*: *StringTail*;

Begin
  If *ThisString* = **Nil Then** { *Do nothing* }
  Else
  Begin
    With *ThisString^* **Do**
      RefCount := *RefCount* – 1;
    If *ThisString^.RefCount* < 1 **Then**
    Begin { *Was the only ref. to this string* }
      ThisTailChunk := *ThisString^.TailChunks*;
      dispose(*ThisString*);
      While *ThisTailChunk* <> **Nil Do**
      Begin
        NextTailChunks := *ThisTailChunk^.FurtherTailChunks*;
        dispose(*ThisTailChunk*);
        ThisTailChunk := *NextTailChunks*
      End
    End;
    ThisString := **Nil**;
  End;
End{ *FinalSTRING* };

```
Procedure SetToFirstPosSTRING(Var FirstPos:PosInString;
                                Var ThisString: String);
{
* FirstPos initialized to point to the first char of ThisString
*
* pre-condition
*    ThisString <> ''
}
Begin
  With FirstPos Do
  Begin
    InFirstChunk := true; { FirstChunk record }
    HeadChunkContainingPos := ThisString;
    IndexInChunk := 1
  End;
End{ SetToFirstPosSTRING };

Procedure MoveToNextPosSTRING(Var ThisPos: PosInString;
                                Var CharAtThisPos: Char);
{
* ThisPos is advanced to point to next char in its string and
* current char returned in CharAtThisPos
*
* pre-condition
*    ThisPos initialized by call to SetToFirstPosSTRING
*    and not at end of string
}

Var NextChunk: StringTail;

Begin
  With ThisPos Do
    If InFirstChunk Then
    Begin { header record }
      CharAtThisPos :=
        HeadChunkContainingPos^.FirstChunk[IndexInChunk];
      If IndexInChunk <> ChunkSize Then
        IndexInChunk := IndexInChunk + 1
      Else
      Begin
        IndexInChunk := 1;
        NextChunk := HeadChunkContainingPos^.TailChunks;
        { change variant }
        InFirstChunk := false;
        TailChunkContainingPos := NextChunk
      End
    End
    Else
```

```
Begin { tail record }
  CharAtThisPos :=
    TailChunkContainingPos^.ThisTailChunk[IndexInChunk];
  If IndexInChunk <> ChunkSize Then
    IndexInChunk := IndexInChunk + 1
  Else
  Begin
    IndexInChunk := 1;
    TailChunkContainingPos :=
      TailChunkContainingPos^.FurtherTailChunks
  End
  End
End { MoveToNextPosSTRING };

Procedure InitValParamSTRING(ThisString: String);
{
* Initializes ThisString, which should be a value parameter, to be
* safely usable within the current procedure.
*
* Increase ref. count for a by-value param.
}
Begin
  If ThisString <> Nil Then
    With ThisString^ Do
      RefCount := RefCount + 1
End{ InitValParamSTRING };

Procedure AssignSTRING(Var lhs: String; rhs: String);
{
* lhs := rhs
}
Begin
  InitValParamSTRING(rhs);
  FinalSTRING(lhs);
  If rhs = Nil Then { Empty string }
    lhs := Nil
  Else
  Begin
    lhs := rhs; { Ref. copy }
    With rhs^ Do RefCount := RefCount + 1
  End;
  FinalSTRING(rhs)
End{ AssignSTRING };

Function AssignFuncResultSTRING(Var ThisString:String):String;
{
* Returns ThisString, and finalizes ThisString (sets to empty).
}
Begin
  { As FinalSTRING(ThisString), but without the actual
    reclaiming of storage }
```

```
   If ThisString <> Nil Then
      With ThisString^ Do
         RefCount := RefCount - 1;
   AssignFuncResultSTRING := ThisString;
   ThisString := Nil
End;

Procedure CopySTRING(Var lhs: String; rhs: String);
{
* lhs := rhs (forces a string copy)
}

Var TailChunkCount: Nat0;
    i: Nat1;
    TailChunk, LeftTailChunk, RightTailChunk: StringTail;

Begin
   InitValParamSTRING(rhs);
   FinalSTRING(lhs); { For reference counting, we are going to
                        assign a value to this variable }

   new(lhs);
   { Copy string FirstChunk }
   lhs^.length := rhs^.length;
   lhs^.FirstChunk := rhs^.FirstChunk;
   With lhs^ Do
   Begin
      RefCount := 1; { This one }
      TailChunkCount := (rhs^.length - 1) Div ChunkSize;
      TailChunks := Nil;
      { Allocate and link in any extra string TailChunks needed }
      For i := 1 To TailChunkCount Do
      Begin
         new(TailChunk);
         TailChunk^.FurtherTailChunks := TailChunks;
         TailChunks := TailChunk
      End
   End;
   { Loop through copying string tail if required }
   LeftTailChunk := lhs^.TailChunks;
   RightTailChunk := rhs^.TailChunks;
   For i := 1 To TailChunkCount Do
   Begin
      LeftTailChunk^.ThisTailChunk :=
                        RightTailChunk^.ThisTailChunk;
      LeftTailChunk := LeftTailChunk^.FurtherTailChunks;
      RightTailChunk := RightTailChunk^.FurtherTailChunks
   End;

   FinalSTRING(rhs);
End{ CopySTRING };
```

```
Function ConcatSTRING(s1, s2: String):String;
{
* Concatenates the string s1 with s2, returning a new string
* containing the result.
}

{ Reuses memory from string s1 if there are no other references to
  it.
}

Var null: Char; { set to chr(0) }
    result:String;
    LengthOfS1:Integer;
    ExtraTailChunkCount:Integer;
    ExtraTailChunkList:Stringtail;
    NextResultChunk:Stringtail;

    Procedure BuildExtraChunks(Var ChunkList:StringTail;
                               Var ChunkCount:Integer);
    {
    * Computes in ChunkCount the number of tail chunks needed
    * to append s2 on the back of result, and builds that many
    * into ChunkList
    }
    Var ResultChunk:Stringtail;
        i:Integer;
    Begin
      { Compute number of extra string chunks needed }
      ChunkCount := ((result^.length – 1) Div ChunkSize)
                      – (LengthOfS1 – 1) Div ChunkSize;
      { Build list of extra chunks }
      ChunkList := Nil;
      For i := 1 To ChunkCount Do
      Begin
        new(ResultChunk);
        ResultChunk^.FurtherTailChunks := ChunkList;
        ChunkList := ResultChunk
      End;
    End;

    Procedure AppendTailOnResult(ChunkList:StringTail;
                                 Var NextChunk:StringTail);
    {
    * Add on ChunkList to result, and find NextChunk, = pointer
    * to first tail chunk to contain a char after the old s1
    }
    Var ResultChunk:StringTail;
    Begin
      With result^ Do
```

```
If TailChunks = Nil Then
Begin
  TailChunks := ChunkList;
  NextChunk := ChunkList;
End
Else
Begin
  ResultChunk := TailChunks;
  While ResultChunk^.FurtherTailChunks <> Nil Do
    ResultChunk := ResultChunk^.FurtherTailChunks;
  ResultChunk^.FurtherTailChunks := ChunkList;
  If LengthOfS1 Mod ChunkSize = 0 Then
    NextChunk := ResultChunk^.FurtherTailChunks
  Else
    NextChunk := ResultChunk;
  End
End;

Procedure CopyS2ToResult(NextResultChunk:StringTail);
{
* copy s2 onto the back of result. NextResultChunk is the first
* StringTail chunk where any characters from s2 go.
}
Var S2CharPos:PosInString;
    ResultChunkStartPos:Integer;
    S2CharCount:Integer;
    ResultChunkPos:Integer;

    Procedure CopyCharFromS2(Var ch:char);
    Begin
      If S2CharCount >= s2^.length Then
        ch := null
      Else
      Begin
        MoveToNextPosSTRING(S2CharPos,ch);
        S2CharCount := S2CharCount + 1;
      End;
    End;

Begin { of CopyS2ToResult }
  { Loop through copying s2 to end of result char by char! }
  SetToFirstPosSTRING(S2CharPos,s2);
  S2CharCount := 0; { How many copied so far }
  If LengthOfS1 >= ChunkSize Then{ start in a tail chunk }
    ResultChunkStartPos :=
                    LengthOfS1 Mod ChunkSize + 1
  Else
  Begin
    { Copy from s2 into FirstChunk of result }
    For ResultChunkPos := LengthOfS1 + 1 To ChunkSize
    Do
       CopyCharFromS2(result^.FirstChunk[ResultChunkPos]);
    ResultChunkStartPos := 1;
  End;
```

```
            { Now fill up the tail chunks }
            While NextResultChunk <> Nil Do
            Begin
              With NextResultChunk^ Do
                For ResultChunkPos :=
                      ResultChunkStartPos To ChunkSize Do
                    CopyCharFromS2(ThisTailChunk[ResultChunkPos]);
                ResultChunkStartPos := 1;
                NextResultChunk := NextResultChunk^.FurtherTailChunks;
              End;
            End;

Begin { of ConcatSTRING }
  null := chr(0);
  InitValParamSTRING(s1);
  InitValParamSTRING(s2);
  InitSTRING(result);

  { Deal with trivial cases first }
  If s1 = Nil Then
    AssignSTRING(result,s2)
  Else
  If s2 = Nil Then
    AssignSTRING(result,s1)
  Else
    { Both s1 and s2 are non-empty }
  Begin
    { Obtain convenient copy of length of s1 }
    LengthOfS1 := s1^.length;

    { If there were no references to s1 beforehand, then we can reuse
      that string in the answer }
    If s1^.RefCount = 1 Then { Note: reference has been incremented
                                    by InitValParamSTRING }
      AssignSTRING(result,s1)
    Else
      CopySTRING(result,s1);

    { Now fill in the answer }
    With result^ Do
    Begin
      { Set length }
      length := LengthOfS1 + s2^.length;
      BuildExtraChunk(ExtraTailChunkList,ExtraTailChunkCount);

      { Append new chunks on end of result }
      AppendTailOnResult(ExtraTailChunkList,NextResultChunk);

      { At this stage, result contains (a copy of) s1, and enough chunks
        for s2. NextResultChunk points to the tail chunk to be next used
        for copying s2 }
```

```
      CopyS2ToResult(NextResultChunk);
    End{ With result^ };
  End;

  FinalSTRING(s1);
  FinalSTRING(s2);
  ConcatSTRING := AssignFuncResultSTRING(result);
End{ ConcatSTRING };

Function MakeLimitedSTRING(
                    Var static: Packed Array [lo..hi:Integer] Of Char;
                    limit: Integer):String;
{
* Converts a static Pascal string into a (dynamic) String.
* From lo to limit rather than hi. Note: assumes limit > 0.
* This internal procedure may be made generally available
* should there be a demand.
}

Var null: Char; { set to chr(0) }
    StaticLength: Nat1;
    i, TailChunkCount, CurrentLength: Nat0;
    result: String;
    TailChunk: StringTail;
    StaticPos: Integer;
    FirstChunkPos,ThisTailChunkPos: 1..ChunkSize;

Begin
  null := chr(0);
  { InitSTRING(result) not needed, as created here }

  StaticLength := limit - lo + 1;
  TailChunkCount := (StaticLength - 1) Div ChunkSize;
  { Copy into String FirstChunk }
  new(result);
  With result^ Do
  Begin
    length := StaticLength;
    RefCount := 1; { this one! }
    TailChunks := Nil;
    StaticPos := lo;
    CurrentLength := 0;
    { Copy string, null padding if necessary }
    For FirstChunkPos := 1 To ChunkSize Do
      If FirstChunkPos > StaticLength Then
        FirstChunk[FirstChunkPos] := null
      Else
      Begin
        FirstChunk[FirstChunkPos] := static[StaticPos];
        StaticPos := StaticPos + 1;
        CurrentLength := CurrentLength + 1;
      End;
```

```
    { Allocate and link in any extra string chunks needed }
    For i := 1 To TailChunkCount Do
    Begin
      new(TailChunk);
      TailChunk^.FurtherTailChunks := TailChunks;
      TailChunks := TailChunk
    End;
    { Loop through copying string tail if required }
    TailChunk := TailChunks;
    While TailChunk <> Nil Do
    Begin
      With TailChunk^ Do
      Begin
        { Copy string, null padding if necessary }
        For ThisTailChunkPos := 1 To ChunkSize Do
          If CurrentLength >= StaticLength Then
            ThisTailChunk[ThisTailChunkPos] := null
          Else
          Begin
            ThisTailChunk[ThisTailChunkPos] := static[StaticPos];
            StaticPos := StaticPos + 1;
            CurrentLength := CurrentLength + 1;
          End
      End;
      TailChunk := TailChunk^.FurtherTailChunks
    End{ While }
  End{ With };

  { Return the newly created dynamic string }
  MakeLimitedSTRING := AssignFuncResultSTRING(result);
End{ MakeLimitedSTRING };

Function MakeSTRING(
        static: Packed Array [lo. .hi:Integer] Of Char):String;
{
* Converts a static Pascal string into a (dynamic) String.
}
Begin
  MakeSTRING := MakeLimitedSTRING(static, hi)
End{ MakeSTRING };

Function CharToSTRING(ThisChar: Char):String;
{
* Converts a character into a string of length 1
}

Var OneCharStaticString: Packed Array [1 .. 1] Of Char;

Begin
  OneCharStaticString[1] := ThisChar;
  CharToSTRING := MakeSTRING(OneCharStaticString)
End{ CharToSTRING };
```

Function *LengthOfSTRING*(*ThisString*: *String*):*Nat*0;
{
* *Returns the length of a dynamic string*
}
Begin
  InitValParamSTRING(*ThisString*);
  If *ThisString* = **Nil Then**
    LengthOfSTRING := 0
  Else
    LengthOfSTRING := *ThisString*^.*length*;
  FinalSTRING(*ThisString*);
End{ *LengthOfSTRING* };

Function *EmptySTRING*: *String*;
{
* *Returns the empty or null string* ''
}

Begin
  EmptySTRING := **Nil**
End{ *EmptySTRING* };

Function *IndexSTRING*(*ThisString*: *String*; *i*: *Nat*1):*Char*;
{
* *Returns ThisString*[*i*]
*
* *pre-condition*:
*   *i* <= *LengthOfSTRING*(*ThisString*)
}

Var *j*: 2. .*maxint*; *chunk*: *StringTail*;

Begin
  InitValParamSTRING(*ThisString*);
  With *ThisString*^ **Do**
    If *i* <= *ChunkSize* **Then**
      IndexSTRING := *FirstChunk*[*i*]
    Else
    Begin
      chunk := *TailChunks*;
      For *j* := 2 **To** (*i* − 1) **Div** *ChunkSize* **Do**
        chunk := *chunk*^.*FurtherTailChunks*;
      IndexSTRING :=
        chunk^.*ThisTailChunk*[(*i* − 1) **Mod** *ChunkSize* + 1]
    End;
  FinalSTRING(*ThisString*);
End{ *IndexSTRING* };

Procedure *MakeStaticSTRING(*
                 dynamic: *String*;
                 Var *static*: **Packed Array**[*lo. .hi*:*Integer*] **Of** *Char*);
{
* *Converts a dynamic string into a static string.*
* *'static' is space padded if necessary.*
* *Info will be lost if LengthOfSTRING(ThisString) > hi − lo + 1.*
}

Var *PosInStatic*: *Integer*;
    LengthCopiedSoFar: *Nat1*;
    LengthOfDynamic: *Nat0*;
    ch : *Char*;
    PosInDynamic: *PosInString*;

Begin
   InitValParamSTRING(dynamic);

   LengthCopiedSoFar := 0;
   LengthOfDynamic := *LengthOfSTRING(dynamic)*;
   If *LengthOfDynamic* <> 0 **Then**
     SetToFirstPosSTRING(PosInDynamic, dynamic);
   For *PosInStatic* := *lo* **To** *hi* **Do**
     If *LengthCopiedSoFar* < *LengthOfDynamic* **Then**
     Begin
       MoveToNextPosSTRING(PosInDynamic, ch);
       static[*PosInStatic*] := *ch*;
       LengthCopiedSoFar := *LengthCopiedSoFar* + 1
     End
     Else
       static[*PosInStatic*] := ' ';

   FinalSTRING(dynamic);
End{ *MakeStaticSTRING* };

Procedure *ReadlnSTRING*(**Var** *TextFile*: *Text*; **Var** *result*: *String*);
{
* *Reads a string from text file TextFile; eoln terminating. The file*
* *read position is left pointing after the end of the line.*
*
* *pre-condition*:
* *TextFile open for reading and not eof (TextFile)*
}

Const *BufferLength* = 120; { *Note: not an implementation*
                     restriction, via recursion. }

Var *RestOfLine* : *String*;
    PartialLineLength : *Nat0*;
    PartialLine : **Packed Array** [1. .*BufferLength*] **Of** *Char*;
                        { *maybe all* }

```
Begin
  InitSTRING(RestOfLine);

  PartialLineLength := 0;
  While Not eoln(TextFile)
        And (PartialLineLength <> BufferLength) Do
  Begin
    PartialLineLength := PartialLineLength + 1;
    read(TextFile, PartialLine[PartialLineLength])
  End;
  If PartialLineLength = 0 Then
    AssignSTRING(result, EmptySTRING)
  Else
    AssignSTRING(result, MakeLimitedSTRING(PartialLine,
                                PartialLineLength));

  { Check for more characters on the input line }
  If Not eoln(TextFile) Then
  Begin
    { Get the rest }
    ReadlnSTRING(TextFile, RestOfLine);
    AssignSTRING(result, ConcatSTRING(result, RestOfLine))
  End
  Else
    get(TextFile);

  FinalSTRING(RestOfLine);
End{ ReadlnSTRING };

Procedure ReadSTRING(Var TextFile: Text; Var result: String;
                     Function stop(c:Char):Boolean);
{
* Reads a string from text file TextFile. The string is terminated by
* eoln(TextFile) or stop(TextFile^) returning true, whichever occurs
* first.
* In either case, the file read position is left at (not after) the
* terminator.
*
* pre-condition:
*    TextFile open for reading and not eof(TextFile)
}

Const BufferLength = 120; { Note: not an implementation
                              restriction, due to recursion. }

Var RestOfLine : String;
    PartialLineLength : Nat0;
    PartialLine : Packed Array [1 .. BufferLength] Of Char;

Begin
  InitSTRING(RestOfLine);

  PartialLineLength := 0;
  While Not eoln(TextFile)
        And (PartialLineLength <> BufferLength)
        And Not stop(TextFile^) Do
```

Begin
  PartialLineLength := *PartialLineLength* + 1;
  read(*TextFile*, *PartialLine*[*PartialLineLength*])
End;
If *PartialLineLength* = 0 **Then**
  AssignSTRING(*result*, *EmptySTRING*)
Else
  AssignSTRING(*result*, *MakeLimitedSTRING*(*PartialLine*,
                                      PartialLineLength));

  { *Check for more characters on the input line* }
  If Not *stop*(*TextFile*^) **And Not** *eoln*(*TextFile*) **Then**
  Begin
    { *Get the rest* }
    ReadSTRING(*TextFile*, *RestOfLine*, *stop*);
    AssignSTRING(*result*, *ConcatSTRING*(*result*, *RestOfLine*))
  End;

  FinalSTRING(*RestOfLine*);
End{ *ReadSTRING* };

Function *GetSubSTRING*(*ThisString*: *String*;
                            FromPos:*Nat*1; *ToPos*: *Nat*0):*String*;
{
* *Returns ThisString*[*FromPos*,. . .,*ToPos*]
* *Extracts a substring of ThisString.*
* *returns ' ' if FromPos and ToPos not in range.*
}

Const *MaxBufferLength* = 512; { *Note*: *not an implementation*
                                 restriction, due to recursion
                                 and concatenation. }

Var *result*: *String*;
    BufferLength, *i*, *StopPos*: *Nat*1;
    ch: *Char*;
    PosInS: *PosInString*;
    StaticBuffer: **Packed Array** [1..*MaxBufferLength*] **Of** *Char*;

Begin
  InitValParamSTRING(*ThisString*);
  InitSTRING(*result*);
  If (*ToPos* <= *LengthOfSTRING*(*ThisString*)) **And**
    (*FromPos* <= *ToPos*) **Then**
  Begin
    { *convert (max MaxBufferLength) chars to fixed string* }
    If *ToPos* – *FromPos* + 1 > *MaxBufferLength* **Then**
      StopPos := *FromPos* + *MaxBufferLength* – 1
    Else
      StopPos := *ToPos*;
    BufferLength := 0;
    SetToFirstPosSTRING(*PosInS*, *ThisString*);
    For *i* := 1 **To** *FromPos* – 1 **Do**
      MoveToNextPosSTRING(*PosInS*, *ch*);

```
      For i := FromPos To StopPos Do
      Begin
        MoveToNextPosSTRING(PosInS, ch);
        BufferLength := BufferLength + 1;
        StaticBuffer[BufferLength] := ch;
      End;
      { Convert to String }
      If BufferLength <> 0 Then { positive slice }
        AssignSTRING(result,MakeLimitedSTRING(StaticBuffer,
                                                    BufferLength));
      { check any more left }
      If ToPos <> StopPos Then
        AssignSTRING(result,
                    ConcatSTRING(result,
                              GetSubSTRING(ThisString,
                                          StopPos + 1,
                                          ToPos)))
   End;
   FinalSTRING(ThisString);
   GetSubSTRING := AssignFuncResultSTRING(result);
End{ GetSubSTRING };

Function CompareSTRING(left, right: String):StringCompareResult;
{
* Compares left with right
}
{ Comparison in whole chunks is valid even for the last (possibly
  incomplete) chunk, since chunks are filled up with the smallest
  value of Char (chr(0)) and due to the property that
  for-all ThisString:String, i:Char.
        ThisString < ThisString Concat [i] }

Var LeftLength, RightLength: Nat0; LeftTail, RightTail: StringTail;
    state: (GoOn, Less, Greater, Stop);
Begin
  InitValParamSTRING(left);
  InitValParamSTRING(right);
  LeftLength := LengthOfSTRING(left);
  RightLength := LengthOfSTRING(right);
  { Do trivial cases first }
  If LeftLength = 0 Then
    If RightLength = 0 Then
      CompareSTRING := StringEqual
    Else
      CompareSTRING := StringLessThan
  Else
  If RightLength = 0 Then
    CompareSTRING := StringGreaterThan
  Else
```

```
Begin
  { Non-trivial cases – both left and right are non-empty }
  LeftTail := left^.TailChunks;
  RightTail := right^.TailChunks;
  If left^.FirstChunk < right^.FirstChunk Then
    state := Less
  Else
  If left^.FirstChunk > right^.FirstChunk Then
    state := Greater
  Else
    state := GoOn;
  { Check tails if necessary }
  While state = GoOn Do
    If (LeftTail = Nil) Or (RightTail = Nil) Then
      state := Stop
    Else
    If LeftTail^.ThisTailChunk < RightTail^.ThisTailChunk Then
      state := Less
    Else
    If LeftTail^.ThisTailChunk > RightTail^.ThisTailChunk Then
      state := Greater
    Else
    Begin
      LeftTail := LeftTail^.FurtherTailChunks;
      RightTail := RightTail^.FurtherTailChunks
    End;

  { Final check for differing lengths }
  Case state Of
    Less: CompareSTRING := StringLessThan;
    Greater: CompareSTRING := StringGreaterThan;
    Stop: If LeftLength < RightLength Then
            CompareSTRING := StringLessThan
          Else
          If LeftLength > RightLength Then
            CompareSTRING := StringGreaterThan
          Else
            CompareSTRING := StringEqual
  End
  End;
  FinalSTRING(left);
  FinalSTRING(right);
End{ CompareSTRING };

Function EqualSTRING(left,right: String):Boolean;
{
* left = right
}
Begin
  InitValParamSTRING(left);
  InitValParamSTRING(right);
  EqualSTRING := CompareSTRING(left, right) = StringEqual;
```

```
    FinalSTRING(left);
    FinalSTRING(right);
End{ EqualSTRING };

Function NotEqualSTRING(left,right: String):Boolean;
{
* left <> right
}
Begin
    InitValParamSTRING(left);
    InitValParamSTRING(right);
    NotEqualSTRING := CompareSTRING(left, right) <> StringEqual;
    FinalSTRING(left);
    FinalSTRING(right);
End{ NotEqualSTRING };

Function GreaterOrEqualSTRING(left,right: String):Boolean;
{
* left >= right
}
Begin
    InitValParamSTRING(left);
    InitValParamSTRING(right);
    GreaterOrEqualSTRING :=
          CompareSTRING(left, right) <> StringLessThan;
    FinalSTRING(left);
    FinalSTRING(right);
End{ GreaterOrEqualSTRING };

Function LessOrEqualSTRING(left,right: String):Boolean;
{
* left >= right
}
Begin
    InitValParamSTRING(left);
    InitValParamSTRING(right);
    LessOrEqualSTRING :=
          CompareSTRING(left, right) <> StringGreaterThan;
    FinalSTRING(left);
    FinalSTRING(right);
End{ LessOrEqualSTRING };

Function LessSTRING(left,right: String):Boolean;
{
* left < right
}
Begin
    InitValParamSTRING(left);
    InitValParamSTRING(right);
    LessSTRING := CompareSTRING(left, right) = StringLessThan;
    FinalSTRING(left);
    FinalSTRING(right);
End{ LessSTRING };
```

Function *GreaterSTRING(left,right: String):Boolean*;
{
* *left > right*
}
Begin
  InitValParamSTRING(left);
  InitValParamSTRING(right);
  GreaterSTRING := CompareSTRING(left, right) = StringGreaterThan;
  FinalSTRING(left);
  FinalSTRING(right);
End{ *GreaterSTRING* };

Function *PosOfStringInSTRING(ThisString,*
                                    PossibleSubString: String):Nat0;

{
* *Returns position of PossibleSubString in ThisString or 0 if not present.*
* *Empty strings are not considered present*!
}

Var *LengthDiff, LengthOfS, LengthOfPat, OuterMatchPos,*
       InnerMatchPos: Nat0;
     ContinueOuter, ContinueInner, MatchesAtInnerPos: Boolean;

Begin
  InitValParamSTRING(ThisString);
  InitValParamSTRING(PossibleSubString);

  LengthOfS := LengthOfSTRING(ThisString);
  LengthOfPat := LengthOfSTRING(PossibleSubString);
  If (*LengthOfS = 0*) **Or** (*LengthOfPat = 0*)
                       Or (*LengthOfPat > LengthOfS*) **Then**
    PosOfStringInSTRING := 0
  Else
  Begin
    OuterMatchPos := 0;
    LengthDiff := LengthOfS – LengthOfPat;
    ContinueOuter := true;
    While *ContinueOuter* **Do**
    Begin
      OuterMatchPos := OuterMatchPos + 1;
      InnerMatchPos := 0;
      ContinueInner := true;
      While *ContinueInner* **Do**
      Begin
        InnerMatchPos := InnerMatchPos + 1;
        MatchesAtInnerPos :=
            IndexSTRING(PossibleSubString, InnerMatchPos)
          = IndexSTRING(ThisString,
                          OuterMatchPos + InnerMatchPos – 1);
        ContinueInner := MatchesAtInnerPos
                         And (*InnerMatchPos <> LengthOfPat*);
      End;

```
          ContinueOuter := Not MatchesAtInnerPos
                           And (OuterMatchPos <= LengthDiff );
     End;
     If MatchesAtInnerPos Then
        PosOfStringInSTRING := OuterMatchPos
     Else
        PosOfStringInString := 0
  End;

  FinalSTRING(ThisString);
  FinalSTRING(PossibleSubString);
End{ PosOfStringInSTRING };

Function ReplicateSTRING(RepString: String; RepCount: Nat0):String;
{
* [[ Returns RepString * RepCount ]]
* Replicates RepString, RepCount times.
}

Var null : Char; { set to chr(0) }
    ch: Char;
    LengthOfRepString, ResultLength: Nat0;
    i, TailChunkCount, CurrentLength: Nat0;
    result: String;
    TailChunk: StringTail;
    RepStringPos: Integer;
    FirstChunkPos,ThisTailChunkPos: 1..ChunkSize;
    PosInRepString: PosInString;

Begin
  null := chr(0);
  InitValParamSTRING(RepString);
  InitSTRING(result); { Note: also sets to EmptySTRING }

  LengthOfRepString := LengthOfSTRING(RepString);
  ResultLength := LengthOfRepString * RepCount;

  If ResultLength <> 0 Then
  Begin
     TailChunkCount := (ResultLength – 1) Div ChunkSize;
     { Copy into String FirstChunk }
     new(result);
     With result^ Do
     Begin
       length := ResultLength;
       RefCount := 1; { this one }
       TailChunks := Nil;
       SetToFirstPosSTRING(PosInRepString, RepString);
       CurrentLength := 0;
       RepStringPos := 1;
       { Copy string, null padding if necessary }
```

```
    For FirstChunkPos := 1 To ChunkSize Do
      If FirstChunkPos > ResultLength Then
        FirstChunk[FirstChunkPos] := null
    Else
    Begin
      MoveToNextPosSTRING(PosInRepString, ch);
      If RepStringPos = LengthOfRepString Then
      Begin
        RepStringPos := 1;
        SetToFirstPosSTRING (PosInRepString, RepString)
      End
      Else
        RepStringPos := RepStringPos + 1;
      FirstChunk[FirstChunkPos] := ch;
      CurrentLength := CurrentLength + 1;
    End;
    { Allocate and link in any extra string chunks needed }
    For i := 1 To TailChunkCount Do
    Begin
      new(TailChunk);
      TailChunk^.FurtherTailChunks := TailChunks;
      TailChunks := TailChunk
    End;
    { Loop through copying string tail if required }
    TailChunk := TailChunks;
    While TailChunk <> Nil Do
    Begin
      With TailChunk^ Do
      Begin
        { Copy string, null padding if necessary }
        For ThisTailChunkPos := 1 To ChunkSize Do
          If CurrentLength >= ResultLength Then
            ThisTailChunk[ThisTailChunkPos] := null
        Else
        Begin
          MoveToNextPosSTRING(PosInRepString, ch);
          If RepStringPos = LengthOfRepString Then
          Begin
            RepStringPos := 1;
            SetToFirstPosSTRING(PosInRepString, RepString)
          End
          Else
            RepStringPos := RepStringPos + 1;
          ThisTailChunk[ThisTailChunkPos] := ch;
          CurrentLength := CurrentLength + 1;
        End
      End;
      TailChunk := TailChunk^.FurtherTailChunks
    End{ While };
  End{ With };
End;
```

```
    FinalSTRING(RepString);
    ReplicateSTRING := AssignFuncResultSTRING(result);
End{ ReplicateSTRING };

Procedure ChangeCharInSTRING(Var UpdateString: String;
                                 UpdatePos: Nat1;
                                 UpdateChar: Char);

{
* Updates the string UpdateString at position UpdatePos
* with the char UpdateChar.
* If UpdatePos > LengthOfSTRING(UpdateString), UpdateString is first
* space filled upto UpdatePos.
}

Var i: 2..maxint;
    TailChunk: StringTail;
    NewPartOfString, Spaces: String;

Begin { of ChangeCharInSTRING }
  If UpdateString <> Nil Then
    If UpdateString^.RefCount > 1 Then
      { Make a unique copy before update }
      CopySTRING(UpdateString, UpdateString);
      { Note: careful (!) use of var and value parameters. }
  If UpdatePos <= LengthOfSTRING(UpdateString) Then
    With UpdateString^ Do
      If UpdatePos <= ChunkSize Then
        { pos is in string FirstChunk }
        FirstChunk[UpdatePos] := UpdateChar
      Else
      Begin
        { Find tail chunk containing pos. UpdatePos }
        TailChunk := TailChunks;
        For i := 2 To (UpdatePos - 1) Div ChunkSize Do
          TailChunk := TailChunk^.FurtherTailChunks;
        TailChunk^.ThisTailChunk[(UpdatePos - 1) Mod ChunkSize + 1]
                                                  := UpdateChar
      End
  Else
  Begin
    { Inefficient but rare case }
    InitSTRING(NewPartOfString);
    InitSTRING(Spaces);
    AssignSTRING(Spaces,
                 ReplicateSTRING(CharToSTRING(' '),
                                 UpdatePos -
                                     LengthOfSTRING(UpdateString) - 1));
    AssignSTRING(NewPartOfString,
                 ConcatSTRING(Spaces, CharToSTRING(UpdateChar)));
    AssignSTRING(UpdateString, ConcatSTRING(UpdateString,
                                            NewPartOfString))
  End
End{ ChangeCharInSTRING };
```

Procedure *WriteSTRING*(**Var** *TextFile*: *Text*; *ThisString*: *String*);
{
* *Write the dynamic string ThisString to file TextFile*
*
* *pre-condition*:
*   *TextFile open for writing*
}

Var *TailChunk*: *StringTail*;
     TailChunkNumber: *Nat*1;
     TailChunkCount: *Nat*0;

Begin
  InitValParamSTRING(*ThisString*);

  If *ThisString* = **Nil Then** { *Do nothing if string* = '' }
  Else
  Begin
    With *ThisString*^ **Do**
    Begin
      TailChunkCount := (*length* – 1) **Div** *ChunkSize*;
      If *length* > *ChunkSize* **Then**
        write(*TextFile*, *FirstChunk*:*ChunkSize*)
      Else
        write(*TextFile*, *FirstChunk*:*length*);
      TailChunk := *TailChunks*;
      { *Output any tail chunks* }
      For *TailChunkNumber* := 1 **To** *TailChunkCount* **Do**
        With *TailChunk*^ **Do**
          If *TailChunkNumber* <> *TailChunkCount* **Then**
          Begin
            write(*TextFile*, *ThisTailChunk*);
            TailChunk := *FurtherTailChunks*
          End
          Else
            write(*TextFile*,
                  ThisTailChunk:((*length* – 1) **Mod** *ChunkSize*) + 1)
    End;
  End;

  FinalSTRING(*ThisString*);
End{ *WriteSTRING* };

Procedure *WritelnSTRING*(**Var** *TextFile*: *Text*; *ThisString*: *String*);
{
* *Write the dynamic string ThisString to file f followed by an eoln*
* *marker*
*
* *pre-condition*:
*   *TextFile open for writing*
}
Begin
  InitValParamSTRING(ThisString);
  WriteSTRING(TextFile, ThisString);
  writeln(TextFile);
  FinalSTRING(ThisString);
End{ *WritelnSTRING* };

Begin
  { *Put your main program here.* }
End.

Bibliography

Adams D. (1979). *The Hitch Hiker's Guide to the Galaxy.* London: Pan Books.

British Standards Institution (1982). *BS6192: 1982 Specification for Computer programming language Pascal.* May be purchased from BSI Sales Department, Newton House, 101 Pentonville Road, London N1 9ND, UK. Alternatively, the standard is also included in Wilson I.R. and Addyman A.M. (1982). *A Practical Introduction to Pascal – with BS6192* 2nd edn. Basingstoke: Macmillan

British Standards Institution (1988). *VDM specification language protostandard.* (Ritchie, B., ed.). Technical Report BSI IST/5/50. London: BSI

Conway R., Gries D. and Zimmerman E. C. (1976). *A Primer on PASCAL.* Winthrop.

Galler B.A. and Fischer M.J. (1964). An improved equivalence algorithm. *Communications of the ACM*, **7**(5), 301–3.

Henderson P. and Snowdon R.A. (1972). An experiment in structured programming. *BIT*, **12**, 38–53

Jones C.B. (1990). *Systematic Software Development Using VDM* 2nd edn. Englewood Cliffs, NJ: Prentice-Hall

Naur P., ed. (1963). Revised report on the algorithmic language ALGOL 60. *Communications of the ACM*, **6**(1), 1–17

Answers to exercises

Chapter 1

1.1 If your answer was a program, you were wrong! The correct answer is something like: 'Because I don't have enough information. I don't know what kind of average, what kind of numbers, how many numbers, where the numbers are, where the result goes and what accuracy of result is required.'

1.2 Item (a) is an element of the type Nat-seq as defined in this exercise. Item (b) is too, even though it is an infinite sequence. Item (c) is not an element, as it is a sequence of real numbers. Item (d) is an element because a sequence may have just one element. Item (e) is not an element, as the data type $\mathbb{N}$ is not a sequence.

1.3 Yes, the suggested implementation does satisfy the specification as it stands. To make the specification reflect the intention of doubling, and nothing else, it must be stated that the value of in does not change. That would mean the final value of out must be twice the original value of in. The simplest way to state that the value of the variable in does not change is to make its mode read only (rd).

1.4 A pre-condition of true means that *nothing* may be assumed about the values of the external variables before the operation executes. A false pre-condition would mean that *everything* could be assumed, including that true is equal to false. Not surprisingly, one should never write such a pre-condition.

1.5 Sequences are indexed from one upwards, and so the expression has no value – it is **undefined**.

1.6 The first loop would not write anything. For the second, the output would be repeated forever – or at least until the user got bored with the results and aborted the program!

1.7 The diagram for an identifier shows that there is no maximum length. (In the bad old days, it was the case that only the first eight characters of an identifier were significant, the rest being ignored by the compiler. Now, standard compilers must allow any length of identifier and all characters must be significant.)

1.8 The first is an expression which has the value *false*. The second is a statement which adds one to the variable *x*.

1.9 The program will write to the standard output the sum of the first ten natural numbers. That is, it will write the value 55.

Chapter 2

2.1 Parts (a) and (c) are red herrings designed to discourage you from thinking too much about the other parts. They are both false. If you thought part (b) was true, then you really are upside down! If you thought part (d) was false, then maybe you use a calculator too often – perhaps you used one here? On the other hand, if you thought part (d) was true, you have already learned about precedence. Part (e) is false – Bodmas was never a professor.

2.2 You should be able to show this by a truth table with four lines:

p	q	not p and q	not (p or not q)
T	T	F	F
T	F	F	F
F	T	T	T
F	F	F	F

2.3 Sad days – your car is ruined! Its pre-condition was violated. But, don't worry – petrol pumps *never* deliver water, because the garage staff *ensure* only petrol can ever come out. So don't bother checking – it's messy and leaves a nasty taste in your mouth!

2.4 The second alternative is slightly more efficient because it is not necessary to compare the first salary with the previous highest found. However, the difference in efficiency is practically insignificant, and not worth losing any sleep over!

Chapter 3

3.1 For case (a) the best number is 6. For case (b), however, the best number would be 0, but that is cheating.

3.2 Note the extra brackets which have been inserted around the expanded sub-expressions.

(a) $(-b + ((b^2 - 4ac)^{1/2}))/2a$

(b) $(x - y)/(1 + (x - y) * (x - y))$

(c) $(((a + b + c)/2) * (((a + b + c)/2) - a) *$
       $(((a + b + c)/2) - b) * (((a + b + c)/2) - c))^{1/2}$

3.3 The following would be true:

current-player = computer and input = [6]

3.4 Whilst the move-limit was ensured to be not more than the pile to begin with, the pile will reduce as the game proceeds.

3.5 (a)   It is a special case because the rules of the game insist that at least one match is taken, but the best move would be to take no matches.

(b)   Yes, any value between one and the value of pile, but not more than that of move-limit could have been specified. The value one was chosen to prolong the game in the hope that the opponent does not know the winning strategy or will make a mistake.

3.6 The variable, x, could have *any* value, because the operation has write access to it and it is not mentioned in the post-condition.

3.7 The completed truth table is:

p	q	not (p and q)	(not p) or (not q)
T	T	F	F
F	T	T	T
T	F	T	T
F	F	T	T

3.8   **Program** *FindLargest* (*input,output*);

Var *NumberOne, NumberTwo, GreatestNumber* : *Integer*;
Begin
    write(output, 'What is the first number? ');
    readln(input,NumberOne);
    write(output, 'and the second number? ');
    readln(input,NumberTwo);
    If *NumberOne > NumberTwo* **Then**
        GreatestNumber := *NumberOne*
    Else
        GreatestNumber := *NumberTwo*;

> *writeln(output, 'The largest of '.NumberOne,' and ', NumberTwo,*
> *' is ', GreatestNumber)*
>
> **End.**

3.9 Yes.

Chapter 4

4.1 There are many questions about the customer's requirement statement, for example:

What does 'control' of a taxi fleet encompass? Is it just the management of assigning cars to customers, or does it involve things such as keeping accounts for each taxi, or working out shifts of taxi drivers?

What is a taxi-fleet? Is there a fixed, variable or maximum number of cars in the fleet? How must the program respond to such events as a taxi breaking down?

What is the 'best car' to answer a call? (The nearest car not already having a customer?) What is the 'best route'? The shortest? The fastest? One using least petrol? What does the phrase 'or the cost' mean? Should this be 'and the cost'? How is the cost calculated? Is there a meter in the car, or is it some function of the distance, type of route and time of day?

The program is required to 'keep track of the whereabouts of a car'. Is this at every point on its journey, or at fixed times or fixed check points? Is it reasonable to assume that each car has radio contact with a central control? How does information from the taxi driver reach the control program? Should the information be displayed in some pictorial manner?

Are there any regular customers such as schoolchildren with disabilities or people travelling to work? Should special provision be made for entering this type of customer into the control program?

4.2 (a)   {A,B,C}

(b)   { [ ] , { } , { { } } }

(c)   {X,Y,Z,x,y,z}

4.3 One would expect a field for each of the attributes mentioned. The types of the fields would depend on the context. For example, the country of origin might be a string of characters, or a value from some enumerated set depending on how flexible the specification is to be. Taste would almost certainly be chosen from a set of values such as 'med-dry' and 'sweet'.

4.4 It is the positive square root function, defined implicitly, giving no hint as to how it can be implemented.

4.5 A valid implementation could produce a report sequence *longer* than the input sequence of telegrams. This may happen, if for example, an implementor decided it would be more efficient always to have a report sequence with a total length (in bytes) divisible by some weird number, such as a disk block size. The implementor could achieve this by adding on an extra report occupying the appropriate number of bytes. (An implementation could not produce a report sequence shorter than the input sequence, because all indices of the input sequence are considered in the specification of the relationship between the input items and the output items.)

4.6 Part (a) is true. Part (b) is false for sets that overlap. Part (c) is true. Part (d) is not true for any sequence containing duplicates.

4.7 The set is

$$\{ [ ] , [a] , [b] , [c] , [a,b] , [a,c] , [b,a] , [b,c] , [c,a] , [c,b] \}$$

4.8 The correct answers to the first five questions concerning the requirements are as follows:

Q1: Yes, over-length words are charged as normal words.

Q2: No, over-length words are not modified for output.

Q3: Both letters and digits should be included in the length of words to say if they are overlength.

Q4: Just the fact that over-length words exist is reported.

Q5: It is the chargeable words that are counted for the output, not all words.

4.9 (a) and (b) are true, (c) is false.

4.10 It is true for all s1 and s2, such that each of those sequences consists of zero or more repetitions of the same sub-sequence. For example:

$$[a,b,c,a,b,c,a,b,c] \frown [a,b,c] = [a,b,c] \frown [a,b,c,a,b,c,a,b,c]$$

The more obvious special cases are when either s1 or s2 is empty (zero repetitions of the common sub-sequence), when s1 and s2 are the same (one repetition of the common sub-sequence each), and when s1 and s2 both consist of only one and the same element (the common sub-sequence is just one element).

4.11 (a)   ` monkey'
   (b)   'monk'
   (c)   'The animal is a monkey'<new-line>
   (d)   `   '<new-line>

Chapter 5

5.1 (a) Eleven.   (b) { }.

5.2 It has no base case, but it does need one. If you were to try to evaluate say, fact(5), you would have to compute an infinite number of multiplications:

$$5 * 4 * 3 * 2 * 1 * 0 * -1 * -2 * -3 \ldots$$

5.3 (a) The value is [ ].   (b) The value is 2 (note *not* [2]).   (c) An example is

   [[1]]

In fact, any sequence such that the first element is a non-empty sequence will do.

5.4 reverse : (s : Seq of X) → Seq of X
   reverse(s) △
     if s = [ ] then [ ]
     else reverse(tl s) ⌢ [hd s]

5.5 Perhaps the most obvious one is square root. Its inverse is the function which squares, and that is certainly more easily defined than some explicit square root function.

5.6 (a)   The number of seconds from the start of the year, y, up to, but excluding the quarter, q.

   (b)   The most useful function is the one given in part (a). The number of seconds in a quarter is the number of seconds up to the start of the next quarter, minus the number of seconds up to the start of the quarter in question. For the last quarter, the number of seconds in the year must be calculated, by taking the number of seconds up to the start of the following year, minus the number of seconds up to the given year. This gives a problem for when the given year is 99, which can be resolved by observing that the pattern is repeated every 4 years.

quarter-year-size : (q : Quarter-no , y : Year) → Time-second
quarter-year-size(q,y)△
  if q < 4 then
    q-s(q + 1, y) - q-s(q, y)
  else
    year-seconds((y mod 4) + 1) - year-seconds(y mod 4) - q-s(q, y)

5.7 first-item takes a sequence of characters, and returns a leading portion of it. There are two cases: when the first character is a dollar, and when it is not. If it is a dollar, the leading portion is a mnemonic, starting and ending with a dollar. (Of course, it might not be one of the recognized mnemonics.) The ending dollar can be assumed to exist, because of the pre-condition. If the first character is not a dollar, the result is the longest leading portion not containing a dollar.

5.8 Because you know that programs should be indented as they are written, not after!

5.9 Suppose there is an odd number of dollars, and the number of characters in the format is equal to the maximum. Changing the final character to a dollar produces an even number of them only if it is not one already. If it is, it is sensible simply to discard it.

5.10 Many operating systems have no concept of stopping – you simply switch the machine off.

5.11 This is not as difficult as you might think! The top-level of the design of the procedure might be (assuming the type Time from the chapter):

```
find-elapsed-time (time1,time2 : Time;
                      var elapsed-time : Time)
begin
  abstract-time( retrieve-time(time1) -
                    retrieve-time(time2) , elapsed-time)
end
```

This employs a procedure and a function:

```
abstract-time ( time-as-second : Integer;
                var time-as-record : Time)
function retrieve-time(time-as-record : Time) : Integer
```

The chapter gives an explicit definition of retrieve-time, which could be used as the basis of a design. The procedure abstract-time is almost the same as the procedure get-time in the chapter, except that it is given the time value in seconds as a parameter, rather than accessing it directly from the *wallclock* function.

5.12 (a)   The function Perfect-list produces a sequence of natural numbers which are all the perfect numbers greater than 1, but less than the argument of the function N. A perfect number is one whose factors (excluding the number itself) add up to that number, for example 6 = 3 + 2 + 1. Each perfect number is not duplicated in the sequence, but their order is not specified.

(b)   The specification can be implemented by a loop that works through all the numbers, checking to see if each is perfect. The sum of the factors of each number could be calculated by another loop, trying all numbers smaller to see if they are factors.

5.13 (a)   *multiply* takes two arguments, x and y. There are three cases, depending on the value of x being less than (1), equal to (2) or greater than (3) zero. In case (1), the function terminates if its recursive call does, and that is a case (3). For case (2), the function clearly terminates as this is the base case. For case (3), there is a recursive call where the argument is one less than the value of x, and hence is nearer to the base case.

(b)   The loop of the iterative version repeatedly adds the value of y on to the result, each time decrementing the value of x. The loop terminates when x has the value of zero.

Chapter 6

6.1 No, that would violate the transitivity rule. If any member of gang A was also a member of gang B, all members of gang A would have to be members of gang B, and vice versa.

6.2 Questions about the customer's requirements include: What information is on the payroll records? Presumably there will be things such as the National Insurance number, information as to whether the employee is paid weekly or monthly, type of payment to be made, amount earned so far this year, tax code, ... It is not clear which of this information needs to be updated from the customer's requirements. For example, the updating of some fields in the record, such as amount earned so far this year, may depend on updating other fields, such as salary, and how frequently the salary is to be paid. Some fields may be rarely updated (type of payment to be made) and others may never be updated (National Insurance number).

What does 'update' mean? Records may need to be added and deleted as employees start and leave their jobs, as well as being amended. Should the updating be done interactively or via some regular batch job? How should the information to be updated be input? Are salary records sorted, perhaps by employee number? May update transactions be duplicated for a particular employee?

How should errors be handled? It may be sensible to abort the whole update run rather then risk updating information incorrectly. What about the security aspects of updating such sensitive information? Must the program deal with this?

6.3 (a) True.   (b) True.   (c) False (c is missing).

6.4 Nothing. (Perhaps now it is a *little* clearer why the operator is called implication.)

6.5 T = {1}

In fact, it could be any set with only one member.

6.6 1 + 2 * 1 000 000 * 1 000 000

6.7 Convinced? If not, see that if p1 and p2 are the same, then s1 and s2 will be the same. Thus the union of s1 with s2 is equal to s1 (and also s2), and is precisely the set missed from the first comprehension. Try an example!

6.8 (a) True.   (b) True.   (c) False – the intersection is empty.
(d) True (for example, [1,2,3,4]).   (e) False (for example, [4,3,2,1]).

6.9 (a) Legal.   (b) Illegal (where is the 'q'?).   (c) Illegal.   (d) Legal.

6.10 Because the initialize command discards all the current equivalences, it is important that the operation is not performed by accident! Hence there is a requirement of some confirmation in the concrete syntax, that is, a question like 'Do you really want to initialize?' will be asked. If none of the legal characters is typed in reply, it is safe, and hence sensible, to treat the input as though it were 'N'.

6.11 Now read on!

6.12 function root(p:Part-number):Part-number
    { find the root of the tree containing p. This has a side-effect on
    the concrete value of database, by making p point directly to its
    root. The abstract value is not changed }
    var start-part : Part-number
    begin
        start-part := p
        while database.follower[p] ≠ p
            p := database.follower[p]
        root := p
        database.follower[start-part] := p
    end

6.13 The value of *i* is undefined, and that of *start* is 124.

6.14 Note the lack of space after the 3:

Part number 3is equivalent to 361

6.15 (a)   The specification is of an operation that removes one instance
            of the smallest element from a sequence of naturals, s. The
            order of the remaining elements is not necessarily the same as
            in the sequence s before the operation was performed. There
            always does exist a minimum element because the pre-
            condition says that s is not the empty sequence.

   (b)   The sequence is represented by a record containing an array
            of integers which holds the elements in the sequence, and a
            length field which holds the length of the sequence. The
            procedure compares each element with the one at the end of
            the list, and swaps them if necessary so that the smaller of the
            two is placed at the end. Once all elements have been treated
            thus, an instance of the smallest element in the whole se-
            quence will be at the last place. The length of the sequence is
            then reduced by one to remove that minimum element.

6.16 (a)   The specification describes a palindrome-checker. Function
            X checks whether the argument is equal to its reverse. The
            function Y reverses the word. An empty word is regarded as
            a palindrome.

   (b)   The Pascal function X compares the first element with the
            last, the second with the penultimate, and so on. Note that,
            because of the commutativity of equality, there is no need to
            compare all of the word with all of its reverse. Representative
            examples may be used to convince oneself of the correctness
            of the function. Cases to demonstrate are the empty word, a
            word of even length and a word of odd length.

6.17 (a) The function Y returns a natural number which occurs the most frequently in a sequence of natural numbers. A number is always returned as the pre-condition ensures that the sequence is never empty.

(b)
```
Const MaxSeqLength = ??
Type Nat = 0 .. MaxInt;
     NatSeq = Record
                   value : Array[1..MaxSeqLength] Of Nat;
                   length : Nat
              End;

Procedure FindMostFrequent(ThisSeq : NatSeq; Var result : Nat);

Var ValHereHasOccurred : Array [1..MaxSeqLength] Of Boolean;
    MostFrequentValue, MaxNoOfOccurrences,
    CurrentValue, NoOfOccurCurrentValue,
    ThisPosition, PossibleOtherPlace : Nat;

Begin
  { initialize }
  MaxNoOfOccurrences := 0;
  For ThisPosition := 1 To ThisSeq.length Do
    ValHereHasOccurred[ThisPosition] := false;
  For ThisPosition := 1 To ThisSeq.length Do
  Begin
    If Not ValHereHasOccurred[ThisPosition] Then
    Begin
      ValHereHasOccurred[ThisPosition] := True;
      CurrentValue := ThisSeq.value[ThisPosition];
      NoOfOccurCurrentValue := 1;
      For PossibleOtherPlace := (ThisPosition + 1) To
                                   ThisSeq.length Do
        If CurrentValue =
               ThisSeq.value[PossibleOtherPlace] Then
        Begin
          NoOfOccurCurrentValue :=
                  NoOfOccurCurrentValue + 1;
          ValHereHasOccurred[PossibleOtherPlace] := True
        End
      If NoOfOccurCurrentValue > MaxNoOfOccurrences Then
      Begin
        MaxNoOfOccurrences := NoOfOccurCurrentValue;
        MostFrequentValue := CurrentValue
      End
    End;
  End;
  result := MostFrequentValue
End;
```

6.18 (a)   The result of the function X is the mean average line length of the given piece of text, which is assumed to have at least one line. (The function Y produces the sequence of line lengths and Z adds them up.)

(b)   One design for this procedure reads in a text file, *TextFile*, and has two nested while loops. The outer loop counts the number of lines in the text file and is terminated when *eof* (*TextFile*) is true. The inner loop reads and counts the number of characters in the file, line by line, and is terminated when *eoln*(*TextFile*) is true. Once all the characters have been read, the average may be calculated by dividing the number of characters by the number of lines.

Chapter 7

7.1 Questions about the requirements include the following: What sort of texts are liable to be input? Program texts? Books? The length of the text and the number of noise words may affect the program design. What if the text contains non-alphabetic characters? Should these be ignored or be incorporated somehow?

How should the output be presented? Perhaps each line contains a word, followed by the line numbers of where that word occurs in the text. What if the word occurs more than once on a line – should the line number be repeated? Should the output be sorted? Alphabetically?

What words are 'noise' words? How are they to be given to the program? (As a separate file?) What is the user interface?

7.2 (a) True, because 'c' is less than 'e'. (b) False, because [48,19] is less than [48,19,17]. (c) True because 3 is less than 4.

7.3 (a)   Yes – as long as all the significant rotations appear, it would not matter if any extra entries occurred also. (They cannot appear in the output from the program, because the specification of KWIC also says the length of the output is equal to the number of occurrences of significant words in the input.)

(b)   If titles[i] is the empty sequence, its index set is the empty set, so the universally quantified disjunct is trivially true.

7.4 (a)   The function X counts the number of words occurring in some text made up from sequences of lines of characters. A word either starts a line or is preceded by a space, but does not itself begin with a space.

(b)   The following is a proposed implementation of the function:

```
Procedure WordCount ( Var InFile : Text;
                      Var NoOfWords : Integer);

Var LastWasSpace, FirstOnLine : Boolean;

Begin
  reset (InFile);
  NoOfWords := 0;
  While Not eof (InFile) Do
  Begin
    LastWasSpace := false;
    FirstOnLine := true;
    While Not eoln(InFile) Do
    Begin
      If InFile^ <> ' ' Then
      Begin
        If FirstOnLine Or LastWasSpace Then
          NoOfWords := NoOfWords + 1;
        LastWasSpace := false
      End
      Else
        LastWasSpace := true;
        FirstOnLine := false;
        get(InFile)
    End;
    readln(InFile)
  End
End { WordCount };
```

7.5   The specification allows multiple occurrences of a value in the input sequence to be removed, or more to be added.

7.6   Yes.

7.7   Such a solution would cause as many recursive calls to sort as there are elements in the sequence (assuming that we don't try to sort the single item removed each time!). Thus, for a sequence with N items, there would be $N - 1$ trivial split operations and $N - 1$ merge operations. Each merge would need to process all the items in the two sequences it is merging. The number of such elements would be N for the merge at the outermost level, $N - 1$ for the next in; an average of $N/2$ items. Thus the time taken to execute the sort would be proportional to

$$(N - 1) * (N / 2)$$

(It would be said to be **of order N^2.**)

7.8 If on average the length of the sub-sequences were half the length of the given sequence, there would still be $N - 1$ merges, but the average number of elements in each merge would be the logarithm to the base 2 of N. (If N was 1024, the average number of elements in each merge would be 10.) Assuming that splitting was still easy (just hack the sequence in half) the time of execution would be proportional to

$$(N - 1) * \log N$$

Even if the splitting was not trivial and was proportional in time to the number of elements in the sequence being split, the overall time would be proportional to

$$2 * (N - 1) * \log N$$

(It would be said to be **of order $N \log N$,** which is *far* less than order N^2.)

7.9 The pre-condition could be

$$s \neq [\,]$$

and the split operation would still be defined. If the sort performed split when given only a single length sequence, it would still work, but would be (a little) less efficient because there would be approximately twice as many calls to the procedure.

7.10 Comparison (a) would be true on Rita's machine, but false on the other. Comparison (b) would be false on both. Comparison (c) would be false on Rita's but true on the other. Comparison (d) would be false on both.

7.11 (a) The value of *ch* is unchanged (assuming it is not undefined beforehand). (b) The value of *ch* becomes '0'. (c) The value of *ch* becomes '8'. (d) The value of *b* becomes false.

7.12 Read on in the chapter, and you'll find out!

7.13 (a)   The invariant inv-Hand defines that a hand comprises up to 13 distinct cards.

(b)   A hand may be implemented by a record which contains the size of the hand and the cards which are held in an array. A card may be implemented as a record, mirroring the specification. Any standard sorting algorithm may be used in the implementation of the procedure. As a guide, here is a

bubble sort procedure for sorting an array of 1000 integers:

```
Const IntArraySize = 1000;

Procedure sort (Var v:IntArray);
Var scan, pair, swap : Integer;
Begin
  For scan := IntArraySize Downto 2 Do
    For pair := 1 To scan - 1 Do
      If (v[pair] < v[pair + 1]) Then { compare }
      Begin { exchange }
        swap := v[pair];
        v[pair] := v[pair + 1];
        v[pair + 1] := swap
      End
  End { sort };
```

Chapter 8

8.1 Recursive version:

```
Function PolyEval (CoEffs : SeqOfReal; x : Real): Real;
Begin
  If CoEffs = Nil Then PolyEval := 0
  Else PolyEval := CoEffs^.ThisCoEff +
                       x * PolyEval(CoEffs^.rest,x)
End { PolyEval };
```

Iterative version:

```
Function PolyEval (CoEffs : SeqOfReal; x : Real): Real;
Var SumOfCoEffs, PowerOfX : Real;
Begin
  SumOfCoEffs := 0;
  PowerOfX := 1;
  While CoEffs <> Nil Do
  Begin
    SumOfCoEffs := SumOfCoEffs +
                       CoEffs^.ThisCoEff * PowerOfX;
    PowerOfX := PowerOfX * x;
    CoEffs := CoEffs^.rest
  End;
  PolyEval := SumOfCoEffs
End { PolyEval };
```

The recursive version mirrors the specification and so is more obviously correct. However, there is a memory and time overhead due to the number of recursive calls (space is needed for remembering where to continue execution, and for the instances of the value parameters). On the other hand, the iterative version uses up a constant amount of memory, however large the polynomial, but it is harder to reason that it implements the specification.

8.2 Using the same data type word-set, such a procedure could be:

```
add-on-end-of-word-set(w:word; var ws:word-set)
var new-node : word-set
begin
  if ws = nil then
    new(new-node)
    ws := new-node
  else
    new-node := ws
    while new-node ^.next ≠ nil
      new-node := new-node ^.next
    new(new-node ^.next)
    new-node := new-node ^.next
  end-of-if
  new-node ^.this-word := w
  new-node ^.next := nil
end
```

8.3 No, because the value of length would be undefined when the algorithm first tried to increment it.

8.4 Given the context of the chapter, you would be excused if you thought this was an exercise in the use of linked lists – that was what we were hoping for you to practise. Such a solution involves reading the file line by line, storing each line in a linked list and counting its length. After reading each line, its length is compared with that of the longest line found so far, and the copy of the line is kept if it is longer. Having read all the lines, the program simply writes out the longest line. You should consider the possibility of the file being empty. In this case, the specification indicates that an empty line is to be output.

However, a simpler solution is one that reads the file twice. The first pass through counts the lines, and the length of each line. While doing this, it remembers the position and the length of the longest line found so far. Once this is complete, the position of the longest line is known, so the second pass simply skips lines up to that point and then copies the longest line from the file to the output. A slight complication is that Pascal does not define the effect of a *reset* on the input file, therefore a program may not be able to read the input file twice. To get round this, the program below makes a copy of the input to another file as it reads it the first time. You should check that the program works for an empty file:

```
Program PrintLongestLine (input,output);
{
* prints the longest line from the input file
* (blank line if input empty)
}
Var
   SizeOfLongestSoFar, SizeOfCurrentLine,
   NumberOfCurrentLine, NumberOfLongestSoFar : 0 .. MaxInt;
   CopyOfInput : Text;
   i : Integer; ch:Char;

Begin
   SizeOfLongestSoFar := 0;
   NumberOfCurrentLine := 0;
   NumberOfLongestSoFar := 0;
   rewrite(CopyOfInput);
   While Not eof (input) Do
   Begin
     NumberOfCurrentLine := NumberOfCurrentLine + 1;
     SizeOfCurrentLine := 0;
     While Not eoln(input) Do
     Begin
       SizeOfCurrentLine := SizeOfCurrentLine + 1;
       read(input,ch);
       write(CopyOfInput,ch)
     End;
     readln(input);
     writeln(CopyOfInput);
     If SizeOfCurrentLine > SizeOfLongestSoFar Then
     Begin
       SizeOfLongestSoFar := SizeOfCurrentLine;
       NumberOfLongestSoFar := NumberOfCurrentLine
     End
   End;
   { now second pass }
   reset(CopyOfInput);
   For i := 1 To NumberOfLongestSoFar - 1 Do
     readln(CopyOfInput);
   For i := 1 To SizeOfLongestSoFar Do
   Begin
     read(CopyOfInput,ch);
     write(output,ch)
   End;
   writeln(output)
End.
```

On computers with very fast disks and large memory buffers, this program could be more efficient than building linked lists. However, it has the disadvantage that all the input must be stored, which could be a headache if there was likely to be a very large amount.

8.5 (a) The specification requires a sequence of integer numbers (already unique and in order) to be extended with a further integer number, i, in the correct position, if it is not already present.

(b) The cases to consider are when *ThisList* is empty, when the element is already in the list, and when it is a new element. The sub-cases of this latter case are for when the new number would be at the front of the list, in the middle somewhere and at the end.

Note the role of the **Var** parameter in procedure *Rec* in remembering the link from the previous position in the list.

8.6 The order of the statements

left := *left^.tail*;
If *left^.head* <> *right^.head* **Then** *IsPalindrome* := *false*;

must be swapped for the function to work correctly. A small worked example, paying attention to the variable and value parameters of *Check*, will help to illustrate that the corrected function then implements the specification.

8.7 An example of an array representation is

Type *SeqOfInt* = **Record**
                elements : **Array** [1. .*MaxLength*] **Of** *Integer*;
                length : *Integer*
            End;

An array limits the sequence to be of a fixed maximum length. An array is often easier to code and can be efficient in use of space, and the elements may be accessed randomly. However, if the maximum length of the sequence is much larger than the average length, it can be inefficient in use of space, because the maximum space always has to be allocated, even if it is not all used.

An example of a linked list representation is

Type *SeqOfInt* = ^ *SeqOfIntRec*;
      SeqOfIntRec = **Record**
                    head : *Integer*;
                    tail : *SeqOfInt*
                End;

A linked list allows one to implement unbounded sequences and also sequences that are bounded, but their maximum length is very large and their actual length is variable. It is efficient in memory usage because one uses exactly what is needed. However, if a more-or-less fixed length is always used then this implementation will use more memory than an array and will have a slower access time. This is because elements can be accessed only by working along the list in one direction (extra pointers may be needed to access in more than one direction) rather than randomly, as in an array.

An example of a file representation is

Type *SeqOfInt* = **File Of** *Integer*;

A file is useful for implementing an enormous sequence that will not all fit in memory. The operations on a file are very limited – sequential input and output – and hence some algorithms are extremely inefficient. The end of the sequence is marked by the end of the file. Because of the limited operations, the coding is very simple, if that representation is suitable.

Chapter 9

9.1 Ambiguities and omissions to the customer's requirements include the following points: In what language are the documents written? English, American? What is a 'document'? – assume it is a text file and check with the customer. Should a particular dictionary be used as the definition of known words? The choice may be affected by the machine being used and any performance considerations. For example, is the spelling checker program to be interactive or run in a batch mode? Again, in relation to the user interface, how should unknown words be reported? Should they be accompanied by the line number in which they occur in the document? By the line in which they occur? Should they be written to a file, written to the screen, or both?

As far as dealing with obvious grammatical rules – is this feasible? The English language is notoriously full of exceptions to rules: the plural of sheet is sheets, but the plural of sheep is sheep. A feasibility study of this should be made before coming to any conclusions. For example, it may be possible to hold a list of exceptions to some rules.

9.2 Always absent, yes and it makes no difference whether the string occurs once or many times on a line (respectively).

9.3 File (for example, **File Of** *Char*). Although values of type **File Of** *Char* have all the necessary properties they are usually associated with disks or other, relatively slow, storage media.

9.4 Use your imagination!

9.5 (a) The function F takes a sequence of natural numbers and produces a sorted sequence of the same elements, but with any duplicates removed. The output is sorted in ascending order.

  (b) The sorting process may be achieved, using the given ADTs, by forming the set of elements of L, then successively extracting the largest element from this set and appending it to the front of the result (originally an empty sequence) until all elements have been removed.

9.6 (a) Queue may be represented by a linked list built with pointers. An extra pointer is needed to access the end of the queue, to add on an element efficiently without having to search through the entire list. With this representation, there is no arbitrary limit to the size of the queue.

  (b) The headings of the procedures and function are given below.

> **Procedure** *newQ* (**Var** *qu* : *Queue*)
> **Procedure** *enQ* (*e* : *Qel*; **Var** *qu* : *Queue*)
> **Procedure** *deQ* (**Var** *qu* : *Queue*; **Var** *e* : *Qel*)
> **Function** *isemptyQ* (*qu* : *Queue*) : *Boolean*

Chapter 10

10.1 It is not a true function because it has a side-effect on its argument.

10.2 Of course you can guess! If you want to know, you should see Chapter 12!

10.3 The difference is that the *ReadSTRING* procedure does not skip the end of line when there are no characters on the line for which the stop function is true. This is justified because it is consistent with the behaviour when a character is found for which the stop function is true. That is, the terminating character is not read.

10.4 The first part of Cynthia's post-condition does not say anything about the value of UpdateString at the places other than UpdatePos. Rita corrected this tactfully. She may have written:

post if UpdatePos $\leqslant$ len ($\overline{\text{UpdateString}}$) then

  UpdateString = $\overline{\text{UpdateString}}$[1 , . . . , UpdatePos $-$ 1]

     $\frown$ [UpdateChar]

     $\frown$ $\overline{\text{UpdateString}}$[UpdatePos $+$ 1

          , . . . , len $\overline{\text{UpdateString}}$]

 else

  UpdateString = $\overline{\text{UpdateString}}$

     $\frown$ spaces(UpdatePos $-$ len $\overline{\text{UpdateString}}$ $-$ 1)

     $\frown$ [UpdateChar]

10.5 (a) The fact that i cannot be greater than j. (b) Remove the conjunctions specifying that i must be less than or equal to j and broaden the range of i and j in the quantifiers to include 0 and len ThisString $+$ 1. (c) The first.

10.6 **Function** *NoOfLinesContainingSobStory*(**Var** *TextFile*: *Text*):*Nat0*;

 { Count the number of lines that contain the string 'sob story'. }
 Var *CurrentLine, DynamicSobStory*: *String*;
  NoOfLinesFoundSoFar: *Integer*;
 Begin
  InitSTRING(DynamicSobStory);
  InitSTRING(CurrentLine);
  reset(TextFile);
  NoOfLinesFoundSoFar := 0;
  AssignSTRING(DynamicSobStory, MakeSTRING('sob story'));
  While Not *eof (TextFile)* **Do**
  Begin
   ReadlnSTRING(TextFile,CurrentLine);
   If *PosOfStringInSTRING(CurrentLine,DynamicSobStory)* <> 0 **Then**
    NoOfLinesFoundSoFar := *NoOfLinesFoundSoFar* + 1
  End;
  NoOfLinesContainingSobStory := *NoOfLinesFoundSoFar*
  FinalSTRING(CurrentLine);
  FinalSTRING(DynamicSobStory);
 End;

10.7 You may well have fallen into the trap of assuming that replace does not occur in replacement! If you did, say 'oops' and try again before reading on.

  Here is one solution – note the initialization and finalization.

 Function *ReplaceString(main,replace,replacement:String):String*;
 Var *result* : *String*;
 Begin
  InitValParamSTRING(main);
  InitValParamSTRING(replace);
  InitValParamSTRING(replacement);
  InitSTRING(result); *{ Note: sets to empty string }*

```
While NotEqualSTRING(EmptySTRING,main) Do
Begin
  NextReplacePos : = PosOfStringInSTRING(main,replace);
  If NextReplacePos = 0 Then
  Begin
    AssignSTRING(result,ConcatSTRING(result,main);
    AssignSTRING(main,EmptySTRING);
  End
  Else
  Begin
    AssignSTRING(result,ConcatSTRING(result,
                                 GetSubSTRING(main,1,
                                 NextReplacePos - 1);
    AssignSTRING(result,ConcatSTRING(result,replacement);
    AssignSTRING(main,GetSubSTRING(main,
                                 NextReplacePos +
                                 LengthOfSTRING(replace),
                                 LengthOfSTRING(main)));
  End;
End;

FinalSTRING(main);
FinalSTRING(replace);
FinalSTRING(replacement);
ReplaceString : = AssignFuncResultSTRING(result);
End;
```

10.8   A Pascal type definition could be:

```
InfPosInt = ^ InfPosIntRec;

InfPosIntRec = Record
                 SixDigits : 0. .999999;
                 NextDigits : InfPosInt
               End;

InfInt = Record
           Sign : { plus,minus };
           LongInt : InfPosInt
         End;
```

The following example illustrates how this representation relates to the corresponding abstract values:

Abstract value : – 12345678901234567890

Representation:

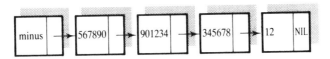

The operation headings are as follows:

Function *AddInfInts* (*InfInt1*,*InfInt2* : *InfInt*):*InfInt*

Subtract, multiply, div and mod are similar to add.

Procedure *AssignInfInt*(*InfInt1*:*InfInt*; **Var** *InfInt2*:*InfInt*)
Procedure *InputInfInt*(**Var** *Infile*:*Text*; **Var** *ToInfInt*:*InfInt*)
Procedure *OutputInfInt*(**Var** *Outfile*: *Text*; *FromInfInt*:*InfInt*)

10.9 (a)   X is commonly called a 'stack' (like a stack of plates in a cupboard). Y is a queue (such as a queue of people in the Post Office or at a bus stop).

(b)   X may be implemented by a linked list in which elements may be added to and removed from the front.

Type *Nat* = 0 .. *MaxInt*;
      SeqOfN = ^ *SeqOfNRec*;
      SeqOfNRec = **Record**
                      Value : *Nat*;
                      Next : *SeqOfN*
           End;

Procedure *add*(*x*:*Nat*; **Var** *s* : *SeqOfN*);
Var *xrec* : *SeqOfN*;
Begin
  new(*xrec*);
  xrec^.value : = *x*;
  xrec^.next : = *s*;
  s : = *xrec*
End;

Procedure *remove*1(**Var** *s* : *SeqOfN*; **Var** *r* : *Nat*);
Begin
  r : = *s^.value*;
  s : = *s^.next*
End;

(c)   For the datatype Y, removing the elements from the end of the list would involve a search through all the elements to reach the end.

      An alternative structure would be to have a pointer to the end of the linked list and regard this as the beginning of the sequence, so that elements could be added to this end.

Elements would be removed from the beginning of the linked list (end of sequence) in the same manner as before.

Chapter 11

11.1 Questions include: What does it mean to 'manage' a shift rota? Assume it means to allocate staff to particular shifts. How are staff to be chosen? Arbitrarily? Taking into account their preferences? How long is a shift? How many shifts are there in 24 hours? Do shifts overlap at all?

'A shift must comprise within one half of the total number of staff available.' Is this feasible, assuming that shifts are less than 12 hours long and that staff have break days and holidays (another area to be explored)?

The term SRN and its implications needs clarification. Does it include students? The phrase 'three weekends from four' is similarly vague. Is there some rigid four weekly system in operation, or will an average over the year be alright?

11.2 There are two obvious but different ways of writing it: either implicitly or explictly.

min : (n1 : $\mathbb{N}$, n2 : $\mathbb{N}$) → $\mathbb{N}$
min (n1,n2) △
   if n1 < n2 then n1
   else n2

min : (n1 : $\mathbb{N}$, n2 : $\mathbb{N}$) → (m : $\mathbb{N}$)
post (m = n1 or m = n2)
    and m ⩽ n1
    and m ⩽ n2

11.3 One.

11.5 (a) 3. (b) – 3. (c) 7. (d) 8. (e) – 8. (f) – 4. (g) 4.

11.6 display-matrix = array [1. .x-max, 1 . .y-max] of Char

max-bird : (f : forest) → (m : $\mathbb{N}$)
post (∃ x ∈ {1, . . . ,x-max}, y ∈ {1, . . . , y-max} • m = f [x,y].bird)
   and
   not (∃ x ∈ {1, . . . ,x-max}, y ∈ {1, . . . , y-max} • m < f [x,y].bird)

bird-output-representation : (f : Forest) → (d : display-matrix)
post let display-scale = least-scale-needed(max-bird(f)) in
    ∀ x ∈ {1, . . . ,x-max}, y ∈ {1, . . .,y-max} •
    d[x,y] = output-char(f[x,y].bird,display-scale)

11.7   **Procedure** *SetSpaces*(**Var** *ThisArray* : **Array** [*Xlo* .. *Xhi* : *Integer*;
                                                    Ylo .. *Yhi* : *Integer*] **Of**
                                                    Char);

   Var *x,y* : *Integer*;
   Begin
     For *x* : = *Xlo* **To** *Xhi* **Do**
       For *y* : = *Ylo* **To** *Yhi* **Do**
         ThisArray[*x,y*] : = ' '
   End;

11.8   comment-skip
         var skip:boolean
         begin
           skip : = true
           while skip
             if eof(bb-data)
               skip : = false
             else
             if eoln(bb-data) or (bb-data ^ = '!')
               readln(bb-data)
             else
               skip : = false
         end

11.9   This would need an extra variable to remember the number of the
         line of the file which is currently being read. It would be set to
         one to begin with, and incremented each time a new-line was
         encountered (wherever a *readln* occurs in the data reading
         routines). The error routine would output the line number in
         addition to the error message.

11.10 (a)   The function profs-meeting returns all the times when all of
              the three professors are free.

     (b)   **Const** *NineAm* = 9; *FivePm* = 17; *mon* = 1; *fri* = 5;

           Type *Periods* = *NineAm* .. *FivePm*; { 9–10 a.m., 10–11 a.m.,
                                               and so on. }
                 WeekDays = *mon* .. *fri*;
                 Day = **Set Of** *Periods*;
                 DeskDiary = **Array** [*WeekDays*] **Of** *Day*;

           Procedure *ProfsMeeting* (**Var** *FreeTimes* : *DeskDiary*;
                           *prof*1, *prof*2, *prof*3: *DeskDiary*);
           Var *Wday* : *WeekDays*;
           Begin
             For *Wday* : = *mon* **To** *fri* **Do**
               FreeTimes[*Wday*] : = [*NineAm* .. *FivePm*] –
                                   (*prof*1[*Wday*] + *prof*2[*Wday*] +
                                   *prof*3[*Wday*])
           End; { *ProfsMeeting* }

11.11 (a)   This describes a function magic which checks whether a square matrix of natural numbers has the property that the sum of each of its rows and each of its columns and each of the two long diagonals (from bottom left to top right and from top left to bottom right) add up to the same value.

(b)   The matrix may be implemented by a two-dimensional array, similar to its specification. magic may be implemented by a Pascal function with subsidiary functions mirroring those in the specification. The function *magic* is as follows (assuming the subsidiary functions):

```
Function magic (m : matrix) : Boolean;
Var CoOrd, RowSum, ColumnSum, tlbrSum, bltrSum,
        MagicSum : Integer;
    IsMagic : Boolean;
Begin
    tlbrSum := SumtlbrDiag(m);
    bltrSum := SumbltrDiag(m);
    IsMagic := tlbrSum = bltrSum;
    MagicSum := tlbrSum;
    CoOrd := 1;
    While IsMagic And (CoOrd <= squaresize) Do
        Begin
            RowSum := SumRow (m,1,CoOrd,1,0);
            ColumnSum := SumColumn(m,CoOrd,1,0,1);
            IsMagic := IsMagic And (RowSum = ColumnSum)
                            And (RowSum = MagicSum);
            CoOrd := CoOrd + 1
        End;
    magic := IsMagic
End;
```

Chapter 12

12.1 (a)   The output o from the operation D is the same as the input i, except it is in reverse order and all the occurrences of the character c (if any) are omitted.

Sensible names for L, D, n, i and o are line, delete-and-reverse, multiplicity, in-line and out-line respectively.

(b)   Note that the question asks for a program. The input file and output file may be assumed to be of type *Text*. in-line is then the first line of the input file and out-line is the first line of the output file. The character to be deleted may be assumed to be read in from the standard input. in-line may be read into an array of size 100, filtering out the character to be deleted and keeping a count of the number of characters read in to the array. The characters in the array may then be written out to out-line in reverse order.

(c)   If p < q, the line would not be reversed. Thus the input line would not need to be stored in the implementation, the program would simply filter the character to be deleted and output all other characters to out-line.

12.2   (a)   The argument to func is a sequence of characters. The result of func is an array indexed by the lower case letters of the alphabet. The array maps each letter on to the ratio of the number of occurrences of it in the argument to the number of occurrences of all lower case letters. To be precise, we must not forget that the argument might not contain any lower case letters, in which case the result can be anything.
      Better names for func, argument and result are letter-frequency-count, input-text and letter-ratios respectively.

(b)   type letter-ratio-array = array ['a'..'z'] of real;

      letter-frequency-count (var input-text: text;
                              letter-ratios:letter-ratio-array);
      var letter-count : integer;

      begin
        reset input-text
        initialize all elements of letter-ratios to 0
        letter-count : = 0

        while not end of input-text
          read a character
          if character is lower case
            increment count at appropriate array position
            increment letter-count
        end-of-while
        divide each element of the array by letter-count
      end

12.3   (a)   D is an implicitly defined function from a sequence of reals to a sequence of reals. Each sequence represents a polynomial. D models the operation of differentiating a polynomial. For example, the polynomial

$$3.0x^2 + 2.0x + 10.3$$

would be represented by the sequence

$$[10.3, 2.0, 3.0]$$

Applying the function D to the example would give the following result:

$$D([10.3, 2.0, 3.0]) = [2.0, 6.0]$$

which is equivalent to $6.0x + 2.0$.

(b)   **Function** D (s : *SeqOfReal*) : *SeqOfReal*;

Var *result, RestOfResult*: *SeqOfReal*;
     PowerOfx : *Integer*;

Begin
  new(*result*);
  If $s\textasciicircum.tail$ = **Nil Then**
  Begin
    result$\textasciicircum$.*head* := 0;
    result$\textasciicircum$.*tail* := **Nil**
  End
  Else
  Begin
    PowerOfx := 1;
    $s := s\textasciicircum.tail$;
    RestOfResult := *result*;
    Repeat
      RestOfResult$\textasciicircum$.*head* := *PowerOfx* * $s\textasciicircum$.*head*;
      $s := s\textasciicircum.tail$;
      PowerOfx := *PowerOfx* + 1;
      If $s <>$ **Nil Then**
      Begin
        new(*RestOfResult*$\textasciicircum$.*tail*);
        RestOfResult := *RestOfResult*$\textasciicircum$.*tail*
      End
    Until s = **Nil**;
    RestOfResult$\textasciicircum$.*tail* := **Nil**
  End;
  $D := result$
End;

12.4 (a)   matches is an operation that checks whether a given sequence of characters matches the external sequence of characters pattern. An asterisk in the pattern can match with any sub-string (including empty), other characters only match with themselves. For example, given the string "Rita" and pattern "R*a", matches would return a true result. However, with the string "BigMac" and pattern "B*Magic", matches would return false.

(b) *MatchRemaining* matches the rest of the strings from the given argument positions, calling itself recursively to continue matching. It is only when the end of the *pattern* string is reached that a decision is made as to whether the strings match. If *ThisString* is longer, then they don't. If there are no wild cards, the match is simple, just recursively calling *MatchRemaining* with positions in the strings incremented. If *pattern* contains '*', the rest of *ThisString* is searched to see if it matches with the rest of the pattern, starting at every position in *ThisString* after the current position. All the results of these attempted matches are **Or**ed together so that, if there is one successful match, this will return a true value and the procedure *matches* will return a true result. The procedure is not very efficient, as it continues to look after a match has been found.

Index

Page references in *italic* refer to examples and uses of the keyword.

Specification notation

Pascal notation

General index